HELLO, CHATTANOOGA!

Famous People
Who Have Visited the Tennessee Valley

To Mary and Patrick!

David Carroll

2023

HELLO, CHATTANOOGA!

Famous People
Who Have Visited the Tennessee Valley

David Carroll

Fresh Ink Group
Guntersville

Hello, Chattanooga!
Famous People Who Have Visited the Tennessee Valley

Copyright © 2021
by David Carroll
All rights reserved

Fresh Ink Group
An Imprint of:
The Fresh Ink Group, LLC
1021 Blount Avenue #931
Guntersville, AL 35976
Email: info@FreshInkGroup.com
FreshInkGroup.com

Edition 1.0   2021

Book design by Amit Dey / FIG
Cover design by Stephen Geez / FIG
Associate publisher Lauren A. Smith / FIG

Cataloging-in-Publication Recommendations:
HIS036120 HISTORY / United States / State & Local / South
(AL, AR, FL, GA, KY, LA, MS, NC, SC, TN, VA, WV)
PER009000 PERFORMING ARTS/Reference
BIO006000 BIOGRAPHY & AUTOBIOGRAPHY / Historical

Library of Congress Control Number: 2021911771

ISBN-13: 978-1-947893-97-9 Papercover
ISBN-13: 978-1-947893-96-2 Hardcover
ISBN-13: 978-1-947893-95-5 Ebooks

ACKNOWLEDGMENTS

With special thanks to John Shearer, author of numerous Chattanoogan.com columns, and the book "Chattanooga Trivia; Barry Courter, longtime entertainment editor and reporter for the *Chattanooga Times Free Press*; David Jenkins; Sportswriter and editor of "Baseball in Chattanooga"; Mark McCarter, longtime Chattanooga sportswriter and author of "Never a Bad Game," Nick Wilkinson, executive director of the Tivoli Foundation; Dave Holscher, general manager of the Tivoli Theater and Memorial Auditorium; Ken Kapelinski, former director of the UTC Arena; John Wilson of Chattanoogan.com; the staff at the Chattanooga Public Library; the Chattanooga Times Free Press, Cherokee Regional, Libraries Stephen Geez of Fresh Ink Group; Hugh Moore, Jr (The Man of a Thousand Concerts), and the extraordinarily cooperative and generous people at Newsbank, Inc.

I must also thank my great family for their patience and good advice: my wife Cindy, and my sons, Chris and Vince.

Without these people, this book would simply not have been possible:

Michael Alfano, Gary Behler, Thom Benson, Bob Boyer, Jim and Rhonda Catanzaro, Shaina Chandler, Pat Charles, Wayne Cropp, Mitzi Morgan Derryberry, Mike Dougher, Johnny Eagle, Bryan Eley, Anne Exum, Eric Foster, Jay Fowler, James Fox, Randall Franks, Earl Freudenberg, Greg Funderburg, Marilyn Garner, Austin Garrett, Ted Gocke, Gary Goforth, Talley Green, Pamela Hammonds, Julie Harding, Gator Harrison, Steve Hartline, Linda Hisey, David Johnson, Steve Johnson, Harmon Jolley, Jamie Jones, Chris Keene, Barbara Kennedy, Ron Littlefield, Michael Loftin, Cindy Lowery, Davis Lundy, Don Luzynski, Angie McGregor, Bobby McKeel, Linda McReynolds, Ralph Miller, Norma and Olan Mills II, Allen Mincey, Richard

Mooney, Charlie Moore, Bob Mulkey, Jack Mullins, Wayne Murphree, Rick Norton, Buddy O'Guin, Greg "Styckman" Owens, Bob Payne, Bill Peterson, Jerry Pond, McCracken Poston, Carla Pritchard, Steve Reno, Bill Steverson, Neil Thomas, Chuck Thornton, Melissa Wagner, Zach Wamp, Dave Weinthal, Becky White, Mark Wiedmer, Pat Wilcox, and Angie Williams.

INTRODUCTION

"Hello Chattanooga!" I have heard that dozens of times in my life, shouted from just about every stage in the city. You could add "Hello Tennessee," "Hello Georgia," and similar lines spoken by the biggest names in entertainment.

I have resolved countless arguments about whether Elvis Presley ever played Chattanooga (he did not), if Bruce Springsteen sold out the Soldiers and Sailors Memorial Auditorium during his one appearance (not even close), and if Babe Ruth and Lou Gehrig actually struck out against a teen girl at Engel Stadium (absolutely).

This project, which took several years to complete, began on a much smaller scale. I posted a blog on my website (ChattanoogaRadioTV.com) about the UTC Arena, also known as McKenzie Arena, or the Roundhouse. During its heyday in 1980s and 1990s, Tennessee Valley music fans enjoyed big-name concerts in the Arena almost every week. Then suddenly, the shows dried up. In my story, I explained how a combination of factors resulted in artists bypassing the Arena for newer, more attractive venues in surrounding cities.

Each time someone commented on the story, they would try to recall their favorite UTC Arena concert. "I saw Jimmy Buffett there. Or was it at Memorial Auditorium?" (It could have been either one.) "I attended the Huey Lewis show, and that's the night I proposed to my wife. I wish I had saved the ticket stub. I've always wondered what day it was." (February 17, 1987.) "I saw Taylor Swift, but she was someone's opening act. I wonder how old she was then?" (She was 17 when she opened for Brad Paisley on April 26, 2007.)

As the questions poured in, I decided to compile a complete list of the UTC Arena concerts as you will see in Chapter 4. That posting also elicited a huge response, and it led to more questions. "Can you do Memorial Auditorium?" "What about a list of Tivoli Theater shows?"

"We used to go to Lake Winnie for the free concerts every Sunday. Can you list those shows too?"

I decided to go for it. I had obtained the UTC Arena concert list with one easy e-mail. Thanks to former Arena director Ken Kapelinski, I had all the data within 24 hours. It was basically a cut-and-paste job. So, I thought, I'll just request the same information from the other popular Chattanooga area stages, and I'll have an instant book.

If it had been that easy, you would have been holding this book a long time ago. I barked up a lot of wrong trees. I was chasing down theater managers who had passed away, dealing with venue owners who had not kept records of shows, and family members who had thrown away old ledgers. After all, who in their right mind would care about concerts that took place fifty years ago? Me, that's who.

However, I had already started my journey down this rabbit hole, and just like that classic oldie, it was "Too Late to Turn Back Now." (By the way, the group that sang that one, the Cornelius Brothers and Sister Rose, played Ross's Landing in 1991. See Chapter 7.)

One thing led to another. If I'm going to list all the Lake Winnie shows, I should do the same for Chattanooga's annual Riverbend Festival. If I'm listing the nationally-known singers and bands who have appeared at local night clubs, how about the big-time comedians who have played the Comedy Catch?

While tracking down all those shows, I would see newspaper stories about famous political figures, even presidents who have visited the area. In an effort to verify some of those stories, friends would ask, "Are you going to mention the time Mickey Mantle of the New York Yankees opened his clothing store at Eastgate Mall?" When soliciting more information, people would send clippings or photos of famous folks who had visited the Tennessee Aquarium, attended a local party, or stopped by to visit their relatives.

The Chattanooga area has welcomed hundreds of familiar faces at charity benefits, golf tournaments, and telethons. We have spotted movie stars quietly stopping in at restaurants, hotels and tourist attractions thinking they will go unnoticed (and no doubt some of them did.) We have seen relatively unknown actors, singers, and musicians appear on our stages before they achieved great fame. Frank Sinatra, Jimi Hendrix, and John Goodman were among them. Now, I can tell you where they appeared, and what they were doing in Chattanooga in their early twenties.

Memorial Auditorium and Tivoli Theater ledgers dating back to the 1920s.

There is some risk in doing a book like this. For starters, it is not complete. On several occasions, I thought it was "a wrap." A few minutes later, I would discover another famous visitor. Despite years of poring over ledgers, letters, e-mails, ticket stub collections, concert notes, and newspaper archives, I could never include every famous person who has visited the Chattanooga area. Nor can I include all of the great local entertainers who have played and sung their hearts out on our stages. I assure you, no exclusion is intentional. Despite the assistance of various people who helped compile the data, this was basically a one-person project. A person, I might add, who stopped and started a few hundred times due to the distractions of work and life.

So, please accept my apologies in advance for the inevitable errors and omissions. Every effort was made to enlist the cooperation of venue managers, past and present. Some were eager to help, some were unable to help, and others were unwilling to help. But rather than dwell on

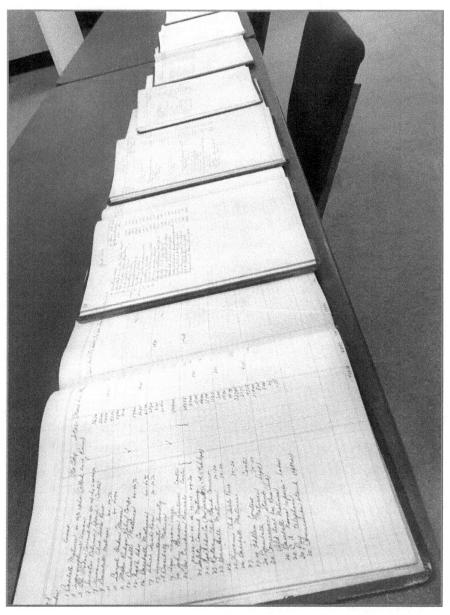

The Auditorium and Tivoli records were an important source of information on events at both venues.

1

October, 1963

1963	Events	Gross
Oct. 2	Concert + Dance - Sam Cooke	3250 00
3	Wrestling	2200 00
7	Kiwanis Travelogue	3000 00
10	Wrestling	2200 00
12, 13	Shrine Circus	6740 00
15	Chatt. Citizens Council Mtg - Geo. Wallace	8130 00
17	Wrestling	2200 00
18	Gospel Concert	3080 00
21	Musicale - New Zion Baptist Church	3000 00
24	Wrestling	2200 00
28	Kiwanis Travelogue	3000 00
29	Concert + Dance - Little Stevie Wonder	3079 77
30	Community Concert	3000 00
31	Wrestling	2200 00

Rentals, Etc.

Fortunately for the author, those who kept the records had excellent handwriting skills.

what may not be listed, enjoy what you find here. Hopefully this work will enlighten, inform and entertain you. The past hundred-plus years has been a great time to be alive and in Chattanooga, Tennessee. Thanks to our location, our philanthropists, our beautiful performing venues, and our friendly people, we have heard the "Hello Chattanooga" greeting from the most famous and talented people in the world. My goal in offering this book is to jog your memory, and to celebrate the performances, speeches, and athletic feats that have played such a huge role in our community.

I hope you will give special attention to our two incredible downtown theaters, both built in the 1920s. The Soldiers and Sailors Memorial Auditorium and the Tivoli Theater are proud old warriors. They have withstood the Great Depression, World War II, the introduction of television, various economic slowdowns, competition from larger (and smaller) venues, periods of disinterest by political and civic leaders, inconsistent management, outdated infrastructure, occasional neglect and disrepair, and the ravages of time.

They are still standing thanks to forward-thinking managers and elected officials, concerned citizens, skilled laborers, and thousands of fans like you who enjoy a good show. Here's wishing both venues a successful second century.

Now, turn the page, and take a trip back in time.

David Carroll, 2021
(Cover photograph: for KING & COUNTRY at the Tivoli Theater in 2019
(Mitchell Schleper)

TABLE OF CONTENTS

CHAPTER 1

Soldiers and Sailors Memorial Auditorium

For everyone living in the Chattanooga area in the 21st century, the Soldiers and Sailors Memorial Auditorium has been a constant in our lives. The Auditorium, at 399 McCallie Avenue, has hosted more famous people than any other facility in our region. For longtime city residents, it's the only auditorium we have ever known. But it was not the first.

The old City Auditorium on East 9th Street (now Martin Luther King Jr. Boulevard) burned in 1916. It hosted a variety of shows and

The original Chattanooga City Auditorium (Chattanooga Public Library)

1

stars, including the actress Sarah Bernhardt on March 16, 1906. (She arrived in her private train as part of her farewell tour.) There were also occasional live vaudeville-type performances at the Bijou Theater, which opened in 1906 at 601 Walnut Street, the site of the current Courts Building.

When the City Auditorium was destroyed by fire, Chattanooga residents no longer had a large venue to host live events. A temporary tabernacle was built at the site of the current Miller Park, at Market and 9th Streets to provide a space large enough to accommodate the crowds to see evangelist Billy Sunday, among others.

In 1918, the Chattanooga Kiwanis Club began making plans for a new auditorium that would honor the soldiers and sailors who died during the World War (which later became known as World War I). The project would be the largest undertaking of its kind in the history of the city.

The Kiwanis Club recommended that the city of Chattanooga issue $400,000 in bonds "for the purpose of building a memorial auditorium." Voters approved the auditorium by a 3-1 margin on March 11, 1919. A Soldiers and Sailors Memorial Auditorium Commission was appointed, and the Commission paid $100,000 to James A. Caldwell for the land at the intersection of McCallie Avenue and Lindsay Street covering the entire block toward Oak Street. Caldwell's home was demolished, allowing the project to go forward.

Dr. Alexander Guerry chaired the project, and R. H. Hunt was selected as the architect. Construction began in 1922, and the cornerstone was laid on November 11, 1922, the fourth anniversary of the armistice that ended the World War. the new facility opened on February 22, 1924. The final cost was $700,000.

The auditorium's birth spanned the terms of three mayors: it was planned under Jesse Littleton, built under A.W. Chambliss, and dedicated during the term of Richard Hardy.

The primary hall seated approximately five thousand people, with an additional "little theater" upstairs with a capacity of about eight hundred. In the early years, most of the auditorium's entertainment bookings were operatic in nature.

Mayors Littleton, Chambliss, and Hardy (Chattanooga Public Library)

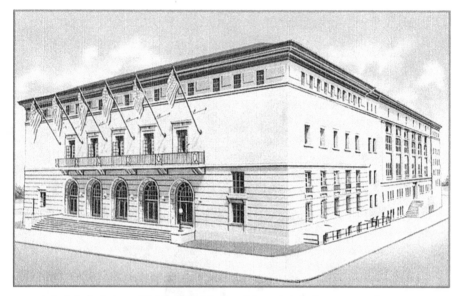

*Artist's depiction of Soldiers and Sailors Memorial Auditorium in the 1920s
(Chattanooga Public Library)*

1924

108,000 attended programs at the new auditorium during the first month. During the first year, there were art shows, home shows, war veterans reunions, an auto show, high school graduations, religious services, business conventions, pipe organ concerts, lectures and plays in the Little Theater. Edwin H. Lamare was the city's municipal organist.

2/22-23 Dedication with Chicago Civic Opera "The Jewess," and remarks by US Sen. Kenneth McKellar, Maj. Gen. James G. Harbord, Tenn. Gov. Austin Peay, Chattanooga Mayor Richard Hardy, and former South Carolina Gov. Richard Manning

2/26 Anna Pavlova (Russian ballerina)

3/9- 4/6 Gipsy Smith (British Evangelist), 4 week revival

3/18 Cho Cho the Health Clown

4/23 Rosa Ponselle (soprano)

9/27 Funeral for Dr. Jonathan Waverly Bachman, pastor of First Presbyterian Church

10/11 Maria Jeritza (soprano)

10/16 John Philip Sousa and his Band

10/27 Admiral Sumner Kittelle (Navy Day program)

10/28 *"Don Pasquale"* comic opera

10/30 Democratic campaign rally with Gov. Austin Peay, and US Rep. Sam McReynolds

11/4 Election returns presented by Chattanooga Times

11/17 Harry Houdini- Magician (newspaper review called his performance "stupid." According to the review, Houdini did more lecturing than magic, to the disappointment of the audience.)

11/18 Vladmir de Pachmann (pianist)

11/25 John Randall Dunn (lecture on Christian Science)

1925

(There were still various "road shows" playing at the Bijou Theater, including Will Rogers on Dec. 6, 1925. During that year, the new auditorium hosted Better Homes and Gardens expos, organ recitals, flower shows, a Halloween costume ball, fiddlers conventions, American Legion meetings, war veteran reunions, high school graduations, dog shows, high school "basket ball" tournaments, automobile shows, lectures and plays in the Little Theater, and a Boy Scout convention.)

1/17 Paul Whiteman and Orchestra (jazz)

1/20 The Marriage of Figaro (comic opera)

1/22 Louis Graveure (Belgian baritone)

1/26 Denishawn Dancers

2/10 Homer Rodeheaver (gospel singer)

2/12 First recital with new Austin Pipe Organ (project organized by Chattanooga Music Club, and purchased by the city, with support from local civic clubs for $44,549)

2/23-24 Thais (Chicago Civic Opera with Mary Garden)

2/27 John Charles Thomas (baritone)

3/4 Pablo Casals- Cellist

3/14 Lt. "Smiling Jack" Harding, world flyer with movies of his flights

5/4-7 Xerxes (opera)

6/29- 7/5 "*Captain Blood*" motion picture

7/18-19 "*Evolution*" motion picture

10/23 Claudia Muzio (Italian soprano from Chicago Opera Company)

11/13 Louis Graveure (Belgian baritone)

11/17 Sweethearts (Victor Hugo operetta)

11/20 Pailey-Oukrainsky ballet

1926

New additions this year included a Chattanooga Products Expo, a police and fireman's ball, oratorical contests, occasional movies like "The Naked Truth," "Julius Caesar," "Birth of a Nation." and "The Big Parade" and public debates on whether to allow boxing in the auditorium. Polk Smartt was auditorium manager.

2/1 Ignacy Jan Paderewski (Polish pianist)

2/6 Albert Spaulding (violinist) and Charles Stratton (tenor)

2/11 New York Celtics vs. Chattanooga Rail-Lites "basket ball." The Celtics featured Johnny Beckman, Nat Holman, Pete Barry, Davey Banks, Dutch Dehnert, Chris Leonard, Horse Haggerty and Joe Lapchick. It was at this game the Celtics accidentally invented the pivot play, which became a standard pattern of offense.

2/27 *"Carmen"* opera featuring Mary Garden of Chicago Civic Opera Company

3/1-4 Jane E. Castle (mentalist)

3/11 Kathryn Meisle (contralto, Chicago Opera)

3/16-17 Dr. Charles Popplestone (speaking on salesmanship)

3/19 Tony Sarg's Marionettes

3/20 Georgia Tech Glee Club

3/29 Former Gen. William Mitchell, US Army speaking on importance of aviation

4/21 Amelita Galli-Curci (soprano)

5/4 Evangelist John "Brother" Brown

5/10 Reinald Werrenrath (baritone)

8/28 Dr. Frederick Bowles (evolutionist, atheist)

9/13 Marion Talley (soprano)

10/23 Mexican Tipica Orchestra

10/28 Claudia Muzio (soprano)

11/2 Namiko-San & Pagliacci (opera) Pailey-Oukrainsky ballet and Manhattan Opera Company

11/11 John Philip Sousa band with Marjory Moody (soprano)

11/29 US Navy Band

11/30 Philip Manuel (pianist) and Gavin Williamson (harpsichordist)

12/9 Barber of Seville opera with Feodor Chaliapin (basso)

12/16 Roland Hayes (tenor)

12/28 Yale Banjo and Glee Club

12/29 Rhondda Singers

1927

(New additions included Kiwanis and American Legion conventions, "music memory" contests, a Boy Scouts Indian Pow-Wow, and several small productions in the little theater)

1/17 Will Rogers (humorist) addressed "large crowd"

1/21 "Fire Clown" Harry "Smoky" Rogers at Fire Prevention program

2/8 New York Celtics (featuring "best player in basket ball" Nat Holman) vs. Tepco Rail-Lites

2/25-26 Il Trovatore, Madame Butterfly, Masked Ball (Chicago Civic Opera)

3/22 Ruth St. Denis & Ted Shawn (modern dance company)

4/1-2 Macbeth, Hamlet (Robert Mantell, Genevieve Hamper)

4/7-9 Vitaphone audible motion picture demonstration

5/19-21 "Birth of a Nation" film

6/18 Jess Young "champion fiddler" with Allen Brothers, "latest song and dance hits"

8/18 Funeral service for former Mayor Richard Hardy

9/21 Kansas City Nighthawks (jazz dance band)

October: World Series results (with magnetic player board, thousands attended)

11/27 Memorial program for the late Prof. Joseph Cadek (3,000 in attendance)

12/8 Jose Echaniz (pianist) and Glenn Drake (tenor)

1928

New additions included the Chattanooga Music Club, Meat Shop Owners, Rotary Convention, volleyball, organ recitals, square dances, Moose Club meetings, church conventions, baseball radio broadcasts, safety meetings, a retail grocers convention, and an increase in "moving pictures." It was a presidential election year, and various nationally known political figures brought the campaign to Chattanooga.

2/2 New York Celtics vs. Chattanooga Rail-Lites ("basketball")

2/6 Westminster Choir from Dayton, Ohio

2/23-24 I Pagliacci (Chicago Civic Opera, starring soprano Mary Garden)

3/12-17 "Mary" George M. Cohan play (in Little Theater)

3/26 Grace Moore (soprano from Tennessee)

5/31-6/2 Showing of movie *"Hunchback of Notre Dame"*

9/7 US Sen Joseph Robinson (D-Ark) VP candidate (Alfred Smith was the presidential candidate)

9/17 *"Abie's Irish Rose"* (in the Little Theater)

10/12 Democratic presidential candidate Alfred Smith speaks at rally

10/18 Idaho Sen. William Borah speaks for Herbert Hoover presidential campaign

10/24 Paul Whiteman Orchestra

10/26 Former TN Gov Malcolm Patterson for Alfred Smith presidential campaign

10/30 US Sen. Carter Glass (D-VA) rally for Alfred Smith presidential campaign

11/1-3 American Opera Company

11/6 Presidential Election voting results (Herbert Hoover defeated Alfred Smith)

11/7 Theodor Kosloff (Russian ballet in Little Theater)

11/12 *"Rio Rita"* (play)

1929

(The auditorium added various boxing and wrestling events, power and engineering shows, a household appliance expo, an auto show, and WDOD radio co-owner Earl Winger was asked to install amplifiers to improve the big hall's acoustics, a problem that would plague the auditorium for decades.)

1/21 *"King of Kings"* film

1/28 Sewanee Glee Club

2/1 Cleveland Rosenblums vs. Chattanooga Rail-Lites basketball

2/26 Prohibition debate: Attorney Clarence Darrow vs. US Rep. William Upshaw (D-GA)

3/8 City Annexation Parade and Concert

4/25 *"The Vagabond King"* operetta

April-August: July: Chattanooga Lookouts baseball results each afternoon on magnetic board ("baseball matinee," good attendance)

5/9 Oscar Seagle (world renowned baritone, born in 1877 in Ooltewah, TN)

6/9 Boxing begins: out-of town promoter calls it "Best Ring Set-up in the South"

6/24 Erwin McConnell, blind organist, replaces Edwin H. Lamare as auditorium's municipal organist

6/25 US Rep. Oscar DePriest "Negro Congressman from Chicago"

9/4 Radio Show (displaying new radio models, would become an annual event, 3,000 in attendance)

9/30 Annexation Celebration featuring University of Chattanooga Band

October: *Chattanooga Times* "Magnetic Scoreboard" with results of the World Series

11/12 US Army band (2 performances, well attended)

12/2-4 Pennsylvania Opera Company

12/13-14 Jimmie Rodgers ("The Singing Brakeman," "Father of Country Music")

The 1930s

In the 1930s, Soldiers and Sailors Memorial Auditorium was featuring professional wrestling on Tuesday nights. Regular events included cooking shows, church conventions, flower shows, home shows, automobile shows, American Legion conventions, fiddlers conventions, monthly Sunday organ concerts, children's shows, Golden Gloves boxing, fashion shows, local opera performances, circus acts, a weekend skating rink, World War and Spanish-American war veteran reunions, high school commencement programs, basketball games (usually featuring the Tennessee Electric Power Company "Tepcos") and miniature golf.

Many traveling production companies declined to play the Auditorium due to poor reviews of the acoustics, citing a distracting echo.

A new front door "exclusively for Negroes" was installed in December 1930. According to news reports, it was called the "colored entrance," and the front left balcony was reserved for that portion of the audience as well. Prior to this, their only entrance was at the rear of the Auditorium, and city leaders agreed that more people from the "colored community" would attend events if they could enter the building from the front.

The racial attitudes of the era are evident in newspaper clippings. When the "colored" pianist Lil Armstrong performed on the Auditorium stage in 1935, a Chattanooga newspaper reviewer wrote, "She is one of the best of her race."

In 1930 "amplifiers" or loud speakers, to help with acoustics were added, with limited success. There had been numerous complaints that Chattanooga was lacking "cultural events," due in part to poor sound.

Among performers of note was Jackie Coogan, the former child star who was 21 when he performed with his orchestra in 1937. Three decades later, he was better known as Uncle Fester on TV's "The Addams Family." Actor Cesar Romero appeared in a 1930 play, long before becoming a film star, and "The Joker" on TV's "Batman." Olympic track and field Gold Medalist Jesse Owens appeared in 1937 with a 12-piece jazz band.

Tommy Thompson was named auditorium manager in 1932 and served in that capacity for more than three decades, until his death in 1963.

1930

1/21-22 *"A Connecticut Yankee"* (Mark Twain musical, poor attendance)

1/23 St. Olaf Lutheran Choir of Minnesota

1/31 Tony Sarg's Marionettes (2 shows)

2/4 Sir Harry Lauder (Scottish musician/comedian)

3/5 Charles Doenberger & his 11-piece Victor Orchestra

4/15 Jack Dempsey refereed boxing exhibition (4,000 fans)

6/30 Dr. John B. Cline's Sexual Hygiene Lectures (poor attendance, canceled after one day)

9/9-12 Chattanooga Radio Show (selling radios) with Harriet Lee, CBS Radio entertainer

Early October: Audio play-by-play of World Series, with "Player board" on display"

10/13 Republican rally with Congressman Will Taylor

11/3 John Philip Sousa conducted local high school bands (2 performances)

11/13 Colleen Moore in *"Cindy"*

11/19 *"Cherries Are Ripe"* play (acoustical problems)

12/25 *"Strictly Dishonorable"* play (with Cesar Romero)

1931

1/2 *"Flying High"* (musical)

1/19 Roland Hayes (tenor)

1/21 New York Celtics basketball

1/28 Ignacy Jan Paderewski (Polish pianist) (good turnout) (first played Chattanooga in 1895 at the Opera House at 6ᵗʰ and Market Streets)

2/13 Chicago Bruins (American Basketball League) game

2/25 Admiral Richard Byrd

3/12 USMC Major Gen. Smedley Butler (decorated veteran of Mexican Revolution and World War)

3/16 Boxing exhibition with Champ Max Schmeling vs. Young Stribling

4/6 *Hamlet/As You Like It* (two performances, total attendance 4,000)

5/18 President Woodrow Wilson memorial film (attendance 3,200)

6/9 Wrestler Jim Londos defeated Jim Katan (record attendance estimated at 6,000)

Late Sept.- Early October: Audio play by play of World Series, with "player board" on display

12/4 *"Elijah"* presented by Cadek Choral Society/Metropolitan Opera (attendance 5,500)

12/15 World Champion wrestler Jim Londos vs. Milo Steinborn of Germany

1932

1/13 New York Celtics basketball

1/18 Wrestling champion Jimmy Londos vs. Pat O'Shocker

2/17-18 *"The Apple Cart"* play by George Bernard Shaw ("disastrous" attendance)

3/2 *"The Student Prince of Heidelberg"* play (poor attendance)

3/22 Bill Tilden vs. Albert Burke (tennis)

4/5 Fred Stone musical comedy show (poor acoustics led to no further "road shows" for many years)

9/22 Vice President Charles Curtis (campaigning for Pres. Hoover) 4,700 attendance

10/19 Joe DeVito vs. Jim Londos (wrestling champion)

10/25 3rd District Congressional rally with Sen. Kenneth McKellar, Rep. S. D. McReynolds

10/29 Southern Fiddlers Championship

11/3 U.S. Sen. Cordell Hull (D-Tenn)

1933

(There was talk among city officials of closing the facility in 1932-33. Many suggested a velour curtain splitting the size of the main hall, reducing the size of the audience, hopefully resulting in better acoustics.)

1/11 New York Celtics basketball vs. Chattanooga Dynamos

3/25 Gene Austin's Broadway Rhapsody

9/1 Cotton Ball (The first of what would become an annual Chattanooga event)

9/9 Hi-De-Ho Queen (Blanche Calloway, older sister of Cab)

10/16 Boxing: Clyde Chastain vs. Maxie Rosenbloom (big crowd)

10/21 Tennessee-Alabama football (shown on Grid-Graph board)

1934

1/8 New York Celtics basketball team (attendance 5,000)

1/29 President Franklin D. Roosevelt Birthday Ball

1/30 Earl Hines and his Grand Terrace Orchestra

Tennessee-born actress singer Grace Moore was greeted by 4,000 fans during "Grace Moore Week" in Chattanooga in 1934 (Chattanooga Public Library)

2/27 Noble Sissle Orchestra

3/10 Sister Aimee Semple McPherson (evangelist, two lectures)

3/23 Walter Barnes Orchestra

5/3 Don Redman Orchestra

6/14 Jim Londos vs. George Zaharias (wrestling)

6/21 Claude Hopkins Orchestra

7/3 Don Curtez Orchestra, singer Jennie Lou Peck

8/2 Duke Ellington (5,000 in attendance)

9/11 Cab Calloway & Cotton Club Orchestra (6,000 in attendance)

10/14 Bozo the Wonder Dog (magic)

10/21 McConnell Erwin (organist)

10/25 Buck Weaver wrestling (All American football player)

10/29 Democratic rally (Gov. Hill McAlister, Sen. Kenneth McKellar, Sen. Nathan Bachman)

11/5 Mills Brothers and Tiny Bradshaw (big crowd)

11/26 Grace Moore (Tennessee-born actress-singer) (4,000 attendance)

1935

1/14 New York Celtics basketball (5,000 fans)

2/11 Zach Whyte & his Chocolate Beau Brummels (orchestra)

3/31 Dr. Bob Jones (president of Bob Jones College in Cleveland, TN)

4/5 Duke Ellington Orchestra

5/14-18 Second National Folk Festival

8/12 Jimmie Lunceford & Columbia Broadcasting Orchestra

9/10 Lil Armstrong (Louie's wife, a pianist) and her Kings of Rhythm

10/3 Fats Waller Orchestra

12/6 Wayne King, the Waltz King

12/7 Southern Champion Fiddlers Contest

12/31 Cotton Club Revue

1936

(Professional wrestling was scheduled on most Thursday nights, which would continue for decades)

1/4 Sally Rand (fan dancer) poor attendance

1/17 Champion New York Celtics basketball

2/11 Joe Sanders and Famous Nighthawk Orchestra

2/21 Homer Challiaux, American Legion president, anti-Communist rally

3/25 Babe Zaharius vs. Marshall Blackstock wrestling (5,500 fans)

5/12 Blanche Calloway Orchestra

6/1 Jan Garber orchestra (sellout)

8/25 Glen Gray & Casa Loma Orchestra

9/9 Joe Lipps vs. Berry Baggett boxing

9/10 Earl Browder, Communist party presidential candidate

9/16 Norman Thomas, Socialist party presidential candidate

10/11 Homer Rodeheaver, gospel singer (4500 in attendance)

11/2 Gordon Browning, Democratic candidate for Tenn. Governor

11/7 Nino Martini, Metropolitan Opera star

11/27 Rita Rio and the Rhythm Girls

12/1 "George White's Scandals"

1937

1/10 New York Celtics basketball

1/28 Female Wrestling Mildred Burke vs. Clara Mortensen (6,000 attendance)

2/3 Kay Kyser Orchestra

2/9 Ted Shawn dancers

2/11 Clara Mortensen vs. Mildred Burke wrestling (4,200 fans)

3/20 Ellsworth Vines vs. Frederick John Perry (tennis)

4/6 Don Bestor Orchestra

4/7 Harlem Play Girls Orchestra

4/10 Jesse Owens (1936 Olympic track and field winner of 4 Gold Medals), with 12-piece jazz band

4/23 Orlando Roberson Orchestra

4/28 Glen Gray & Casa Loma Orchestra

5/8 Andy Kirk and his Clouds of Joy orchestra

6/8 Jan Garber orchestra

6/25 Clyde McCoy orchestra

8/10 Fats Waller Orchestra (sellout)

8/24 Louis Armstrong and band

8/31 Jackie Coogan (later "Uncle Fester" on Addams Family) and orchestra

9/24 Little Jack Little & orchestra

9/29 Freckles Ray ("Our Gang" comedies) and his 16 Swing Gangsters

10/20 Don Redman orchestra

10/26 Shep Fields orchestra (Fields' "Ripplin' Rhythm" was believed to be inspiration for Lawrence Welk's "champagne music")

11/19 Mordkin Imperial Russian Ballet (4,000 attendance)

12/28 Ella Fitzgerald with Chick Webb & Savoy String Orchestra

12/31 Adrian McDowell and NBC Orchestra

1938

1/14 New York Celtics basketball

2/7 University of Tennessee vs. University of Chattanooga basketball

2/11 Fats Waller Orchestra

2/18 New York Celtics basketball

2/22 David Rubinoff, violinist

3/16 Noble Sissle Orchestra

4/5 Count Basie and his Orchestra

4/22 Ted Shawn Dancers

5/20 Professional tennis: Ellsworth Vines vs. Fred Perry

5/27 George Hall Orchestra

6/4 Fats Waller Orchestra

7/23-24 T Perry Brannon (evangelist)

8/1 US Sen. George Berry (D-Tenn)

8/2 Tenn. Gov Gordon Browning

9/23 Don Bestor Orchestra, Johnny Hamp Orchestra

9/24 Barn Dance Jamboree: Tex Marvin, Hollywood Ranch Boys

10/26 Little Jack Little Orchestra

11/18 US Navy Band

12/17 Jascha Herfetz (violinist)

1939

1/2 Jumbo Circus

1/13 New York Celtics basketball

2/6-10 Golden Gloves/ Colored Golden Gloves

2/14 Ted Lewis Orchestra

3/1 La Meri (Japanese dancer)

3/25 Dave Rubinoff Violin

3/27 Nelson Eddy, baritone singer (5,000 attendance)

4/24 Larry Clinton Orchestra with vocalist Bea Wain

5/12 Dale Carnegie lecture

5/17 Count Basie Orchestra

8/31 Roland Hayes (tenor)

9/12 First Lady Eleanor Roosevelt speech (with Howard High School Choir)

9/25 Jan Garber orchestra

10/27 Southern Aires

11/1 Henry Busse band

11/15 Helen Jepson (soprano)

11/20 Russ Morgan Orchestra dance

11/29 Ella Fitzgerald (6,100 attendance)

11/22-26 Adams Rodeo

12/4-5 *"Tobacco Road"* play

12/16 H.V. Kaltenborn (news commentator who incorrectly predicted FDR would not run for 3rd term in 1940)

The 1940s

In the 1940s, Roller Derby was a frequent attraction. Professional wrestling continued as a weekly event on Thursday nights, although late in the decade outdoor matches were held at Engel Stadium. Several dances were advertised as "for colored" audiences. The Auditorium also hosted several University of Chattanooga basketball games.

In 1949, Mayor Ed Bass called the facility "a money-losing white elephant."

However, the 1940s brought some young people who would soon become household names, including Rev. Billy Graham, Eddy Arnold, Minnie Pearl, Louis Armstrong, Doris Day, the Carter family, Chet Atkins, Kitty Wells, Nat King Cole, Victor Borge, and Ella Fitzgerald.

Of one future superstar, a Chattanooga newspaper reviewer wrote, "(The Tommy Dorsey Show) featured teen-aged Connie Haines, and male singer Frank Sinatra, who presented their numbers well."

The auditorium also welcomed some of the biggest stars of the era, including Bob Hope, Roy Acuff, and Nelson Eddy, along with top bandleaders Duke Ellington, Cab Calloway, Guy Lombardo, Harry James, and Count Basie.

This decade could be considered the beginning of the Golden Age of entertainment on the Auditorium stage. Chattanooga's railroad station made the city a convenient stop for performers on their way to and from larger cities. Highway improvements also enabled "hillbilly" performers from Nashville, Knoxville, Georgia and Alabama to make a quick trip to Chattanooga, much to the delight of local audiences.

Frank Sinatra in 1940 with Tommy Dorsey Orchestra (origin unknown)

1940

1/9 Artie Shaw Orchestra under direction of Georgie Auld

1/10 Yehudi Menuhin (violinist)

1/23 Cab Calloway dance

2/21 Allan Jones (tenor), Irene Hervey

3/5 New York Celtics basketball

4/9 Ink Spots dance (6,100 attendance)

4/25 Professional wrestling refereed by former heavyweight boxing champ Jack Dempsey

4/30 Tommy Dorsey Orchestra dance (4,000 in attendance) featuring 24-year-old "male singer" Frank Sinatra and 22-year-old drumming sensation Buddy Rich

5/2 Philadelphia Orchestra directed by Eugene Ormandy

6/8 Presidential candidate Sen. Robert Taft (R-Ohio)

7/3 Duke Ellington dance

8/13 Ella Fitzgerald dance

10/14 Democratic meeting: US Rep. Arthur Mitchell (D-Illinois), the first African-American elected to Congress

10/25 Democratic meeting: US Sen. Kenneth McKellar (D-Tenn), Gov. Prentice Cooper (D-Tenn.), Rep. Estes Kefauver (D-Tenn) (attendance 3500)

11/7 Larry Clinton orchestra

11/17 Josef Hoffmann, pianist

12/6 US Rep. Martin Dies D-Texas, Chairman Of House Committee Investigating UnAmerican Activities (attendance 4,000)

12/13 Ted Lewis dance

12/31 Louis Armstrong dance

1941

1/13/15 Passion Play with Josef Meier

1/17 New York Celtics basketball

1/28 Allan Jones (tenor)

1/29 Roller Derby (26 consecutive nights)

3/2 Roy Acuff, Minnie Pearl, Bashful Brother Oswald, Pee Wee King, "Grandpappy" (Archie Campbell)

3/5 Nelson Eddy (baritone)

3/21 Paul Whiteman orchestra (4,000 attendance)

3/23 St Louis Symphony Orchestra

3/31 Ballet Russe de Monte Carlo

4/8-10 Water Follies (Buster Crabbe)

4/21 Lawrence Tibbett (baritone) almost 5,000 in attendance

5/8 Pro wrestling with former heavyweight boxing champ Jack Dempsey as referee

5/12 & 14 Jean Watson, Canadian opera singer

6/6 Guy Lombardo dance

6/9 Roy Acuff

6/24 Ink Spots dance

8/19 Erskine Hawkins orchestra

10/3 Cotton Ball (Actress Susan Hayward attended)

10/17 Jan Garber Orchestra

10/20 *"Barber of Seville"* by Metropolitan Opera Company

10/23 Vronsky and Babin (dual pianists)

10/25-28 Buster Crabbe Water Follies

11/20 Marian Anderson (African-American opera singer "welcomed by admiring members of her race," according to newspaper story)

11/21 John Whitaker, foreign correspondent *Chicago Daily News* (warned about Hitler wanting to take over the world) attendance 3,000

11/26 Earl Hines Orchestra dance

11/29 Don Cossack Russian Choir

12/8 Doris Doe, Metropolitan Opera star

12/22- 1/4 Roller Derby

1942

(Regular events included Wrestling, Golden Gloves Boxing, and Square Dances)

1/21 Philadelphia Symphony conducted by Eugene Ormandy

1/23 New York Celtics basketball

1/28 Fletcher Henderson Revue

2/15 Roy Acuff, Eddy Arnold, Minnie Pearl, Bashful Brother Oswald, Pee Wee King

2/19 Hellzapoppin

2/20 Tennis exhibition: Don Budge/Bobby Riggs, Fred Perry, Frank Kovacs

2/26 Grace Moore (soprano, Tennessee native)

3/4-10 Shrine Circus

3/28 War bonds broadcast on Mutual Radio Network

4/12 Renfro Valley Barn Dance (Range Riders)

4/13 Albert Spalding, violinist

5/5 Fla. Sen. Claude Pepper "Victory Bond" rally

5/28 Count Basie Orchestra

7/13 Jimmie Lunsford "dance for colored"

7/23 Wrestling (6,000 fans, a record)

7/28 Erskine Hawkins "dance for colored"

8/13 Jimmie Lunceford

8/26 Tiny Bradshaw "dance for colored"

9/1 Greer Garson war bonds rally with WWI Hero Alvin York

9/18 Snookum Russell "dance for colored" (his big hit: "Your Feets Too Big")

9/22 Jeannette McDonald Army Relief concert (4,600 fans)

10/9 Andy Kirk "dance for colored"

10/10 Radio Hillbilly Jamboree ("Grandpappy" Archie Campbell)

10/14 Ted Lewis Orchestra (dance)

10/17 Radio Hillbilly jamboree ("Grandpappy" Archie Campbell, Cowboy Copas, Fiddlers Contest)

10/20-23 Skating vanities (featuring Gloria Nord)

10/31 Radio Hillbilly Jamboree (John "Slim" Totten, Pete Cassell, Riley Puckett, Cas Walker's Smoky Mtn. Hillbillies)

11/6 La Boheme (Chattanooga Civic Chorus)

11/7 Radio Hillbilly Happy Valley Jamboree (Pete Cassell, Riley Puckett)

11/14 Happy Valley Jamboree (Pete Cassell)

11/21 Happy Valley Jamboree (Shorty Sharp, Eddie Hill)

11/28 Happy Valley Jamboree (Bill Carlysle)

12/5 Happy Valley Jamboree (Cowboy Copas)

12/12 Happy Valley Jamboree (Bonnie Jones, Curley Fagen)

12/14 Robert Casadeus (pianist)

12/26 Happy Valley Jamboree (Pete Cassell, Hoyt Pruett, Riley Puckett)

12/27-1/11 Roller Derby

1943

(The auditorium turned a profit in 1943 for the first time in its 19-year history)

1/16 Happy Valley Jamboree (Bill Shepherd's Melody Rangers)

1/21 Ballet Russe de Monte Carlo

1/23-24 Happy Valley Jamboree (Ernest Tubb, Melody Ranch Boys)

1/29 New York Celtics basketball

1/30 Happy Valley Jamboree (Texas Daisy, Lowell Blanchard)

1/31 Bill Monroe and his Bluegrass Boys, Stringbean, Clyde Moody

2/5 Tiny Bradshaw Orchestra

2/6 Happy Valley Jamboree (Lloyd Back)

2/13 Happy Valley Jamboree (Cas Walker & Smoky Mtn. Hillbillies)

2/16 Minneapolis Symphony

2/20 Happy Valley Jamboree (Curly Fox, Texas Ruby)

2/27 Happy Valley Jamboree (Carter family, Rex Griffin)

3/6 Happy Valley Jamboree (Cackle Sisters)

3/13-14 Happy Valley Jamboree (Delmore Brothers)

3/22-27 Great American Indoor Circus

3/30 Coast Guard band from St. Louis

4/12 Andy Kirk orchestra

4/14 Lily Pons (opera soprano) 5,000 attendance

5/14 Ink Spots

5/15 WAPO Barn Dance (Kitty Wells, Natchee, the Arizona Indian)

5/31 Sigmund Romberg (operatic composer)

7/16 Tommy Reynolds (clarinetist) and his orchestra, with singer Bonnie Baker

7/30 Erskine Hawkins

8/22 Ernest Tubb, Minnie Pearl

9/1 Andy Kirk orchestra

9/3 Hillbilly Jamboree (Pete Cassell)

9/24 Cootie Williams Orchestra ("colored" dance)

10/20 Marian Anderson (opera singer)

10/23 Tito Guizar (Latin singer)

10/29 "*Faust*" (opera)

11/5 Tiny Bradshaw Orchestra

11/15 Sigmund Romberg (operatic composer)

11/17 Fletcher Henderson Orchestra ("colored dance")

11/29 Larry Adler (harmonica) Paul Draper (tap dancer)

12/11 Frank Buck (humanitarian hunter)

12/14-20 Skating Vanities

12/25-1/23 Roller Derby

1944

1/26 Lucky Millinder Orchestra

2/3 "Die Flidermaus" (The Bat) performed by Philadelphia Opera

2/4 Helen Traubel (soprano)

2/6 Roy Acuff, Rachel & Oswald, Jimmie Riddle

2/11 Blossom Time operetta (4,000 fans) Sigmund Romberg

2/15 Minneapolis Symphony

2/20 Southernaires

3/6 Eddie Durham band ("colored dance")

3/10 Zino Francescatti (French violinist)

3/28 Jimmie Lunceford orchestra

4/25-30 Hollywood Ice Revels of 1944

5/12 Buddy Johnson ("colored dance")

5/28 Dunninger, mentalist

5/30 Ink Spots, Ella Fitzgerald, Cootie Williams

6/29 Al Jolson War Bonds show, with Lt. William Holden, Benny Goodman, John Payne, David Rose, broadcast nationally by Mutual, via WDEF radio, 5,000 people in attendance

8/2 Erskine Hawkins Orchestra

8/18 Jimmie Lunsford orchestra

9/4 Silas Green Minstrels

9/8 Lucky Millinder orchestra

9/20 Louis Jordan (swing music, "King of the Jukebox") and his Tympany Five

9/30 Alec Templeton (concert pianist)

10/16 *"Kiss and Tell"* (play)

10/20 Buddy Johnson orchestra

10/6 Alec Templeton (pianist)

10/24 *"The Merry Widow"* (opera)

10/30 Rally in support of President Franklin Roosevelt with Georgia Gov. Ellis Arnall, and Senator Lister Hill (D-Alabama)

10/31 "La Traviata" (opera)

11/1 Thomas Dewey for President rally with Roscoe Simmons ("Negro orator")

11/15 Artur Rubenstein (pianist)

11/18 Barn Dance Revue (Rufe Davis)

12/4 *"Naughty Marietta"* (opera)

12/5 Southernaires

12/18-19 Harry Blackstone Sr. the Magician

12/25- 1/10 Roller Derby

Rev Billy Graham in 1945 (Billy Graham Evangelistic Association)

1945

1/17 International Sweethearts of Rhythm (integrated all woman jazz band)

1/21 Minnie Pearl and Pee Wee King with his Golden West Cowboys

1/24 Ballet Russe de Monte Carlo

2/6 Sons o' Fun (Ole Olsen & Chic Johnson comedy revue)

2/16 Helen Jepson (soprano) and Charles Kullman (tenor)

2/20 Trapp Family Singers (from Austria, memorialized in "The Sound of Music")

2/24 Minneapolis Symphony

2/25 "Win The War" rally with 3rd Dist. Rep. Estes Kefauver (D-TN)

3/2 Victory Parade of Spotlight Bands: Les Brown and his Band of Renown, and singers Morton Downey and Doris Day (attendance 5,000 textile workers, who were granted free admission. The radio show was broadcast over the Blue network, a predecessor of the ABC radio network)

3/4 Roy Acuff, Rachel & Oswald, Sonny Day, Pap and his Jug Band

3/12 Sigmund Romberg

3/14 Mia Slavenska dance ensemble

4/2 "Martha" (opera)

4/3 Tiny Bradshaw ("King of the Jitterbugs")

4/12 "Carmen" (opera)

4/15 City-wide memorial service for Pres. Franklin Roosevelt, who had died three days earlier

6/9 Rev. Billy Graham (age 26) and Central High School Band (Youth for Christ rally) attendance 1,800

6/13 Earl "Fatha" Hines dance band

7/3 Louis Armstrong dance

7/21 Hamilton County Singing Convention with Sand Mountain Quartet

7/30 Luis Russell orchestra, singer Savannah Churchill, Deek Watson and his Brown Dots

8/3 Ted Fio Rito Orchestra

8/8 Charles Coolidge Day (Local WWII Medal of Honor recipient honored)

8/13 Silas Green from New Orleans ("all colored show")

8/15 Tex Ritter and comedian Dub Taylor

8/22 Hepsations (band led by Dizzy Gillespie), Nicholas Brothers

8/31 Lucky Millinder (began integrating his formerly all-Black band) plus Sister Rosetta Tharpe

9/16 Grand Ole Opry: Uncle Dave Macon, Curly Fox, Texas Ruby

9/21 Woody Herman Orchestra

9/30 Grand Ole Opry: Duke of Paducah, Bailes Brothers

10/5 Erskine Hawkins orchestra

10/27 Tex Ritter Hollywood Hillbilly Jamboree with comedian Dub Taylor

10/29 "*Rigoletto*" (opera)

10/31 Atlantic City Follies

11/6 Victor Borge, comedy pianist

11/13 Earl Carroll Vanities

11/15 Cootie Williams orchestra with singer Ella Fitzgerald

11/16 Pittsburgh Symphony Orchestra

11/27 Bill "Bojangles" Robinson

12/27-1/13 Roller Derby

1946

1/17 Don Cossack Chorus

2/7 Sammy Kaye Orchestra (5,000 people)

2/15 Eleanor Stieber (soprano)

2/18 Minneapolis Symphony Orchestra

2/22 Sigmund Romberg (opera) sellout

2/25 Jascha Heifetz (violinist)

2/27 Count Basie dance

3/1 Jose Iturbi, Spanish pianist (4,500 in attendance)

3/6 Jimmy Dorsey Orchestra (jitterbug dance, 3500 fans)

3/29 Cincinnati Symphony

4/1 Louis Jordan dance

4/16 Tommy Tucker dance band

4/23 James Melton, tenor

4/30 "Desert Song"

5/10 Benny Carter dance

5/22 "*Rigoletto*" (opera) Jan Pearce, Ezio Pinza, Patrice Munsel, Lucille Browning (Mezzo Soprano) 5,000 in attendance

7/14 Grand Ole Opry with Eddy Arnold, Tennessee Plowboys, Rod Brasfield

7/19 Wally Fowler and his Georgia Clodhoppers (for Ned Carmack U.S. Senate campaign)

9/7 Glen Gray & Casa Loma jazz orchestra

9/21 Jerry Wald & his Orchestra

10/7 Phil Spitalny & and his all-girl orchestra

10/25 Guy Lombardo Orchestra (5,000 attendance)

10/27 Pee Wee King and his Golden West Cowboys (Grand Ole Opry)

10/28 "*Il Trovatore*" (opera, sellout)

11/4 Cootie Williams Orchestra

11/6-10 Skating Vanities of 1947

11/21 Louis Jordan dance

11/25 Strauss Festival with Oscar Straus

11/29 Glenn Miller Orchestra (dance) led by Tex Beneke, pianist was Henry Mancini

12/1 Xavier Cugat Orchestra (big crowd)

12/7 Spike Jones Orchestra

12/11 Ballet Russe

12/17 Woody Herman Orchestra

12/27- 1/14 Roller Derby

1947

1/15 Sammy Kaye Orchestra (sellout)

1/20 Eugene List (pianist)

1/28 Ink Spots Dance, with Johnny Otis Band

2/3 Golden Gloves Boxing (6,000 in attendance)

2/8 Jussi Bjoerling (Swedish Tenor)

2/10 Cab Calloway dance

2/22-27 Holiday On Ice

3/10 Duke Ellington dance

3/12 Gene Krupa (drummer, orchestra leader)

3/13 Wrestling with former boxing champion Jack Dempsey as referee

3/21 "*Hamlet*" with Maurice Evans

4/7 Tony Pastor Orchestra

4/12 Lauritz Melchior with orchestra (Danish tenor)

4/23 New York Philharmonic Symphony Orchestra

5/6 Harry James Orchestra

6/6 Jimmy Dorsey Orchestra

6/23 Bob Wills & his Texas Playboys (King of Western Swing), Tex Ritter

6/27 Miss Chattanooga Pageant

7/30 Cab Calloway dance

8/8 Miss Tennessee Pageant

9/19 Louis Jordan dance

9/18 Wrestling with former heavyweight boxing champ Jack Dempsey as referee

10/7-12 Skating Vanities of 1948

11/10 Rose Bampton (soprano)

11/11 Roy Milton (R & B bandleader)

12/12 Erica Morini (violinist)

12/27- 1/13 Roller Derby

1948

1/19 Christopher Lynch (Tenor, Voice of Firestone)

1/21 Gene Krupa (drummer, bandleader)

1/26 Don Cossack Chorus

1/31 University of Chattanooga vs. University of Tennessee basketball

2/16-22 Holiday On Ice

2/27 Buddy Johnson orchestra

3/12 Rosario & Antonio (Spanish dancers)

3/13 WAGC Teen Timers show live broadcast starring singer Johnny Desmond (broadcast nationally by Mutual Network)

3/22 Nelson Eddy

3/23 Former child star Freddie Bartholomew starred in "The Hasty Heart" in the Community Theater

3/28 Detroit Symphony Orchestra

3/30 Count Basie Orchestra

4/5 Aida (Metropolitan Opera)

4/15 Tommy Dorsey Orchestra

4/17 WAPO Hillbilly Jamboree: The Delmore Brothers (Grand Ole Opry)

4/30 Miss Chattanooga pageant

5/4 Philadelphia Symphony Orchestra, conducted by Eugene Ormandy

7/30 "Grandpappy" Archie Campbell, Homer and Jethro, Chet Atkins

10/11 "Home to the Hermitage" play, starring Walter Pidgeon in NBC national broadcast via WAPO

10/13 The Ravens, George Hudson orchestra (dance)

10/17 Democratic VP candidate Sen. Alben Barkley of Kentucky

10/18 Lily Pons, soprano

10/19 Philadelphia all-girl Orchestra

10/25 Louis Jordan dance

10/27 *"Romeo & Juliet"* (Wagner Opera Company)

11/3 Marian Anderson (opera singer)

11/12 Harry James orchestra

11/19 Lionel Hampton orchestra

11/23-28 Skating Vanities of 1949

12/27- 1/14 Roller Derby

Bob Hope, Doris Day and Les Brown in 1949 (origin unknown)

1949

1/18 Ballet Russe de Monte Carlo

1/29-2/3 Holiday On Ice

2/18 Spike Jones Orchestra, Doodles Weaver

2/25 James Melton, tenor

3/21 Dinah Washington, Ravens, Cootie Williams Orchestra

4/11 *"Annie Get Your Gun"*

4/23 Bob Hope, Doris Day, Les Brown orchestra, and Irene Ryan (4,000 in attendance)

4/29 Dizzy Gillespie Orchestra

4/30 Dixieland Jamboree (The Hartman Brothers)

5/13-14 American Rose Society national convention

5/16 Guy Lombardo Orchestra

6/11 Dick Contino (teenage accordionist)

6/12 Renee Martz (8-year-old evangelist) 5,000 people

6/13 King Cole Trio (including Nat King Cole)

7/5 Amos Milburn (R & B band)

10/4 Louis Jordan dance

10/24 I Pagliacci (Wagner Opera)

11/8-13 Skating Vanities

11/14 Horace Heidt orchestra

11/15 Ravens, Dinah Washington

11/18 Bidu Sayao (opera)

12/17 University of Chattanooga vs. University of Dayton (Ohio) basketball

The 1950s

For many reasons, the 1950s was a most challenging decade for the auditorium. The facility had endured almost three decades of wear and tear, and it was starting to show. Paint was peeling, electrical wiring was long outdated, lighting was subpar, the ceiling and roof were in need of repairs, and the acoustics were still a problem. The city agreed to fund the renovations, and the building was closed for five months.

At the reopening, WDEF radio personality Luther Masingill was asked to help test the new sound system. He noted the improved sound quality, and commented, "Entertainers will no longer call it a barn, because the echoes are gone."

Unfortunately, that did not solve all the problems. Professional wrestling, which did not rely on lighting or sound quality, helped keep the auditorium afloat with steady crowds. But when television came to Chattanooga in 1954, its presence was felt at the auditorium box office. Some people wondered why they should spend money to see entertainers who were appearing in their living room free of charge.

By 1957, the auditorium was losing some of its signature events. The Home Show had moved to the Warner Park Field House. Several musical programs opted for the Chattanooga High School auditorium. Holiday on Ice, long a reliable draw, canceled a date. Roller derby attendance began to drop, resulting in cancellations. A news report quoted Mrs. William Montague of the Chattanooga Symphony and Opera as saying, "The auditorium is not good for anything except wrestling matches."

Still, the 1950s decade had its moments. From time to time, national radio broadcasts originated from the auditorium stage. Musical shows ranged from big bands, to gospel groups, to Grand Ole Opry stars, to rhythm and blues singers, to the pioneers of rock and roll. Radio station WDXB promoted several teen dances.

Throughout the decade, WDEF radio and the Kiwanis Club hosted a Christmas Eve party for children that packed the hall each year.

The first local telethon was held on behalf of Cerebral Palsy in April 1958 by WTVC Channel 9, then in its third month on the air. Then little-known game show host Johnny Carson emceed the event, four years before he would begin his long reign on NBC's "Tonight Show."

The auditorium enforced the social norms of the era, prohibiting any multi-racial shows. An evening's entertainment was all-white, or all-black. As "race" music (later known as rhythm and blues, or soul) gained popularity, younger white music lovers wanted to attend the shows. They could do so, but were seated in their own section, away from the black audience. When racial tensions flared up across the nation, particularly in the south, some disagreements spilled out into the audience, and outside the auditorium.

In 1959, the city was asked to provide $700,000 to modernize the heating and air conditioning system, add new curtains, and to install an escalator. The request was tabled. The optimism that accompanied the "improved" sound system in 1950 had been dampened by negative reviews calling it "a disappointment."

It would remain to be seen if the city would continue investing into a facility that no longer had widespread community support.

A full house at WDEF Kiwanis Club Christmas party for children in 1950 (WDEF)

1950

1/14 Artur Rubenstein (pianist)

1/25 Julius Caesar (Webster Shakespeare Company)

1/27 (Dave) Rubinoff and his Violin

1/30 Ballet Russe De Monte Carlo

2/4 University of Chattanooga vs. University of Georgia basketball

2/13-16 Holiday On Ice

3/7 Cincinnati Symphony Orchestra

3/8 Gene Autry, Rufe Davis, Melody Ranch Boys (2 shows)

3/28 Bob Astor and his Orchestra

3/29 Grand Ole Opry: Red Foley, Minnie Pearl, Hank Snow, Ernest Tubb, Rod Brasfield (Mayor Hugh Wasson presented Foley with a gold record for "Chattanooga Shoe Shine Boy")

3/31 Bidu Sayao (soprano)

4/3-5 *"Oklahoma"*

4/18 Amparo and Jose Sturbi (brother and sister concert pianists)

4/19 Feruccio Tagliavini (tenor)

5/7 Grand Ole Opry, 2 shows: Little Jimmy Dickens, Bill Monroe, Uncle Dave Macon

5/10 Charles Brown and the Smarties

REMODELING AND RENOVATIONS TOOK PLACE FROM MAY THROUGH OCTOBER 1950

10/13 Zino Francescatti (violinist)

10/17 Louis Jordan (dance)

10/30 Gladys Swarthout (soprano) with Chattanooga Symphony

11/7-12 Skating Vanities of 1951

11/16 Royal Philharmonic Orchestra of London

12/11 Margaret Truman (singer-pianist, daughter of President) with Chattanooga Symphony

1951

1/17 University of Chattanooga vs. Mississippi Southern basketball

2/5-9 Holiday on Ice

2/19 Harry Shub (violinist) with Chattanooga Symphony

2/23 Elena Nikolaidi (opera)

3/5 Harlem Globetrotters (5,000 fans)

3/12 Oscar Levant (concert pianist) with Chattanooga Symphony

3/13 *Don Juan in Hell* starring Agnes Moorehead, Charles Laughton, Charles Boyer

3/16 Spike Jones Orchestra (4,500 fans)

4/28 Hormel Girls (all-female drum and bugle corps, with dancers) on NBC and CBS radio

4/30 Lionel Hampton orchestra

6/22 Miss Chattanooga pageant

10/17-20 Shrine Circus

10/23 Johnny Otis/Little Esther

10/25 Patrice Munsel, vocalist with Chattanooga Symphony

12/4 Yehudi Menuhin (violinist)

1952

1/21 Alec Templeton (blind pianist)

1/23 New York Ballet Theater

1/25 Gospel Concert with Big Jim Waits, Speer Family

2/4-8 Holiday on Ice

2/12 Arthur Rubenstein (pianist) with Chattanooga Symphony

2/22 Guy Lombardo Orchestra

2/26 Dorothy Kirsten (soprano) with Pittsburgh Symphony Orchestra

2/29 Harlem Globetrotters

3/3 Isaac Stern (violinist) with Chattanooga Symphony

3/5 Billy Eckstine/Count Basie

4/4 Jussi Bjoerling (tenor)

4/25 Adolph Busch (violinist) and Rudolph Serkin (pianist)

5/2 Gospel concert: Bobby Strickland and Crusaders, Blue Ridge Quartet, Homeland Harmony Quartet

5/9 Gospel concert: Wally Fowler, Blackwood Brothers, Statesmen quartet

5/16 Miss Chattanooga pageant

9/24 Eisenhower for President rally with Sen Everett Dirksen (R-Illinois)

10/21 Jose Iturbi (Pianist)

10/22 Louis Jordan dance

10/24 Danish National Orchestra

10/28 Benny Goodman (clarinetist) with Chattanooga Symphony

11/25 Harry Shub (Violinist) with Chattanooga Symphony

12/5 Gene Autry (2 shows for Police Welfare Fund) 6,500 fans) with Smiley Burnette, Johnny Bond and Pat Buttram

12/6 Robert Shaw Chorale

12/27-1/4 Roller Derby

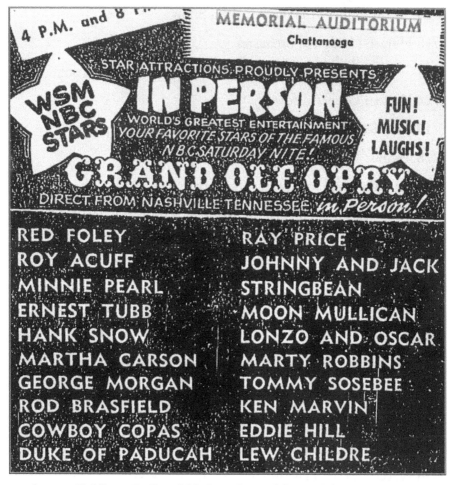

Star-studded lineup for Grand Ole Opry show at Memorial Auditorium in 1953

1953

1/17 Ballet Theater

1/19 Claudio Arrau (pianist) with Chattanooga Symphony

2/3-7 Holiday On Ice

2/9 Vronsky & Babin (pianists)

2/11 Robert Merrill (baritone) with Chattanooga Symphony

2/13-14 Bill Bailey All-Star Minstrel Show

2/18 Horace Heidt and orchestra

2/20 Gospel show (Bobby Strickland and the Crusaders, Sunshine Boys)

2/24 Harlem Globetrotters

3/10 Ossy Renardy (violinist) with Chattanooga Symphony

3/28 Tennis: Jack Kramer vs. Frank Sedgman

4/5 Rev. Billy Graham (Easter sunrise service)

4/5 Grand Ole Opry (Roy Acuff, Minnie Pearl, Little Jimmy Dickens, Ernest Tubb, Red Foley, Rod Brasfield, Hank Snow, George Morgan, Cowboy Copas, Duke of Paducah, Ray Price, Stringbean, Lonzo and Oscar, Marty Robbins, Moon Mullican) 2 shows

4/26 Boston Symphony

4/27 Tiny Bradshaw (dance)

5/2 Roy Rogers (2 sold out shows) with Dale Evans, Pat Brady

5/25 Sammy Thompson dance

5/29 Gospel Singing (Imperials, Crusaders)

7/1 Roy Milton orchestra, Camille Howard

7/26 WAGC Tenn. Hayloft Jamboree (Smokey Mtn. Quartet, Chester Allen)

8/24 Clovers, Ruth Brown

8/28 Gospel Concert (Crusaders, Happy Goodman family)

9/5 Tenn. Hayloft Jamboree (Bob Sanders, The Alabama Kid)

9/9 Wrestling with former boxing champion Jack Dempsey as referee

9/19 Tenn. Hayloft Jamboree (Bob Sanders, Little Haskett Brothers)

9/30 Wrestling with Fred Blassie

10/9 Wayne King (waltz bandleader)

10/26 Rise Stevens (soprano)

10/31 Dorothy Lamour

11/6 Grand Ole Opry, George Morgan

11/13 Agnes DeMille Dance Theater

11/16 St. Paul's Choir of London

12/28- 1/17 Roller Derby

1954

2/1-5 Holiday on Ice

2/9 Rudolf Serkin (pianist)

3/5 Harlem Globetrotters

3/15-17 *"South Pacific"*

3/29 Billy Eckstine, Nipsey Russell, Charles Brown, Ruth Brown, Clovers (sellout)

4/2 US Army Band

4/28 Clovers, Fats Domino, Charles Brown, Amos Milburn, Margie Day

4/30 Gospel show: Happy Goodman Family

5/18 America's Town Meeting (ABC live radio broadcast, via WAPO) "Is TVA Good for the Country?"

5/28 Gospel Melody Quartet, Revelaires

6/12 Pee Wee King Orchestra (national CBS radio broadcast via WDOD)

9/15 Nat King Cole dance, with Ella Johnson and Nolan Lewis, Buddy Johnson Orchestra

10/5 Louis Jordan dance

10/29 Gospel show: Melody Makers, Dixie Rhythm Boys, Crusaders

11/5 Amsterdam Royal Orchestra

11/14 Grand Ole Opry: Webb Pierce, Cowboy Copas, Martha Carson, Audrey Williams

11/16 Muddy Waters, Ray Charles, Ruth Brown, Charles Brown, Lowell Fulson

11/23 Lily Pons (soprano)

12/27- 1/16 Roller Derby

1955

1/19 Whittemore and Lowe (pianists)

2/2 *"Caine Mutiny"* with Paul Douglas and Wendell Corey

2/16 Boston Pops Orchestra conducted by Arthur Fiedler

2/25-26 Harlem Globetrotters

3/2 Yma Sumac "Bird Woman of the Andes"

3/3 Gospel: Harvesters, Keymasters

3/7 Clovers, Joe Turner, Moonglows, Bill Doggett

3/12 Horace Heidt Orchestra, Inks Spots, Eddy Arnold (NBC radio broadcast, and first live national TV broadcast from Chattanooga, both via WDEF)

3/25 Ballet Russe de Monte Carlo

3/28- 4/1 Holiday on Ice

4/16 Gospel: Chuck Wagon Gang, Harmonees, Revelaires

4/22 Dr Norman Vincent Peale

5/20 Hank Snow All-Star Jamboree with Faron Young, Wilburn Brothers, Duke of Paducah, Mother Maybelle & Carter Sisters (Elvis Presley was part of this tour group, but for reasons unknown, did not accompany the troupe to Chattanooga)

5/27 Roy Hamilton, Drifters, Erskine Hawkins, Lavern Baker, The Spaniels

7/16 Gospel: Marksmen, Rebels Quartet, Melody Makers

8/1 Sarah Vaughan, Al Hibbler, Moonglows

9/27 Bo Diddley, Etta James, Clovers, Faye Adams, Joe Turner, Bill Doggett, The Charms

10/1 Gospel show: Leroy Abernathy Quartet, Harvesters Quartet, Melody Makers

10/2 Roy Acuff, Kitty Wells, Johnnie & Jack

10/14 Buddy Johnson/Chuck Berry/Arthur Prysock

10/18 Boston Symphony

10/25 Grand Ole Opry: Little Jimmy Dickens, Rod Brasfield, Ray Price, Wilburn Brothers, Moon Mulligan

11/8 US Marine Band

11/18 Ballet Espagnols

11/28 Grand Ole Opry: Ferlin Husky, Martha Carson, Bill Carlisle

12/5 Rudolf Furkusny (pianist)

1956

1/16 Fabulous Harlem Magicians (Goose Tatum basketball)

1/18 Gladys Swarthout (soprano) and Eugene Conley (tenor)

1/30 Roy Hamilton, Platters, Drifters, Bo Diddley, Lavern Baker, Joe Turner (brawl…according to news reports, "9 Negroes jailed for disorderly conduct, 6 hospitalized..bottles and chairs thrown, after a Hamilton group member sat in a section reserved for white spectators")

2/3-7 Holiday on Ice

2/10 Gospel: Speer Family, Wally Fowler, former Louisiana Gov Jimmie Davis

2/21-22 Harlem Globetrotters

3/2 Robert Shaw Chorale

3/18 Gospel: Wally Fowler, Chuck Wagon Gang, The Statesmen, Hovie Lister

3/26 Joe Tex, Little Willie John, Five Royales

4/9 George London (baritone)

4/23 Grand Ole Opry: Duke of Paducah, George Morgan

4/25 Ruth Brown, Little Richard, Fats Domino, Clovers, Little Willie John, Cadillacs

5/10 Gospel: Moses Family, Revelaires

5/21 Bill Haley and his Comets (2 shows) Platters, Lavern Baker, Clyde McPhatter, Joe Turner, Teenagers, Bo Diddley, the Drifters (poor attendance, possibly due to concern over racial issues)

5/25 Gospel: Wally Fowler, Archie Campbell, Oak Ridge Quartet, The Moses Family

6/22 Gospel: Statesmen, Melody Makers, Blackwood Brothers, Crossroads Quartet

10/8 Grand Ole Opry (Hank Snow, Faron Young, Johnny Cash, Johnny Horton, Roy Orbison, Duke of Paducah, Sonny James)

11/2 Grand Ole Opry (Roy Acuff, Kitty Wells, Johnnie & Jack, Willis Bros.)

11/5 Little Richard, Etta James, Bill Doggett, Big Joe Turner, Moonglows, Robins

11/20 Ballet Russe le Monte Carlo

1957

1/15 Fabulous Harlem Magicians basketball

2/6 Eileen Farrell (soprano)

2/24 Gospel: Big Jim Waite, Keymasters, Melody Makers

3/7 Harlem Globetrotters

3/8 Carroll Glenn (violinist) and Eugene List (pianist)

Carl Smith, Goldie Hill, and Red Sovine in 1957 (origin unknown)

3/11 Bill Carlisle, Ray Price, Lester Flatt and Earl Scruggs

3/14 US Navy Band

3/18 B B King, Ruth Brown, Chuck Willis

4/9 Les Brown and his Band of Renown dance

4/14 Philip Morris Country Show (Carl Smith, Red Sovine, Goldie Hill)

8/8 Little Richard, Bobby Blue Bland

9/24 Fats Domino, Chuck Berry, Drifters, Frankie Lymon, Clyde McPhatter, and LaVern Baker. (Paul Anka, Buddy Holly, and the Everly Brothers were also part of this tour, but Chattanooga was one of five cities in which black and white performers were forbidden to appear together on stage. The other cities were Birmingham, New Orleans, Memphis and Tulsa.)

10/24 American Ballet Theater

11/13 Roy Hamilton, Clovers, Spaniels

11/18 Louis Kentner (Hungarian pianist)

Barbara Molloy and Jim Nabors in 1958 (Barbara Molloy)

For Jim Nabors, it all started in Chattanooga

Jim Nabors did so much in a career that spanned more than six decades. But he is forever ingrained in our memories for twenty-three episodes of Andy Griffith's show that originally aired from 1962 to 1964. He was Gomer Pyle. Remember "Citizens' Array-est!" If not, don't worry, it will be on TV somewhere very soon.

After leaving the Griffith show, he starred in his own sitcom, "Gomer Pyle USMC," and "The Jim Nabors Hour," a variety show, both on CBS. His recording and concert career was hugely successful, giving him a chance to showcase the rich baritone singing voice that surprised so many when it was unveiled on national TV.

That brings me to my Chattanooga Jim Nabors story. His employment at Channel 3 in the late 1950s is said to have "started it all." The Sylacauga, Alabama native moved to Chattanooga in 1957 to join the crew at the one-year-old station, then known as WRGP, with studios at 1214 McCallie Avenue across from Warner Park.

Long before the proliferation of national network and syndicated programming, local stations like Channel 3 produced variety shows, staged in a tiny, cramped studio under hot lights. Local TV was then considered to be "radio with pictures," and they took it quite literally. It was not uncommon for a host to hold up a copy of "Life" or "Look" magazine, or a book of travel photos, and just hold it up to the camera and flip through the pages while an instrumental record played in the background.

Eventually the station enlisted live entertainers. Local singers, musicians and dancers were invited to appear, and that worked out pretty well, except for one thing. If they called in sick, or got snowed in, the TV host still had an hour to fill. One day, such an occurrence changed the life of Nabors, who up until then, had been behind the scenes.

"Jimmy" Nabors, as they called him then, was 26. Back home in Alabama, he had sung in high school and church, and had acted in a few plays while attending the University of Alabama. To get his foot in the door of a TV station, he took the Channel 3 job. He was responsible for "cutting," or editing the film that was aired in commercials and news stories.

One afternoon, while the daily "Holiday for Housewives" hour was airing, a scheduled guest didn't show up, and the host realized he had several minutes left in the show. He sent an assistant scrambling through the station's offices, asking co-workers if they had any hidden talents. Nabors popped out of the film room. In his natural Alabama drawl he said, "Well, I can sing" (although that word sounded like "sang" coming out of his mouth).

There was no time to check the accuracy of his claims, so he was rushed into the studio, and the host hoped for the best.

What happened next was a TV miracle, the stuff of which legends are made. The film cutter with the high-pitched, twangy accent opened his mouth, and out came the richest, purest baritone anyone had ever heard. When he finished, studio crew members looked at each other in amazement, and then looked at Nabors. "Wow, we had no idea, you were absolutely great!" He just smiled and said, "Well, I told ya I could sang…"

1958

1/14 Gene Vincent dance (big)

2/1 Roberta Peters (opera)

2/4 Chuck Berry, Larry Williams, Midnighters, Five Royales

2/9-12 Holiday On Ice

2/14 Junior Miss pageant followed by Valentine Dance with Buddy Knox

3/2 Gospel: Blackwood Brothers, Statesmen Quartet

3/28 WDXB dance: Fabian, Jerry Lee Lewis, Jimmy Bowen, Tommy Sands, Buddy Knox

4/12-13 Cerebral Palsy telethon on WTVC (Johnny Carson, Roberta Quinlan, Vivian Dorsett, Jim Nabors, Barbara Molloy)

4/18 Roy Hamilton, Clovers, Thurston Harris, Donnie Elbert, Shirley and Lee

4/19 WAPO country show: Patsy Cline, George Morgan, Little Jimmy Dickens, Warner Mack

4/20 Victor Borge

5/21 Midnighters, Five Royales, Little Willie John

10/28 LaVern Baker, Jerry Butler & the Impressions, Jackie Wilson, Bobby Day, Lloyd Price

11/7 WDXB dance (Brenda Lee, Johnny Cash, Ray Stevens)

11/24 Highland Dancers of the Scots Guards

12/11 Cesar Siepi (bass)

1959

1/16 Goose Tatum basketball

1/27-30 Golden Gloves

2/8-11 Holiday on Ice

2/16 Philadelphia Orchestra directed by Eugene Ormandy

2/18 Five Royals, James Brown, Midnighters, Bobby Blue Bland

2/24 WDXB dance (Jerry Lee Lewis)

3/7 Lisa Della Casa (soprano)

3/13 Turtle Derby with Minnie Pearl, Carl Butler, and Bob Brandy

3/14 Mull's Singing Convention (also **5/15**, **9/18**)

3/31 Spivakovsky violin duo

4/8 Frankie Lymon, Lavern Baker, Coasters, Little Anthony, Lloyd Price, Clyde McPhatter

4/21 Duke of Paducah (country comedian)

6/10 Sam Cooke, Jackie Wilson, Jesse Belvin, Marv Johnson, Hank Ballard & the Midnighters

7/27 Clyde McPhatter, Bo Diddley, Chubby Checker, the Crests

9/7 Dee Clark, Ruth Brown, Drifters, Wilbert Harrison

10/9 Gospel: Speer Family, Wally Fowler, Prophets, Speer Family, LaFevre trio

10/19 Brook Benton, Ruth Brown, the Pips (news reports of "racial disturbance" after show)

10/28 Fred Waring & Pennsylvanians

11/9 Five Royales, Midnighters, Flamingos, Baby Cortez

12/14 Eileen Farrell (soprano)

The 1960s

Like everything else in the entertainment business, Soldiers and Sailors Memorial Auditorium got a huge boost from the baby boomers who had matured into ticket-buying rock and roll fans. Multi-act traveling shows backed by Motown, Dick Clark, and radio stations WDXB and WFLI filled the main hall on a regular basis. Ray Charles, Jackie Wilson, Chattanooga's own Impressions, and James Brown consistently drew big crowds.

Country and Western music was surging as well, and radio stations WMOC and WDOD promoted "country shindigs" and "showers of stars" featuring Grand Ole Opry entertainers. Christian minister and religious broadcaster J Bazzel Mull used his weekly Chattanooga television program to promote a successful series of gospel shows throughout the decade, and beyond. And for the "squares," Lawrence Welk and Fred Waring brought their nostalgic sounds to the non-rocking crowd.

Along with the top record-sellers of the 1960s, the auditorium also hosted numerous dramatic plays, operas and musicals, and internationally known musicians and actors like Leonard Bernstein, Bette Davis, Mahalia Jackson, Dinah Shore, Van Cliburn, Liberace, Johnny Mathis, and the Boston Pops.

The "Before They Were Stars" category includes names like 13-year-old Stevie Wonder in 1963, 20-year-old Patti LaBelle, then an opening act for Jerry Butler, 22-year-old Jimi Hendrix (then playing guitar for Jackie Wilson) in 1964, using the name Maurice James, 21-year-old Gladys Knight in 1965, 25-year-old Neil Diamond (three times in 1967), and 21-year-old Dolly Parton in 1968.

Holiday on Ice was a perennial audience favorite, as was the comedy basketball troupe the Harlem Globetrotters (and their various offshoots).

Early in the decade, air conditioning was installed, much to the relief of frequent visitors.

Dick Clark brought his Caravan of Stars to Chattanooga in the 1960s, promoting the event on his ABC "American Bandstand" show.

Tommy Thompson, who had managed the auditorium since 1932, died on March 11, 1963. Ben Landress was hired as the new manager and would serve until 1970.

The long-debated (and long overdue) renovations, once estimated at $700,000, grew to more than two million dollars' worth of improvements, and was finally approved in 1964. The project was the result of a campaign led by John Stophel and Alex Guerry Jr. It would result in a five-month shutdown in the summer and fall of 1966. Wrestling shows were temporarily moved to the National Guard Armory, and many musical acts had to settle for the smaller Tivoli Theater, or other venues.

Most of the top presidential candidates (and their surrogates) drew big crowds to the auditorium during elections seasons in 1960, 1964, and 1968. The civil rights conversation picked up steam in the 1960s, and crowds gathered to hear Rev. Martin Luther King Jr., and Jackie Robinson.

Forty-two years after its opening, the auditorium was rededicated on November 5, 1966, with few changes during the next quarter-century. Its seating capacity was now 4,843.

Ray Charles Band Plays Here Tuesday

Ray Charles and his orchestra, featuring the Raelets, will be starred in a concert and dance at Memorial Auditorium Tuesday night at 8 o'clock.

A special section has been reserved for white spectators.

Newspaper article promoting a 1960 Ray Charles show mentions a "special section for white spectators."

1960

1/25 Vienna on Parade

2/7-10 Holiday on Ice

2/16 Lorin Hollander (14-year-old child prodigy pianist)

2/17 Goose Tatum Basketball

2/19 *"The World of Carl Sandburg"* play with Bette Davis and Barry Sullivan

2/21, 4/9, 5/13 Mull's Singing Convention

3/4 Ray Charles and the Raelettes

3/9 Melissa Hayden, ballerina and Chicago Opera Ballet

3/11 Harlem Globetrotters

3/16 Four Freshmen (Community Theater)

3/30 Don Cossack Chorus and Dancers

5/2 Lloyd Price, Clyde McPhatter, Lavern Baker, Coasters, Little Anthony, Bo Diddley

6/13 B.B. King, Roy Hamilton, Clarence "Gatemouth" Brown, Shirley and Lee, Little Willie John

7/11 Jackie Wilson, Arthur Prysock

9/16 Leonard Bernstein & New York Philharmonic Orchestra

9/19 US Marine Band

9/24 Jerome Hines (opera)

9/30 Sen. Lyndon Johnson of Texas (Democratic candidate for Vice President) 2,000 people

10/1 Jerry Lee Lewis

10/11 Sen. Barry Goldwater (R-Arizona) speaking at Richard Nixon for President rally

10/19 Fabian, Brenda Lee, Duane Eddy, Jimmy Clanton, Freddie Cannon

10/26 Fred Waring & Pennsylvanians

10/28 Sam Cooke, Lavern Baker, Jerry Butler, Hank Ballard and the Midnighters, Little Willie John, Marv Johnson

11/22 Ray Charles and the Raelettes

11/23 Whittemore & Lowe (dual pianists)

12/30 Dr Martin Luther King Jr., Emancipation Day speaker (3500 people attended, he said "Let freedom ring from Lookout Mountain." Heavy security, fewer than 25 white attendees)

1961

1/18 Roger Williams (pianist)

1/28 Ernest Tubb, Grandpa Jones, Wilma Lee

2/24 Goose Tatum Basketball

2/26 Hank Snow, Archie Campbell, Kitty Wells, Johnnie and Jack, Skeeter Davis, Carl Smith, Jean Shepard, Hawkshaw Hawkins, Willis Brothers, Duke of Paducah, Bill Monroe, Stonewall Jackson (2 shows)

3/26-30 Holiday on Ice

4/1 George Jones

4/16 Baseball legend Jackie Robinson spoke to NAACP

4/19 Fats Domino, Chubby Checker, Shirelles, Bo Diddley, Drifters, Chuck Jackson

8/11 WDXB dance: Jerry Lee Lewis, Bill Black Combo

8/27 Brother Dave Gardner (comedy)

10/3 Jackie Wilson, Jerry Lee Lewis, Coasters, Ruth Brown, Bo Diddley, Chris Kenner

11/7 Roy Hamilton, Drifters, Chuck Berry, Lloyd Price

11/18 Roger Wagner Chorale

12/8 Mahalia Jackson

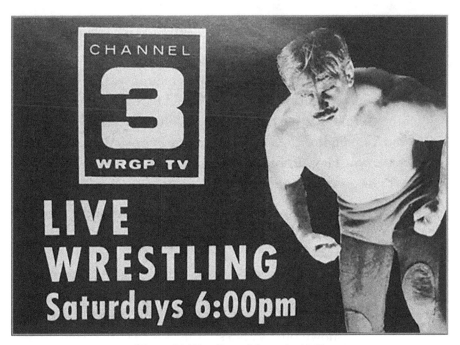

Channel 3 Wrestling ad from the 1960s

Wrestling helped keep the Auditorium afloat

Those of us who grew up watching Chattanooga TV in the "baby boomer era" surely remember these names: Jackie and Tojo. If we were lucky, we got to see them in person at Soldiers and Sailors Auditorium.

Jackie Fargo was one of our first TV superstars. We would watch "Live Wrestling" on Saturday afternoons because there was a good chance that Jackie would be trading one-liners with ringleader Harry Thornton.

Early is his career, Jackie (born Henry Faggart in North Carolina) started out as a "heel," a bad guy. By the 1960s, Jackie had evidently seen the light, and turned into a good guy with a hint of mischief. His usual opponents were introduced as Japanese or German, and fans were happy to see Jackie cheat a little to pay them back for World War II.

Thornton, the master promoter, knew a goldmine when he saw it. Every year or so, he made sure Jackie would have a bitter feud with either the Germans or the Japanese. Quite often, Jackie's foe was the evil Tojo Yamamoto. Tojo's real name was Harold Watanabe, and he was born in Hawaii. But Thornton told us he was from Japan, and that was good enough for me.

Tojo was a scowling presence. On Saturdays, Jackie would appear on the Chattanooga wrestling show for a friendly interview to promote a favorite charity. And then out of nowhere, Tojo would wage a sneak attack on Jackie with a wooden shoe. Jackie, caught by surprise, would wipe away blood (or something that looked like it) and vow revenge. Harry would arrange a grudge match between the two, but it would not be shown on TV. No sir, this was so big, it would have to be staged in front of 5,000 screaming fans at the Auditorium, all of whom were more than willing to cough up five bucks to see how it played out.

Those of us fortunate enough to go, saw a longer version of the weekly TV slugfest. The rest of us would have to depend on newspaper accounts, friends who had attended, or we'd have to wait until the next Saturday when Harry would report the outcome.

Saturday wrestling was my original Must-See-TV, and I later learned that the weekly matches at the Auditorium helped keep it afloat during slow periods when concerts and plays were not attracting much business.

When I was "all grown up," I learned that Jackie Fargo had retired to North Carolina. I figured someday I might make a visit and tell him how much I appreciated his style and showmanship. I'd thank him for entertaining folks from 4 to 104, getting their minds off their problems for an hour or two each week.

I waited too late. Jackie died in 2013, just before his 83rd birthday. I hope that somewhere, in that big wrestling ring in the sky, Jackie, Tojo, and Harry are having some laughs as they swap stories about those good times at Memorial Auditorium.

1962

1/3 Harlem Magicians

1/20 The Escorts (with Charlie McCoy)

1/26 Pete Fountain (clarinetist)

1/29 Van Cliburn (pianist)

2/10-16 Holiday On Ice

2/19 Fred Waring and the Pennsylvanians

2/23, 4/27, 5/11, 8/17 Mull's Singing Convention

3/14 *"The Music Man"*

3/18 Bandleader Lawrence Welk was on stage, with performers from his TV show, including JoAnn Castle, Larry Hooper, the Lennon Sisters, Myron Floren, Norma Zimmer, Dick Dale, Bobby Burgess and Barbara Boylan, and Joe Feeney (Record crowd)

3/21 Boston Pops conducted by Arthur Fiedler

4/24 B.B. King, Sam Cooke, Gladys Knight & Pips, Solomon Burke, Dion, Ral Donner, Drifters, Dee Clark

5/15 Rev Martin Luther King Jr. (speaking to Southern Christian Leadership Conference)

5/19 Tony Martin (365 Club benefit)

7/27 James Brown

8/7, 8/14 Roller Derby

8/15 Jackie Wilson

9/19 Ray Charles

10/20 Chubby Checker

1963

1/5 National Ballet of Canada

1/18 Pete Fountain

1/26 Harlem Magicians basketball

2/11 Detroit Symphony

2/19-22 Holiday On Ice

2/25 James Brown

3/9 Ronald Turini (Canadian pianist)

3/11 Count Basie Orchestra

3/24, 10/18, 12/27 Mull's Singing Convention

3/28-30 *"My Fair Lady"*

4/3 Ferrante & Teicher

4/17 Mahalia Jackson

4/28 Dinah Shore, Vaughn Meader (JFK impersonator) huge crowd, 365 Club benefit

5/13 Sam Cooke, The Drifters, Jerry Butler, Crystals, Solomon Burke, Dionne Warwick

5/25 Webb Pierce (2 shows)

9/5 Grand Ole Opry: Sonny James, Roy Acuff, Curly Fox, Archie Campbell, Lefty Frizzell, Country Boy Eddie

9/11 James Brown, Martha and Vandellas, Jimmy Reed, Inez Foxx, Drifters, Doris Troy, The Crystals

10/2 Sam Cooke, Dion, Bobby Blue Bland, Little Willie John, Freddie Scott

10/15 Ala. Gov. George Wallace (2500 people) speaking out against President Kennedy, joined by former Tenn. Gov. Prentice Cooper

10/29 Little Stevie Wonder (age 13), Miracles, Marvin Gaye, Martha & Vandellas, Mary Wells, Kim Weston, Contours (Motortown Revue)

10/30 Royal Philharmonic Orchestra of London

11/11 Koutcv Bulgarian National Ensemble

11/12 Hootenanny folk singers (Glenn Yarbrough, Journeymen, Geezinslaw Brothers, Jo Mapes, Halifax III)

11/19 James Brown

11/20 *"Tosca"* by Goldovsky Opera

12/13 Harlem Globetrotters

1964

1/11 Tommy Scott Medicine Show

1/24 Harlem Magicians

2/2 Peter, Paul and Mary (Big crowd)

2/10-13 Holiday on Ice

2/18 Liberace (concert was attended by members of the Jimmy Hoffa trial jury)

2/22, 4/11, 5/15, 10/16, 12/5 Mull's Singing Convention

2/25 Grant Johannsen (pianist)

3/7 Smothers Brothers (Big crowd)

3/14-15 Beatles Washington DC Coliseum concert (**2/11/64**) closed circuit broadcast

4/4 Fats Domino, Jerry Butler, Impressions, Gene Chandler, Drifters, Barbara Lewis, Major Lance, Sam and Dave

4/6 Birgitt Nilsson (soprano)

Poster for 1965 Motown concert

5/13 Kingston Trio/Frank Fontaine (as Crazy Guggenheim) 365 Club benefit (BIG)

7/25 Grand Ole Opry: Lonzo and Oscar, Jan Moore, Archie Campbell

9/21 Jerry Butler, Solomon Burke, Betty Everett, Chuck Jackson, Drifters, Carla Thomas, Patti LaBelle

10/7 Al Hirt

10/10 Richard Nixon Republican rally (big crowd, he campaigned for presidential candidate Barry Goldwater)

10/24 Jackie Wilson/Sam Cooke (Jimi Hendrix, then known as Maurice James, backed up Jackie Wilson on guitar as part of the Gorgeous George Band), Garnet Mimms, Hank Ballard & Midnighters

11/13 "*La Bohème*" by Goldovsky Grand Opera

11/22 Hank Williams Jr. (in conjunction with release of movie "Your Cheatin' Heart") with his mother Audrey Williams, Roger Miller, Jean Shepard, Stonewall Jackson, Curley Fox

12/6 Dick Clark's Caravan of Stars: Two shows. Dick Clark was on stage with Sonny Knight, Bobby Freeman, the Supremes, Johnny Tillotson, Brian Hyland, Drifters, Hondells, Crystals, Dee Dee Sharp, Mike Clifford, Velvettes

12/8 Arthur Gold & Robert Fitzdale (dual pianists)

1965

1/1, 1/23, 2/7, 3/20, 5/8, 10/8 Mull's Singing Convention

1/22 Peter, Paul and Mary (Big crowd)

1/30 Harlem Magicians basketball

2/5 Berlin Philharmonic Orchestra

3/3 Johnny Mathis/Young Americans

3/5 Sam Cooke memorial (he died in December 1964)

3/6 Chicago Opera Ballet

3/7 Grand Ole Opry: Billy Grammer, Osborne Brothers

3/19 WFLI Spectacular # 1 (Jan and Dean, Johnny Rivers, Jerry Lee Lewis, Bobbi Martin, Sue Thompson, Jimmy Cross, Missing Links)

4/6 Harlem Globetrotters

4/10 Connie Francis/Morey Amsterdam (365 Club benefit) 6,000 attendance

4/14 Richard Tucker (Metropolitan Opera tenor)

4/19 Jackie Wilson, Solomon Burke, B.B. King, Little Stevie Wonder, Ben E. King, Gladys Knight & the Pips

4/23 WDOD 40th anniversary Jamboree: Bill Anderson, Roy Drusky, Lonzo & Oscar, Charlie Louvin

5/9 Gene Pitney, Vic Dana, Reflections, Crystals, Bill Black Combo, Dobie Gray, Brian Hyland, Gene Pitney, Bobby Goldsboro, Gary Lewis and the Playboys, Hullabaloos

5/11 Jerry Butler, Joe Tex, The Impressions, Gene Chandler, Major Lance, The Drifters, Betty Everett

5/20 Chet Atkins, Floyd Cramer, Boots Randolph

5/25 Sonny Liston/Cassius Clay closed circuit heavyweight boxing championship match

6/21 Marvin Gaye, Jr. Walker, Martha and the Vandellas, Four Tops, Brenda Holloway, Willie Tyler and Lester, Choker Campbell Band (Motortown Revue)

7/12 Joe Tex, Otis Redding, Billy Stewart, Gladys Knight and The Pips, William Bell

7/16 Beach Boys (attendance 1500, sponsored by WMOC)

8/2 James Brown (big crowd, sponsored by WMOC)

Singer Lesley Gore at WFLI Spectacular in 1966 (Johnny Eagle)

8/20 WMOC Dick Clark Caravan of Stars (Peter and Gordon, Tom Jones, Turtles, Shirelles, Ronnie Dove, Mel Carter, Brian Hyland, Billy Joe Royal)

9/10 Gene Pitney's Bonanza of Stars: Gene Pitney, Bobby Goldsboro, Edwin Starr, Dixie Cups, Bobby Vee, Gary US Bonds, Chiffons (Sonny and Cher were promoted, but did not show up, much to the dismay of audience members)

9/20 Jackie Wilson, Chuck Jackson, Temptations, Bobby Blue Bland, The Drifters

10/4 Solomon Burke

11/2 The Impressions, Jerry Butler, Gene Chandler, Ikettes, Major Lance, William Bell, Gladys Knight & The Pips

11/6 Mantovani and his Orchestra

11/12 Pete Fountain

11/14 Liberace

11/19 James Brown

11/24 Norman Luboff Choir

1966

1/15 Lee Luvisi (pianist)

2/8 Jose Molina (flamenco dancer)

2/27 *Pinocchio*

3/5 Mary Costa (soprano)

3/19 WFLI Spectacular # 2 (2 shows) (Lou Christie, Paul Revere and the Raiders, Vogues, Lesley Gore, Ronnie Dove, Hullabaloos)

3/30 Harlem Globetrotters

4/2 Peter, Paul and Mary (big crowd)

4/11 Jackie Wilson, Impressions, Ben E. King, Lavern Baker, Drifters, B. B. King, Manhattans

4/15 Mary Costa (opera, Tennessee Native)

4/16 "Gomer Pyle" (Jim Nabors), Teresa Brewer (365 Club)

5/4 James Brown

5/13 *"Where the Action Is"* tour: Gary Lewis & Playboys, Paul Revere and the Raiders, Billy Joe Royal, Steve Alaimo, Linda Scott

5/14 WDOD Country Music Spectacular # 1 (Hank Snow, Sonny James, Johnny Paycheck, Warner Mack, Stonewall Jackson, Tommy Cash)

5/20 Chet Atkins, Floyd Cramer, Boots Randolph

5/31 Mahalia Jackson

JUNE-NOVEMBER: Auditorium renovation

11/5 Rededication of Soldiers and Sailors Memorial Auditorium

11/11 Paul Revere & Raiders, Turtles, Ian Whitcomb (big, WMOC)

11/29-12/4 Holiday On Ice

12/7 James Brown (WMOC)

12/9 WFLI Spectacular # 3: Roy Orbison, Sam the Sham, Byrds, Lou Christie, David Houston, Billy Joe Royal, Sandy Posey, McCoys, Newbeats, Question Mark and Mysterians

12/11 WDOD Country Music Spectacular # 2: George Jones, Don Gibson, Del Reeves, Tompall and the Glaser Brothers, Lefty Frizzell, Johnny Darrell, Jan Howard, Dalton Roberts (2 shows)

WFLI Spectacular ad in 1967

*Peter Noone of Herman's Hermits signs autograph while enjoying a day
at Chickamauga Lake after the August 17, 1967 WFLI Spectacular.
WFLI manager Johnny Eagle is seated at left. (Steve Johnson)*

*Roger Daltrey and Keith Moon of the Who enjoy a day at Chickamauga Lake after the
August 17, 1967 WFLI Spectacular. (Steve Johnson)*

"All on One Stage! The Jet-FLI Spectaculars"

What if you heard this announcement today? "Coming Saturday to Memorial Auditorium! See the hottest recording acts in the world, all performing their hits LIVE on stage! TWO great shows, Saturday, at 5 and 8 p.m.! Tickets are on sale now for only twenty dollars!"

That is so ridiculous, right? First, if all the hottest acts bothered to come to Chattanooga, the ticket prices would be astronomical. Not to mention the ego-fueled battles over billing, who would close the show, who would have the largest dressing room, and other details.

Yet in the 1960s, it did work. Ask any baby boomer who grew up in Chattanooga about the Jet-FLI (WFLI radio) Spectaculars, and they will testify. On any given night, more than half of the acts in Billboard's Top Ten would be in Chattanooga, on the Auditorium stage, one right after another. Ticket prices ranged from $2.50 to $3.50.

If you missed Paul Revere and the Raiders this year, don't worry. They just might be back next year. Same goes for Lou Christie and other repeat visitors. Here's the story behind the most amazing series of live performances ever staged in Chattanooga, before or since.

WFLI's strong signal captured most of the teen and young adult audience as soon as it signed on in 1961, and the station got even stronger when the Beatles and other British acts shook up the music world a few years later. WFLI was among a group of stations owned in part by the Brennan family of Alabama. The others were in Birmingham, Montgomery, and Jacksonville, Florida. The stations pooled their resources to create multi-star shows twice a year at each station, making it convenient for the artists. For example, they'd schedule shows Friday in Chattanooga, Saturday in Birmingham and Sunday in Montgomery, so the artists had an easier flight schedule.

Ticket prices were low, according to WFLI's first general manager Johnny Eagle, to allow as many people as possible to attend.

"It wasn't meant to be a money-maker," he said. "Our owner Billy Benns just wanted to promote the radio station, and boy did it ever work!"

The first Spectacular was staged on March 19, 1965, and for the next six years, the twice-yearly shows were enormously popular. Listeners anxiously awaited the announcements of the lineups for the summer and winter shows.

The deejays would promote about five acts for a few weeks, and then just before the show, a "surprise special guest" would be added. With great fanfare, they would tell us that Johnny Rivers or Andy Kim or some other big name "has just been added...you'd better get your tickets now!"

In that pre-internet era, ticket sales were handled literally by hand, by the WFLI staff. People sent cash in self-addressed, stamped envelopes, or drove to the studio to get them in person.

"We handled everything, from setting up the sound, hiring the security, making travel arrangements, and getting the stars to and from the airport," Eagle said. "Peter Noone and Herman's Hermits got here three days early in the summer of 1967, and we put them up in the Downtowner Motel, across from the Read House. They had a great time water skiing at Lake Chickamauga." (It should also be noted that the Who was on the bill that night, along with Neil Diamond and others).

It didn't always go smoothly. A few days before a heavily promoted show, Eagle heard about some confusion on the part of Paul Revere and the Raiders. They had the number-one song in the nation, and were outselling the Beatles. But the Raiders management had mistakenly booked two shows in Atlanta on the same day as the

WFLI shows. "We freaked out," Eagle said. "Nobody wanted to go on stage and tell five thousand screaming kids that the Raiders were not going to play. We arranged for our co-owner Bill Brennan, down in Birmingham to fly his private jet to Atlanta, pick up the Raiders after their 3:00 show, get them to Chattanooga in time to open our 5:30 show, fly them back to Atlanta to open their 8:00 show, and then fly them back here to close our 9:00 show. We paid police escorts to get them to and from the airport twice, and hired a crew to haul Paul Revere's instruments on and off the stage, every time."

The falsetto-voiced Lou Christie ("Lightning Strikes") was a local favorite who caused a different kind of problem. "He turned the gals on," Eagle said. "He would rip off his shirt, and that was considered racy back then. It would get the teenage girls too excited. He did it at the 5:30 show, and the police told us if he did it again at 9:00, we'd have to close the curtains."

Not every act caused a headache. Eagle speaks fondly of Roy Orbison. "He just stood there on stage, didn't say much and didn't move a muscle, but that boy could sing," Eagle said. "The girls loved his voice, and the guys loved his guitar playing."

Eagles said Kenny Rogers was among the nicest stars. "He carried his own equipment, he had no help, no ego. With all those big stars in the lineup, it was hard to get anybody to open the show. I'd go up to Kenny, kind of embarrassed, and ask him if he would be kind enough to open the show, and he'd say absolutely, whatever you need. He had more hits than anybody, but he didn't act like it. He couldn't have been any nicer. It was no surprise to me that he went on to be more successful than any of them."

There were various other multi-star shows at the Auditorium from the 1950s to the 1970s. Nashville's Grand Ole Opry would send a troupe of entertainers, often packing a lot of star power into one night. Prior to WFLI's emergence, radio station WDXB would sponsor similar lineups, although many are lost to history. American Bandstand's Dick Clark, singer Gene Pitney, and Motown Records sent caravans of stars on multi-city trips also, occasionally including Chattanooga on their tours. Chattanooga country radio stations WMOC and WDOD staged "Country Shindigs" and "Showers of Stars" drawing a somewhat older crowd to the Auditorium.

But none are as widely remembered as the Jet-FLI Spectaculars, which gave Chattanooga area teens a chance to scream for their musical idols in their own hometown.

1967

1/1 Mull's Gospel: Speer Family, Dottie and the Singing Rambos, Statesmen Quartet, Imperials, Scenicland Quartet

1/25 Arthur Fiedler & New Orleans Philharmonic Orchestra

1/28 WDOD Country Spectacular # 3 (Porter Wagoner, Norma Jean, Loretta Lynn, Wilburn Brothers, Billy "Crash" Craddock, Little Jimmy Dickens, Chuck Wagon Gang)

1/29 Harlem Magicians basketball

2/6 Vronski and Babin (Dual Pianists)

3/8 Al Hirt (trumpeter)

3/10 WDOD Country Spectacular # 4 (Carl and Pearl Butler, Webb Pierce, Kitty Wells, Johnny Wright, Stonemans, Little Jimmy Dickens, Joe Maphis, Justin Tubb)

3/15 Pearl Buck (author)

4/1 Sandor Konya (tenor)

4/4 Harlem Globetrotters

4/11 Jackie Wilson, B.B. King, Drifters, Freddie Scott, Johnny Guitar Watson

4/16 *Where the Action Is* tour: (Neil Diamond, P.J. Proby, Tommy Roe, Billy Joe Royal, Keith Allison, Freddie Cannon, Dale Wright, Men of Action, Hard Times, Baby Ray and the Precious Few, Action Kids)

4/17 Robert Shaw Chorale

4/23 Dinah Shore, Rowan and Martin (365 Club benefit)

5/19 WMOC Country Shindig # 1 Loretta Lynn, Wilburn Brothers, Sonny James, Ralph Emery, Jim and Jesse

6/9 James Brown

6/27 Jerry Butler, Ben E. King, Chi-Lites, Tyrone Davis, Chuck Jackson, Maxine Brown, Patti LaBelle

7/1 WFLI Spectacular # 4: Paul Revere and Raiders, Lou Christie, Gary Lewis & Playboys, Every Mother's Son, Billy Joe Royal, Steve Alaimo, Roy Head (2 shows, both sold out)

7/21 Dave Clark 5 (small crowd, estimated at 300-500)

8/4 Country Shindig #2: Hank Williams Jr., Jerry Lee Lewis, Conway Twitty, Tom Pall and the Glaser Brothers, Charlie Louvin, The Cheatin' Hearts, The Lonesome Blue Boys, Lamar Morris, Jeff Simmons

8/9 Gov. George Wallace Stand Up for America (attendance 4,000)

8/15 Jackie Wilson, B.B.King, Linda Jones, Freddie Scott, Drifters, Major Lance

8/17 WFLI Spectacular # 5: Herman's Hermits, The Who, Neil Diamond, Blues Magoos, Jon & Robin, The In Crowd (tickets $3.50) (2 shows)

8/18 Mull's Gospel: Happy Goodmans, LeFevres, Prophets, Florida Boys, Dixie Echoes, Scenicland Quartet

9/2 Masters Festival of Music: Chet Atkins, Boots Randolph, Floyd Cramer

9/29 WMOC Country Shindig #3 Ernest Tubb, Waylon Jennings, Billy Walker, Don Gibson, Skeeter Davis, Chuck Wagon Gang

11/4 Liberace

Waylon Jennings at Memorial Auditorium in 1968 (Jack Mullins)

11/20 Ivan Davis (pianist)

11/23 Mull's Gospel: Oak Ridge Boys, Blackwood Brothers, Scenicland Quartet, Statesmen Quartet

11/25 WFLI Spectacular # 6: Tommy James & Shondells, Neil Diamond, Association, Billy Joe Royal, Charlie McCoy & Escorts, Ohio Express, Joe South, the Rose Garden (2 shows)

12/9 James Brown

12/11 Harry Simeone Chorale

1968

1/3 American Ballet Theater

1/13 Loretta Lynn, Conway Twitty, Doyle Wilburn, Faron Young, Tammy Wynette

1/17-21 Holiday On Ice

1/22 Preservation Hall Jazz Band

1/24-26 Up with People

1/27 Eddy Arnold, Don Bowman

1/28 Stoneman Family (Community Theater)

1/29 Roberta Peters (soprano)

2/3 Harlem Magicians

3/1 WMOC Country Shindig # 4: Sonny James Trio, Faron Young and the Country Deputies, Conway Twitty and the Lonely Blue Boys, Jimmy Dickens and the Country Boys, Norma Jean

3/2 WFLI Spectacular # 7 Gary Puckett & Union Gap, American Breed, John Fred & Playboy Band, Lou Christie, Hollies, Jay and the Techniques, Bobbi Lynn & the Blynnders (two sold-out shows)

3/4-5 Rev. Bob Harrington

3/23 WMOC Country Shindig # 5: Porter Wagoner, Dolly Parton, Connie Smith, Bill Monroe, George Hamilton IV, Stonewall Jackson

5/18 WMOC Country Shindig # 6: Buck Owens, Wynn Stewart, Waylon Jennings, Sheb Wooley

5/24 James Brown

6/12 Gov. George Wallace (D-Alabama) presidential campaign rally

6/28 WFLI Spectacular # 8: Roy Orbison, Mitch Ryder & Detroit Wheels, Buckinghams, Tams, Gene & Debbe (2 shows)

7/20 WMOC Country Shindig # 7 Bill Anderson, Carl Smith, Kenny Price, Willis Bros., Osborne Bros.

7/23 Lawrence Welk Show stars: Jo Ann Castle, Arthur Duncan, Joe Feeney, Dick Dale, Larry Hooper

7/26 Young Rascals

8/9 Marty Robbins

8/15-16 Rev. Bob Harrington

8/31 Chet Atkins, Floyd Cramer, Boots Randolph, Jerry Reed

9/21 Eric Burdon and the Animals

9/27 WMOC Country Shindig # 8 George Jones, Grandpa Jones, Arthur Smith, Don Gibson

9/27 Richard Nixon for President (10,000 people, overflow crowd)

10/9 Temptations/Marvellettes

10/23 Andy Williams/Roger Miller (sold out)

10/25 Mull's Gospel: LeFevres, Jimmie Davis, Statesmen, Speer Family

10/30 Mantovani and his Orchestra

11/15 WFLI Spectacular # 9: Paul Revere and the Raiders, Sam the Sham & the Pharoahs, Brian Hyland, Ohio Express, Bobby Boyd and the Playboy Review (2 shows)

11/23 WMOC Country Shindig # 9: Loretta Lynn, Conway Twitty, Sonny James, Doyle Wilburn, Jack Green

12/3 *Funny Girl* (Marilyn Michaels)

12/5 Former heavyweight boxing champion Joe Louis referees wrestling

1969

1/25-26 March of Dimes Telerama # 3 David Canary, Linda Cristal

2/4-9 Holiday On Ice

3/21 WMOC Country Shindig #10: Porter Wagoner, Dolly Parton, Loretta Lynn, Glaser Brothers, Mel Tillis, Osborne Brothers

3/26 Harlem Globetrotters

4/4 Mull's Gospel: Singing Rambos, LeFevres, Statesmen, Blackwood Brothers, Prophets

5/13 Billy Joe Royal (at Junior Achievement Awards banquet)

5/24 James Brown (fight broke out later, James Brown helped break it up)

6/19 Bobby Blue Bland

6/20 WMOC Country Shindig #11: Jerry Lee Lewis, Merle Haggard, Jean Shepard, Linda Gail, Bonnie Owens

8/1 WFLI Spectacular #10: Tommy James and the Shondells, Cowsills, Box Tops, Mercy, Andy Kim (2 shows)

8/15 WMOC Country Shindig # 12: Tammy Wynette, George Jones, Norma Jean

8/16 Mull's Gospel: Jimmie Davis, Chuck Wagon Gang, Downings, Speer Family, LeFevres

9/26 Mull's Gospel: Swanee River Boys, Happy Goodman Family, Florida Boys, Inspirations, Steve Sanders

11/14 Mull's Gospel: Oak Ridge Boys, Thrasher Brothers, Downings, Inspirations

11/21 WMOC Country Shindig # 13: Merle Haggard, Jack Greene, Jeannie Seely, Osborne Brothers, Bonnie Owens

11/28 WFLI Spectacular #11: Grassroots, Kenny Rogers & First Edition, Bobby Sherman, Melanie, Ray Stevens, Buckinghams, Canned Heat (2 shows)

12/6 Chet Atkins, Boots Randolph, Floyd Cramer, Homer & Jethro

12/21 Harlem Globetrotters

The 1970s

The calm before the storm, or more accurately put, it may have been the storm before the calm. The 1970s decade brought more capacity crowds than ever before to the auditorium. The now half-century old venue was enjoying a temporary resurgence, as the much larger UTC Arena was in the planning stages.

Multi-act "package" shows were on the decline, soon to be replaced by headline acts drawing huge crowds on their own. A hard-fought three-way top-40 radio station battle (between WFLI, WGOW, and WDXB) resulted in concerts featuring the hottest acts on the charts. Country music's steady growth, credited in part to the top-rated "Hee Haw" television show, also brought big stars to the auditorium stage, sponsored by competitors WDOD and WMOC. Chattanooga's proximity to Nashville almost ensured that any country artist with a number one record would appear in the Scenic City. The Mull's Singing Convention gospel shows were frequent and well-attended.

Artists as diverse as James Brown, Chet Atkins, Conway Twitty, the Bill Gaither Trio, Liberace, and Goose Creek Symphony were frequent and reliable crowd-pleasers throughout the decade.

In 1973, a trio of young Texas rockers calling themselves ZZ Top made their first Chattanooga appearance. There would be many more, on several local stages.

In what became a cherished Chattanooga memory, the annual March of Dimes Telerama was presented each January, with sponsoring stations WRCB and WTVC bringing in top Hollywood stars performing for charity. The broadcasts usually ran for about 19 hours, from 11 p.m. Saturday night, to 6 p.m. Sunday evening.

Top national political figures, including several presidential hopefuls and Vice President Spiro Agnew visited the auditorium. A 1973 highlight was an appearance by the Apollo 11 astronauts.

Some of the nation's most famous TV evangelists were also popular draws, including Jimmy Swaggart, Bob Harrington (the Chaplain of Bourbon Street), and Ernest Angley.

Roller Derby, professional wrestling, Golden Gloves boxing, circus acts, professional tennis exhibitions, Holiday on Ice, the Harlem Globetrotters and other non-musical attractions remained popular in the 1970s.

In 1975, a popular tradition began when Bethel Bible School (later Bethel Bible Village) recruited Tom T. Hall to headline a multi-star benefit concert. Pat Boone took over hosting duties in 1978 and brought in big-name entertainers annually for more than twenty years.

Near the end of the decade, longtime radio and TV comedian Red Skelton made the first of two Auditorium appearances, charming the crowd during a 150-minute show, with no opening act, and no intermission. He seemed to enjoy the show as much as (or more than) the audience. As the show passed the 90-minute mark, he would occasionally shout, "You want more?" The answer was always "YES!" He attracted media attention earlier in the day while buying props for his act at the Hill's Department Store on Brainerd Road, cheerfully interacting with customers.

There were bumps in the road, most dangerously the riot that broke out in 1971 when soul music star Wilson Pickett refused to play, claiming he was supposed to be paid in advance. There were acts of vandalism, with the Tennessee Highway Patrol and National Guard called in to restore order.

When the controversial play "Jesus Christ Superstar" came to town, the streets outside the auditorium were filled with protesters. However, they were far outnumbered by two sellout audiences.

On May 13, 1974, the Doobie Brothers headlined a show (promoted by Chattanooga native Dennis Haskins before his acting days), and their post-show behavior resulted in a ban from the auditorium. Group members were unwinding, celebrating the final show of their spring tour, and began throwing cream pies around the stage, some of which landed on the venue's upholstered chairs. Security officers called in the police, who put a scare into the Doobie Brothers, according to Haskins. The group was inducted into the Rock and Roll Hall of Fame in 2020.

On April 26, 1976, the young artist hailed as "Rock's New Sensation" by Time and Newsweek magazines made his first and only Chattanooga appearance. Our town was a bit late to the Springsteen party, with fewer than one thousand fans in the seats.

Two top-selling singers, Helen Reddy and Mac Davis co-headlined a show on July 27, 1973. Ironically, they died on the same day, September 29, 2020.

Another music superstar, Charlie Daniels made his first Chattanooga appearance at the Auditorium on September 26, 1973. He would go on to perform in Chattanooga more often than possibly any other nationally known headline act. Sadly, he had scheduled another auditorium show for August 8, 2020, which had already been canceled due to the coronavirus pandemic. He died on July 6, 2020 at the age of 83.

Still another sadly historic footnote occurred in the career of the southern rock band Lynyrd Skynyrd. In late 1973, they made their first

Auditorium appearance as the opening act for Jo Jo Gunne. "Skynyrd" became another Chattanooga mainstay, soon moving up to headline status. The band was scheduled to play the Auditorium on October 25, 1977. Five days earlier, three group members, including lead singer Ronnie Van Zant were killed in a plane crash. Many fans have kept their tickets to the show to this day.

Clyde Hawkins took over from Ben Landress as Auditorium manager in 1970, a position he would hold for the next eighteen years.

1970

1/17 Mull's Gospel: Happy Goodmans, Florida Boys, Inspirations, Scenicland Quartet, Steve Sanders

1/23 WMOC Country Shindig # 14: Porter Wagoner, Dolly Parton, Kitty Wells, Johnny Wright, Wynn Stewart

1/24-25 March of Dimes Telerama # 4 (Mark Slade, Maureen Arthur, Gretchen Wyler)

2/11 Stevie Wonder

2/13-20 Rev Bob Harrington (8 dates)

2/26 Ga. State Rep. Julian Bond (D)

2/27 James Brown

3/10-15 Holiday on Ice

3/27 Mull's Gospel: Singing Rambos, Downings, LeFevres, Speer Family

3/20 Country Shindig # 15: Loretta Lynn, Osborne Bros., Wilburn Bros., Peggy Sue, Del Reeves, Sonny Wright

4/17 WFLI Spectacular # 12 (2 sold-out shows) Paul Revere and Raiders, Canned Heat, The Guess Who, Grassroots, Michael Parks, Frijid Pink, Tony Joe White

5/1 WMOC Country Shindig # 16: Conway Twitty, Bill Anderson, Jan Howard, Jim Ed Brown

5/18 Three Dog Night (sellout)

6/26 WDOD Shower of Stars # 1: Jerry Lee Lewis, George Jones, Tammy Wynette

7/28 Stars of *Lawrence Welk Show*: Myron Floren, Bobby Burgess & Cissy King, Dick Dale, Joe Feeney, Arthur Duncan, Clay Hart

8/1 Steppenwolf (sellout)

8/14 WDOD Shower of Stars # 2: Merle Haggard, Bonnie Owens, Tompall and the Glaser Brothers, Penny DeHaven

8/15 Mull's Gospel: Happy Goodmans, Downings, Inspirations, Florida Boys

9/11 James Brown

9/26 Mull's Gospel: Four Galileans, Monarchs, Inspirations, Statesman Quartet

9/29 Tennessee US Sen. Albert Gore Sr. (D) Rally

10/24 WDOD Shower of Stars # 3: Sonny James, Jack Greene, Jeannie Seely, Warner Mack, Mac Wiseman

11/21 WFLI Spectacular # 13 (2 sold-out shows) Tony Orlando & Dawn, Michael Nesmith, Paul Revere and the Raiders, Grassroots, Badfinger

11/23 Dr. Norman Vincent Peale

12/4 Chet Atkins, Floyd Cramer, Boots Randolph

12/5 Harlem Globetrotters

12/30 Hank Williams Sr. Memorial (big crowd) Conway Twitty, Osborne Brothers, Hank Williams Jr., Duke of Paducah, Merle Kilgore, Connie Smith, the Drifting Cowboys, Del Reeves

1971

Dolly Parton and Porter Wagoner at Memorial Auditorium in 1971 (Jack Mullins)

1/1 Mull's Gospel: Wendy Bagwell & Sunliters, LeFevres, Downings, Hopper Bros. & Connie

1/22 WDOD Shower of Stars # 4: Jerry Lee Lewis, Jim Ed Brown, Faron Young, Crystal Gayle

1/23 Harlem Magicians

1/24 Atlanta Vice Mayor Maynard Jackson (voter registration rally)

1/30-31 March of Dimes Telerama # 5 (David Hartman, Crystal Gayle, Maureen Arthur, Clu Gulager)

2/8 Liberace

2/27 Mull's Gospel: LeFevres, Naomi & the Segos, Florida Boys, Scenicland Quartet

3/5 WDOD Shower of Stars # 5: Porter Wagoner, Dolly Parton, Mel Tillis, Tompall and the Glaser Brothers, Speck Rhodes

3/16-21 Holiday On Ice (8 shows)

4/1 Debate: Liberal Frank Mankiewicz vs. Conservative James Kilpatrick

4/10 Johnny Cash (2 shows) June Carter Cash, Carter Family, Carl Perkins, Statler Brothers

4/30 Blood, Sweat, and Tears (big crowd)

5/21 Wilson Pickett (refused to perform because he was not paid in advance. Major riot, vandalism. The Tennessee Highway Patrol and later, the National Guard were called in)

6/11 James Brown

7/10 Steppenwolf (big crowd, 2nd year in row)

8/7 Mull's Gospel: Happy Goodmans, Florida Boys

8/14 *Jesus Christ Superstar* (2 sellout shows, lots of protests) with Yvonne Elliman

9/3 Country Shindig # 17: Conway Twitty, Earl Scruggs Revue, Bobby Bare

10/3 Bread

10/22 The Guess Who (big crowd)

11/5 US Sen. Henry (Scoop) Jackson (D- Wash) '72 presidential candidate

11/14 Carpenters (HUGE, fastest sellout in auditorium history)

11/22 Art Linkletter (drug abuse talk, large crowd)

11/26 Mull's Gospel: Singing Goffs, Inspirations, Happy Goodman Family

12/3 WFLI Spectacular # 14 (small crowd compared to previous spectaculars, resulting in this being the final one): Hamilton, Joe Frank & Reynolds, Grassroots, Five Man Electrical Band, Stampeders, Pacific Gas & Electric

12/20 Harlem Globetrotters

12/29 Hank Williams Sr. Memorial (big crowd) with Hank Williams Jr., Porter Wagoner, Dolly Parton, Faron Young, Tompall and the Glaser Brothers, Duke of Paducah, Merle Kilgore

1972

1/7 Riverside vs. Howard high school basketball 6,000 fans

1/15 Mull's Gospel: Scenicland Quartet, Statesmen, Blackwood Brothers

1/29-30 March of Dimes Telerama #6: Don Galloway, Roy Clark, Richard Dawson, Barbara Sharma, the Hagers

2/5 B. J. Thomas/Crabby Appleton

2/8 James Brown

3/4, 4/21, 8/5, 9/30, 11/24 Mull's Singing Convention

3/5 Fifth Dimension (big crowd)

3/12 WDOD Shower of Stars # 6: Charley Pride, Jack Greene, Jeannie Seely, Johnny Duncan (big crowd)

3/28-4/2 Holiday On Ice

4/28 Gov. George & Cornelia Wallace (presidential campaign)

6/26 B. B. King

7/14 Curtis Mayfield

9/9 Rare Earth/White Witch

9/21 Vice President Spiro Agnew (attendance 5,000)

10/1 Doc Severinsen (Tonight Show bandleader)

10/16 Steve Miller Band

11/2 Country Shindig # 18 Loretta Lynn, Conway Twitty, Mel Tillis, Ray Griff

11/3 Byrds/Goose Creek Symphony

11/11 Harlem Globetrotters

12/1 Chet Atkins, Floyd Cramer, Boots Randolph, Jethro Burns

12/9 Humble Pie/Roxy Music/Flash

Some of the nation's biggest stars filled the Auditorium stage each January for the March of Dimes Telerama (Irv Prevou family/WRCB)

Telerama guest Donna Douglas, who played Elly May on "The Beverly Hillbillies" with Shane Hullender in 1974 (Shane Hullender)

"Live from the Auditorium: the March of Dimes Telerama!"

For eleven years, (1967-77), Chattanooga television viewers watched a 19-hour annual telethon, from 11:00 p.m. Saturday to 6:00 p.m. Sunday, for the March of Dimes. Broadcast live for the first two years from the Tivoli Theater, and then the Memorial Auditorium, the stage was filled with stars, all with a common goal: raising money to fight birth defects.

Similar telethons were broadcast by stations nationwide beginning in the early 1960s. Local singers and bands were recruited to perform, with national celebrities providing the star power. Some would sing or dance on the shows. Others would simply appear on stage, make personal appeals for donations, and help answer the phones. Fans who attended the shows often got autographs from the stars.

Perhaps the biggest star to appear was Michael Landon in 1967. His western series "Bonanza" was riding high in the ratings, and everybody loved "Little Joe." Landon made a tearful (and effective) plea for viewers to donate.

Each year, we would anxiously await the announcement of the next Telerama stars. In 1968, Leonard Nimoy was the headliner. That was a bit of a letdown after Landon's appearance. It sounds strange now, but "Star Trek" wasn't that popular when it originally aired, so an appearance by "Mr. Spock" didn't create much excitement at the time. Sharing the bill with Nimoy were James Drury of "The Virginian," "King of the Road" singer Roger Miller, and country comedian Minnie Pearl.

In the years to come, guests included David Canary of "Bonanza," "Hee Haw" stars Roy Clark, Gunilla Hutton, and Roni Stoneman, "Laugh-In" cast member Richard Dawson, Peter Marshall of "Hollywood Squares," Anson Williams of "Happy Days," Robert

Reed of "The Brady Bunch," Donna Douglas of "The Beverly Hillbillies," and singer Crystal Gayle.

Local telethons eventually faded out, giving way to national extravaganzas like Jerry Lewis's annual Muscular Dystrophy Telethon, which is now also a thing of the past. But for more than a decade, viewers were treated to an annual gathering of national talent that filled the stage of Memorial Auditorium.

1973

1/16 *Jesus Christ Superstar* (big crowd)

1/20, 3/3, 4/27, 7/3, 8/11, 9/29, 11/23 Mull's Singing Convention

1/23 Lester Flatt, Bill Monroe, the Osbornes, Jim & Jesse

1/27-28 March of Dimes Telerama #7 Roy Clark, Peter Marshall, Gunilla Hutton, OB McClinton, Sammi Smith

2/4 Blood, Sweat and Tears

2/22 Apollo 11 astronauts Harrison Schmitt, Eugene Cernan, Ronald Evans

3/6 ZZ Top

3/14 Black Oak Arkansas/Jo Jo Gunne/Gentle Giant

3/22 Rev. Rex Humbard (*Cathedral of Tomorrow*)

3/23 Richie Havens

4/5 Royal Lippizan Stallions

4/8 Stamps Quartet with J.D. Sumner, the Statesmen with Hovie Lister

4/10 Isaac Hayes

4/20 Goose Creek Symphony

5/7 Bobby Womack/Ohio Players

5/23 Harold Melvin and the Blue Notes

6/1 B.J. Thomas

6/20 War/Wet Willie

6/22 Blue Oyster Cult/Bachman Turner Overdrive

6/26 Carpenters/Skiles and Henderson (sold-out)

7/19 Dr. John/Kinky Friedman

7/27 Helen Reddy/Mac Davis (big crowd)

8/3 James Gang /Rufus (big crowd)

8/10 Danny Davis & Nashville Brass

8/12 Frankie Valli and 4 Seasons

9/1 Grand Funk/Wet Willie (big crowd)

9/12 Goose Creek Symphony

9/14 Kris Kristofferson/Rita Coolidge

9/26 Charlie Daniels Band/Marshall Tucker Band

10/3 Mott the Hoople

10/17 Black Oak Arkansas

10/23 ZZ Top

10/26 Burl Ives Show, emceed by Hugh O'Brian

10/27 Jerry Wallace, Roni Stoneman

11/11 Mountain/Foghat

11/19 Harlem Globetrotters

11/25 J. Geils Band

12/9 Country Shindig # 19 (2 shows) Conway Twitty, Loretta Lynn, Nat Stuckey, Johnny Russell

12/16 Johnny Winter/the Stories

12/26 Jo Jo Gunne/Lynyrd Skynyrd

1974

1/11 Porter Wagoner, Dolly Parton, Speck Rhodes

1/21 Goose Creek Symphony

1/25 Country Shindig # 20 Donna Fargo, Freddie Hart, Johnny Rodriguez

1/26-27 March of Dimes Telerama # 8 (Lloyd Haynes, Donna Douglas, Dave Madden, Diana Trask, Snooky Lanson) first time on WTVC after being telecast on WRCB from 1967-1973

2/26 Marshall Tucker Band/ Charlie Daniels Band

3/2, 6/22, 8/3, 10/26, 11/23 Mull's Gospel

3/5 Humble Pie, Spooky Tooth, Montrose

3/15 Royal Lippizan Stallions

3/20 Bee Gees with Nashville Symphony, and Jim Stafford

4/11-14 Holiday on Ice

4/20 Johnny Cash, June Carter Cash, Mother Maybelle Carter, Carl Perkins

5/6 Edgar Winter/Rick Derringer/Dan Hartman/Humble Pie/Roxy Music (BIG)

5/13 Doobie Brothers (banned from the Auditorium for throwing cream pies after the show, damaging the upholstery)

5/22 Earth, Wind and Fire

7/1 Del Reeves

7/15 Kool and the Gang

7/17 Poco/Wet Willie

8/20-22 Rev. Jimmy Swaggart

10/6 Mac Davis

10/30 America/Douglas Ross

11/11 Foghat/Montrose

11/22 Black Oak Arkansas/Goose Creek Symphony

11/24 Earth Wind and Fire

11/27 Todd Rundgren

11/29 Boots Randolph, Floyd Cramer, Brenda Lee

12/2 Harlem Globetrotters

12/5 Johnny Winter/Hydra

12/6 James Brown

1975

1/2 Bachman Turner Overdrive/Bob Seger

1/24, 3/22, 6/27, 8/2, 9/27, 11/15, 11/28 Mull's Gospel

1/25-26 March of Dimes Telerama #9 (Anson Williams, Cris Connelly, Maureen Arthur, Bob Luman)

1/28 Liberace

2/25 Joe Walsh/Charlie Daniels Band

2/28 Country Shindig # 21 Conway Twitty/Loretta Lynn/Cal Smith

3/19 Lynyrd Skynyrd/Bonnie Bramlett (sold out)

3/26-30 Holiday on Ice

5/20 Linda Ronstadt/Earl Scruggs Revue

5/23 Bethel Bible School concert: Tom T. Hall, Johnny Rodriguez, Connie Smith, Dickey Lee, Chet Atkins, Marilyn Sellars, Jerry Reed, Ralph Emery

6/16 Marshall Tucker Band/James Gang

6/17 Bee Gees/Revelation

6/18 Average White Band (DISORDER FOR SMOKING, 100 people ejected)

7/16 Seals and Crofts (sold out)

7/25 Rufus w/Chaka Khan, Bohannon

8/14 Jethro Tull/Alex Harvey Band (big crowd)

8/20 BT Express

8/28 Graham Central Station

9/10 KISS/Slade

9/12 Bill Gaither Trio

10/1 Charlie Daniels Band/Goose Creek Symphony (big crowd)

10/28 Edgar Winter Group/Rick Derringer/Amazing Rhythm Aces

11/1 *Jesus Christ Superstar*

11/2 Rev. Ernest Angley

Ad for a poorly-attended Bruce Springsteen show in 1976

1976

1/3 Roscoe Tanner tennis matches (Dennis Ralston, Harold Solomon, Bob Lutz)

1/21 Sweet/Eric Carmen

1/23, 3/6, 5/15, 6/26, 8/6, 9/18, 11/13 Mull's Gospel

1/24-25 March of Dimes Telerama # 10 Richard Anderson, Don Galloway, Elizabeth Baur, Lee Majors, James Rogers

2/25 Marshall Tucker Band/Elvin Bishop/Outlaws

3/5 Conway Twitty/Crystal Gayle/Mickey Gilley

3/12 Joe Cocker/Atlanta Rhythm Section

3/30 Neil Sedaka/Kiki Dee

4/14 Rufus w/Chaka Khan/The Dramaticx

4/15 Foghat/Montrose

4/26 Bruce Springsteen (small crowd)

5/12 Santana/Wet Willie

5/14 Bethel Bible School concert: Tom T. Hall, Jerry Clower, Johnny Rodriguez, Dickey Lee

5/16, 7/31, 8/1, 11/28-30 Rev. Ernest Angley

5/21 People's Choice/Willie Hutch

6/4 Mel Tillis

6/28 Earth, Wind and Fire

7/20 Blue Oyster Cult/Rush

8/30 Robin Trower/Mother's Finest

9/14 O'Jays (big crowd)

10/6 Charlie Daniels Band/Wet Willie (Tennessee Democratic Party fundraiser)

Poster for Dolly Parton show in 1977

10/12 Parliament/Funkadelic/Bootsy's Rubber Band/Hugh Masekela

10/26 Ted Nugent/Montrose

11/3 Harlem Globetrotters

11/10 Leon Russell

12/10 Wild Cherry

1977

1/7, 1/28, 4/16, 11/19 Mull's Singing Convention (gospel)

1/18 Marshall Tucker Band/Pure Prairie League

1/22 March of Dimes Telerama (#11 and final) Kristy McNichol, Gary Collins, Mary Ann Mobley, Tiny Tim

1/30 Statler Brothers, Tammy Wynette, Ronnie Milsap (big crowd)

2/10 Waylon Jennings/Jessi Colter/Amazing Rhythm Aces

2/15 Kansas/Rush

2/27-3/1 Rev. Ernest Angley

3/3 Gary Wright/Robert Palmer

3/4 Conway Twitty/Loretta Lynn (big crowd)

3/15 Willie Nelson/Jerry Jeff Walker (Walker was reportedly intoxicated, Nelson was not happy)

3/22 Rev. Jimmy Swaggart

3/31 Bill Gaither Trio

4/18 Bootsy Collins' Rubber Band

4/25 Jimmy Buffett

5/13 Bethel Bible Village concert: Tom T. Hall, Helen Cornelius, Ralph Emery, Pee Wee King, Dickey Lee, Larry Gatlin, Marty Robbins, Jeannie C. Riley, Johnny Rodridguez

6/14 Seals and Crofts (big crowd)

6/19-21 Rev. Ernest Angley

6/28 Hall and Oates/Little River Band

7/6 Commodores/Emotions (sold out)

8/5 "Chaplain of Bourbon Street" Rev. Bob Harrington & Madelyn Murray O'Hair (debating atheism)

8/14 Brothers Johnson/Maze (big crowd)

8/17 Leo Sayer/Melissa Manchester

8/20 Mull's Gospel: Goffs, Kingsmen

10/1 Mull's Gospel: Happy Goodmans, Kingsmen

11/17 Rose Royce/LTD

11/18 Dolly Parton (big crowd)

11/26 Charlie Daniels Band/Sanford Townsend Band

*Chuck and Mike Crowder get autographs from the Captain and Tennille after
a 1978 concert (The Crowders)*

1978

1/6 Mull's Gospel: Jerry & the Singing Goffs, Cathedral Quartet, Kingsmen

1/7 Happy Goodmans, Florida Boys, Dixie Echoes

2/2 Liberace (big crowd)

2/5 Charley Pride/Dave & Sugar (sold out)

3/5 Mull's Gospel: Jerry & Singing Goffs, Statesmen, Kingsmen

3/8 Outlaws/Wet Willie

3/16 Conway Twitty/Loretta Lynn (big crowd)

3/21 Rush/Babys

3/23 Johnny Guitar Watson/Bar-Kays (big crowd)

3/30 Bill Gaither Trio

4/5 Rev. Jesse Jackson (4,000 in attendance, Operation PUSH)

4/21 Millie Jackson/Floaters

4/27 Bootsy's Rubber Band/Raydio

5/3 Harry Chapin

5/11 O'Jays/Enchantment (big crowd)

5/19 Bethel Bible Village concert: Pat Boone, Dickey Lee, Jim Chesnut, Jim Owen

6/12 BT Express

6/20 Doug Henning (magician) (big crowd)

6/30 Mull's Gospel: Chuck Wagon Gang, Jimmie Davis, Lamar Sego Family

7/2 Black Oak Arkansas/Sweet

7/12 Foreigner (big crowd)

7/27 *The Wiz* (sold out)

7/29 Mull's 20th anniversary gospel: Jerry & the Singing Goffs, Kingsmen, Blackwood Brothers

8/2 Jimmy Buffett/Little River Band (Buffett had recently broken his leg, played to big crowd anyway)

8/4 Gospel: Scenicland Quartet, Hinsons, Happy Goodmans

8/30 Brothers Johnson

9/17 Evangelist Richard Roberts

9/20 Captain & Tennille/Larry Groce (big crowd)

9/22 Gov. John Connally (campaigning for GOP presidential nomination in 1980, entertainment by fiddler Curly Fox)

9/29 Lettermen

10/4 ConFunkShun/Bohannon

10/12 Kenny Rogers/Dottie West (sold out)

11/5 Johnny Paycheck/Mickey Gilley/O.B. McClinton/Walker Sisters

11/20 Tony Orlando

11/22 Mulls' Gospel: Happy Goodman Family, Inspirations

12/1 Statler Brothers/Barbara Mandrell (big crowd)

12/28 Bar Kays/Evelyn "Champagne" King

12/29 Outlaws/Pat Travers Band

12/31 Rev. Ernest Angley

1979

1/6 Gospel: Scenicland Boys, Florida Boys

1/20: Mull's Gospel: Singing Goffs, Hinson Family, Kingsmen Quartet

1/24 Charlie Daniels Band/Pure Prairie League

Comedy legend Red Skelton entertains a packed house at Memorial Auditorium in 1979 (Wayne Murphree)

2/2 Conway Twitty/Marty Robbins

2/13 Triumph/Brownsville

2/15 Waylon Jennings/ Crickets with Sonny Curtis

3/2 Sha Na Na (sold out)

3/6 Harry Chapin

3/15 Rush/Molly Hatchet

3/16 Charlie Rich/Ronnie Milsap/Janie Fricke (big crowd)

3/18 Peabo Bryson

3/30 Atlanta Rhythm Section/LeRoux (big crowd)

4/7 Red Skelton (sold out)

4/20 Billy "Crash" Craddock/Sonny James/Jeanne Pruett

5/18 Pat Boone/Bethel Concert (with Debby Boone, Trini Lopez, Jim Chesnutt, Mayf Nutter, Barry Williams, Jim Owen)

5/19 Mull's Gospel: Singing Cookes, Hinson Family, Kingsmen Quartet

5/27 Rev. Ernest Angley

6/15 Patti LaBelle/Sister Sledge

6/20 Nazareth/Raggedy Ann

6/29 Larry Gatlin & Gatlin Brothers, Con Hunley

7/24 Bay City Rollers

8/4 Mull's Gospel: Singing Cookies, Hinson Family, Kingsmen Quartet

8/21 *Eubie!* (musical featuring Jackee Harry)

9/21 Triumph/YIPES

10/9 Mother's Finest/Jay Ferguson

10/24 Peter Frampton/Simms Bros. (big crowd)

10/31 Gamma/Mistress

11/9 Chuck Mangione

11/20 Harlem Globetrotters

11/21 Mull's Gospel: Rex Nelon/Henson Family/Singing Cookes

11/29 Statler Brothers/Barbara Mandrell (big crowd)

Multi-talented Barbara Mandrell at Memorial Auditorium in 1979 (Wayne Murphree)

11/30 Sea Level/Dixie Dregs

12/2 Rev. Ernest Angley

12/27 Atlanta Rhythm Section/Wet Willie (big crowd)

The 1980s

The 1980s began much as the 1970s ended for the Auditorium, with superstar acts like the Oak Ridge Boys, Molly Hatchet, Waylon Jennings, Conway Twitty, and the Statler Brothers packing the house, as always. But when the UTC Arena (capacity: 11,200) opened in 1982, many of the artists who once headlined the Auditorium opted for the larger venue. Willie Nelson, Alabama, Jimmy Buffett, and Kenny Rogers were among the first headliners at the Arena, setting the tone for other emerging acts who would bypass the Auditorium.

Some performers evidently preferred the cozier confines of the Auditorium. Charlie Daniels, Conway Twitty, Waylon Jennings, Prince, and Mickey Gilley seemed more at home in the smaller venue. The Statler Brothers played the UTC Arena once, but soon switched back to their old stomping grounds.

Among the soon-to-be-famous names who appeared at the Auditorium during the decade were Kathie Lee Johnson (who would become better known as Kathie Lee Gifford), 26-year-old Reba McEntire (opening for Mickey Gilley in 1981), 23-year-old Prince (a "one-hit wonder" in 1981),

By the mid-80s, the frequent barrage of shows at UTC began taking their toll on the Auditorium. The bookings were fewer, and despite constant acoustical problems at the new Arena, the newness had not worn off. The appeal of seeing superstars like Lionel Richie, Elton John, and Rod Stewart could not be denied, and such acts could no longer fit their audience inside a 4,843-seat hall.

To add insult to injury, professional wrestling, a dependable weekly Auditorium draw for fifty years, finally began to fade. Local television stations could no longer compete with the wilder wrestling shows on cable. Without the weekly local TV push, attendance plummeted. By 1984, wrestling was rarely booked at the Auditorium, and bigger events promoted by the World Wrestling Federation (WWF) became an occasional program at the UTC Arena.

Gospel music acts, including younger-skewing Contemporary Christian artists helped fill the void created by the UTC Arena. Also, the Tivoli Theater proved to be a better fit for most touring plays and musicals.

In 1987, the smaller Community Theater (upstairs, with a capacity of 800) reopened after several years of neglect and disrepair. The theater attracted acts with smaller followings, and also hosted local lectures and films.

Longtime manager Clyde Hawkins waged a David vs. Goliath style battle to keep the Auditorium open, booked and relevant, turning to more Broadway-style shows that were not intended for Arena-size audiences. In 1985, Hawkins and architect Ted Franklin convinced city leaders that converting the Auditorium into a performance-oriented hall would enable it to compete with other local facilities.

After eighteen years on the job, Hawkins left in 1988 to head up the new Northwest Georgia Trade Center in Dalton, Georgia. His assistant, David Johnson was named manager, and took on the task of modernizing the Auditorium, which would have a dramatic new look at the dawn of the 1990s. The Auditorium would be closed for eighteen months beginning in the summer of 1989, but the final result would prove worth the wait.

1980

1/18 Oak Ridge Boys, Johnny Rodriguez, Charly McClain, Joe Sun (big crowd)

1/19 Mull's Gospel: Kingsmen, Cathedrals, Rex Nelon Singers

2/14 Sandler & Young

3/1 Charlie Rich

3/5 Molly Hatchet (big crowd)

3/14 Waylon Jennings, Jessi Colter, The Crickets (sold out)

3/16 Harry Chapin

3/21 Don Williams/Ronnie Milsap/Zella Lehr (sold out)

3/26 Rufus with Chaka Khan, Brothers Johnson

4/17 Bar Kays

4/18 Conway Twitty/T. G. Sheppard (big crowd)

5/16 Pat Boone, Dickey Lee, Barry Williams (for Bethel Bible Village)

5/17 Mull's Gospel: Kingsmen, Singing Cookes, The Gems

6/24 Rossington Collins Band/Johnny Winter

7/3 Charlie Daniels Band/Pure Prairie League (big crowd)

7/20 Rev. Ernest Angley

8/17 Allman Brothers Band/Henry Paul Band

9/30 *A Chorus Line* (big crowd)

10/16 Mickey Gilley/Johnny Lee

10/20 Little River Band/Dirt Band

11/7 Emmylou Harris/Con Hunley

11/25 Harlem Globetrotters

12/7 Rev. Ernest Angley

12/26 Atlanta Rhythm Section/Mothers Finest (big crowd)

1981

1/13 *Dancin'* (choreographed by Bob Fosse)

1/25 Oak Ridge Boys/Gail Davies (sold out)

3/5 *They're Playing Our Song* (Lorna Luft)

3/11 Bar Kays

3/12 Molly Hatchet/.38 Special (big crowd)

3/15 Rev. Ernest Angley

3/26 Con Funk Shun/Slave

3/27 Conway Twitty/TG Sheppard (sold out)

4/2 Liberace (sold out)

5/1 Alabama/Con Hunley/Kendalls (big crowd)

5/13 Gap Band/Yarbrough & Peeples

5/15 Pat Boone/BJ Thomas/Debby Boone/Jordanaires, Kathie Lee Johnson (later known as Kathie Lee Gifford) for Bethel Bible Village

6/7 Don Williams/David Frizzell & Shelley West

7/16 Ted Nugent (big crowd)

8/19 Mother's Finest/Point Blank

8/20 Smokey Robinson/Evelyn "Champagne" King

9/17-19 Rev. Kenneth Copeland

9/26 *Sugar Babies* (Eddie Bracken, Mimi Hines, Toni Kaye)

10/4 Statler Brothers/Margo Smith (big crowd)

10/25 Mickey Gilley/Johnny Lee/Reba McEntire (big crowd)

11/19 *Best Little Whorehouse in Texas* (sold out)

11/22 Ronnie Milsap/Kippi Brannon/Leon Everette

11/25 Four Tops/Luther Vandross

11/27 Mull's Gospel: Teddy Huffam & the Gems, Jerry & the Singing Goffs, Singing Echoes, Hinson Family

12/16 Prince/The Time

12/28 Atlanta Rhythm Section/Mother's Finest

12/31 Mull's Gospel: Heaven Bound Singers, Primitive Quartet, Singing Cookes, Gold City Quartet

WTVC news anchor Bob Johnson with Teddy Gentry, Jeff Cook, Randy Owen, and Mark Herndon of Alabama in 1982 (John Creel)

The Boys from Fort Payne, Alabama

In 1980, country music was at a weird intersection. Longtime stars like Loretta Lynn, Conway Twitty and George Jones were competing with the more youthful sounds of the Urban Cowboy era. Mickey Gilley and Kenny Rogers were topping the charts, with George Strait and Lee Greenwood on the way.

The charts were dominated by solo acts, with the exception of the Statler Brothers and Oak Ridge Boys, established groups that had been around for decades.

Then, seemingly out of nowhere came an "overnight success" that was actually years in the making. Randy Owen, Jeff Cook and Teddy

Gentry were literally country cousins who had played the bars and clubs for years under the name "Wild Country."

Throughout the 1970s the cousins, backed by various drummers, took all sorts of odd jobs to help keep their musical dreams alive. At nights and on weekends, they would back up big-name artists who came through the area, and eventually relocated to Myrtle Beach, South Carolina where they played a club called The Bowery. There, they played nightly for tips, performing whatever was hot on top-40 and country radio at the time. Lynyrd Skynyrd, Merle Haggard, you name it, they played it.

They put out a few records on small labels, but nothing clicked. Finally they took in Mark Herndon, a drummer with a rock background, and found some success with a single called "I Wanna Come Over." It wasn't a huge hit, but it got the attention of an RCA Records executive in Nashville.

He saw them perform live at a "New Faces" concert, where they shared the stage with another up-and-coming artist named Reba McEntyre. In April 1980, RCA offered them a contract. Folks, when the label that sold millions of Elvis records offers you a deal, you should probably sign the dotted line. The Alabama boys did, and the rest is in the Country Music Hall of Fame history books.

The numbers are staggering. Starting with "Tennessee River," the group scored 21 consecutive number-one hits, an unprecedented winning streak. There was one great song after another: "My Home's In Alabama," "Feels So Right," "Love in the First Degree," and my personal favorite, "Old Flame." Not bad for a bunch of cotton-picking country boys!

Soon, they were racking up every major industry award, and selling out big arenas. Who made up their audience? These were not the middle-aged folks who stood in line to buy Conway and Loretta tickets. Alabama, with their longish hair and upbeat songs, were opening country music up to a younger crowd.

After about 20 years, the hits stopped coming quite so frequently, as newer artists captured the radio spotlight. Randy and the boys stepped aside for a while to raise their kids and work on solo projects. Now and then, they'd reunite for a charity show. Randy, in particular, adopted St. Jude Children's Hospital in Memphis, raising millions of dollars with his music, and his personal appeals.

Alabama also generously gave back to their community. They truly never forgot where they came from.

1982

1/12 Harlem Globetrotters

1/17 Alabama/Janie Fricke (big crowds, 2 shows)

1/24 Rev. Ernest Angley

1/25 *A Chorus Line*

2/7 Hank Williams Jr/Gail Davies/Burrito Brothers

2/17 Bar Kays/Chocolate Milk

2/26 Conway Twitty/Ronnie McDowell (big crowds, 2 shows)

3/4-6 *Annie*

4/30 Millie Jackson/Manhattans

5/21 Pat Boone, BJ Thomas, Ed Ames (for Bethel Bible Village)

7/30 Toto

8/1 Rainbow/Krokus

9/3 Kansas/Johnny Van Zant Band

11/11 Prince/Time with Morris Day/Vanity 6 (big crowd)

11/19 Don Williams/Bellamy Brothers

12/12 Rev. Ernest Angley

12/26 Charlie Daniels Band (the band played extra because opening act Gary Morris was snowed in)

Singer Tom Jones with David Carroll in 1983.

1983

1/23 Conway Twitty/Ronnie McDowell (HUGE, 2 shows)

2/4 George Jones/George Strait (big crowd)

3/4 Hank Williams Jr./Earl Thomas Conley

3/6 David Frizzell/Shelly West/John Conlee

3/15 George Clinton/Parliament/Funkadelic

3/24 Bill Gaither Trio (big crowd)

Conway Twitty at Memorial Auditorium in 1984 (Cindy Lowery)

5/8 Loretta Lynn/Lee Greenwood

5/20 Pat Boone/Russ Taff/Debby Boone/James Ward/Desiree Daniels (Bethel Bible Village)

6/29 Maze/Lakeside

7/15 Thrasher Brothers

8/6 Mull's Singing Convention 30th anniversary with Mike & the Payne Family, Primitive Quartet

8/7 Tom Jones/comedian George Wallace (big crowd)

8/19 Waylon Jennings/Jerry Reed/Jessi Colter

10/18 *Evita*

10/26 Mitzi Gaynor

11/13 Rev. Ernest Angley

11/29 Petra

(WRESTLING WAS WEEKLY THROUGH 9/83, THEN MONTHLY IN OCTOBER AND NOVEMBER, AND THEN DISCONTINUED ON A REGULAR BASIS)

1984

1/29 Conway Twitty/Ronnie McDowell (big crowd, 2 shows)

2/2 *Oliver!*

3/1 Mickey Gilley/Charly McClain

3/24 Hank Williams Jr./Big Al Downing/Merle Kilgore

4/6 George Jones/Con Hunley

4/7 Wayne Newton/Freddie Roman (sellout)

4/8 Dirt Band/Boys at Heart (from Lafayette, GA)

4/21 Jesse Jackson for President rally

5/11 Bobby Womack/SOS Band

6/8 Pat Boone (Bethel Bible Village) Glen Campbell, Debby Boone

6/10 Shirley Caesar

7/7 Gap Band/One Way/Jocelyn Brown

7/19 Imperials

8/1 Patti LaBelle

9/7 Walter Mondale for President rally

9/24 Amy Grant/David Meece

Mickey Gilley at Memorial Auditorium in 1984 (Cindy Lowery)

11/2-4 *Sesame Street Live*

11/16 Dallas Holm and Praise

11/17 Jeffrey Osborne/Patrice Rushen

11/23 Ed Bruce/Becky Hobbs

11/30 Millie Jackson/Manhattans/Dells

12/8 Shirley Caesar

1985

1/19 Mylon LeFevre

1/25 Conway Twitty/Reba McEntire (big crowd)

2/3 Liberace (sold out)

2/21 Petra

2/23 Gary Morris/Forester Sisters

3/7 Hank Williams Jr (big crowd)

3/21 Roger Whittaker

3/29 Sandi Patti (big crowd)

4/19 Russ Taff/David Meece

5/7 David Copperfield (magician)

5/19 Lee Greenwood/Exile

6/1 Kendalls/Boys at Heart

6/7 Pat Boone, Dion, Sandi Patti (for Bethel Bible Village)

6/19 Rev. Jim Whittington

7/28 Mikhail Baryshnikov (ballet)

11/1 Anne Murray (big crowd)

11/3 Freddie Jackson/Melba Moore (big crowd)

11/22 James Brown

11/23 PDQ Bach with Chattanooga Symphony

12/7 Frankie Beverly and Maze

12/14 DeGarmo & Key

1986

1/8 Rev. Jim Whittington

1/10 Mylon LeFevre

1/31 George Strait/Kathy Mattea

2/1 Harvest

2/11 Dallas Holm and Praise

2/15 Wendy Bagwell & Sunliters, Teddy Huffman and the Gems, Gold City Quartet

Perry Como, John Gary, and Pat Boone at Memorial Auditorium in 1986 (Becky White)

2/22 Temptations/Platters

3/1 2nd Chapter of Acts

3/14 Latimore/Bobby Rush

4/15 David Copperfield (sold out)

4/18 Judds/Forester Sisters/Mark Gray (big crowd)

4/25 Pat Boone, Perry Como, John Gary (Bethel Bible Village) (sold out)

5/9 Charly McClain/Wayne Massey/Eddy Raven/Danny Shirley (Red Food Cancer Control benefit)

5/17 Ronnie Milsap/John Schneider

7/11 Mike Warnke

7/17 Merle Haggard/T. Graham Brown

9/27 Inspirations, Kingsmen, McKameys

10/10 Ricky Skaggs/Randy Travis

11/1 Bill Gaither Trio

11/15 The Hinsons, Heaven Bound, Singing Cookes

1987

(WRESTLING RETURNED 1/24)

1/31 George Strait/O'Kanes

2/18 Ready for the World/Bobby Brown (big crowd)

2/26 Anne Murray (big crowd)

3/27 George Jones/ TG Sheppard/Sweethearts of the Rodeo (big crowd)

4/23 Gary Morris/Sawyer Brown

4/24 Floyd Cramer with Chattanooga Symphony

5/1 Gallagher (big crowd)

5/8 Pat Boone (Bethel Bible Village benefit) Perry Como, Greg X. Volz, Twila Paris

5/9 Cathedrals

5/29 Mylon LeFevre/DeGarmo & Key

7/20 Johnny Winter (at reopening of Community Theater)

7/31 Lee Greenwood/90 Proof Band

8/29 Tony Bennett/Henny Youngman (Siskin Star Night)

9/18 Imperials

10/16 Carman

10/31 Night Ranger/Helix

11/8 Stars of *Lawrence Welk Show* (Ava Barber, Ken Delo, Arthur Duncan, Aldridge Sisters, Jim Turner)

11/8 George Winston (Community Theater)

11/13 Bobby Rush

11/20 Larnelle Harris (gospel)

11/22 Statler Brothers/Sylvia (big crowd)

1988

1/19 Harvest

1/22 Harlem Globetrotters

1/29 Chippendales

3/8 Roger Whittaker

3/13 Conway Twitty/Loretta Lynn (sold out)

4/7 Dallas Holm & Praise

4/9 Mull's Gospel: Primitve Quartet, Singing Cookes, McKamey Family, Spencer Family

4/16 Tom Jones (big crowd)

4/21 Reba McEntire/Steve Wariner (big crowd)

5/13 Pat Boone, Debby Boone, Greg Volz (Bethel Bible Village)

6/10 George Jones/Mark Gray/Shenandoah/Benny Berry

8/5 Ray Stevens/Ethel & the Shameless Hussies (big crowd)

8/19 Amy Grant (big crowd)

9/10 Phil Cross

9/24 DeGarmo & Key

10/2 Ronnie McDowell, Eddy Raven, Billy Joe Royal

11/20 George Strait/Patty Loveless (big crowd)

1989
(WRESTLING ENDED AGAIN ON A REGULAR BASIS 4/27)

1/31 George Winston

2/5 Ricky Van Shelton/Shenandoah (big crowd)

2/19 Statler Brothers/Girls Next Door (big crowd)

2/24 Steve Green

3/10 Judds/TG Sheppard (big crowd)

3/17 Carman

4/17 Red Man Concert Tour: Rodney Crowell, Sweethearts of the Rodeo, Michael Johnson, Shooters

5/12 Pat Boone (Bethel Bible Village), Roy Clark, John Gary, Terri Gibbs, George "Goober" Lindsey, Foster Brooks

7/8 Michael Warnke

(RENOVATION BEGINS, CLOSED UNTIL FEBRUARY 1991)

The 1990s

The Memorial Auditorium "redevelopment plan," under the direction of former Mayor Robert Kirk Walker, had been approved in October 1985, and took more than three years to get off the ground. The architects were Selmon T. (Ted) Franklin and Robert A. Franklin. From July 1989 to January 1991, excitement built over one long-overdue change: a sloped floor. The level floor had been perfect for tennis, wrestling, basketball, roller derby, ice skating, and various exhibitions. But it was often a drawback for concert-goers who had to crane their necks to see over the head of the person seated in front of them.

The new sloped floor offered a better view of the performers on the wider, renovated stage. Seating was reduced from 4,843 to 3,800. The slightly more intimate setting also provided more leg space and comfort.

The first performance in the redeveloped Auditorium was headlined by Shirley Jones, who shared the stage with a 340-member festival chorus and orchestra led by Dr. Glenn Draper, and the Southern College Symphony Orchestra, under the direction of Orlo Gilbert. The following night, a still youthful Red Skelton, at the age of 77, filled the house with laughter as he had done in 1979. During the next few weeks, superstar acts Eddy Arnold, Charlie Daniels, Travis Tritt, and Rudolf Nureyev would follow, ensuring a strong comeback for the refreshed 66-year-old venue.

The smaller capacity proved to not be a deterrent, as sellouts had already become less frequent than in the Auditorium's heyday. The massive re-design also resulted in a major sound upgrade, in a facility often marred by poor acoustics. Such sound problems continued to be an issue at the UTC Arena, so many artists who insisted on top quality sound opted for the Auditorium.

During the 90s decade, some of the world's biggest stars, covering all genres of entertainment, graced the Auditorium stage. Ballet dancers Rudolf Nureyev and Mikhail Baryshnikov appeared just a few months apart in 1991. World renowned violinists Itzhak Perlman and Isaac

Stern performed with the Chattanooga Symphony Orchestra. Jay Leno, Garth Brooks, David Copperfield, Prince, Tony Bennett, Bob Dylan, Wayne Newton, B.B. King, Kenny G, Steven Curtis Chapman, Barry Manilow, Tom Jones, Reba McEntire, the Statler Brothers, Amy Grant, Della Reese, and Kenny Rogers, all of whom frequently played larger halls, entertained packed houses. Nationally known comedians like Jeff Foxworthy, D.L. Hughley, Bernie Mac, and Gallagher proved to be big draws. As always, the ever-popular Southern Gospel and Contemporary Christian acts were an Auditorium mainstay.

Broadway touring productions of *The Wiz, Cats, A Chorus Line, Annie, Phantom of the Opera, Les Miserables, and Oh Calcutta!* Proved the Auditorium could still attract crowds for plays and musicals. Two decades after creating protests and controversy, *Jesus Christ Superstar* returned to the Auditorium for numerous shows, with original lead Ted Neeley. Theodore Bikel, who played Tevye more than any other actor in history, appeared in *Fiddler on the Roof.*

Among new discoveries was 25-year-old country singer Kenny Chesney, who opened for Confederate Railroad in 1994. A Chattanooga newspaper reviewer was not impressed, writing "Chesney looked like a kid dressed in his dad's 10-gallon hat, hanging down halfway across his face. He waved, Gomer Pyle-like to individuals in the audience." He soon went on to become one of the biggest superstars in the music business.

The jam band Widespread Panic, which included two Chattanooga natives, also played numerous shows, to bigger crowds each time.

In 1998, 17-year-old Britney Spears, who had just released her first single, opened for the boy band NSYNC. Within weeks, she would become a household name.

On February 21, 1999, almost seventy-five years to the day since the Soldiers and Sailors Memorial Auditorium was opened to the public, comic superstar Bill Cosby played two sold-out shows, celebrating the grand old hall's anniversary in style.

1990

(Memorial Auditorium main hall was closed all year, while being renovated for improved sight lines with sloped concert seating. All listed performances in 1990 were in the Community Theater.)

Red Skelton at Memorial Auditorium (Wayne Murphree)

2/10 Michael Card

2/23 Leon Russell

5/5 Bobby Blue Bland

11/1-3 "*Love Letters*" starring Eli Wallach & Anne Jackson

11/14 Michael Hedges (singer, acoustic guitarist)

Garth Brooks meets "Big Jon" Anthony of US-101 at Memorial Auditorium in 1991 (WUSY)

1991

(MAIN HALL REOPENED ON JANUARY 31, 1991)

1/31 Shirley Jones

2/1 Red Skelton

2/8 Eddy Arnold

2/9 Charlie Daniels Band/Travis Tritt

Jay Leno with Cindy Carroll after his 1991 Memorial Auditorium show (Mike Dunne)

2/15 Rudolf Nureyev (ballet)

2/16 Bill Gaither Trio

2/22-24 *Peter Pan* (Cathy Rigby)

3/1 Jay Leno

3/8 Garth Brooks/Joe Diffie

3/27 Teenage Mutant Ninja Turtles

3/30 Kentucky Headhunters

4/2-3 *A Chorus Line*

4/12 Anne Murray

4/27 Mull's Gospel with Primitive Quartet

5/3 Phil Driscoll

5/10 Pat Boone, Paul Overstreet, Terri Gibbs (for Bethel Bible Village)

5/15 Michael W. Smith

5/19 Mikhail Baryshnikov (ballet)

6/14-16 *Cats*

7/19 Sharon, Lois and Bram

7/20 Mull's Gospel: McKameys, Trailblazers

8/17 Freddie Jackson

9/7 Steven Curtis Chapman

9/13 Goose Creek Symphony (Community Theater)

9/14 Gold City, Inspirations

9/20 Ronnie Milsap, Tams (for VITAL Center)

9/27 Cathedrals/Talleys

10/26 Kingsmen

11/20 Vince Gill/Patty Loveless

11/24 *Annie*

11/30 Jethro Tull/Chrissy Steele

1992

1/3 David Copperfield (magic)

1/4 O'Jays

1/23 *Oh Calcutta!*

2/5-6 Travis Tritt/Marty Stuart (2 sold out shows)

2/29 Roger Whittaker

3/14 Steve Green

3/27 Teenage Mutant Ninja Turtles

5/13 Patti LaBelle

5/16 Gallagher

7/27 Wayne Newton

9/12 Gold City

9/14 Steven Curtis Chapman

9/15-16 The *Wiz* (Stephanie Mills)

9/25 Kenny Rogers, Paulette Carlson, Billy Joe Royal

10/5 Black Crowes/Urban Shakedancers

10/17 Miss Tennessee USA pageant with Lee Greenwood

10/27 Righteous Brothers/Tim Wilson

11/6 HBO Comedy Jam (Bernie Mac/Bill Bellamy)

11/10-11 *Sesame Street Live*

11/20 Bill Gaither Trio/Michael English/Happy Goodmans

12/15 Billy Dean

1993

1/14 *Phantom of the Opera*

1/20 Teenage Mutant Ninja Turtles

1/23 All Star Comedy Jam (featuring D.L. Hughley)

1/30 Gold City/Kingsmen

2/5 Tanya Tucker/Gibson-Miller Band

2/6 *The Music Man*

2/13 White Heart (contemporary Christian)

2/27 Delbert McClinton (Community Theater)

2/28 Lorrie Morgan/John Michael Montgomery/Mark Collie

3/8 .38 Special (Community Theater)

3/18 Johnny Winter (Community Theater)

3/19 Michael English/ 4HIM

3/26 B B King/ Bobby Blue Bland

3/30 *Beauty and the Beast*

4/16-18 Last of the Red-Hot Lovers (Don Knotts, Barbara Eden)

5/7 Pat Boone, John Gary (Bethel Bible Village)

6/1-6 *Les Miserables* (8 shows)

6/10 Cathedrals, Speer Family

7/27-28 *Cats*

9/11 Gold City, Hoppers

10/2 DeGarmo & Key

10/16 John Stewart (Community Theater)

10/18 *Aladdin*

10/22 Ray Charles, Regina Belle

10/29 Sammy Kershaw, Martina McBride

10/30 *Wizard of Oz*

11/9-10 *Sesame Street Live*

11/15 Barry Manilow

11/19 Temptations/Drifters

12/6 Tom Jones

1994

1/15 Newsong

1/20 *Porgy and Bess*

2/6 Confederate Railroad/Kenny Chesney

2/15 Newsong

2/17 *Man of LaMancha*

3/3 George Jones, Brother Phelps

3/5 Steve Green

3/26 Silk

3/29 Dan Fogelberg

4/9 Mark Lowry

4/15 Tony Bennett

5/6 DC Talk

5/7 Bob Dylan

5/27 Bernie Mac

6/17 Isley Brothers/Angela Winbush

7/14-15 Jeff Foxworthy

8/18 Frankie Beverly/Maze

8/21 Kirk Franklin

8/26 Squire Parsons

9/10 Kingsmen/Bishops

9/24 Bill Gaither/Mark Lowry

10/4-5 Rockettes/Susan Anton

10/12 Della Reese

10/16 Phish

10/22 4Him

11/5 Isaac Stern with Chattanooga Symphony

11/8-9 *Sesame Street Live*

11/10 Boys Choir of Harlem

11/12 Sammy Kershaw/Rick Trevino/Don Cox

11/28 Steven Curtis Chapman/Newsboys

12/17 Gallagher

12/27-29 *Cats*

1995

1/10-11 *Fiddler on the Roof* (Theodore Bikel)

1/28 Newsong/Bryan Duncan

2/11 Kingsmen/Bishops

2/12 Dramatics, Delfonics

2/22 Jazz Explosion: George Duke, Sheila E

2/24 Ray Boltz

2/25 Diamond Rio, George Ducas

2/28-3/2 *Will Rogers Follies*

3/3 John Hinton/Bill Bellamy (comedy)

3/20 Twila Paris/Phil Keaggy

3/26 Peter, Paul and Mary

4/1 Gold City/The Greens

4/7 *Passion Play*

7/22 Kirk Franklin

7/29 Kenny G (sold out)

9/9 Kingsmen, Gold City, The Bishops

9/12-13 *Tommy* (the musical)

9/21-22 Josh McDowell/Newsboys

10/13 John P. Kee (gospel)

10/14 Nickelodeon "*Wild and Crazy Kids*" game show

10/18 *Jesus Christ Superstar* (Ted Neeley)

10/19-21 Miss Tennessee USA pageant

10/28 Petra

11/4-5 *State Fair* (John Davidson, Kathryn Crosby, Donna McKechnie, Andrea McArdle)

11/7-8 *Sesame Street Live*

11/9 Clay Walker/Terri Clark

11/18 Mark Lowry

12/29 Widespread Panic

1996

1/5 David Copperfield (sold out)

1/13 Newsong

3/2 Steve Green

3/3 Gallagher

3/15 Bernie Mac

3/26-28 *Grease* (Adrian Zmed, Mackenzie Philips, Sally Struthers, Sutton Foster)

4/11 DC Talk (sold out)

4/27-28 *Joseph and the Amazing Technicolor Dreamcoat* (Brian Lane Green)

5/22 Itzhak Perlman with Chattanooga Symphony

6/13 *Jesus Christ Superstar* (Ted Neeley)

9/7 Kingsmen

9/19 Newsboys/Geoff Moore & the Distance

9/28 Bill Gaither & Friends/Mark Lowry (sold out)

10/11-13 *Stomp*

10/19 Widespread Panic/Leftover Salmon

10/24 4Him/Point of Grace

11/3 Bob Dylan/Kenny Wayne Shepherd

11/12-13 *Sesame Street Live*

11/13 Bela Fleck (Community Theater)

12/4 Johnny Paycheck/Andy Childs

12/6 *The Sound of Music*

1997

1/11 D.L. Hughley (comedy)

1/14-16 *Cats*

1/18 Newsong

2/15-16 *West Side Story*

2/21 Twila Paris

2/28 David Copperfield (magic)

3/21 Doc Watson (Community Theater)

3/24 Gold City

3/28 Inspirations

5/10 Ray Boltz

6/8 Lou Christie, Dickie Lee, Shangri-las

6/27 Anthony Burger, Happy Goodmans

7/23 *Grease*

8/16 Bernie Mac

8/23 Tommy Dorsey Orchestra

10/1-5 *Les Miserables*

10/11 Coasters, Drifters, Platters

10/25 Bill Gaither & Friends

11/18-19 *Sesame Street Live*

11/23 Jars of Clay

11/29 *A Chorus Line*

12/9 4Him/Point of Grace

12/10 Glenn Miller Orchestra

12/14 Bellamy Brothers, Andy Childs

1998

1/31 Newsong

2/20 Clay Crosse

2/21 *Bye Bye Birdie* (Troy Donahue)

3/14 Steve Green

4/10 Inspirations

4/15 Indigo Girls

4/16 Jamie Foxx/Spike Davis

4/25 *Damn Yankees*

4/28 Amy Grant

5/7 Prince/Larry Graham (sold out)

6/14 Dickie Lee, Little Eva

7/30 Anthony Burger

8/21 Jeff Foxworthy/Ritch Shydner (sold out)

8/22 Patti LaBelle (sold out)

9/15 Michael W. Smith/Chris Rice

9/25-27 *Goosebumps*

10/22-23 Usher (capacity crowds, free shows)

10/24 *Fiddler on the Roof*

11/10 Newsboys

11/21-22 *Sesame Street Live*

11/25 Widespread Panic

11/30 Ray Boltz

12/4 Jim Brickman

12/9 B.J. Thomas/Heather Myles

12/11 *Big* (the musical)

12/12 NSYNC/Britney Spears (sellout)

1999

1/13 Kirk Franklin/CeCe Winans

1/15 *Smoky Joe's Café*

1/16 Newsong

2/5 Bernie Mac

Reba McEntire with Ken Hicks of US-101 in 1999 (WUSY)

2/9-10 *Stomp*

2/21 Bill Cosby (2 sold out shows, Auditorium 75th anniversary)

2/23 Point of Grace

2/26 Statler Brothers/Tara Lynn

3/25-26 Mark Lowry/Anthony Burger

3/30-4/4 *Riverdance* (8 shows)

5/17 Natalie Merchant

5/19 America/Nelson

6/22 Bonnie Raitt/Jon Cleary

7/6-7 *Cats*

7/17 Najee

8/28 Cathedrals

10/12 *Annie*

10/23 Avalon/Annointed

10/29-30 Big Apple Circus

11/2 Chonda Pierce (comedy)

11/4 Reba McEntire

11/6 Sinbad

11/9 Twila Paris

11/11 *Porgy and Bess*

11/12 O'Jays (sellout)

11/19-21 *Sesame Street Live*

11/27 Steven Curtis Chapman (sellout)

12/3 Gene Watson

12/8 *Lord of the Dance*

The 2000s

By now, the Auditorium had settled into a comfortable groove. The renovations of a decade ago had paid off with better sound and sight lines, making the big hall a desirable venue for singers, musicians, and actors.

Local promoter Alan Knowles of Dove Ministries booked dozens of popular Contemporary Christian shows. The touring plays and musicals that once shunned the Auditorium were now on the big stage almost monthly. Rock bands, comedians, and country artists that didn't want to play the 11,000 seat UTC Arena were quite comfortable filling the 3,800 seat Auditorium.

Def Leppard, David Copperfield, Jerry Seinfeld, Jeff Foxworthy, Kenny Chesney, Steve Harvey, Sandi Patty, George Jones, Harry Connick Jr., Chonda Pierce, and Travis Tritt were among the biggest draws. Other headline names ranged from the slapstick comedy of Tim Conway to the poetry of Maya Angelou.

Before they became household names, Larry the Cable Guy, Ron White, Nickel Creek, and Lady Antebellum opened the show for bigger-named acts.

In 2004, the newly restored Austin Pipe Organ was a featured attraction, the result of a twenty-one-year campaign spearheaded by the Chattanooga Music Club.

David Johnson retired as Auditorium manager in 2004 after a sixteen-year run. He returned the following year to assist Missy Crutchfield, who had been named as the city's director of Education, Arts, and Culture. He continued in that role until 2012.

The Tivoli Auditorium Promotion Association (TAPA) was formed as a non-profit and was responsible for bringing in many of the Broadway touring shows each year.

Although Auditorium patrons were still enjoying live performances, some warning signs were beginning to emerge. From fiscal year 2001 to fiscal year 2003, the number of events at the Auditorium declined 29 percent, and attendance dropped 40 percent. After a strong start to the decade, the shows had dwindled by 2009, signaling some major changes in the decade ahead.

2000

1/22 Def Leppard/Billionaire (sold out)

1/25-27 *Chicago* (the musical, with Alan Thicke)

2/5 Jeff Foxworthy/Ron White/Bill Engvall (2 sold out shows)

2/16 *Be Careful What You Pray For* (play, starring Cuba Gooding Sr.)

2/20 Sammy Kershaw/Aaron Tippin

3/7 *Showboat*

3/14 David Copperfield (Magic)

4/7 Cedric the Entertainer

4/18 Third Day/Jennifer Knapp (Dove)

4/21 Good Friday Sing (Kingsmen, Gold City)

5/4 Merle Haggard/Bonnie Owens, Chris Knight, Ty Tyler

5/5 Ray Boltz (Dove)

8/1 Mary J. Blige/Jagged Edge, Carl Thomas

9/20 *Music of Andrew Lloyd Webber* (Europa Philharmonia)

9/26 Sisters in the Spirit (Mary Mary, Yolanda Adams, Shirley Caesar)

10/8 Jars of Clay/Jennifer Knapp (Dove)

11/3 Michael Card (Dove)

11/24 Kenny Chesney/Phil Vassar (sold out)

11/25 *Dr. Jekyll & Mr. Hyde*

12/1 Ronnie McDowell/Exile

12/10 Jaci Velasquez (Dove)

12/11 *Peter Pan*

12/2 Steve Green (Dove)

2001

2/9-11 *Blues Clues*

2/27-28 *Fame*

3/16 Chris Rice (Dove)

3/17 George Jones/Mustang Sally (sold out)

3/24 Platters with Chattanooga Symphony Orchestra

4/19 Chonda Pierce (Dove)

4/13 Good Friday Sing (The Inspirations)

5/17 Plus One, Stacie Orrico, Rachael Lampa (Dove)

5/31 Drifters/Tams

7/27 Hoppers, Dove Brothers, Galloways (Gospel)

6/22 Steve Harvey

6/23 Happy Goodmans

6/29-7/1 *Bear in the Big Blue House*

9/8 Michael Combs (gospel)

George Jones was one of the longest-running headliners at Memorial Auditorium from the 1960s, until shortly before his death in 2013 (Cindy Lowery)

9/29 Avalon (Dove)

10/16 Sandi Patty

10/26 *My Fair Lady*

11/9 Cedric the Entertainer

12/4-9 *Riverdance*

2002

1/7 *Annie Get Your Gun*

1/25 Newsboys/Newsong

1/31 David Copperfield (Magic) 2 shows

2/26-28 *Veggie Tales Live*

3/2-3 *Rent*

3/8 Sheryl Underwood (comedy)

3/9 Crabb Family (Dove)

3/15 Jars of Clay

3/20-24 *Beauty and the Beast*

4/6 George Jones

4/15 Temptations

5/1-2 *Ragtime*

5/9 Third Day (Dove)

5/14 Fernando Ortega (Dove)

5/21 The Impressions

5/30 Sha Na Na

9/14 Richard Smallwood/Donald Lawrence (gospel)

9/20 *Spirit of the Dance*

9/24 Jackie Joyner-Kersee (Olympic track and field gold medal winner, spoke to 2,000 students)

9/27 Chonda Pierce

10/12 Steven Curtis Chapman/Nichole Nordeman

10/27 Kirk Franklin/Yolanda Adams

12/5 Ricky Van Shelton

12/6 *Lord of the Dance* (Michael Flatley)

2003

1/8 *Cinderella*

2/1 Gold City, Singing Cookes

2/4-9 *Miss Saigon*

2/12 Merle Haggard/Eric Heatherly

3.4 *Copacabana* (musical)

3/8 Crabb Family, Heirline (gospel)

3/12 Jars of Clay (gospel)

4/1 *South Pacific*

4/18 Inspirations

5/23 Jerry Seinfeld (sold out)

6/4 *Grease*

6/17 The Wilburns (gospel)

7/26 Darryl Wheeler Jr. AKA Lil D

8/23 Larry Gatlin and the Gatlin Brothers/Chattanooga Symphony Orchestra

9/16 Nickel Creek

9/26 Chonda Pierce

10/10 Travis Tritt/Bill Engvall

10/14 Widespread Panic

11/1 Inspirations Reunion

11/7 Chris Rice

11/11 *Saturday Night Fever*

11/20 David Copperfield (Magic) 2 shows

12/5 Juice Newton

2004

2/2 *The Music Man*

2/7 Gold City/Crabb Family

2/13 Tim Conway/Harvey Korman

2/24 *Kiss Me Kate*

2/25 Maya Angelou

3/6 Mercy Me/Amy Grant/Bebo Norman

3/7 *Til Death Do Us Part* (play)

3/12 Jeff Foxworthy/Larry the Cable Guy

3/13 Heirline/Michael Combs

3/19 Hoobastank/Lost Prophets/Ima Robot

3/30 *"If These Hips Could Talk"* (play with Billy Dee Williams/Robin Givens)

4/1 Avalon/Mark Schultz

4/9 Inspirations/McKameys

4/20-21 *Sesame Street Live*

5/8 Mark Lowry/Stan Whitmire/LordSong

5/11-12 *Madea's Class Reunion* (Tyler Perry)

6/6 Gary Puckett/Anita Cochran

6/11 Rickey Smiley (comedian), in the Community Theater

6/14 Chattanooga Music Club patriotic concert with Dr. Jonathan Crutchfield playing the partially restored Austin pipe organ

6/15 Harry Connick Jr.

9/17 Chonda Pierce/Sandi Patti

9/25 Dove Brothers, Chuck Wagon Gang, Talley Trio

10/1 Ricky Skaggs/Chattanooga Symphony Orchestra

10/27 *Cats*

11/11 Third Day/Toby Mac

11/13 Ron White (comedian)

11/30 *Fosse* (musical)

12/10 B B King/Kate Fenner

12/11 John Anderson/Daniel Lee Martin

2005

1/3 Celebration of Life for hometown football star Reggie White, who had died Dec. 26, 2004 at the age of 43

1/12 Alison Krauss & Union Station

1/14-16 *Sesame Street Live*

1/20 Eddie & Gerald Levert/Johnny Gill

2/1-2 *Riverdance*

2/4 *Guilty Until Proven Innocent* (Gospel play with K-Ci and JoJo)

2/5 Gold City/Crabb Family

2/19 Larry the Cable Guy

2/20 *Porgy and Bess*

2/22 *Smokey Joe's Cafe*

3/12 Michael Combs/Heirline

3/25 Inspirations, McKameys, Kingsmen

3/29 Widespread Panic (sold out)

3/30 *Fiddler on the Roof*

6/4 Joe Diffie

7/7 Jerry Seinfeld

7/30 Greater Vision/Talley Trio/New Ground (Gospel)

8/5-7 *Dragon Tales Live*

8/18 Bruce Hornsby

10/6 *42nd Street*

12/4 *1964* (Beatles Tribute)

12/11 Michael Card

2006

1/7 Gospel: Michael Combs, Heirline

1/24 "*The Man of Her Dreams*" (play, starring Jackee Harry)

2/4 Gold City, Crabb Family

2/18 Casting Crowns/Nichole Nordeman

3/11 Legacy Five/Dove Brothers

3/31 Third Day/David Crowder Band

4/14 Inspirations, Kingsmen, McKameys, Gold City

4/20 Chonda Pierce

4/27 Nickel Creek/Ditty Bops

5/4 *Veggie Tales Live*

6/1 George Jones, Confederate Railroad

6/2 *"Marrying Up"* play with Thea Vidale

6/3 Mark Chesnutt/ 3 Fox Drive

9/23 *Joseph and the Amazing Technicolor Dreamcoat*

9/30 Classical Mystery Tour (Beatles tribute) with Chattanooga Symphony Orchestra

10/15 Widespread Panic

10/21 BluesFest with Clarence Carter

11/7 *Men, Money and Gold Diggers* (Robin Givens, Carl Payne)

12/2 Bowzer, Crystals, Tokens

12/6 Toby Mac, Hawk Nelson

12/7 *Cirque Dreams Jungle Fantasy*

2007

1/19-22 *Sesame Street Live*

2/3 Crabb Family, Gold City, Mike Bowling Group

2/10 Goo Goo Dolls/Augustana (sold out)

2/14 Rickey Smiley

2/27 Chris Tomlin/Louie Giglio

3/3 Sugarland/Little Big Town

3/5 Kingsmen Reunion

3/10 Heirline, Hoppers, Michael Combs, Greesons

3/15 *Camelot*

4/6 McKameys, Inspirations, Primitive Quartet

4/17 Hinder

4/19 John Tesh (syndicated radio host, pianist)

4/21 Alison Krauss & Union Station, Tony Rice, Jerry Douglas

6/1 Sammy Kershaw/Whitney Duncan

6/4 *Celtic Woman*

7/2 Organists Richard Peter Conte & Hector Olivera (Dedication of restored Austin Pipe Organ, 21 years in making thanks to Chattanooga Music Club, attendance 3,000)

7/20 *"Earthquake"* Joe Torry/Lavell Crawford (comedy)

7/25 Zig Ziglar (motivational speaker) with University of Tennessee coaches Bruce Pearl and Phil Fulmer (4,000 attendance)

8/17 Ron White

9/13-14 *Evita*

9/15 Chonda Pierce

9/29 *Phantom of the Opera* (CSO)

10/5 Toby Mac/BarlowGirl/Thousand Foot Krutch

10/30 Widespread Panic

11/8 Sara Evans

11/25 *Rent*

11/30 Billy Joe Royal/BJ Thomas "Raindrops and Boondocks" concerrt

12/8 *Cats*

2008

1/15 *Dirty Rotten Scoundrels* (Play)

1/18-20 *Sesame Street Live*

1/26 Lil Wayne/Yo Gotti

2/10 Brian Regan (comedian)

2/15 George Jones/Janie Fricke/Jason Bird

2/16 Temptations/Four Tops

2/21 Trace Adkins/Jason Michael Carroll

2/22 *Lord of the Dance*

3/3 *Chicago* (play)

3/8 Michael Combs/Heirline

3/14 Steven Curtis Chapman

3/15 Plies/Lil Derrick (rapper)

3/21 *My Little Pony* (live)

3/30 B B King

4/17 Rodney Carrington (comedian)

4/23 Robert Plant, Alison Krauss, T-Bone Burnett (sold out)

5/29 *Jesus Christ Superstar* (Ted Neeley, 35 years after first playing the role of Jesus)

5/31 Mike Epps (comedy)

6/1 Pam Tillis/Daniel Lee Martin

7/1 Chattanooga Music Club patriotic concert with organist Robert McDonald

8/2 Bar-Kays, Midnight Star, Brick, Dazz Band

8/6 Merle Haggard

9/13 Chonda Pierce

10/2 *Veggie Tales Live*

10/23 Jason Aldean/Lady Antebellum

11/8 Kutless, Pillar, Thousand Foot Krutch

11/14 The Wiggles (children act)

11/25 *Annie* (musical)

12/5 Drifters/Tams

12/12 *Movin Out* (Billy Joel/Twyla Tharp play)

2009

1/31-2/1 *Hairspray* (musical)

2/13 Denise LaSalle/Latimore

3/6 *Meet the Browns* (Play)

3/7 Hoopers, Michael Combs/Heirline

3/24 Papa Roach/Avenged Sevenfold

4/4 Celtic Celebration with CSO, Eileen Ivers of *Riverdance*

4/10 Inspirations, McKameys

5/1 George Jones

5/28 Jason Aldean/Colt Ford

6/4 *Bob the Builder*

6/7 Joe Diffie

6/18 *Rain* (Beatles tribute)

7/2 Chattanooga Music Club patriotic concert with organist Nicholas Bowden

8/19 Mike Brooks/Shucky Ducky (comedy)

9/5 Frankie Beverly & Maze/Brownstone

10/10-11 *Wizard of Oz*

10/24 *Celtic Woman*

11/22 Mannheim Steamroller

11/27 Oak Ridge Boys

12/3 Skillet, Hawk Nelson

12/6 New Rascals

12/16 Kenny G

The 2010s and Beyond

You may have noticed a downturn in shows at the end of the previous decade. The Auditorium's slow bookings reflected the recession that was plaguing America. The city of Chattanooga was facing some severe economic cutbacks, and there were some who suggested closing the Auditorium. Newspaper editorials were calling for the resignations (or dismissal) of those in charge of operating the facility.

But as was the case in years past, the economy gradually bounced back, and the grand old building survived. In 2010, a campaign had been established to restore the Community Theater, in hopes of making it more viable for performers who preferred a venue of its size.

In the early part of the decade, touring troupes of Broadway plays and musicals continued to be an Auditorium fixture, with *Cats* the most frequent booking. Tyler Perry's plays were also a perennial favorite. Still, compared to years past, the number of shows was in decline.

Among veteran performers making their Auditorium debuts were Steve Martin, and Crosby Stills and Nash. In 2013, Black Jacket Symphony, made up of top session musicians, began a long run at the Auditorium (and Tivoli Theater) playing note-for-note re-enactments of classic rock albums. Chris Stapleton opened the show for Little Big Town on March 8, 2015, shortly before attaining superstar status. Later that year, the Avett Brothers sold out the main hall, which was by that time a rare occurrence.

On March 26, 2013 the Auditorium hosted one of the final performances by country music superstar George Jones, who passed away five weeks later.

In 2015, Mayor Andy Berke established the Tivoli Foundation to handle the operations of both the Auditorium and the Tivoli Theater. The Foundation launched a massive renovation project in the Community Theater, which would reopen on October 14, 2017 as the Robert Kirk Walker Community Theater, honoring the late mayor who had been a key supporter of the Auditorium and the Tivoli Theater. The once rarely-used hall, now commonly referred to as the Walker Theater, was soon transformed into one of the city's busiest stages.

AC Entertainment, a Knoxville-based live entertainment and facilities management group headed by Ashley Capps, was contracted by the Tivoli Foundation to operate both faciliites. AC's track record in hosting the annual Bonnaroo Festival in nearby Manchester, Tennessee and in booking other venues proved to be beneficial to the Chattanooga halls. By decade's end, local music fans who once complained of a lack of live entertainment now had multiple options, almost every night.

Nick Wilkinson, executive director of the Tivoli Foundation, and Dave Holscher, who managed the daily operations of the Auditorium and Tivoli, were busily lining up shows, keeping both stages busy. Concerts were never more plentiful, occurring on an almost nightly basis. Unfortunately, operations ground to a halt on March 13, 2020 when COVID-19 safety concerns forced both venues to pause live performances until public gatherings could be held safely.

2010

2/9 *Cabaret*

2/18 *Madea's Big Happy Family* (starring Tyler Perry)

2/19 Chonda Pierce

3/5 Michael Combs/Heirline

3/21 Sir Charles Jones/Latimore

4/2 Gold City, McKameys, Kingsmen

4/15 Heart

4/28 Alice in Chains/Shooter Jennings

(May) Travis Porter/SwaggBotz

5/3 *The Color Purple*

5/4 Widespread Panic

5/18-20 *Riverdance*

6/6 Lee Greenwood

6/29 Chattanooga Music Club patriotic concert with organist Dr. Jeannine Jordan

9/17-18 *Legally Blonde*

10/1-2 *Fiddler on the Roof*

10/29-30 *Irving Berlin's White Christmas*

11/13 Lady Antebellum/ David Nail

11/19 Phillips Craig & Dean (Dove)

12/3 Sheryl Underwood

12/5 Aaron Tippin

12/7 *Cats*

12/10 *Rent*

2011

3/5 Inspirations/McKameys

3/10 *In the Mood* (1940s musical revue)

3/15 *A Chorus Line*

3/21 Airmen of Note (US Air Force jazz band)

4/16 Trans-Siberian Orchestra

5/5 *Celtic Woman*

5/17 Third Day

5/26 Steve Martin/Steep Canyon Rangers

5/27 Marvin Sapp (gospel)

6/5 B. J. Thomas/Billy Joe Royal

6/20 *Beauty and The Beast*

6/30 Chattanooga Music Club patriotic concert with organist Dr. Steven Ball

7/7 Jeff Dunham

8/13 Hoppers, Gold City

9/10 Garrison Keillor/Sara Watkins

9/29 3 Doors Down/Theory of a Deadman/Pop Evil

10/1 Billy Currington/Brantley Gilbert

10/15 *The Haves and Have-Nots* (play written by Tyler Perry)

10/29 Amy Grant/Michael W. Smith

11/14 Mannheim Steamroller

12/2 Lorrie Morgan/The Wright Kids

12/5 Oak Ridge Boys

12/31 Bruce Bruce (comedy)

2012

2/2 *Monty Python's Spamalot*

2/10 Arnez J (comedy)

3/3 Inspirations/McKameys/Heirline

3/20 Trans-Siberian Orchestra

3/25 Tyrese Gibson/Chrisette Michelle/Aaron Bing

3/29- 4/1 *Smoke on the Mountain*

5/31 Yanni

6/1 The Association/Regie Hamm

6/26 Chattanooga Music Club patriotic concert with Tom Trenney (organist)

7/10 Crosby Stills and Nash

7/26 Blue Man Group

7/28 Rickey Smiley/Mark Curry

9/25-26 *Sister Act*

10/13 Mike Epps (Comedy)

11/23-25 *Sesame Street Live*

12/7 John Michael Montgomery/Morgan Frazier

12/10 Hall & Oates

2013

1/18 Black Jacket Symphony: Fleetwood Mac *Rumours*

1/19 TK Soul, Bobby Rush

2/12 *Lord of the Dance*

2/15 Sheryl Underwood

3/2 Inspirations/McKameys

3/22 George Jones (He died on **4/26/13**, just a month later), also Wilson Fairchild

4/19 *Celtic Woman*

5/8 "*Love Lies*" play starring Brian McKnight

5/24 K-Ci and Jo-Jo, Jagged Edge, and Silk

5/31 Family Stone/Hey Elsten

7/1 Chattanooga Music Club patriotic program with organist Walt Strony

8/29 Black Jacket Symphony performing Rolling Stones "*Some Girls*" album

9/13 ZZ Top

9/15 Anthony Hamilton

11/1-2 *West Side Story*

11/8 Gaither Vocal Band (Mark Lowry, Michael English, David Phelps, Wes Hampton and Bill Gaither)

11/16 Straight No Chaser

12/6 Tracy Lawrence/Rick Huckaby

2014

1/5 Mindless Behavior (boy band)

1/12 Fresh Beat Band

2/4 *Hell Hath No Fury* (Tyler Perry play)

2/26 U.S. Navy Concert Band

3/1 Inspirations, McKameys

5/12 Brit Floyd (Pink Floyd Tribute group)

7/1 Chattanooga Music Club patriotic program with organist Frederick Hohmann

8/29 Casting Crowns

10/11 The Hoppers, Triumphant Quartet

11/6 *Elf the Musical*

11/22 Old Crow Medicine Show/Marty Stuart

12/4 Bobby Jones Gospel Band

12/5 Diamond Rio/Raquel Cole/Truman Brothers

12/9 Joe Bonamassa

12/18 *Cirque Dreams Holidaze*

2015

1/27 Blue Man Group

3/7 McKameys, Gold City, Inspirations

3/8 Little Big Town/Chris Stapleton

3/8 Ben Vereen (Community Theater)

4/9 Celtic Woman

4/18 T. Graham Brown (Community Theater)

4/28 Chicago (band)

5/29 Starship/Cumberland Blue

5/31 Rickey Smiley

6/30 Chattanooga Music Club patriotic program with organist Jelani Eddington

8/16 Garrison Keillor/Sarah Jarosz

9/12 Avett Brothers (sold out)

10/16 Katt Williams (comedy)

10/17 Gold City, Kingsmen

10/24 Chris Young, Eric Paslay, Clare Dunn

11/3 Fred Hammond, Donnie McClurkin (gospel)

11/6 *The Illusionists*

11/7 Christoper Titus (Community Theater)

11/13 *"Brand New Man"* with Julie Roberts

12/4 Lonestar/Brent Rupard

2016

3/5 McKameys, Inspirations

4/20 Widespread Panic (sold out)

4/24 *Mamma Mia*

5/4 Old Crow Medicine Show/Brandi Carlile/Secret Sisters

6/3 Sister Hazel

6/28 Chattanooga Music Club patriotic program with organist Peter Richard Conte

7/16 Gaither Vocal Band

7/30 Maxwell/Fantasia/Ro James

Todd Rundgren performing on stage at the Walker Theater, formerly known as the Community Theater. (Dave Weinthal)

*Charley Pride posed with fans Chris and David Carroll after his
Memorial Auditorium show in 2017.*

9/30 Legends of Southern Hip-Hop (Mystikal, Juvenile)

10/16 Impractical Jokers

10/21 Nate Bargatze (Community Theater)

10/22 Anthony Hamilton/Lalah Hathaway/Eric Benet

11/19 Triumphant, the Hoppers

12/4 Neal McCoy

2017

(On October 14, 2017, the Community Theater became known as the Walker Theater. Shows in that venue are denoted as "W")

1/14 Katt Williams

3/5 McKameys, Inspirations

3/15 Earth Wind and Fire

3/21 Brit Floyd (Pink Floyd Tribute)

6/4 Maxwell/Ledisi

6/27 Chattanooga Music Club patriotic program with organist Dr. John Schwandt

7/24 Michael McDonald (Community Theater)

8/9 Mary Chapin Carpenter (Community Theater)

8/10 Todd Rundgren (Community Theater)

9/22 Newsboys

10/14 Delbert McClinton (Walker Theater)

10/21 Willie Nelson/Dwight Yoakam (sold out)

10/23 Turnpike Troubadors (W)

10/28 Lyle Lovett/John Hiatt (W)

11/18 Charley Pride/Sammy Kershaw/Collin Raye/James Otto

The newly renovated Walker Theater was unveiled in 2017, and immediately became one of Chattanooga's most popular performance venues (Tivoli Foundation)

Organist Richard Hills plays the Austin pipe organ at the 2018 Chattanooga Music Club patriotic program at Memorial Auditorium.

11/30 Scotty McCreery (W)

12/4 Joe Bonamassa

12/12 Steve Earle (W)

12/15 John Berry (W)

12/16 Puddles Pity Party (W)

Weird Al Yankovic's devoted fans, like Courtney and Kelly Treece, were always in attendance at his Chattanooga shows. (Kelly Treece)

2018

1/11 Henry Rollins (W)

1/25 Neko Case (W)

2/9 Steep Canyon Rangers (W)

2/16 Jim Brickman (W)

Maxwell is pictured with WMPZ/WJTT radio personality Magic Crutcher at his 2017 show at Memorial Auditorium (Magic Crutcher)

2/17 Todd Snider/Rory Carroll (W)

2/23 Jonny Lang (W)

3/8 Steve Martin/ Martin Short

3/9 Steven Curtis Chapman (W)

3/15 Travis Tritt (W)

3/16 Wood Brothers (W)

3/24 Marty Stuart (W)

3/29 Indigo Girls (W)

3/31 Shovels and Rope (W)

4/7 112/Ginuwine/Jagged Edge/Guy

4/13 Weird Al/Emo Phillips (W)

4/14 Philip Phillips/The Ballroom Thieves (W)

5/3 Mavericks (W)

5/4 Henry Cho (W)

5/11 Edwin McCain (W)

6/26 Chattanooga Music Club patriotic program with organist Richard Hills

7/24 Michael McDonald (W)

8/9 Mary Chapin Carpenter (W)

8/10 Todd Rundgren (W)

8/16 Heather Land

8/25 Trish Suhr/Leanne Morgan/Karen Mills (W)

9/15 Sam Bush (W)

9/30 Drive By Truckers (W)

10/6 Lee Ann Womack (W)

10/11 Eric Johnson (W)

10/12 Alice Cooper

10/13 Ron White

10/14 Eva Schloss (holocaust survivor)

10/18 Chris Robinson Brotherhood (W)

10/30 Lyle Lovett/Robert Earl Keen (W)

11/9 Psychedelic Furs (W)

11/10 Triumphant Quartet/Hoppers

11/10 Allen Stone/Nick Waterhouse (W)

11/11 100th anniversary Armistice concert sponsored by Chattanooga Music Club (organist Ken Double, Chattanooga Symphony Orchestra conducted by Kayoko Dan, and Lee University Singers)

Alice Cooper made his first Chattanooga concert appearance at Memorial Auditorium in 2018. (Angie Williams)

11/13 Lindsey Buckingham (W)

11/16 The Band Perry (W)

11/17 Mac DeMarco (W)

11/23 Hip Hop Nutcracker

11/30 Black Violin (W)

12/1 Eli Young Band (W)

12/3 David Cross (W)

12/19 Wynonna & The Big Noise (W)

12/20 Dancing with the Stars Live

12/31 Blackberry Smoke

Morgan Wallen performed as part of US-101's "Heart Strings for Hope" concert at Memorial Auditorium in 2019. The annual show is a fundraiser for St. Jude Children's Research Hospital in Memphis. (Don Luzynski)

2019

1/9 Riley Green (W)

1/19 Art Garfunkel (W)

1/23 Tedeschi Trucks Band

2/1 Steeldriver (W)

2/2 Drew and Ellie Holcomb (W)

2/9 McKameys Final Chapter

2/19 Christopher Cross (W)

3/2 Wild Kratts Live

3/5 Luke Combs, Jon Pardi, Randy Houser, Morgan Wallen, Kelley Lovelace, Channing Wilson

3/7 "Friends" (musical parody) (W)

3/8 Trae Crowder (W)

3/9 Marc Broussard (W)

3/16 "Whose Live is it Anyway" with Greg Proops, Chip Esten, Joel Murray and Jeff Davis (W)

3/21 Ben Rector

3/23 Graham Nash (W)

3/28 Mac Powell & the Family Reunion (W)

3/29 Steep Canyon Rangers (W)

4/12 Leon Bridges

4/14 Jeff Tweedy (W)

4/18 Mandolin Orange (W)

4/19 David Sedaris (W)

4/30 Melissa Etheridge (W)

5/1 Blue October (W)

5/9 *Madea's Farewell* (Tyler Perry)

5/11 Preacher Lawson (W) 2 shows

6/20 Puddles Pity Party (W)

6/21 Rob Bell (W)

6/22 Todd Snider (W)

6/27 Andrew Schaeffer, organist at Chattanooga Music Club patriotic concert

7/11 Welcome to Nightvale (W)

7/28 Hannibal Burress (W)

9/29 Lucinda Williams (W)

10/11 Langhorne Slim/Katie Pruitt (W)

10/12 Delbert McClinton (W)

11/9 Ryan Bingham (W)

11/14 Corey Smith (W)

11/15 Jay and Silent Bob (Silent Reboot Roadshow) (W)

11/16 Jeff Dunham

11/21 Kathleen Madigan (W)

11/23 Heather McMahon (W)

12/6 Colter Wall (W)

12/7 Heather Land (W)

12/13 Dave Barnes (W)

12/15 Robert Earl Keen (W)

12/19 Wynonna Judd & Big Noise (W)

12/23 Jim Brickman (W)

Hamilton County Chief Deputy Austin Garrett poses with Ashley McBryde, one of the stars of the 2020 Heart Strings for Hope concert. (Austin Garrett)

2020

1/15 Jonny Lang (W)

1/21 Citizen Cope (W)

1/29-30 Indigo Girls (W)

1/31 Tig Notaro (W)

2/6 Marty Stuart (W)

2/11 Matt Kearney (W)

2/13 Wood Brothers (W)

2/24 Walk Off The Earth (W)

3/3 Joe Bonamassa

3/5 Big Bad Voodoo Daddy (W)

3/6 Stassi Schroeder podcast (W)

3/7 Jim Breuer (W)

3/7 Triumphant Quartet, Inspirations, Karen Peck and New River

3/10 Kelley Lovelace, Ashley McBryde, Hardy, Tyler Farr, Kip Moore

3/12 Marc Broussard (W)

On March 13, 2020 the City of Chattanooga declared its facilities would be closed until further notice, citing government safety guidance regarding the COVID-19 pandemic. Live shows resumed at Memorial Auditorium on August 10, 2021.

2021

8/10 George Thorogood and the Destroyers (W)

8/13 Theresa Caputo (The Long Island Medium)

9/13 David Sedaris (W)

9/28 Santana

10/1 Allman Betts Band (W)

10/5 Shinedown

CHAPTER 2

Tivoli Theater

"The Jewel of the South," located at 709 Broad Street in Chattanooga, has certainly lived up to the expectations of those who created a magnificent theater. As the March 19, 1921 opening day program stated, "The management of the Tivoli pledges its every effort for your comfort and delight." It also promised "a rich mezzanine, and conveniences afforded in the finely appointed lounge and rest rooms." In fact, many visitors were dazzled by the fact there were so many rest rooms, a rarity in public buildings of the era.

Patrons could look forward to "the rarest works of the greatest photoplay directors…enhanced by the (twenty piece) Tivoli symphony orchestra and Bennett organ…setting a new standard for entertainment in the Southland."

The Tivoli was the dream of F.H. Dowler Jr., who was president of Tennessee Enterprises, and the Signal Amusement Company. He had long held the belief that the city deserved a better entertainment venue than those that were already in operation.

The facility was built at a cost of just under a million dollars, and the architect was R. H. Hunt. Construction had begun in 1919, and the building took two years to complete. The capacity was 2300. For most of the theater's first forty-two years, it was primarily used for film showings, with occasional live performances and programs. Emmet Rodgers was theater manager from 1921 to 1957.

In 1924 the Paramount-Publix theater chain bought the Tivoli.

The Tivoli was the first Chattanooga establishment with air conditioning, installed in 1926. At the time, there were very few buildings in the nation with air conditioning. Keep in mind, the "air conditioning" units of the 1920s were quite primitive, unlike the cooling systems of today. They were essentially heating systems modified with

1 Program cover for "Mary of Scotland" with Helen Hayes at the Tivoli in 1935

refrigeration equipment that distributed water-cooled air through floor vents, resulting in hot, muggy conditions at upper levels and much colder temperatures at lower levels, where patrons sometimes resorted to wrapping their feet with newspapers to stay warm. Although the air conditioning was a great promotional tool for such a theater in the early days, it was soon outdated, but remained in place for decades.

The first renovation was done in April 1939.

Tivoli Theater Pre-1960s

3/19/1921 Opening day: silent film actress Mae Murray made a personal appearance. M.B. Ochs, Dr. Spencer McCallie and Chattanooga Mayor Alexander Chambliss spoke at the ceremony. Dr. McCallie had visited Tivoli, Italy, and insisted on reproducing the art and architecture of that region. The Tivoli Symphony Orchestra performed. For the first four nights, the featured movie was Cecil B. DeMille's "Forbidden Fruit." For the next four nights it was Charlie Chaplin's "The Kid."

3/17/24 Organist Edward Lyle Taylor gave the first public recital on a new $30,000 Wurlitzer. Later that week he accompanied the feature film "The Shadows of Paris." The Wurlitzer Style 235 Special Opus 780 included three keyboards and eleven sets of pipes which produced different sounds. Among them were tuba, flute, clarinet, oboe and violin. The new instrument replaced a smaller Bennett organ.

7/18/27 Ginger Rogers (age 16) appeared in vaudeville act

2/21/35 Fanny Brice vaudeville act

3/29/35 Helen Hayes performed in the play "Mary of Scotland"

11/26/35 Earl Carroll's Vanities

4/14/36 Judith Anderson performed in the play "The Old Maid."

12/1/36 Helen Morgan performed in the play "Scandals."

12/8/36 Star Parade of 1937 with Dave Apollon

4/30/37 Tallulah Bankhead performed in play "Reflected Glory."

2/22/39 Alfred Lunt and Lynn Fontanne appeared in the play "Idiots Delight."

1/11/40 Alfred Lunt, Lynn Fontanne, and Sidney Greenstreet appeared in the play "Taming of the Shrew."

1/17/40 Phil Spitalney and All Girl Orchestra

1940 "Gone with the Wind" played to 12 straight sellouts (the Wurlitzer organ was removed at this time, and would be unused until 1963)

2/12/58 Actor/singer Tommy Sands appeared in person to promote his movie "Sing Boy Sing"

The 1960s

The Tivoli closed as a movie theater in August, 1961. The last film shown on the big screen was "Snow White and the Three Stooges." The Tivoli was in danger of closing forever before the city of Chattanooga came to the rescue, leasing the building from a Charlotte, North Carolina subsidiary of American Broadcasting-Paramount Theaters.

An application for the National Register for Historic Places stated, "When the renovated Tivoli reopened as a cultural center on March 5, 1963, it was hailed as the beginning of the revitalization of downtown Chattanooga."

The renovation drive was spearheaded by DeSales Harrison, president of the Chattanooga Chamber of Commerce. The architect was James T. Franklin.

The Tivoli reopened for live performances on March 5, 1963 with the intention of becoming a showcase for the arts, as opposed to its long history as primarily a movie theater. Among notable performers were Louis Armstrong, Victor Borge, Johnny Cash, and one of the nation's hottest comedians, "Brother Dave" Gardner.

There was an increase in bookings for several months in 1966 while Soldiers and Sailors Memorial Auditorium was closed for renovations.

Starting in 1967, a few live local telecasts were beamed from the Tivoli, including the first two eighteen-hour telethons for the March of Dimes ("Telerama") and Tennessee Junior Miss programs. Both events were hosted by WRCB-TV personality Roy Morris. "Bonanza" star Michael Landon was a guest during the program's first year in 1967. The Telerama moved to Memorial Auditorium in 1969.

Although overall bookings trailed the Auditorium, the Tivoli also hosted high school graduations and local symphony, opera and dance productions.

1963

3/5 Leslie Parnas (cellist) and Chattanooga Symphony Orchestra (Grand Opening of Tivoli)

3/14 The Lettermen

3/22 "World's Strongest Man" Paul Anderson

3/23 First Parade of Harmony: Bill Barger played the Wurlitzer Organ, installed in 1924, which had been dormant since 1940.

4/4 Dame Judith Anderson (performing excerpts from *Madea* and *Macbeth*)

5/1 Grand Ole Opry with Lonzo & Oscar, Willis Brothers

5/2/4 *The Sound of Music*

5/16 "Brother Dave" Gardner (comedian)

5/17 *"Here Today"* with Tallulah Bankhead and Estelle Winwood

10/26 Norman Luboff Choir

11/1 Fred Waring and his Pennsylvanians

11/11 Louis Armstrong

11/14 *"Mary Mary"* comedy play

11/29-30 *"How to Succeed in Business (Without Really Trying)"*

12/31 *"A Thousand Clowns"* starring John Ireland

1964

1/27 Jose Greco, Spanish dancer

2/29 *"Seven Ways to Love"* starring Joseph Cotten

3/2-4 *Camelot*

3/16 The Four Freshmen

3/28 Roger Williams, pianist

4/24 Ferrante and Teicher, pianists

10/14 Guy Lombardo orchestra

11/12 Peter Nero, pianist

11/25 *"Who's Afraid of Virginia Woolf"*

12/12 *"Oliver"*

12/5 *"HMS Pinafore"*

1965

2/17 *"Never Too Late"* with Penny Singleton and Lyle Talbot

2/26 Jose Molina

2/28 NBC *Tonight Show* Bandleader Skitch Henderson with Chattanooga Symphony Orchestra

3/7 Fred Waring and his Pennsylvanians

4/3 Jose Greco and his Spanish Gypsy Dancers

5/4 *"Carmen"* opera

10/20 *"Barefoot in the Park"*

11/3-7 *"Hello Dolly"* with Betty Grable

Rev. And Mrs. J. Bazzel Mull of "Mull's Singing Convention, who staged
dozens of gospel shows at the Tivoli Theater and Memorial Auditorium
in the 1960s and 1970s. (WTVC)

Ain't That Right, Miz Mull?

For about 30 years in the Chattanooga area, the faces of Rev. J. Bazzel Mull and his wife Elizabeth (Lady Mull) were as familiar as anyone's.

The Mulls first brought Southern Gospel music to local audiences on WRGP Channel 3 in 1956, then switched to WTVC Channel 9 in 1959. At first, the Mulls did a nightly show, before settling into a Saturday noontime slot from 1960 until 1975, in glorious black and white. For the next several years, their show was seen Sunday mornings, well into the 1980s. They had a long run of loyal sponsors like Soddy Men's Shop, Elm Hill Meats, Mayfield Milk and JFG Coffee.

J. Bazzel, blind since a childhood accident at the age of 11 months, was best known for his raspy voice, and a frequent question to his wife that became a local catch-phrase: "Ain't that right, Miz Mull?" "That's right!" she would cheerily reply. He often wore thick glasses to hide his closed eyelids, and many viewers had no idea he was blind.

From Channel 9's old Signal Mountain studio, and later from the Golden Gateway, the Mulls would introduce performances from the Blackwood Brothers, the Chuck Wagon Gang, and the LeFevres, to name a few. In addition, the Mulls would host live multi-act concerts at Memorial Auditorium, part of local TV's one-two punch of big ticket sellers (Harry Thornton's live wrestling shows also filled the seats). At their peak, they presented 75 live concerts, primarily in the Southeast, every year.

Today's young people might wonder how a weekend gospel music TV show had such a big impact. After all, in today's crowded media universe, it's hard for anyone to get noticed. But in those days, local viewers had only three channels from which to choose. The Mulls had a prime spot of TV real estate, between Saturday cartoons and football games, so it's quite likely their weekly show was must-see TV for many, or just on in the background at the very least.

Plus, it was hard not to notice the voice of J. Bazzel Mull. We didn't know it at the time, but when he would get talk too much and lose track of time, "Lady Mull" would pinch his leg under the desk to let him know it was time to introduce the next group.

Old-timers still enjoy telling their J. Bazzel stories. The preacher loved a good joke, even when the joke was on him. His blindness led to some good-natured pranks in the studio. One former Channel 9 crew member remembers the time Rev. Mull cornered them with some Bible wisdom. Quietly, his captive audience tiptoed away, leaving him preaching to a hat rack for several minutes. Another remembered a Tivoli Theater show in which the person who was supposed to lead him off the stage forgot to do so, leaving Rev. Mull standing awkwardly in front of a singing quartet for most of their song.

He didn't let his blindness keep him from his busy calling. Mrs. Mull, who drove him everywhere, faithfully read the Bible to him daily, and even late in life he had a photographic memory of every chapter and verse. The Mulls owned a Knoxville radio station, and his distinctive voice was also heard on powerful New Orleans station WWL (AM 870) with a nighttime signal that carried into several states. Long distance truckers were among the Mulls' biggest fans.

Both Mulls were inducted into the Southern Gospel Hall of Fame, and are credited with starting the careers of many acts that became household words. They promoted and hosted dozens of shows at the Tivoli Theater and Memorial Auditorium that were among the best attended events of their era.

1966

1/22 Ferrante and Teicher

2/11 Sargent Shriver, former director of Peace Corps, now director of Office of Economic Opportunity, and brother-in-law of the late President John F. Kennedy

2/12 "Brother Dave" Gardner

2/21 *"The Subject Was Roses"*

2/27 Mull's Singing Convention, with the Imperials, Oak Ridge Boys, Blackwood Brothers, Statesmen

3/2 Roger Williams, pianist

3/14 Victor Borge, pianist/comedian

3/26 Carlos Montoya, classical guitarist

6/25 Dr. Billy James Hargis, evangelist

9/30 Mull's: Florida Boys, Dixie Echoes, Happy Goodmans

10/18 *"The Odd Couple"* with Lyle Talbot and Harvey Stone

10/25 Bene Hammel, organist

11/9 Guy Lombardo with Nelson Eddy

11/14 "Brother Dave" Gardner

11/17-18 *"Half a Sixpence"*

11/25 Mull's Gospel: Statesman, Wendy Bagwell and Sunliters, Blackwood Brothers, Naomi and the Sego Brothers

11/29 Lorin Hullander, pianist

1967

1/14 Johnny Cash, the Carter Family, the Statler Brothers, and Carl Perkins

1/17 Morley Meredith (baritone)

1/19 *"Porgy and Bess"*

1/21-22 March of Dimes Telerama # 1 with Michael Landon, the Stonemans, Patricia Harty

2/19 Fred Waring and his Pennsylvanians

3/10 *"Luv"* starring Eileen Brennan

5/2 Sen. Strom Thurmond (R-South Carolina)

10/17 *"The Impossible Years"* starring Tom Ewell

10/18 "Brother Dave" Gardner

10/21 John Gary, singer

10/27 Gen. Mark Clark

11/2 American National Opera Company

11/14 Arthur Fiedler and Nippon Orchestra

12/12 Jean Casedesus, French pianist

1968

1/12 *"Roar of the Greasepaint"*

1/20-21 March of Dimes Telerama # 2 with Leonard Nimoy, Roger Miller, Minnie Pearl and James Drury

2/3 Victor Borge

2/8 Fred Waring and his Pennsylvanians

2/15-17 *"The Fantasticks"*

3/19 Rep. John Ashbrook (R-Ohio)

10/14 Pete Fountain (clarinetist)

10/15 Rex Humbard, evangelist

10/21-23 *"Man of LaMancha"*

11/26 Laurindo Almeida (guitarist)

1969

2/24 Preservation Hall Jazz Band

3/23 Ferrante and Teicher

4/23 Guy Lombardo Orchestra

10/10-11 *"Mame"*

11/14 Victor Borge

11/25 Dave Brubeck Quartet

The 1970s

Entering its second decade of live performances, a few traditions were beginning to emerge. Chattanooga audiences made annual trips to the Tivoli to see the Guy Lombardo Orchestra, the pianist duo Ferrante and Teicher, Fred Waring and his Pennsylvanians, numerous musicals that starred John Raitt, and the remaining stars from the Big Band Era.

Among the big-name entertainers to grace the Tivoli stage were Steve Allen, Rod McKuen, Hal Holbrook, Vincent Price and Rick Nelson.

In 1976, the city of Chattanooga bought the Tivoli Theater for $300,000 from ABC-Southeastern Theaters. Manager Clyde Hawkins believed the city would benefit from showing classic movies in addition to staging live performances. The city budgeted $30,000 for the restoration and improvements for the 1924 Wurlitzer Organ. Jon Robere played the organ for numerous silent films, beginning in the late 1970s.

Among the unknown performers who would later go on to great fame was actor John Goodman. The future "Roseanne" star was only 25 when he appeared in a supporting role in "The Robber Bridegroom" on the Tivoli stage in 1977.

1970

1/10-11 *"Fiddler on the Roof"*

1/18 Ferrante and Teicher

1/29 *"Showboat"* starring Robert Horton

2/1 Fred Waring and his Pennsylvanians

2/9 *"Man of LaMancha"*

2/14 Preservation Hall Jazz Band

2/27-28 *"I Do I Do"* starring Phil Ford and Mimi Hines

3/15 Roger Williams

3/17 Guy Lombardo orchestra

4/3-4 *"Cabaret"* (3 shows)

7/9-11 *"How to Succeed in Business"* starring Bob Cummings and Mamie Van Doren (4 shows)

10/16 Tennessee Republican gubernatorial candidate Winfield Dunn and US Rep. Bill Brock, a candidate for US Senate

10/20 Burch Mann's Ballet America

10/24 *"Will Rogers USA"* starring James Whitmore

10/27 Grant Johannesen, pianist

11/6/-7 *"You're A Good Man, Charlie Brown"* (2 shows)

11/18 Rev. Rex Humbard

11/20-21 *"Zorba"* with Vivian Blaine (3 shows)

1971

1/26 *"1776"*

3/3 *"Plaza Suite"* with Betty Garrett and Larry Parks

3/12-13 *"George M"* (3 shows)

4/24 Mull's: Singing Goffs, Sammy Hall Singers

9/20 Sen. Edmund Muskie (D-Maine), 1972 presidential candidate

10/12 *"Promises Promises"* with Alan North

10/20 Skitch Henderson, bandleader

11/9 *"Last of the Red Hot Lovers"* starring Stubby Kaye

11/18 Jerry Jennings (tenor, New York City opera)

1972

1/11 *"Butterflies are Free"* starring Jan Sterling

1/13 National Ballet of Washington

2/2 *"Company"*

3/10 *"Carousel"* starring John Raitt

3/14 Evelyn Mandac, soprano

4/7-8 *"Who's Afraid of Virginia Woolf"*

9/1 Bar-Kays

10/18 *"Kiss Me Kate"* with John Raitt

10/27 Rod McKuen (American Cancer Society benefit)

10/30 Leontyne Price, soprano

11/6 Big Band Cavalcade with Margaret Whiting, Bob Crosby, Frankie Carle, and Freddie Martin

11/7 *"Sleuth"*

11/15 Mitch Miller, choral leader, former host of NBC's "Sing Along With Mitch"

12/4-5 Rev. Bob Harrington, "Chaplain of Bourbon Street"

12/7 *"Two by Two"* with Shelley Berman

1973

1/29 Addis & Crofut (folk singers)

2/27 *"Applause"* with Patrice Munsel

3/6 Thomas Schumecher (pianist)

3/7 Dick Gregory (comedian)

3/9 Guy Lombardo Orchestra

3/22 *"Godspell"*

10/15 *"No Sex Please, We're British"* with Noel Harrison

10/26 *"Hildegarde"* play

10/30 *"Two Gentlemen of Verona"*

11/23 Richard Tucker, Italian tenor

12/1 *"No No Nanette"*

1974

1/16 Steve Allen

1/18 Ferrante & Teicher

1/23 Fred Waring and his Pennsylvanians

2/15 *"Camelot"* with John Raitt

3/10 Guy Lombardo Orchestra

3/13 *"Grease"*

3/28 *"Prisoner of Second Avenue"* with Imogene Coca and King Donovan

4/17 Jose Greco

5/30 Jack Greene and Jeannie Seely (country singers)

6/6 *"Wizard of Oz"*

9/13 Cannonball Adderley (jazz)

10/25 Bill Gaither Trio

11/1 Lamar Alexander (R) for Governor of Tennessee rally

11/5 *"Seesaw"* with John Raitt and Liz Torres

11/10 Big Band Cavalcade with Helen Forrest, Bob Crosby and Freddie Martin

11/13 *"Don Juan in Hell"* with Ricardo Montalban, Myrna Loy, and Edward Mulhare

11/26 *"Sunshine Boys"* with Robert Alda

1975

1/12 Ferrante & Teicher

1/22 *"Fiddler on the Roof"*

2/13 Carlos Montoya

2/25 Guy Lombardo Orchestra

3/5 Ruby Dee/Ossie Davis

3/6 Victor Borge

3/18 *"Pippin"* with Barry Williams ("Brady Bunch")

8/17 Rev. Ernest Angley

9/29 *"Give 'em Hell Harry"* with Ed Nelson

10/10 *"1776"*

10/24 John Hartford

11/3 *Gene Kelly's Salute to Broadway* with Howard Keel, Ken Berry, Mimi Hines

11/15 *Broadway Hit Parade* with Dorothy Collins

1976

1/17 Ferrante & Teicher

2/1 *"Irene"* with Virginia Graham

2/8 Hal Holbrook in *"Mark Twain"*

2/18 *"Jefferson, Hamilton and Burr"* with Howard Duff, Dana Andrews, and Monte Markham

3/31 *"Man of LaMancha"*

4/4 James Rogers (singer from Fort Oglethorpe)

4/29 Erma Bombeck (humor columnist)

5/7 Faron Young/Margo Smith

10/8 Rev. Bob Harrington

10/19 Lorin Hullander (pianist) with Chattanooga Symphony Orchestra

10/24 *"Naughty Marietta"* with Cyril Ritchard

10/28 "A Little Night Music" with Julie Wilson

11/6 Fred Waring and his Pennsylvanians

11/9 Eileen Farrell (soprano) and Chattanooga Symphony Orchestra

11/18 *"Shenandoah"* with John Raitt

1977

1/27 Ferrante and Teicher

2/4 *"Oklahoma"*

2/8 *"Belle of Amherst"* with Julie Harris

2/15 Benny Goodman with Chattanooga Symphony Orchestra

3/11 *"Sherlock Holmes"*

4/2 Paul Winter Consort

4/24 Jose Molina

10/15 Sir Michael Redgrave in *"Shakespeare's People"*

10/18 Anna Moffo (soprano) with Chattanooga Symphony Orchestra

10/22 Ink Spots, Four Lads, Pied Pipers, Four Freshmen

11/5 Fred Waring and his Pennsylvanians

11/11 *"Robber Bridegroom"* with John Goodman (age 25)

11/14/-16 *Bugs Bunny Follies* (3 shows)

11/18 Peter Nero (pianist) with Chattanooga Symphony Orchestra

1978

1/11 *"Bubbling Brown Sugar"*

1/19 Ferrante & Teicher

2/10 *"My Fair Lady"* with David Mulhare

2/15 *"West Side Story"*

2/17 Gordon MacRae

2/18 Les Brown Band and Paula Kelly

3/5 *"Swan Lake"* performed by Pittsburgh Ballet

3/22 *"Same Time Next Year"* with Kathryn Crosby

9/10 George Beverly Shea and Kurt Kaiser

10/20 *"The Sound of Music"* with Sally Anne Howes

11/7 Ransom Wilson (flutist) with Chattanooga Symphony Orchestra

11/12 Ink Spots, Four Lads, Pied Pipers, Four Freshmen

11/15 *"California Suite"* with Carolyn Jones and James Drury

11/25 Vincent Price as Oscar Wilde in *"Diversions and Delights"*

1979

1/10 Blackstone Jr. (magician)

1/12 Cy Coleman and Billy Taylor with Chattanooga Symphony Orchestra

1/18 Ferrante & Teicher

1/25 *"Side by Side"* with Hermoine Ginggold

2/24 Teddy Huffman and the Gems (gospel)

3/10 Marcel Marceau (French mime artist)

3/27 Lorin Hullander (pianist)

10/3 Gen. Alexander Haig (former NATO commander, considered a potential 1980 Republican presidential candidate

10/9 Rick Nelson

11/7-11 *Bugs Bunny in Space*

11/13 *"Showboat"* with Butterfly McQueen and Forrest Tucker

11/17 Roger Williams (pianist) with Chattanooga Symphony Orchestra

12/6 *"Chapter Two"* with Dawn Wells

Brushes with Greatness

Over the years, I've written about interrupting President Carter's vacation, to his mild annoyance, and the time Kenny Rogers reduced my wife to a stammering puddle with his overpowering Kenny Rogers-ness.

But there are a few stories I have not yet told. Remember singer B. J. Thomas, of "Raindrops Keep Falling on my Head" fame? In the 1980s, I had gotten permission to interview him in his dressing room before a concert at the UTC Arena. At the assigned time, I knocked on his door. A woman answered, not particularly happy to see me and my photographer.

"What are you doing here?" she asked. I told her that B.J's road manager had set up an interview. She rolled her eyes and said, "Mr. Thomas is on a tight schedule, and I didn't know anything about this. Go ahead and set up while I get him, but I'm warning you, you'd better make this quick!" She hustled into a nearby room.

We set up as in a hurry, putting up the lights, leveling the tripod, attaching the camera, and testing the microphone. Five minutes later, B.J. strolled in, all alone, just as cheery as a big star could be. I immediately launched into a medley of apologies about any problems we may have created, and told him we would make this interview super-fast.

"What's the problem?" he asked. I caught my breath and told him that his assistant had warned us to make it snappy, because of his tight schedule.

He laughed, and said, "Take your time. No hurry. Don't pay any attention to her." We did the interview at a leisurely pace, and talked as if we were old friends. I was a fan already, and have been a bigger fan ever since.

There were two other stars who must remain nameless, because I don't enjoy going to court. Both had a reputation for drinking too much, and saying inappropriate things. Both more than lived up to their billing. I interviewed both just before they performed, and they weren't any better on stage. The audience noticed too. They are not stars any more.

I've met and/or interviewed many other celebrities who have played, or given speeches in Chattanooga. All three Mandrell sisters, Bob Hope, Richard Simmons (in his short shorts), Bob Barker, Ted Turner, Tom Jones, and Minnie Pearl, among others. In most cases, our encounters were before the age of selfies. In a way I regret that, but in another way I don't. I'm glad I could just live in the moment, without posing for a silly picture.

Unfortunately, I have never met Willie Nelson, but I know someone who did, and he shared this story. He was setting up the Tivoli Theater stage for Willie at a show in 2001. He pulled out a 1977 magazine with Willie on the cover, and asked him to sign it. Willie said he'd like to look at it first, and took the magazine out to his bus. He returned about an hour later, signed the magazine and said, "Thank you for letting me read that. I don't remember anything from the 70s, and I just learned a lot about myself."

The 1980s

The practice of showing classic movies on the Tivoli's big screen continued, with great success.

Throughout the decade, Tivoli regulars included several of the stars who had begun appearing annually in the 1970s, plus Nashville musicians Boots Randolph (saxophonist) and Floyd Cramer (pianist), silky-voiced singer Roger Whittaker, Danny Davis and the Nashville Brass, comedian Gallagher, Atlanta-based humorist Lewis Grizzard, the Preservation Hall Jazz Band, and many top gospel acts, both traditional and contemporary.

From mid-1987 to early 1989, the Tivoli was closed for renovations.

At decade's end, on March 25, 1989, the classic theater's third "grand opening was held, with Chattanooga Mayor Gene Roberts and University of Tennessee president Lamar Alexander among the guests. Alexander had been the state's governor when $3 million in state funding was secured to assist in the renovation. Chattanooga Times publisher Ruth Holmberg led a campaign to raise an additional $3 million in private funding. The remodeling was designed by Selmon T. Franklin Architects, and the work was completed by Raines Brothers Construction.

Among the major improvements was an expansion of the stage. On May 1, 1989 the national tour of "Gypsy" starring Tyne Daly opened at the Tivoli Theater. Seating for the refurbished Tivoli was listed at 1,762.

1980

1/25 Ferrante & Teicher

3/11 *"Death Trap"*

3/12 Dave Brubeck (jazz pianist)

3/13 Lou Rawls/Deniece Williams

3/15 Earl Wrightson/Lois Hunt and Chattanooga Symphony Orchestra

3/18 Jimmy Tawater (local musician)

3/19 Woody Herman Orchestra

3/25-27 *"Ain't Misbehavin'"*

3/29 Beverly Sills (soprano)

3/31 Donald Byrd (jazz trumpeter)

4/9 Bill Watrous (jazz trombonist)

5/2 Dr. Norman Vincent Peale (minister, author)

9/13 US Army Field Band

1981

1/15 Ferrante & Teicher

1/24 Fred Waring and his Pennsylvanians

2/8 Vienna Boys Choir

2/14 Boots Randolph

3/20 Floyd Cramer

3/21 Roberta Peters

6/14 Jerry Clower

8/29 Raymond Fairchild and the Crowe Brothers/ Dismembered Tennesseans

12/8-10 *"Children of a Lesser God"*

1982

1/24 Boots Randolph

2/2 Irish Rovers

2/6 Royal Winnipeg Ballet

2/12 Ferrante & Teicher

3/7 Alvin Ailey Dancers

3/20 Floyd Cramer

4/3 Ralph Stanley, Gary Davis (bluegrass)

9/29 Cab Calloway

11/21 Jose Greco and Jorge Tuller (Spanish dancers)

12/14 Eugenia Zukerman (flutist)

1983

1/15 Dallas Holm & Praise

1/29 Preservation Hall Jazz Band

2/10 Ferrante & Teicher

2/23 *"The Mikado"*

3/10 Roger Whittaker

3/19 Dave Brubeck

7/6 Gallagher (comedian)

11/16 *"Pump Boys and Dinettes"* with Jonathan Edwards, Nicolette Larson, and Henry Gross

11/17 Alvin Ailey Repertory Ensemble

1984

1/19 *"Best Little Whorehouse in Texas"* with Stella Parton, Blake Emmons

1/28 Ferrante and Teicher

2/4 Philippine Folk Dancers

3/17 Skitch Henderson with Chattanooga Symphony Orchestra

3/23 Chuck Mangione

4/22 Marla Gibbs ("The Jeffersons")

6/7 Gallagher

6/17 George Winston (pianist)

8/9 Turtles, Gary Puckett, Association, Mamas and Papas, Spanky and our Gang

8/24 John Hartford, Curly Fox, Dismembered Tennesseans

11/17 Shirley Jones with Chattanooga Symphony Orchestra

12/9 *"The Nutcracker"* by Scottish American Ballet

12/15 *"Sleeping Beauty"* by Tennessee Ballet Festival

1985

1/12 James Rogers

1/25 Lewis Grizzard (humor columnist, author)

1/26 Mitch Miller

2/2 Preservation Hall Jazz Band

3/8 Danny Davis and Nashville Brass

3/14 James Rogers, Desiree Daniels, Heaven's Echoes

4/12-13 Gallagher

6/14 Cristy Lane/Daniel

9/7 Pearl Bailey (Siskin Star Night)

10/8 Conductor Vakhtang Jordania's debut with Chattanooga Symphony Orchestra

10/24 Leon Patillo (Dove Ministries concert)

11/18 Carman/Eternity Express

11/20 Glenn Draper Singers (UTC)

1986

2/10 Preservation Hall Jazz Band

2/16 Millie Jackson (R & B singer)

3/8-9 Shari Lewis (puppeteer)

6/3 Chuck Mangione

9/13 Marvin Hamlisch (pianist, Siskin Star Night)

10/9 Bash 'n the Code (Dove)

11/26 Martha Graham Dance Company

1987

1/15 Alexander Toradze with Chattanooga Symphony Orchestra

1/24 David & the Giants (Dove)

2/12 Victoria Mallova (violinist)

The Tivoli Theater marquee is filled with events during the reopening week in 1989.

2/15 Whitney Phipps (gospel)

3/13 Bobby Jones and New Life

3/28-29 Lalo Schifrin (pianist, with Chattanooga Symphony)

3/24 Petra

6/6 Danny Davis and Nashville Brass

Tivoli Theater was closed for twenty months for renovation, and for the installation of the first new air conditioning system since 1926. Grand Reopening was held on March 29, 1989

Carol Channing (right) with Jenifer Anderson at WDEF-TV as she promotes her 1989 appearance at the Tivoli. (Jenifer Anderson)

1989

3/29 Marilyn Horne (mezzo-soprano)

3/31 Carol Channing

4/2 Dismembered Tennesseans, Chattanooga Boys Choir

4/4 Crystal Gayle

4/6 Peter, Paul and Mary

4/7 William Styron (author)

4/8 Ken Noda (pianist)

4/13 "*42nd Street*"

4/28-29 Lewis Grizzard

5/1 "*Gypsy*" starring Tyne Daly (first show of national tour)

5/15 Danny Davis & Nashville Brass

6/14-15 David Copperfield (magician)

6/28 Atlanta Mayor Andrew Young

8/4 "*1964*" Beatles Tribute

9/23 Clint Black/90 Proof

9/30 DeGarmo & Key/DC Talk

10/21 Bill Gaither Trio

11/20 "*Nunsense*" with Dody Goodman

11/25 Wendy Bagwell & Sunliters

12/16 Forester Sisters/Bellamy Brothers

12/31 Trailblazers, Florida Boys/Fay Sims (gospel)

The 1990s

During the 18-month renovation of Soldiers and Sailors Memorial Auditorium (July 1989 to January 1991), the Tivoli stage was busier than ever, hosting its own traditional shows in addition to several others that had usually played the Auditorium.

Live touring shows became a more regular attraction in the 1990s, drawing sizable audiences. The national touring production of "Lost in Yonkers" began its run at the Tivoli on November 1, 1991.

Robert Goulet's "Man of LaMancha" also began its national tour at the Tivoli, on August 23, 1996.

Comedians were a mainstay during the 1990s, ranging from the political humor of Mark Russell, to the envelope-pushing George Carlin, to Southern humorists James Gregory and Lewis Grizzard, to prop comic Carrot Top. Actor Burt Reynolds got lots of laughs as well with his one-man show of career highlights, memories, and stories. During his motivational speech, former NFL quarterback-turned TV commentator Terry Bradshaw reminisced about playing for Louisana Tech against the Chattanooga Mocs in 1969.

Pianist Jim Brickman made the first of many Chattanooga visits in 1996, establishing an annual tradition with thousands of local fans.

Many longtime TV stars attracted big audiences in their musical and acting roles at the Tivoli, including Robert Wagner, Jill St John, Richard Chamberlain, and Peter Marshall.

The Chattanooga Symphony and Opera performed regularly on the Tivoli stage. During the holiday season, the Chattanooga Boys Choir's Singing Christmas Tree and the Chattanooga Ballet's "Nutcracker" productions were beloved traditions.

1990

2/9 Lorrie Morgan/Mark Collie

2/10 Gold City/Inspirations

2/25 *"Phantom of the Opera"*

3/26 Roger Whittaker

4/7 Shirley Caesar

4/12 *"Dreamgirls"*

4/14 Kingsmen (gospel)

4/26 Russ Taff (gospel)

4/27 Sharon, Lois and Bram

5/8 Petra

5/11 Pat Boone, Forester Sisters (Bethel Bible Village benefit concert)

5/21 *"Big River"*

5/23 David Copperfield (2 shows)

6/23 Louise Mandrell

7/29 George Carlin

8/11 Don Williams

8/13 Air Supply

8/21-23 *"Oklahoma"* starring John Davidson, Kathryn Crosby, and Jamie Farr

8/30 The Cathedrals

9/7 Restless Heart/Lee Roy Parnell

9/11/13 *"Jesus Christ Superstar"*

9/15 Gold City, Kingsmen, Singing Cookes

9/21 Ronnie Milsap

9/22 Mylon LeFevre

9/29 James Gregory and Dean Gaines (Chattanooga native)

10/23 *"The Fantasticks"* with Robert Goulet

11/9 Paul Overstreet

11/19 Liz Story/Philip Aaberg

1991

1/5 Flying Karmazov Brothers

1/19-20 *"Into the Woods"*

1/26 *"Hair"* (2 shows)

1/28 *"Rumors"* starring Peter Marshall ("Hollywood Squares")

2/6 Mantovani Orchestra

2/7 Peter, Paul and Mary

2/16 Bill Gaither Trio, Paul Overstreet

3/15 Tommy Dorsey Orchestra

3/17 *"Lend Me a Tenor"* with Barry Nelson

3/23 *"Hello Dolly"* with Mimi Hines and Phil Ford

4/5 Shelby Foote (historian)

4/13 *"Swan Lake"* ballet

5/3 Judy Tenuta/Emo Phillips (comedy)

5/10 Maya Angelou

5/21 Burt Reynolds

5/23 Mark Russell (political humorist)

7/5-6 *"Wicked Ways"* (gospel play)

7/20 James Gregory/Steve Plemmons

8/16 4-HIM

9/7 Paula Poundstone

9/15 Gordon Lightfoot

10/5 Michael Card

10/12 Ronnie McDowell/Billy Joe Royal

10/26 Shirley Caesar

11/1-2 *"Lost in Yonkers"* with Mercedes McCambridge and Brooke Adams (opened national tour)

11/26 Lewis Grizzard

1992

1/11 Mull's Gospel: McKameys, Primitive Quartet, Wilburns

1/12 George Carlin

3/28 *"Madame Butterfly"*

4/9 Vince Dooley (Univ. of GA Athletic Director, former football coach) and his wife Barbara

5/8 Pat Boone, Larnelle Harris (Bethel Bible Village benefit)

8/29 James Gregory

10/20 Mark Lowry

10/27 Suzanne Somers (*"Three's Company"*)

11/27 George Wallace (comedian)

12/26 Lewis Grizzard

1993

2/26 Shirley Caesar

2/27 Hal Holbrook as Mark Twain

3/5 George Winston (pianist)

3/19 NFL star Reggie White

3/20 Mo Funny Comedy Jam with Chris Tucker

3/27 Ricky Van Shelton, Neal McCoy

4/3 Clyde Edgerton and Tarwater Band

5/8 James Gregory

6/24 Terry Bradshaw (motivational speech)

8/28 James Gregory

10/23 Miss Tennessee USA pageant featuring Lee Greenwood

11/15 Nightnoise/Liz Story

1994

1/10 Lee Luvisi (with Chattanooga Symphony Orchestra)

2/9 Billy Dean

3/12 *"My Fair Lady"* (2 shows)

3/20 Gordon Lightfoot

4/27 Robert Cray Band/The Kinsey Report

6/11 Carrot Top

6/15 Jeff Foxworthy

8/27 James Gregory

9/8 Ida and Ana Kafavian (with Chattanooga Symphony Orchestra)

10/6 John Wallace (with Chattanooga Symphony Orchestra)

11/5 Gold City

11/26 Alison Krauss/Cox Family

11/28 Steven Curtis Chapman

1995

2/11 *"Camelot"*

2/16 Jeffrey Kahane (with Chattanooga Symphony Orchestra)

3/2 *"Raisin"* with Philip Bailey and Peabo Bryson

4/9 *"A Closer Walk with Patsy Cline"*

4/17 Cheri Keaggy, Point of Grace

5/6 Banu Gibson (with Chattanooga Symphony Orchestra)

5/11 Larnelle Harris

7/22 Phil Cross, Karen Peck

9/22 Anne-Marie McDermott (with Chattanooga Symphony Orchestra)

10/25 Robert Cray Band/Tinsley Ellis

1996

3/3 *"Seven Brides for Seven Brothers"*

3/12 Mary Wilson/Impressions

3/28 Andre-Michael Schub (with Chattanooga Symphony Orchestra)

3/16 Pat McLaughlin/Nanci Griffith

4/19 Jim Brickman

4/27 Alison Krauss and Union Station

5/4 Shari Lewis

8/2 Tommy Dorsey Orchestra

8/4 Tori Amos/Willie Porter

8/23-24 *"Man of LaMancha"* with Robert Goulet (began national tour)

9/11 Leann Rimes/Paul Jefferson

9/28 Vice President Al Gore campaigning for President Clinton re-election

10/5 Roger Whittaker

10/12 Jim Wann with Chattanooga Symphony Orchestra

11/9 John Prine/Robert Morris

12/18 Glenn Miller Orchestra

1997

2/22 J.D. Sumner & Stamps Quartet and the Hoppers

4/10 Jim Brickman

4/13 *"Zorba the Greek"*

4/27 Alison Krauss and Union Station

11/7 Atlanta Rhythm Section, John Waite, Beth Nielsen Chapman

1998

1/10 Bob Carlisle

2/20 Bill Engvall

3/6 Shirley Caesar

3/27 Kenny Wayne Shepherd/R.B. Morris

3/1 Third Day

4/30 Steve Earle/Son Volt

9/6 *"The King and I"*

9/15 The Coasters

10/9 Faith Hill/Warren Brothers

1999

2/1 Kenny Wayne Shepherd/Bryan Lee

2/2 Carrot Top

2/12 Michael Card

2/14 Willie Nelson/R. B. Morris

3/12 Bill Engvall

4/3 Kingsmen, McKameys, Gold City

4/9 John Prine

5/7 *"Love Letters"* with Robert Wagner, Jill St John

5/18 George Carlin

9/7-8 *"The Sound of Music"* with Richard Chamberlain

9/26 Jonny Lang/Chris Duarte

10/21 Dr. Jane Goodall (primatologist, anthropologist)

*Willie Nelson poses with the backstage crew prior to his 1999
show at the Tivoli. (Chris Keene)*

Jim Brickman and Donny Osmond sign autographs after their 2000 holiday show at the Tivoli. (Cindy Lowery)

The 2000s

Our "Jewel of the South" had its ups and downs at the turn of the century. Increasingly, the stage played host to World War II era nostalgia acts, rock and roll oldies packages, some past-their-prime pop and country artists who could no longer fill larger venues, and a rapidly shrinking number of plays and musicals.

Part of the booking void was filled by productions from the Cumberland County Playhouse, which brought some of its popular plays from nearby Crossville, Tennessee.

One musical production highlight was Tommy Tune's "Dr. Dolittle" which premiered its national tour at the Tivoli on January 13, 2006.

In 2005, top-ranked radio station WUSY (US-101) began a long tradition of benefit concerts for St. Jude Children's Research Hospital called "Heart Strings for Hope," featuring an all-star lineup of country artists.

Alison Krauss, George Carlin, Jim Brickman, Vince Gill, Willie Nelson, Kenny Wayne Shepherd, Gordon Lightfoot, and pianist George Winston were among the repeat performers during the first decade of the century. The Chattanooga Symphony and Opera were frequently on the schedule as well.

The Tivoli was closed twice in 2008 for repairs and renovations, including reupholstered seating. Sandy Coulter was theater manager at the time.

2000

1/23 Alison Krauss/Jerry Douglas

2/18 Dave Brubeck

3/8 Lyle Lovett

3/11 Dino Kartsonakis (pianist)

3/16 Eugenia Zukerman

3/22 Gary Morris

4/27 Fernando Ortega (contemporary Christian)

6/2 Rickey Smiley (comedian)

9/1 Rodney Carrington (comedian)

10/15 Larry Gatlin & Chattanooga Symphony Orchestra)

12/19 Jim Brickman, Donny Osmond

12/28 Kenny Wayne Shepherd/Floodwater

2001

1/18 Steve Earle & the Dukes

2/11 Willie Nelson/Scott Miller

2/7 Hal Holbrook as Mark Twain (same show, same stage as his first appearance on **2/8/76**)

3/31 Joan Faulkner (singer)

4/16 Rubin "Hurricane" Carter (former boxer)

8/3 Gospel: Hoppers, Dove Brothers, Galloways

8/24 *"Honk"*

8/25 *"Smoke on the Mountain"* (from Cumberland County Playhouse)

9/29 Gary Lewis & the Playboys, Sam the Sham, Merilee Rush, Chiffons, Brian Hyland

11/1 Carrot Top

11/9-10 *"Sanders Family Christmas"* (from Cumberland County Playhouse)

11/17 Kingston Trio with Chattanooga Symphony Orchestra

2002

2/8 Three Mo' Tenors

2/22 Ray Boltz

3/23 Gene Chandler, Sonny Geraci, Little Peggy March, Contours, Frankie Ford

4/3-4 *"Cabaret"*

5/16 Dave Brubeck

7/2 Travis Tritt

8/10, 17, 24, 31 *"Smoke on the Mountain"* (from Cumberland County Playhouse)

8/16, 23, 30 *"Spirit of the Mountains"* (from Cumberland County Playhouse)

8/29 Tommy Dorsey Orchestra

10/12 Ben E. King with Chattanooga Symphony Orchestra

10/30 Glenn Miller Orchestra

11/16 & 23 *"Sanders Family Christmas"* (from Cumberland County Playhouse)

11/19 Keith Urban, Blake Shelton, Andy Griggs, Julie Roberts, Kelley Lovelace

2003

1/19 George Winston (pianist)

1/24 *"Swing"*

2/1 Eddie Miles (Elvis Presley tribute)

2/2 *"Music Man"*

2/21 John Prine/Todd Snider

2/25 Rodney Carrington

4/10-11 Jim Brickman

7/19 Earl Scruggs Family & Friends

8/9 John Hiatt

10/15 Carrot Top

10/25 Dismembered Tennesseans

11/20 Clint Black, Trick Pony, Pat Green, Kelley Lovelace, Jim Collins

2004

1/23 George Carlin

4/17 *"Beatlemania"*

5/14 Nanci Griffith, Suzy Bogguss, Pat McLaughlin

6/13 Lewis Black (comedy)

9/16 Willie P. Richardson (comedy)

9/20 Capitol Steps (comedy)

9/28 Bela Fleck and Flecktones

10/9 *"HMS Pinafore"* (CSO)

11/4 Martina McBride, Kim Carnes, Matraca Berg, Gretchen Peters

2005

1/28 Delbert McClinton, Randall Bramlett

2/24 Del McCoury Band, Dismembered Tennesseans

2/28 Flying W Wranglers

3/21 Phil Vassar, Kelley Lovelace, Craig Morgan, Jamie O'Neal

8/13 Lucinda Williams

8/18 Bruce Hornsby

8/26 Clint Black

11/17 Scot Bruce (Elvis Tribute)

12/14 *Memoirs of a Geisha* movie premiere with author Arthur Golden

12/22 Jim Brickman

2006

1/13-14 *"Dr. Doolittle"* with Tommy Tune

1/19 George Winston (pianist)

2/3 Rickie Lee Jones/Pat McLaughlin

2/12 *"Menopause the Musical"*

3/3 Big Head Todd & the Monsters, Jennifer Daniels

3/16 George Thorogood/Cross Canadian Ragweed

3/27 Billy Currington, Josh Turner, Kelley Lovelace, Jason Aldean, Eric Church

3/31 Charlie Wilson/Gap Band/Will Downing

4/20 Vince Gill, Amy Grant, Gretchen Peters, Jeff Hanna, Matraca Berg

5/5 Carrie Fisher (actress, author)

5/25 Dwight Yoakam, Tennessee Rounders

7/9 Chris Tucker (comedian)

7/16 Urban Mystic, Angela Winbush, Jesse Powell

8/19 John Prine

10/2 Colorado Wranglers

10/14 Leslie Jordan (actor from Chattanooga)

10/15 George Carlin

10/17 Glass Hammer

10/20 Ginny Owens (gospel)

12/18 Bucky Covington, Deana Carter, Steve Azar, Julie Roberts, Blue County

2007

2/13 Lyle Lovett, John Hiatt, Gary Clark, Joe Ely

3/9 Cheryl McGuiness (widow of **9/11** victim), Pam Pierce (Christian singer)

3/22 Aaron Lewis (singer, formerly of Staind)

3/24 Michael Card, Nicol Sponberg

3/29 Jon Meacham (historian, author, McCallie School graduate)

4/2 Rodney Atkins, Jason Michael Carroll, Billy Currington, Sarah Buxton, Kelley Lovelace

4/6-7 *"Menopause the Musical"*

5/5 Jerry Butler, the Impressions with Chattanooga Symphony Orchestra

6/23 *"Church Mess"* play

9/6 Buddy Guy

10/13 Corey Smith

10/14 Nickel Creek, Bela Fleck

10/18 Vince Gill

11/9 Oak Ridge Boys

12/12 Jim Brickman

12/15 Colorado Wranglers

2008

1/11 Emmylou Harris, Shawn Colvin, Patty Griffin

2/10 Brian Regan (comedian)

2/13 Gordon Lightfoot

3/6 Ben Folds

3/11 Jackson Browne

3/18 *"Three Ways to Get a Husband"* with Billy Dee Williams

3/21 Three Doors Down

3/22 Superchick (Christian pop band)

4/5 Stamps Quartet, Blackwood Brothers

4/9 Jewel, Ashton Shepherd, Lee Brice, Kelley Lovelace, Jamey Johnson

4/10 Ailey II Dance Company

5/9 Skillet, Nevertheless, Decyfer Down (contemporary Christian)

6/12 Ernie Haase & Signature Sound (gospel)

**** CLOSED FOR 3 MONTHS FOR REPAIRS AND RENOVATIONS ****

9/19 John Hiatt, Randall Bramlett

10/9 *"Sweeney Todd"*

10/30 Terry Fater, Etta May (comedy)

11/13 Vince Gill

11/28-30 *"Oliver"*

**** CLOSED FOR A MONTH FOR SEATING REPAIRS ****

2009

1/21 Morris Dees (attorney, MLK Day of Unity)

2/7 Old Crow Medicine Show/ Felice Brothers

2/27-28 *"La Boheme"* (CSO)

3/24 Sara Evans, Randy Houser, Kelley Lovelace, Jack Ingram, Justin Moore

4/18 Avett Brothers

4/27 John Tesh

5/9 Rickey Smiley

5/17 Loretta Lynn

8/15 Michael Jr. (comedy)

8/21 Ralphie May (comedy) (Chattanooga native)

9/18-19 "*Cinderella*"

9/28 Vince Gill

10/24 "*The Lost Son*" (Christian play)

Singer-songwriter Jackson Browne played to a packed house at the Tivoli in 2008. (Dave Weinthal)

The San Francisco–based rock band Train on stage at the Tivoli in 2011.
(Dave Weinthal)

11/14 "*The Clean Up Woman*" (play)

11/21-22 "*Screwtape Letters*" (play)

11/29 Jim Brickman

The 2010s and Beyond

By the middle of this decade, the Tivoli would come alive like no other
time in its storied history. As mentioned in Chapter 1, Mayor Andy

Berke established the Tivoli Foundation to handle the operations of both the Auditorium and the Tivoli Theater.

AC Entertainment, a Knoxville-based live entertainment and facilities management group headed by Ashley Capps, was contracted by the Tivoli Foundation to operate both venues. AC's track record in booking other venues helped bring in acts to fill the Tivoli in particular. By decade's end, the Tivoli stage was busier than ever.

Among the most frequent acts was the Black Jacket Symphony, made up of musicians and vocalists who faithfully re-created iconic rock albums. The annual US-101 Heart Strings for Hope concert brought in big stars every year in March. Pianist Jim Brickman, Travis Tritt, comedians Ron White and Lewis Black, numerous classic rock and top-40 acts, the Chattanooga Symphony and Opera, and The Price is Right Live show were all frequently on the calendar.

Southern rocker Gregg Allman was scheduled twice in 2017, first on January 21, which was postponed due to illness, and rescheduled for June 9. Sadly, he never recovered and died on May 27, 2017 due to complications from liver cancer.

The Tivoli Foundation suffered a great loss on August 4, 2018 when local philanthropist Bobby Stone died in a boating accident. Stone was among the theater's top supporters for many years. In his honor, the Tivoli established the Bobby Stone Film Series, showing classic movies on selected weekends.

Much like the Auditorium, the Tivoli had a healthy lineup of shows scheduled for 2020, but the COVID-19 pandemic forced the theater to postpone live concerts beginning on March 13 of that year. By fall, the Tivoli began allowing limited numbers of moviegoers to attend occasional showings of classic movies as part of the Bobby Stone Film Series.

2010

1/16 Ron White

1/17 Brian Regan

2/9 *"Cabaret"*

2/27 Dance Theater of Harlem Ensemble

3/2 Eddie Montgomery, Randy Houser, Kelley Lovelace, Luke Bryan, Mallory Hope

3/14 *"Peter Pan"*

3/27 John Prine/Leon Redbone

4/1 Jamey Johnson/Blackberry Smoke

4/3 Yo Gotti

4/7 Ashton Shepherd, Cody McCarver, Larry Stewart, Jeremy McComb, Katie Armiger, Richie McDonald, Bryan White

5/5 Old Crow Medicine Show

6/26 *Dancing With the Stars* with Maksim Chmerkovskiy

8/14 Collingsworth Family (gospel)

8/28 Kelly Price

9/9 Rodney Carrington

9/23 Straight No Chaser (a capella group)

10/7 Daniel Tosh

10/16 Goo Goo Dolls/The Spill Canvas

10/19 Styx

10/26-28 *"Menopause the Musical"*

11/4 Vince Gill

11/6 Shinedown/Will Hoge

11/12 *"Amahl and the Night Visitors"* (Chattanooga Symphony Orchestra)

2011

2/22 Tim Conway/Chuck McCann

3/1 Chris Young, Randy Houser, Kelley Lovelace, Jerrod Niemann, Jacob Lyda, Joey and Rory

3/10 In the Mood (big band)

3/16 Gordon Lightfoot

4/3 LeFevre Quartet, Jeff and Sheri Easter

4/16 David Sedaris (humorist)

5/17 Train/Dirty Guv'nahs

7/29 Tedeschi Trucks Band

8/20 Rachel Boston (actress from Signal Mountain)

9/8 Brian Regan

9/20 Michelle Rhee (educator)

10/24 Willie Kitchens Jr. & the Tri-Octaves

11/6 Glenn Draper Singers reunion with Lee Greenwood

11/10 Black Jacket Symphony: Pink Floyd's *Dark Side of the Moon*

11/11 Vince Gill

12/27 Jim Brickman

2012

1/29 Ailey II Dance Company

2/17 Black Jacket Symphony: *Led Zeppelin IV*

2/18 Jeanne Robertson (comedian)

2/19 *"Behind the Pulpit"* comedy play

2/24 Lewis Black

3/6 Randy Houser, Kelley Lovelace, Lee Brice, Rodney Atkins, Ronnie Dunn, Lauren Alaina, Jerrod Niemann

3/17 Tommy Davidson, Faizon Love

3/18 Don Williams

3/29 B. B. King

4/7 Alison Krauss/Union Station

4/11 Straight No Chaser

4/19 Michael Pollan (food expert)

4/24 Shen Yun (Chinese dance)

4/28 Iron and Wine (singer-songwriter Samuel Beam)

5/4 Bela Fleck (with Chattanooga Symphony Orchestra)

5/5 Bobby Bare, Rachel Holder

5/24 Black Jacket Symphony: *Sgt. Pepper's Lonely Hearts Club*

6/23 *Dancing with the Stars*, with J.R. Martinez

7/28 Indigo Girls (with Chattanooga Symphony Orchestra)

8/10 Kris Kristofferson

8/11 Collingsworth Family, Triumphant Quartet

9/7 Black Jacket Symphony: Eagles' *Hotel California*

10/2 Carl Hurley/Jeanne Robertson (comedy)

10/8-9 Eric Church (recording live album "*Caught in the Act*")

10/26 Vince Gill, Time Jumpers

11/4 Ron White

11/10 John Prine

11/13 Thomas Friedman lecture

11/15 Randy Owen

11/18 Jamey Johnson, Wayne Mills, Chris Hennessee

12/20 Sandi Patty, Jason Crabb

2013

2/9 *"The Screwtape Letters"*

2/13 Merle Haggard/Chris Janson

2/15-16 Doc Severinsen and Chattanooga Symphony Orchestra

2/28 Brian Regan

3/5 Easton Corbin, Kelley Lovelace, Randy Houser, Lee Brice, Jerrod Niemann

3/17 Jim Gaffigan (comedian)

4/6 Chonda Pierce

4/7 Ira Glass (National Public Radio personality)

4/14 Bill Cosby

4/21 *"Rock of Ages"* musical

5/3 Gene Watson

5/14 Lyle Lovett

5/21 *The Price is Right Live*

6/26 Dave Chappelle

6/29 Ralphie May

6/30 Jonas Nordwell (played Wurlitzer Organ)

8/9 *"Menopause the Musical"*

8/13 Bryan Adams

9/21-22 *"Beauty and the Beast"*

11/1 Barenaked Ladies

11/13 Travis Tritt/Kyle Grubb

11/30 Vince Gill

2014

1/14 Shen Yun

1/18 Don Williams/Colm Kirwan

1/21 Tedeschi Trucks Band

1/31 Black Jacket Symphony (Led Zeppelin *"Houses of the Holy"*)

3/5 Sheryl Crow, Kelley Lovelace, Randy Houser, Jerrod Niemann, Tyler Farr

3/29 Jimmy Tawater, Roger Alan Wade (Chattanooga-based singers)

4/25 Ruben Studdard, Lalah Hathaway

4/30 Gillian Welch, Dave Rawlings

5/3 Black Jacket Symphony (Prince *"Purple Rain"*)

6/26 Jerry Seinfeld, Tom Papa

7/31 Mark Lowry, Jason Crabb, The Martins

9/27 Black Jacket Symphony (Michael Jackson *"Thriller"*)

10/2 Yo Yo Ma (with Chattanooga Symphony Orchestra)

10/16 Kip Moore, Sam Hunt, Charlie Worsham

10/30 Kevin James (comedian, *"King of Queens"* star)

10/31 Ray LaMontagne

11/15 *"Pirates of Penzance"*

11/29 Vince Gill

2015

1/3 Gene Watson, Robby Hopkins

1/17 Black Jacket Symphony (AC-DC "*Back in Black*")

1/20 Shen Yun

1/23 Tedeschi Trucks Band

1/31 Ron White

3/3 Thomas Rhett, Kelley Lovelace, Randy Houser, Jerrod Niemann, Hunter Hayes

3/13 Vienna Boys Choir

3/26 Travis Tritt

5/1 Black Jacket Symphony (Beatles "*Abbey Road*" and The Who "*Who's Next*")

5/2 Lewis Black

6/20 *Dancing with the Stars* (Louis van Amstel, Karina Smirnoff)

9/26 Rodney Carrington

10/7 Renee Fleming with Chattanooga Symphony Orchestra

10/9 Warren Haynes, Justin Townes Earle, Chessboxers, Jeff Sipe

11/6 Ben Folds

11/8 Jason Isbell

11/11 Boz Scaggs

11/14 Straight No Chaser

11/20 Brian Regan

12/26 Dave Rawlings Machine

12/27 Jim Brickman

2016

1/14 Vince Gill

1/21 Black Jacket Symphony (Journey "*Escape*")

1/30 Art Garfunkel

2/6 Jonny Lang

2/8 Rain (Beatles tribute group)

2/24 Guy Clark Jr./Muddy Magnolias

3/1 Foreigner

3/2 Kelley Lovelace, Chris Janson, Dustin Lynch, Justin Moore

3/3 "*Million Dollar Quartet*" play

3/17 Pablo Villegas with Chattanooga Symphony Orchestra

3/18 Moody Blues

4/11 Buddy Guy

4/19 Ben Harper & Innocent Criminals, Christopher Paul Stelling

4/30 Black Jacket Symphony (Pink Floyd "*Dark Side of the Moon*")

5/18 Sturgill Simpson

5/22 Rick Springfield

6/18 Jordan Smith/Jessica Lamb (Jordan is an alumnus of Lee University in Cleveland, who won season 9 of NBC's "The Voice." Jared Herzog and Brooke Simpson were among other Lee students who placed highly on the show.)

6/24 John Prine/Amanda Shires

7/9 Weird Al Yankovic

8/20 Lalah Hathaway

8/24 Jill Scott

8/26 Josh Turner/Raquel Cole

9/16-17 Black Jacket Symphony (Eagles *"Hotel California"*)

10/8 Mambo Kings with Chattanooga Symphony

10/9 Jennifer Nettles/Zach Seabaugh

10/21 David Sedaris

10/25 ZZ Top/Tim Montana

Don Lyle with former Tennessee Titans running back Eddie George at STIR restaurant in 2017. George was starring in "Chicago" at the Tivoli Theater. (Don Lyle)

Poster for a scheduled Gregg Allman show at the Tivoli in 2017. The Southern rocker died of liver cancer less than two weeks before the scheduled show date.

10/26 My Morning Jacket

10/28 Blackberry Smoke/The Steepwater Band

11/13 Bob Dylan

11/19 Tempations/Four Tops

11/26 Goo Goo Dolls/Safety Suit

12/30 Gillian Welch/Dave Rawlings

2017

1/13 Ron White

1/17-18 *"Dirty Dancing"*

1/19 Three Dog Night

1/20 Ronnie Milsap/Courtney Cole

1/28 Tedeschi Trucks Band

2/4 Dave Chappelle

2/15-17 *"Chicago"* the musical with Eddie George

2/24 Black Jacket Symphony (Queen *"A Night at the Opera"*)

3/7 Kelsea Ballerini, Randy Houser, LOCASH, Craig Campbell, Kelley Lovelace

3/8-9 *"Rent"*

3/29 *The Price is Right Live*

4/7 Black Jacket Symphony (Fleetwood Mac *"Rumours"*)

4/8 Loretta Lynn

4/15 Home Free (a capella group)

4/18-20 *"Riverdance"*

4/23 Brian Regan

5/2-3 *"Annie"*

5/17 Brian Wilson/Al Jardine/Blondie Chaplin

6/4 Toto

6/15 Gladys Knight

7/18 In This Moment (rock band)

8/11 "*1964*" Beatles tribute band

8/18 Moon Taxi

8/19 Donald Fagen (of Steely Dan)

8/28 Iron and Wine/Lydia Loveless

9/9 Garrison Keillor

9/22 Band of Horses

9/23 Black Jacket Symphony (Pink Floyd "*Wish You Were Here*")

10/4 Kansas

10/26 Bela Fleck with Chattanooga Symphony Orchestra

*Illusionist David Blaine visits with the staff at STIR restaurant after his 2018
show at the Tivoli Theater. (Don Lyle)*

10/27-28 *"The Sound of Music"*

10/29 Danny Gokey, Mandisa, Love and the Outcome

11/2 *The Price is Right Live*

11/4 Emmylou Harris

11/6 Amos Lee

11/8 Straight No Chaser

Original Beach Boys member Mike Love poses with Jennifer Pond after a 2018 holiday show at the Tivoli Theater. (Jennifer Pond)

11/10 Ray LaMontagne/Ethan Gruska

11/13 Beach Boys

11/18 Mannheim Steamroller

11/27 Robert Earl Keen

12/11 Needtobreathe

12/12-14 *"Kinky Boots"*

12/18 Jennifer Nettles

2018

1/17 David Rawlings

1/26-28 *"Cinderella"*

2/9 Kelsea Ballerini/Walker Hayes

2/16 Jim Brickman

2/23 Blackberry Smoke/Lukas Nelson

3/9-11 *"Jersey Boys"*

3/13 Kelley Lovelace, Mitch Rossell, David Lee Murphy

4/13 America

4/17-19 *"Motown the Musical"*

4/22 Jason Isbell

5/2 Celtic Woman

5/5 Black Jacket Symphony (Guns 'n Roses)

5/10 Ghost (Swedish metal band)

5/11-12 *"Stomp"*

5/16 Chicago (band)

6/2 David Blaine

7/16 Modest Mouse

8/2 ABBA Tribute

8/25 Shenandoah

9/7 Little River Band

9/8 Aziz Ansari (comedian)

9/29 Lauren Daigle

10/19-20 *"Wizard of Oz"*

Country star Travis Tritt has been a frequent performer on most of Chattanooga's stages. He is seen here at the Tivoli Theater in 2019. (Angela Shipe)

10/26 Collective Soul

10/28 Bob Dylan

11/10-11 *"Irving Berlin's White Christmas"*

Jazz saxophonist Kenny G on stage at the Tivoli in 2019. (Angela Shipe)

11/14 Danny Gokey

11/16 Beach Boys

11/17 Crossing the Cumberland

11/23 Mannheim Steamroller

12/10 *Celtic Thunder*

12/11 Harry Connick Jr.

12/13 Chris Tomlin

12/18-20 *"The King and I"*

12/30 Moscow Ballet *"Nutcracker"*

2019

1/7 Willie Nelson

1/11-12 Something Rotten

1/29 Elevation Worship

1/31 Brothers Osborne/The Wild Feather

2/19-24 *"The Book of Mormon"*

2/8 *Disney A Capella*

2/28 Home Free

3/1 Black Jacket Symphony (Queen *"A Night at the Opera"*)

3/9 Gabriel Iglesias (2 shows)

3/15 Rain (Beatles Tribute)

3/17 for KING & COUNTRY

3/21 Cat Power

3/29 Bob Weir & Wolf Brothers

3/31 Jackson Browne

4/11-12 *"Carmen"* (Chattanoooga Symphony Orchestra)

4/16-18 *"Spamalot"*

4/26 Brit Floyd

5/1 Needtobreathe

5/2 Postmodern Jukebox

5/19 Travis Tritt

5/22 PJ Masks (children's show)

6/21-22 *"Finding Neverland"*

Poster for two sold out Dave Chappelle comedy shows at the Tivoli in 2019.

6/23 Peter Frampton

6/28 Chris D'Elia (comedy)

8/10 "*1964*" Beatles Tribute

9/10 Dwight Yoakam

9/14 Righteous Brothers

9/21 Amy Grant

10/5 Bill Maher

10/6 Lyle Lovett

10/12 Bernadette Peters (with Chattanooga Symphony)

10/17 Dream Theater

10/18 Alison Krauss (Tivoli Foundation Gala)

Frankie Valli of the Four Seasons is interviewed by WFLI radio personality Gene Lovin before Valli's show at the Tivoli in 2020.

10/27 Straight No Chaser

11/2 Randy Houser/Paul Cauthen

11/5-10 *"Les Miserables"*

11/15 Goo Goo Dolls

11/22 Kenny G

12/3 Chris Tomlin

12/12 Dave Chappelle (2 shows)

12/17-19 *"Beautiful"* the musical (the Carole King story)

12/24 Moscow Ballet

2020

1/24 Frankie Valli & The Four Seasons

1/25 Black Jacket Symphony (Led Zeppelin tribute, 2 shows)

1/29 Nate Bargatze (comedy)

1/31- 2/3 *"Cats"*

2/9 Jo Koi (comedy)

2/12 Drew and Ellie Holcomb

2/17-18 Blue Man Group

2/22 Gordon Lightfoot

2/27 Michael Carbonaro (magic)

2/29 Kansas

3/6 Newsboys United

2021

9/18 Righteous Brothers (Bill Medley and Bucky Heard)

10/2 Monkees (Micky Dolenz and Mike Nesmith)

CHAPTER 3

Lake Winnepesaukah (Lake Winnie)

Lake Winnepesaukah opened May 30, 1925, at 1730 Lakeview Drive in Rossville, Georgia. The owners were Carl and Minette Dixon, and opening day crowds were estimated at 5,000. It was once known as Green's Lake. Winnepesaukah is an Indian word for "Beautiful Lake of the Highlands," or "Bountiful Waters." In recent years, the amusement park has become more commonly known as Lake Winnie.

The park is located near the Catoosa and Walker County lines, just outside Chattanooga, and spans almost one hundred acres.

From 1925 through 1957, the park featured Sunday night concerts with programs of patriotic songs and religious hymns, sung mostly by local singers. Among the most frequently scheduled events were fireworks, swimming parties, swim lessons, fishing tournaments, high school band concerts, beauty pageants, motorcycle races, bicycle races, football games, wrestling matches, boxing matches, hydroplane races, Easter Egg hunts, water carnivals, midget auto racing, trade days, feats of strength, beer drinking contests, and water skiing. Advertisements urged visitors to "swim in the south's largest pool."

Visiting entertainers included tightwire and trapeze acts, acrobats, magicians, daredevil acts, parachutists, bird acts, a Donkey Baseball Circus, elephants, trained bears, and "flying saucers."

Other activities included treasure hunts, an outdoor roller skating rink, an arcade, row boats, mini-golf, plus picnic areas for communities, businesses, churches, and schools. An open air "town hall" featured audience participation quiz games.

In the early years of the park, rides included the Boat Chute, a ferris wheel, a merry-go-round, the Tilt-a-Whirl, kiddie autos and "aer-o-planes." The Boat Chute was designed and built in 1926 by park owner Carl Dixon, and is considered Lake Winnie's longest-running

Lake Winnepesaukah postcard from the early days.

ride. By the 1950s, the Mad Mouse mini-rollercoaster was the park's most popular ride.

Carl Dixon died in 1933, leaving the park's management to his widow Minette, and it has remained in the family ever since.

Memorial Day, Independence Day, and Labor Day were always busy days at the park.

In the 1940s, Lake Winnie attracted large numbers of those stationed in nearby Fort Oglethorpe at the Women's Army Auxiliary Corps. Soldiers and their families were frequent visitors to the park.

Attendance was affected in the late summer of 1941 due to a polio scare, which canceled many leisure activities.

Most of the park's frequent entertainers during the early years were local musicians who played on Chattanooga radio and television

In 1956, the WDEF-TV children's show "Mr. Chickaroonie" visited the outdoor stage at Lake Winnepesaukah, drawing a huge crowd. (WDEF)

programs. Regionally and nationally known entertainers began appearing in the late 1950s.

Entertainers During The Early Years (1939-1958)

5/27/39 Sonora Carver, blind horse-diving act (attendance 15,000)

5/26/40 "Baby June" Scarborough, 2-year-old swimmer and diver

6/30/40 Mary Park "Stratosphere Girl" parachutist (25,000 attendance)

7/27/40 The Frye Band

8/3/40 Harry Porter and his airplane (stunt flying)

1941 Nightly: Town Hall Players perform, with Mr. and Mrs. C.D. Peruchi (Ma and Pa Peruchi)

5/4/41 Grandpappy (Archie Campbell) and his "gang of radio entertainers" (Huge crowd)

5/18/41 Quiz Man and Grandpappy

7/24/43 Rhythm Rangers (musicians heard on WAPO radio)

1944: Sunday night concerts featuring Lola McCormack

6/7/46 (and future Sundays) Johnny Dorsett, Vocalist

7/4/48 Delmore Brothers Hillbilly Band, jitterbug contest

8/22/48 Col. Ira Summers 32 piece concert band

6/18/50 Jay Craven Orchestra featuring Paul Wyatt, Vocalist

7/4/51 Col. Sandy Summers band

7/27/52 Col. Sandy Summers band

7/4/54 Buddy Beason and his Barn Dance Buddies

7/18/54 Charles Epperson, Jon Robere Trio (Epperson, a Chattanooga native, later changed his name to "Tommy Charles," signing with Decca Records, and appearing in the motion picture "Shake Rattle and Roll")

7/25/54 Buddy Beason and his Barn Dance Buddies

8/22/54 Charles Epperson and the Skylarks

5/29/55 Archie Campbell (Grandpappy)

7/3/55 Morris Bales Dixieland Band

7/4/55 Archie Campbell (Grandpappy)

4/29/56 WDEF-TV Chickaroonie Show with Mr. Moon and Miss Ruth

5/6/56 Tennessee Valley Boys

5/13/56 Tennessee Valley Boys

7/4/56 Archie Campbell (Grandpappy)

9/2/56 Archie Campbell (Grandpappy)

6/2/57 Willis Brothers from WRGP-TV

7/4/57 Willis Brothers

9/1/57 Willis Brothers

9/8/57 Morris Bales & Dixieland Band

5/25/58 Morris Bales & Dixieland Band

6/20/58 Bob Brandy of WTVC-TV

6/29/58 O.J. Bailey orchestra

7/5/58 Willis Brothers

8/24/58 Bob Brandy

8/31/58 Morris Bales & Dixieland Band

9/1/58 Hylo Brown and the Timberliners

Country and Western stars play the Outdoor Stage

Carl and Minette Dixon's daughter, Evelyn Dixon White began running the park following Minette Dixon's death in 1958. Starting in 1959, Lake Winnepesaukah began booking Grand Ole Opry stars for occasional weekend shows on the outdoor, "open air" stage. Local television and radio stations had made household names of Stringbean, Cowboy Copas, Stonewall Jackson, Porter Wagoner, Bill Anderson, Patsy Cline and others, who were more than happy to make the two-hour trip to perform three shows on a Sunday in north Georgia. The shows were free to those who had paid regular park admission.

Throughout the 1960s and 1970s, many rising country music stars played before the largest crowds of their young careers.

In August 1960, Carlene Carter, the 4-year-old daughter of June Carter made her stage debut with the famous Carter family.

On Labor Day 1960, June Carter did her own show, accompanied by the Willis Brothers, who had a daily local TV show on WRGP in the late 1950s. Carter would later skyrocket to worldwide fame performing with Johnny Cash after their marriage in 1968.

The Louvin Brothers of nearby Henegar, Alabama, Charlie and Ira were also frequent performers on the park's outdoor stage.

Gene Goforth, who had worked as a local newspaper, radio, and TV advertising salesman, began booking and promoting Lake Winnie acts. The Willis Brothers and the Stoneman family were among his top acts. In 1966, he began producing a nationally syndicated weekly TV series that starred the Stonemans, He famously discovered Jeannie C. Riley, who would soon top the pop and country charts in 1968 with "Harper Valley PTA." Lake Winnepesaukah was her first concert appearance.

On June 25, 1967 the park hosted Tammy Wynette, playing her first show outside of Alabama, where the 25-year-old mother of three had worked as a hairdresser. Successful appearances on a Birmingham television show led her to Nashville, where producer Billy Sherrill convinced her to change her name (she was then Virginia Pugh).

In 1964, five year old Lorrie Morgan was in attendance when her dad, Opry star George Morgan played Lake Winnie, and she returned as a teen, joining him on stage in 1972. By 1979, the 19-year-old headlined three shows of her own at the park. She would soon advance to national stardom.

In August 1969, barely two months after "Hee Haw" had become a CBS-TV Sunday night hit, comedian Junior Samples told his stories on the outdoor stage. Promoter Goforth was close friends with the Stonemans, who also appeared on "Hee Haw," and that family was among his most frequent bookings. Other "Hee Haw" acts such as the Hager Twins, Kenny Price, Grandpa Jones and Archie Campbell also played Lake Winnepesaukah. Campbell had played the park several times in the 1940s and 1950s as the character "Grandpappy" which he had developed while working at WDOD radio in Chattanooga.

One of Goforth's biggest coups was persuading Loretta Lynn to come to the park. Already a consistent chart-topper, her shows on April 26, 1970 drew some of the largest crowds in Lake Winnepesaukah's history. She returned ten years later, and was again welcomed by thousands of fans.

A year later, Loretta's 20-year-old sister Crystal Gayle played three shows at the park, several years before she emerged as a major star in her own right.

In the summer of 1970, Glen Campbell's mom and dad did a show, letting us know where their son got his amazing talent.

The park's first show of 1972 featured another unknown act Goforth found in Nashville. Royce Kendall and his 17-year-old daughter Jeannie were five years away from their first big-selling record. When the Kendalls finally hit it big, Goforth proudly boasted that Lake Winnie had them first.

The April 1973 season opener also featured a future star, although no one could have known at the time. 14-year-old Marty Stuart was in Lester Flatt's band. Eventually he would become one of the most famous names in country music.

Later in 1973, a gospel group called the Oak Ridge Boys played the outdoor stage. A few years later, they shifted their focus to country music, becoming a chart-topping act. They returned to Lake Winnepesaukah in 1977, riding high with two number-one country records.

In addition to stars who were on their way up, the park was also a regular stop for stars who were on the downside of their career. Roy Acuff, Tex Ritter, Hank Snow, Kitty Wells, and Ernest Tubb were no longer topping the country charts, but their long string of hits kept audience members happy.

Locally-based TV entertainers continued to be frequent outdoor stage entertainers. The Bob Brandy Trio, the Willis Brothers, and ventriloquist act Alex Houston and Elmer played Lake Winnepesaukah many times.

Meanwhile, in the amusement park, the Cannonball roller coaster became a huge attraction in 1967, later gaining national attention as a classic roller coaster. A massive fireworks display drew big crowds on Independence Day and Labor Day each year.

Mrs. White announced her retirement and the closing of the park in late 1974, but it bounced back strong in 1977, leased by Fun Town (owner J.D. Floyd) and under the management of Glenn Bergethon. It has remained open ever since.

1959

5/17 Bob Brandy

5/24 Willis Brothers

5/31 Bill Carlisle

6/7 Cowboy Copas

6/10 (and future Wed. nights) O.J. Bailey orchestra

6/14 Justin Tubb

6/21 Stonewall Jackson

7/4 Willis Brothers

7/5 Porter Wagoner

7/12 Stringbean, Willis Brothers

7/19 Roy Wiggins

7/26 Benny Martin, Guy Willis

8/2 Hawkshaw Hawkins

8/9 Bill Monroe and his Bluegrass Boys

8/23 Jimmy Newman

8/30 Carl Butler

9/6 Cowboy Copas

9/7 Willis Brothers/Alex and Elmer of WRGP-TV Channel 3

9/13 Manny Bowen's Dixieland Band

1960

5/1 Cowboy Copas, Billy Walker, Little Roy Wiggins

5/8 Porter Wagoner

5/29 Bill Anderson, Patsy Cline

6/5 George Morgan

6/12 Lonzo and Oscar

6/17 Duke of Paducah, June Carter, Ferlin Husky, Cousin Jody, Bill Carlisle, George Hamilton IV, Louvin Brothers, Billy Grammer, Roy Wiggins, Bill Anderson (all celebrating Country Music Week in Chattanooga)

6/19 Alex and Elmer

7/2 Stringbean

7/3 Bill Carlisle

7/4 Carl Butler

7/10 Bill Monroe

7/17 Billy Walker

7/24 Archie Campbell, Willis Brothers

7/31 "Cousin Jody"

8/14 Roy Wiggins

8/21 The Carter Family (Mother Maybelle, June, Helen, and Anita, plus June's 4-year-old daughter Carlene)

8/28 Cowboy Copas

9/2 Billy Grammer

9/3 Bill Anderson, Willis Brothers

9/4 June Carter, Willis Brothers

1961

4/30 Bob Brandy

6/4 Willis Brothers

6/11 "Cousin Jody"

7/2 Porter Wagoner

7/3 Alex and Elmer

7/4 Carl Butler

8/6 June Carter

8/13 Bill Anderson

9/3 Duke of Paducah

9/4 Bill Carlisle

1962

5/20 Bob Brandy Trio

5/27 Wilma Lee & Stoney Cooper

6/3 Willis Brothers

6/24 Bill Carlisle

7/4 June Carter

7/13 Vivatones ("Teen Dance" most Friday nights)

7/22 Alex & Elmer, Little Roy Wiggins, the Lonesome Travelers

7/29 Roy Drusky

8/5 Skeeter Davis

8/19 Louvin Brothers

9/3 Porter Wagoner

1963

4/28 Country Boy Eddie

5/5 Bob Brandy

5/19 Country Boy Eddie

5/26 Mother Maybelle Carter & family

6/2 Bill Carlisle

6/9 Lonzo & Oscar

6/16 Little Roy Wiggins, Alex Houston & Elmer

6/23 Roy Drusky

7/4 Mother Maybelle Carter & daughters Helen and Anita

7/14 Bill Anderson

7/21 Bob Brandy Trio

7/28 Louvin Brothers

8/4 Tompall and the Glaser Brothers

8/18 Porter Wagoner

8/25 Bill Carlisle

9/1 Marion Worth

9/2 Lonzo & Oscar

1964

4/27 Tompall and The Glaser Brothers

6/14 Bill Carlisle

6/21 Bob Brandy Trio

6/28 Roy Drusky

7/4 The Homesteaders

7/5 The Singing Browns (featuring Jim Ed Brown)

8/2 George Morgan

8/9 Bill Monroe

8/23 Bill Anderson

8/30 Mother Maybelle Carter & family

9/7 Bill Anderson

1965

5/2 Bashful Brother Oswald

5/16 The Fabulous Fables

5/23 Alex Houston & Elmer

5/30 Dick Flood and the Pathfinders

6/13 Willis Brothers

6/27 Tompall & Glaser Brothers

7/4 The Fabulous Fables

7/18 George Hamilton IV

8/1 Warner Mack

8/8 Carter Family

8/15 Billy Grammer

8/29 The Homesteaders

9/6 Alex Houston & Elmer

1966

4/30 George Hamilton IV

5/8 The Homesteaders

5/15 Lonzo and Oscar

5/22 Alex Houston and Elmer

5/29 Tompall and Glaser Brothers

6/5 Willis Brothers

6/19 Johnny Darrell

6/26 Ray Pillow

7/4 Bobby Lord

7/10 Bill Carlisle

7/17 The Blue Boys

7/24 Bashful Brother Oswald

7/31 The Stonemans

8/7 Justin Tubb

8/14 Little Roy Wiggins

8/21 Bill Anderson

8/28 Gordon Terry

9/3 Patsy Stoneman

9/5 Stringbean

1967

5/7 The Carlisles

5/14 Lynn Anderson (age 19)

5/21 George Hamilton IV

5/28 The Homesteaders

6/4 Bob Luman

6/11 Alex Houston & Elmer

6/18 The Stonemans

6/25 Tammy Wynette (first appearance outside Alabama)

7/2 Bun Wilson

7/4 Lonzo & Oscar

7/9 Dr. Paul Moore

7/16 Patsy and Scott Stoneman

7/23 Bashful Brother Oswald & the Smoky Mountain Boys

7/30 Merv Shiner

8/6 Stoneman Family

8/11 Champells, Marvells, Vondells (emceed by WFLI radio deejay Mike King)

8/13 Jim Reeves' Blue Boys

8/20 Willis Brothers

8/27 Little Roy Wiggins

9/4 Dick Flood and the Pathfinders

1968

5/5 Stonemans

5/12 Tompall and the Glaser Brothers

5/19 Willis Brothers

5/26 Warner Mack

6/2 Tex Ritter

6/9 Bill Carlisle and the Carlisles

6/16 Warner Mack

6/23 The Homesteaders

6/30 Tom T. Hall

7/7 George Hamilton IV

7/14 Bobby Lord

7/21 Bun Wilson

7/28 Jim Reeves' Blue Boys

8/4 Roy Acuff

8/11 Lonzo and Oscar

8/18 Johnny Carver

8/25 Merv Shiner

9/1 Jeannie C. Riley

9/2 Kenny Price

1969

5/4 Lonzo and Oscar

5/11 Bill Carlisle

5/18 Bobby Russell

5/25 George Hamilton IV

6/1 Homesteaders

6/8 Alex Houston & Elmer

6/15 Stringbean

6/22 Doug Kershaw

6/29 Ernest Tubb

7/4 Bobby Russell

7/6 Stoneman Family

7/13 Dick Flood & the Pathfinders

7/20 Merv Shiner

7/27 Roy Acuff

8/3 Billy Grammer

8/10 Tom T. Hall

8/17 Tex Ritter

8/24 Junior Samples

8/29 The Champells

8/31 Jim Reeves' Blue Boys

9/1 Carter Family

1970

4/5 Mother Maybelle and the Carter Family

4/12 Don Gibson

4/19 Bobby Wright

4/26 Loretta Lynn (record crowd)

5/3 Jack Greene & Jeannie Seely

5/10 Lynn Anderson

5/17 Stonemans

5/24 Hagers

5/31 Kitty Wells, Johnnie Wright

6/7 Waylon Jennings

6/14 Tom T Hall

6/21 Wes and Carrie Campbell (Glen Campbell's parents)

6/28 Dottie West

7/4 Bobby Russell (his car caught on fire near Murfreesboro, forcing him to hitchhike to Lake Winnie)

7/5 Ernest Tubb

7/10 The Tams

7/12 Del Reeves

7/19 Faron Young

7/26 Roy Acuff

8/2 Osborne Brothers

8/9 Carl Smith

8/16 Hank Snow

9/6 Louie Roberts (age 13)

9/7 Jim Ed Brown

1971

(Local band Buck Turner and Town & Country Boys frequently played shows and backed up other artists)

4/4 Bob Luman

4/18 Stonewall Jackson

4/25 Little Jimmy Dickens

5/2 Mike Holt, Young Nashville

5/9 Louie Roberts

6/20 Tommy Overstreet

6/27 Blake Emmons

7/4 Del Reeves

7/5 Jim Ed Brown

7/11 Crystal Gayle (age 20)

7/25 Stan Hitchcock

8/1 Bobby Harden

8/8 Murry Kellum

8/15 Sue Rymer and Benny Daniel

Country star David Houston performs at Lake Winnepesaukah in 1972. (Jack Mullins)

8/22 Joe Leamon

8/29 Janice and Gayle Leamon

9/5 Louie Roberts

9/6 Sue Rymer and Benny Daniel

Chattanooga's own Buck Turner and the Town & Country Boys frequently played at Lake Winnepesaukah and other local venues.

1972

4/9 The Kendalls

4/16 Bill Phillips

4/30 Buck Turner and the Town & Country Boys

5/7 Stoneman Family

5/21 Dickey Lee

6/18 Cal Smith, The Four Guys

7/2 Joe and Rose Lee Maphis

7/4 Little Jimmy Dickens

7/9 Ruby Wright

7/16 Diana Trask

7/23 Bud Logan and the Jim Reeves' Blue Boys

7/30 Dottie West

8/6 Warner Mack

8/13 David Houston

8/27 George Morgan

9/3 Roy Acuff Jr.

9/4 George Hamilton IV

1973

4/15 Lester Flatt & Nashville Grass (featuring 14-year-old Marty Stuart)

4/29 Tompall & the Glaser Brothers

5/27 Inspirations Quartet

6/10 Archie Campbell

6/17 John Hartford

7/2 Joe and Rose Lee Maphis

7/4 Little Jimmy Dickens

7/29 Hager Twins

8/12 Oak Ridge Boys (then a gospel act)

8/19 Jim McKinney

9/3 Buck Turner with Town & Country Boys

1974

4/28 Jimmy Riddle

5/5 Jamey Ryan

5/19 Roy Drusky

5/26 Blake Emmons

6/9 Ronnie Sessions & Patty Tierney

7/21 Thrasher Brothers

7/28 Ray Pillow

8/18 Wendy Bagwell & the Sunliters

9/2 Scenicland Boys

1975 & 1976 CLOSED

1977

5/23 Sego Brothers and Naomi

6/5 Jeanne Pruett

6/12 Thrasher Brothers

6/19 Trilly Cole

6/24-25 James Rogers

6/26 Wendy Bagwell & Sunliters

7/3 Louise Mandrell

7/10 Bob Luman, Steve Wariner

7/24 Charlie Louvin

7/31 The Kingsmen

Louise Mandrell played Lake Winnepesaukah on several occasions, starting in 1977. (Cindy Lowery)

8/7 Little David Wilkins

8/12 Dr. Shock (Tommy Reynolds) and Dingbat (Dan East) from local TV's "Shock Theater"

8/21 Kenny Price

9/4 Johnny Russell

9/5 Oak Ridge Boys (by 1977 they had become a top country music act)

1978

5/14 Grandpa Jones

5/21 Narvel Felts

6/11 Joe Stampley

6/18 T. G. Sheppard

7/15 Sonny James

7/16 The Kendalls

7/23 The Kingsmen

7/30 Stella Parton

8/6 David Houston

8/13 Florida Boys

8/20 Mel Street

8/25-26 James Rogers

8/27 Johnny Rodriguez

Country star Johnny Rodriguez is embraced by fan Connie DeBord after a 1978 Lake Winnie show. (Connie DeBord)

1979

5/6 Jacky Ward

5/13 Lorrie Morgan (age 19)

6/24 Louise Mandrell

7/1 Hoyt Axton

7/4 Jacky Ward

7/15 The Stonemans

7/22 Ernest Tubb

7/29 Stella Parton

8/19 The Kingsmen

8/26 Stonewall Jackson

9/2 Del Reeves

9/3 Ronnie McDowell (HUGE CROWD)

9/16 Charlie Louvin, Justin Tubb, Del Wood, Stonemans, Osborne Brothers, Vic Willis, Little Roy Wiggins

A New Stage for the Stars

In 1980, the park opened its new Country Junction stage, featuring more space, comfortable dressing rooms, and improved lighting and sound. Gene Goforth used the new stage as a selling point to attract even bigger stars, and they responded. T.G. Sheppard, Gene Watson, Con Hunley, Ronnie McDowell, Steve Wariner, Louise Mandrell, Sylvia, Jerry Lee Lewis, Eddie Rabbitt, Tanya Tucker, and George Strait were among the popular acts who appeared on the new stage.

In 1982, the legendary Ray Charles made his one and only Lake Winnie appearance. Also that year, Goforth began booking "oldies" rock and roll acts, and groups that performed top-40 hits of the 1950s and 1960s. The bookings drew good crowds, prompting him to rename the park's outdoor stage, "The Jukebox Junction" in 1983. During the mid-80s, about half of the bookings were classic pop-rock acts including the Mamas and the Papas, Chubby Checker, The Drifters, Rick Nelson, the Righteous Brothers, The Coasters, Tommy Roe, and Fabian. There were also occasional shows featuring acts that were considered hard rock, like Rare Earth and the Marshall Tucker Band.

On a somber note, two young stars appeared in the 1980s shortly before their deaths. Rick Nelson performed at Lake Winnie in 1983, just two years before he died in a plane crash. In 1988, country singer Keith Whitley appeared with his wife, frequent Lake Winnie performer Lorrie Morgan less than a year before he died of alcohol poisoning at the age of 33.

As always, Lake Winnie fans got to see several acts just before they achieved superstardom. George Strait played Lake Winnie in the summer of 1982, just before he launched a 30-year string of number one country hits. The group Sawyer Brown exploded in the 1990s, but Lake Winnie audiences were able to get up close and personal with the band in 1988. Blake Shelton was another early Lake Winnie discovery, playing the Jukebox Junction stage in 2002. Hometown girl Lauren Suddeth (later known as Lauren Alaina) was only fourteen years old when she appeared with Confederate Railroad in 2008.

Gene Goforth retired around 1990, and Mitzi Morgan began booking and promoting the acts. She was also active in lining up entertainers for the Soldiers and Sailors Memorial Auditorium, the Tivoli Theater, and the UTC Arena.

During the 1990s and 2000s, the successful mix of oldies acts and country singers remained intact. Among the most frequent Lake Winnie performers of that era were Con Hunley, T. Graham Brown, Ronnie McDowell, Gene Watson, Mel McDaniel, and Exile.

One of the park's longest-lasting relationships was with the band Confederate Railroad, which included singer Danny Shirley and other band mates with strong Chattanooga area ties. Beginning in 1998, the group often opened and closed Lake Winnie's season, performing many holiday weekend shows.

In 1998, Evelyn Dixon's daughter, Adrienne White Rhodes took over management of the park, along with her daughters, Talley Rhodes

Green and Tennyson Dickinson, and their family, marking five generations of the Dixon family who have been involved in the park's operation since its founding in 1925.

In 2013, the SOAKya Water Park was added to Lake Winnie's lineup of attractions, and was an immediate hit.

1980

4/13 Lorrie Morgan

4/20 The Kingsmen

4/27 The Thrashers

5/4 Trilly Cole

5/11 Carter Family

5/18 Wendy Holcombe (champion banjo player, age 17)

5/25 Carl Perkins

6/1 Jean Shepard, Vic Willis, Speck Rhodes

6/8 MacKenzie Colt

6/15 Hoyt Axton

6/22 Kitty Wells, Johnnie Wright

6/29 Loretta Lynn (HUGE crowd)

7/6 Gene Watson

7/20 The Kingsmen

7/27 Ernest Tubb

8/3 Jacky Ward

8/10 T. G. Sheppard

8/17 Trilly Cole

8/24 Charly McClain

8/31 Jeannie C. Riley

9/1 Ronnie McDowell

1981

4/19 Steve Wariner

4/26 Charlie McCoy Band

5/3 The Kingsmen

5/10 Jimmy C. Newman

5/16 Jan Howard, Donna Stoneman

6/7 Orion

6/14 Jacky Ward

6/21 Louise Mandrell & R.C. Bannon

6/28 Jerry Lee Lewis

7/4 Carl Perkins

7/5 Bill Anderson

7/11 Happy Harmony Quartet

7/5 Bill Anderson

7/26 Orion

8/9 Ava Barber

8/16 Kitty Wells, Johnnie Wright

8/23 Wendy Holcombe

8/30 Sylvia

9/6 Carl Perkins

9/7 Ronnie McDowell

1982

4/4 Steppe Brothers

4/11 Ivory Jack

4/25 Bandana

5/2 The VanDells

5/9 Terry McMillan

5/16 Marvells

5/23 Tommy Cash

5/30 Jimmy C. Newman

6/20 Ray Charles

6/27 Johnny Rodridguez

7/3 Del Reeves

7/4 Orion

7/5 VanDells

7/18 George Strait

7/25 Dave and Sugar

8/1 Kitty Wells, Johnnie Wright

8/8 Ace Cannon

8/15 The Vogues

8/22 Jacky Ward

8/29 Chubby Checker

9/4 Jim Owen

9/5 Dr. Hook

9/6 The VanDells

1983 (Stage was renamed Jukebox Junction)

4/24 Van Dells

5/8 Drifters with Bill Pinckney

5/15 Del-Vikings

5/22 Marvells

5/29 Kelli Warren

6/5 Rick Nelson

6/12 The Whites, James Rogers

6/19 Helen Cornelius

6/26 Tom Wopat ("Dukes of Hazzard")

7/3 Chubby Checker, The Marvells

7/10 Louise Mandrell

7/17 Boots Randolph

7/24 The Dovells

7/31 Righteous Brothers

8/7 Trilly Cole

8/14 Sons of the Beach

8/21 Carl Perkins

8/28 Kitty Wells, Johnnie Wright

9/3 The Coasters

9/4 Dr. Hook

9/5 The Van Dells

1984

5/6 James Rogers, The Cannons

5/13 Marti Brown

5/20 Jeannie C. Riley

5/27 Marvells

6/3 The Crystals

6/24 Coasters

7/1 Chubby Checker

7/8 Vince Vance and the Valiants

7/15 Tommy Roe, Bobby Vee, Johnny Tillotson

7/29 Irlene Mandrell (Forgotten Child Fund Toy-a-Thon)

8/5 The Diamonds

8/12 Fabian, Chiffons

8/19 Bo Diddley

8/26 Kitty Wells, Johnnie Wright

9/1 Dee Clark

9/2 Marshall Tucker Band

1985

4/28 Stoneman Family

5/12 The Vandells

5/19 Toni Lynn

5/28 Bill Pinckney & Original Drifters

6/2 Mamas and the Papas, Scott McKenzie

6/9 The Shirelles

6/30 Chubby Checker

7/7 Carl Perkins

7/21 Sha Na Na

8/4 Marvells

8/11 Kitty Wells, Johnnie Wright

8/25 Dee Clark

9/1 Freddy Cannon

9/2 Vince Vance and the Valiants

1986

5/4 Irlene Mandrell (Little Miss Lake Winnie pageant)

5/9 Tanya Tucker

5/25 Rare Earth

6/8 Johnny Tillotson/The Marvells

6/22 Con Hunley

6/29 Jr. Walker and the All Stars

7/6 Billy "Crash' Craddock

7/13 The Challengers

7/20 The Vandells

8/3 Kitty Wells, Johnnie Wright

8/10 Gary Lewis and the Playboys

8/17 Mark Gray

1987

5/31 Frankie Ford

Lorrie Morgan and Keith Whitley, married since 1986, performed together on the Jukebox Junction stage in 1988. (Mitzi Derryberry)

1988

4/29 Patty Loveless

5/15 David Slater

5/22 Johnny Tillotson, Charlie McCoy & Hee Haw Band

5/29 Keith Whitley, Lorrie Morgan

6/5 Van-Dells

6/12 Gene Watson

6/19 Con Hunley

Country star T. Graham Brown at Lake Winnie in 1988. (Bryan Eley)

6/26 Sawyer Brown

7/4 Ronnie McDowell

7/10 Asleep at the Wheel

7/24 The O'Kanes

7/31 Bobby Bare

8/7 Jeannie C. Riley

8/21 T. Graham Brown

8/28 Lynn Anderson

9/4 Johnny Lee

9/5 Eddie Rabbitt

1989

5/28 Orion

6/4 Gene Watson

6/11 Sawyer Brown

6/25 Ronnie McDowell

7/2 John Anderson

7/3 Wild Rose

7/4 Vic Willis Trio

7/9 Billy Crash Craddock

7/16 Tams

8/6 Con Hunley

9/3 Drifters with Bill Pinckney

9/4 Gene Watson

Sawyer Brown, the most dominant country band of the 1990s, performed frequently on the Jukebox Junction stage. (Bryan Eley)

1990

5/13 Con Hunley

5/20 Mark Collie

5/27 Orion

6/3 Gene Watson

6/10 Ronnie McDowell

6/17 John Anderson

6/24 Shelby Lynne, Michael Twitty

7/1 T. Graham Brown

7/4 Jason D. Williams

7/8 The Van-Dells

7/15 Jo-El Sonnier

7/22 Mel McDaniel

7/29 The Marvells

8/5 Billy "Crash" Craddock

8/12 Johnny Tillotson and Sons of the Beach

8/19 Exile

8/26 Con Hunley

9/2 Bill Pinckney & Original Drifters

9/3 Gene Watson

1991

5/12 Con Hunley

5/19 Orion

5/26 Wild Rose

6/2 Gene Watson

6/9 Carlene Carter

6/16 Aaron Tippin

6/23 Van-Dells

6/30 William Lee Golden

7/7 Exile

7/14 Michael Twitty & Vickie Byrd

7/21 Bobby Randall

7/28 Ronnie McDowell

8/4 Con Hunley

8/11 Mel McDaniel

8/18 T. Graham Brown

8/25 Marty Stuart

9/1 Gene Watson

9/2 The Van-Dells

1992

5/10 Con Hunley

5/24 Dixiana

6/7 Tracy Lawrence

6/21 T. Graham Brown

6/28 Jett Williams

7/3 Sons of the Beach

7/5 Ray Price

7/12 B.B. Watson

7/19 Billy Joe Royal

7/26 Ronnie McDowell

8/2 The Drifters

8/9 Jason D. Williams

8/16 Exile

8/30 Bill Anderson

9/7 Gene Watson

1993

5/23 Joy Lynn White

5/30 Lou Diamond Phillips & Pipefitters

6/6 Ronnie McDowell

6/13 Jason D. Williams

6/20 Con Hunley

6/27 Brian Hyland, Frankie Ford

7/3 Bob Evans (Badfinger)

7/4 Jett Williams

7/11 Dixiana

7/18 Neal McCoy

7/25 Van-Dells

8/1 Billy Joe Royal

8/8 Palomino Road

8/15 T. Graham Brown

8/22 The Drifters

8/29 William Lee Golden & the Goldens

9/5 Exile

9/6 Gene Watson

1994

5/8 Neal McCoy

5/15 Daron Norwood

5/22 The Thompsons

5/29 Lou Diamond Phillips & the Pipefitters

6/5 Wylie & the Wild West Show

6/12 Jon Brennan

6/19 Bryan Austin

6/26 Ronnie McDowell

7/3 Evangeline

7/10 Marcy Brothers

7/17 Ricky Lynn Gregg

7/24 Ellis Brothers

7/31 Billy Joe Royal

8/7 Twister Alley

8/14 Turner Nichols Band

8/21 Bellamy Brothers

8/28 Boy Howdy

9/4 Pearl River

9/5 Tony Ford

1995

5/14 Tom Wopat

5/28 Tokens

6/4 Billy Joe Royal

6/11 Ricky Lynn Gregg

6/18 Bellamy Brothers

6/25 Dalton Roberts & Chattaboogie Band

7/2 Ronnie McDowell

7/9 Bill Anderson

7/16 Paul Martin

7/23 Davis Daniel

7/30 T. Graham Brown

8/6 Dallas County Line

8/13 Swinging Medallions

8/20 Frazier River

8/27 Gene Watson

9/3 Tom Wopat

1996

6/8 Lee Roy Parnell

7/20 Darryl Singletary

7/28 Frankie Ford

9/1 Highway 101

1997

6/8 Lee Roy Parnell

6/15 38 Special

7/13 Coasters, Drifters, Platters

7/20 Daryle Singletary

8/3 Ronnie McDowell

8/31 Wade Hayes

1998

5/3 Blackhawk

5/31 Confederate Railroad

6/14 38 Special

6/28 Jan and Dean

7/12 Kentucky Headhunters

8/9 Ronnie McDowell

8/23 Grassroots (substituting for Foghat)

9/6 David Kersh

9/7 Gary Puckett

9/13 Bill Anderson

1999

5/2 Keith Harling

5/16 Wilkinsons

6/27 The Lynns

7/25 Randy Scruggs

9/4 Confederate Railroad

9/5 Gene Watson

Confederate Railroad, led by Chattanooga native Danny Shirley, established a long tradition of playing Lake Winnie's Memorial Day and Labor Day shows, always to huge crowds. (Bryan Eley)

2000

5/7 Confederate Railroad

5/21 Molly Hatchet

6/4 The Wilkinsons

6/11 Kentucky Headhunters

6/25 Jaci Velasquez

7/9 The Kinleys

7/23 Joe Diffie

8/6 Andy Griggs

8/20 Brad Paisley

9/3 Confederate Railroad

2001

5/6 Rascal Flatts

5/27 Joe Diffie

6/4 Chad Brock

6/24 Yankee Grey

7/8 4HIM

7/19 Clark Family Experience

7/22 Ty Herndon

8/26 Cheri Keaggy, Ben Glover, Shaun Groves (gospel)

2002

5/5 Confederate Railroad

5/19 Joe Diffie

6/2 Clay Davidson

6/23 Mark Wills

7/7 Eric Heatherly

8/4 Jake and Plus One

8/18 Blake Shelton

9/1 Confederate Railroad

2003

5/4 Confederate Railroad

5/18 Blake Shelton

6/1 Mark Wills

6/22 The Katinas

7/6 Steve Azar

7/20 Darryl Worley

8/3 Andy Griggs

8/17 Natalie Grant

8/31 Eric Heatherly

2004

5/30 Darryl Worley

6/27 Eric Heatherly

7/11 Buddy Jewell

7/25 Cledus T. Judd

8/8 Joe Diffie

9/5 Confederate Railroad

2005

6/5 Aaron Tippin

6/26 Lee Greewood

7/4 Cledus T. Judd

7/17 Mark Wills

7/31 Jimmy Wayne

9/4 Confederate Railroad

2006

6/4 Joe Nichols

6/25 Tracy Byrd

7/9 Craig Morgan

7/23 Josh Turner

8/6 Aaron Tippin

9/3 Confederate Railroad

2007

6/3 Josh Gracin

6/24 Mark Wills

7/8 Rodney Atkins

7/22 Jason Michael Carroll

8/5 Darryl Worley

9/2 Confederate Railroad

2008

5/30 Jake Owen

6/22 John Anderson

7/6 Jason Michael Carroll

7/20 Bucky Covington

8/3 Ashton Shepherd

8/31 Confederate Railroad

2009

5/31 Jimmy Wayne

6/28 John Anderson

7/12 Keith Anderson

7/26 The Lost Trailers

8/2 Eli Young Band

9/6 Confederate Railroad/Lauren Suddeth (who would later become Lauren Alaina)

2010

6/6 David Nail

6/20 Brandon Heath

6/27 Easton Corbin

7/11 Chris Young

7/18 Francesca Battistelli

7/25 Jason Michael Carroll

8/15 Tenth Avenue North

9/5 Confederate Railroad

2011

6/5 Colt Ford

6/12 Sanctus Real

6/26 Tracy Lawrence

7/10 Jerrod Niemann

7/17 Sidewalk Prophets

7/31 Steel Magnolia

8/14 Natalie Grant

9/4 Confederate Railroad

9/18 Colt Ford

2012

5/27 Clay Walker

6/3 Colt Ford

6/24 Sharp Dressed Man (ZZ Top Tribute Band)

7/22 Charlie Daniels Band

9/3 Confederate Railroad

9/17 J. B. and the Moonshine Band

2013

5/19 Colt Ford

9/22 Confederate Railroad

2014

5/25 Confederate Railroad

8/31 Colt Ford

2015

5/31 Big Smo

9/6 Jana Kramer

2018

5/26 Jack and Jack

2019

5/25 MAX, Jake Miller

CHAPTER 4

UTC ARENA (McKenzie Arena)

Known by many names, the UTC Arena, the Roundhouse, or McKenzie Arena has been on the University of Tennessee at Chattanooga campus since 1982.

I t's hard for younger music fans to believe, but during the first twenty years of its existence, the UTC Arena, at 720 East 4th Street, hosted music's biggest names every few weeks.

The Arena opened October 8, 1982. I was there, along with 11,000 other excited music fans. Chattanooga finally had a performing center large enough to attract superstar musical acts. The Tivoli Theater was great for an intimate show, but much too small for a top-selling artist. Memorial Auditorium, with its 3,800 seat hall, had long been surpassed by arena-sized venues in surrounding cities.

From the very first show, UTC's Arena (or as some called it, The Roundhouse) put Chattanooga in the big leagues as a concert town. The opening night headliner was Kenny Rogers, at the peak of his career. Comedian Lonnie Shorr had the thankless task of opening the show, followed by Larry Gatlin and his brothers. Both acts had to compete with chatty opening-night fans, causing Gatlin to stop in mid-song, asking, "Are we bothering y'all?" Eventually the chatter died down and Rogers appeared, singing "Lucille," "The Gambler" and his other hits. We went home happy, awaiting more great shows.

We were not disappointed. During the next few years, superstars appeared regularly in the Arena. Just a few weeks after it opened, Willie Nelson sang everything from "Amazing Grace" to "Whiskey River" to a packed house. Before long we saw Diana Ross, Alabama, Tina Turner, Bob Seger, Cher, Elton John, Heart, Van Halen, Jackson Browne, ZZ Top, Reba McEntyre, Alan Jackson, The Allman Brothers, Bon Jovi, Wynonna Judd, Chicago, The Beach Boys, The Statler Brothers, Sandi Patti, and Aerosmith.

There was a triple-header show with the three biggest country stars on the planet in 1990: Merle Haggard, George Jones and Conway Twitty. In 2004, a new triple-header of superstars were on one bill: Kenny Chesney, Keith Urban, and Dierks Bentley.

Let's not forget Jimmy Buffett, REO Speedwagon, John Denver, Bob Hope, John Mellencamp, Michael Bolton, Clint Black, The Osmonds, Rick Springfield, Barry Manilow, Amy Grant, the Gaither Family, the Oak Ridge Boys, and Kid Rock.

We saw Rod Stewart kicking a soccer ball, the Pointer Sisters energetically outshining headliner Lionel Richie, and Tina Turner commanding the stage. We looked on with amusement as Billy Joel handed off the high notes to a backup singer. We watched Barbara Mandrell play pretty much every musical instrument ever invented, and we saw so much more.

We saw many little-known opening acts, who went on to become major headliners in their own right. Sawyer Brown, Whitesnake, the Bangles, Twisted Sister, Guns N Roses, Toby Keith, Celine Dion, Sugarland, and Little Big Town are among those who paid their dues, warming up the crowd while the star attraction waited in the wings.

The music shows were mixed in with rodeos, monster trucks, wrestling, Disney On Ice, Harlem Globetrotters, Bob Barker's Game Show, circuses and other spectacles.

We thought those days would never end, but they did. The arena that hosted at least 20 big-name shows a year eventually went silent, except for basketball and commencement exercises. Taylor Swift first performed at the Arena in 2007 as an opening act, before her career kicked into high gear the following year. Maroon 5 with Adam Levine, Carrie Underwood, James Taylor, Brantley Gilbert, and Toby Keith have all appeared in the 21st century, but such shows have been few and far between.

Why did the music fade out? Here's the quick answer. Most acts would rather go somewhere else. Since 1982, the Arena has gone from shiny and new, to undersized and outdated. Better-designed venues have sprung up in nearby cities like Nashville, Atlanta, and Huntsville. That means bigger crowds, and more sales of t-shirts, programs and other items that fatten artists' wallets. One source close to the Arena told me, "It's not from lack of trying. We're always trying to attract big shows. Some artists look at us as just a blip on the map."

A 2015 highlight was the appearance of Vice President Joe Biden, who delivered an emotional tribute to Chattanooga's five fallen servicemen, just days after they were killed in a terror attack. His speech was especially powerful as he shared his grief over the recent loss of his own son to cancer. The Arena proved to be an appropriate setting for a patriotic memorial program.

The facility was built to replace Maclellan Gym, considered too small to accommodate the crowds that were supporting the UTC basketball program. Under head coaches Ron Shumate and Murray Arnold, the Mocs basketball team had become a Southern Conference powerhouse, attracting national attention. There was also great potential for concert acts that were bypassing Chattanooga due to its lack of a venue with more than 5,000 seats. The cost of the Arena was $15.5 million, and the facility's first manager was Mickey Yerger.

About the name: In 2000, the UTC Arena, also known by its nickname "The Roundhouse" was officially renamed McKenzie Arena, in honor of Toby and Brenda McKenzie of Cleveland, Tennessee, longtime UTC boosters.

In the early years, the Arena's acoustics and sight lines were a drawback. The uppermost seats, referred to by critics as "the nosebleed section," were considered acceptable for basketball, but not for concerts. Various improvements were made to the sound system, but it has never been considered ideal for an optimum concert experience.

It's My Kenny Rogers Story, and I'm Sticking To It

In the early 1980s, when I was music director for KZ-106, Kenny Rogers released a new album on Liberty Records. A promoter for the label, Bob Alou would visit the station, and ask us to play Kenny's songs. Bob was well known in the industry as a bit of a wild man. Still, one afternoon, I accepted his invitation to take a ride through Red Bank, just long enough to hear Kenny's new album (on cassette) on his car stereo. As he drove down Dayton Boulevard, he decided to light up a joint. The more he inhaled, the louder the music got. He would take long, deep drags, and he was determined to finish the joint before we returned to the radio station.

He'd crank up Kenny's songs even louder, saying "Man, that sounds good!" Thankfully, we were not stopped by the Red Bank police. Even though I wasn't smoking, I was probably high by association, and my clothes smelled like pot. My wife Cindy understood. She had been in radio too.

In fact, that record promoter scored big points with Cindy just a few weeks later. Kenny performed at the UTC Arena, and Bob arranged for us to meet Kenny backstage. Cindy, by then a seasoned news reporter, started thinking about what she would ask him. "What will your next record be?" "Tell us about your new baby boy." "What do all those Grammy nominations mean to you?" She was prepared, as always.

After the show, we were escorted backstage, and there stood Kenny Rogers. Tall, trim, tanned and handsome in his white suit. We exchanged pleasantries, and he thanked me for playing his songs. I nodded to Cindy, as if to say, "Your turn. She was so taken aback by his good looks, she could not speak. A few words came out, but not in the right order. She was starstruck. Kenny smiled and said, "Well, it sure was nice to meet you." Cindy turned three shades of red, and said, "Kerfuffle perdunkin," or something like that. I'd never seen her speechless, before or since. ("I didn't expect him to be so handsome," she would say later.)

Kenny Rogers then walked away, sporting a big smile. It surely wasn't the first time he'd made a pretty girl blush.

Willie Nelson played Chattanooga several times, including for packed houses at the UTC Arena. (Cindy Lowery)

Bob Hope performed in Chattanooga in 1987 after a near four-decade absence, in a benefit for the Medal of Honor Museum. He is pictured backstage with David Carroll and Terry Farriss preparing to tape a public service announcement for the Museum.

UTC Arena performances

10/08/1982 KENNY ROGERS/Larry Gatlin and the Gatlin Brothers/Lonnie Shorr

10/23/1982 JIMMY BUFFETT

11/07/1982 VAN HALEN/Joe Whiting & the Bandit Band

11/16/1982 JOHN MCENROE VS. GUILLERMO VILAS (tennis exhibition)

11/18/1982 BARRY MANILOW

12/03/1982 WILLIE NELSON

01/29/1983 KISS/Night Ranger

02/03/1983 ROSCOE TANNER vs. BJORN BORG (tennis exhibition, attendance 7600)

02/04/1983 BILLY SQUIER/Saga

In 1987, Andy Williams brought his Christmas show to the UTC Arena, backed by the Chattanooga Boys Choir. He is pictured with Patrick Sallee.

02/25/1983 DIANA ROSS

03/02/1983 BOB SEGER/John Hall

03/11/1983 ALABAMA/Janie Fricke

03/12/1983 ALABAMA/Janie Fricke

03/19/1983 REO SPEEDWAGON/Duke Jupiter

04/08/1983 BARBARA MANDRELL/T. G. Sheppard

04/09/1983 DAN FOGELBERG

05/18/1983 DEF LEPPARD/John Butcher Axis/Krokus

05/27/1983 STYX

Country star Billy Dean opened for Clint Black and Merle Haggard in a 1991 UTC Arena show. Dean also visited St. Nicholas School in Chattanooga before the concert. (Cindy Lowery)

06/03/1983 CHICAGO

07/09/1983 IMPERIALS/Sandi Patty/Mylon LeFevre

07/27/1983 RICK JAMES/Mary Jane Girls

07/28/1983 RICK SPRINGFIELD/Sparks

08/04/1983 OSMONDS/Desiree Daniels

08/13/1983 JACKSON BROWNE

09/04/1983 B B KING

09/12/1983 LOVERBOY/Zebra

10/16/1983 OAK RIDGE BOYS/Louise Mandrell

11/03/1983 GAP BAND/Midnight Star/Zapp/New Edition

11/06/1983 KENNY ROGERS/Righteous Brothers/B.J. Thomas

11/12/1983 HEART/KANSAS

01/18/1984 .38 SPECIAL/HUEY LEWIS & THE NEWS

01/23/1984 LIONEL RICHIE/POINTER SISTERS

02/11/1984 BILLY JOEL (sellout)

03/06/1984 WILLIE NELSON

03/29/1984 LUTHER VANDROSS/DeBarge/The Deele

04/20/1984 ALABAMA/Juice Newton

04/21/1984 TED NUGENT

06/09/1984 CAMEO/Dennis Edwards/O'Bryan/Newcleus

06/28/1984 NIGHT RANGER/Tony Carey

08/01/1984 AEROSMITH/Orion the Hunter

09/25/1984 GO-GO'S/Red Rockers

10/04/1984 GATLIN BROTHERS/Janie Fricke

10/05/1984 ELTON JOHN

10/30/1984 BILLY SQUIER/Ratt

11/03/1984 CULTURE CLUB

11/04/1984 KENNY ROGERS/Crystal Gayle/Sawyer Brown

11/15/1984 QUIET RIOT/Armored Saint/Whitesnake

11/25/1984 CYNDI LAUPER/Bangles

12/02/1984 STATLER BROTHERS/Helen Cornelius

12/04/1984 BARRY MANILOW

12/9/1984 BOB BARKER's Game Show

02/19/1985 IRON MAIDEN/Twisted Sister

03/02/1985 CHICAGO

03/05/1985 REO SPEEDWAGON/Survivor

03/08/1985 MIDNIGHT STAR/Shalamar/Klymaxx

04/06/1985 TOM JONES

04/19/1985 NEW EDITION/Jesse Johnson Revue

05/04/1985 HALL & OATES/Til Tuesday

08/01/1985 LUTHER VANDROSS/Cheryl Lynn/The Whispers

08/21/1985 RATT/BON JOVI/Y & T

10/04/1985 BEACH BOYS/Three Dog Night

10/25/1985 BAR-KAYS

11/09/1985 TINA TURNER/Mr. Mister

01/24/1986 JOHN McENROE/MATS WILANDER Tennis Exhibition

02/01/1986 LOVERBOY/HOOTERS

02/23/1986 ZZ TOP/Jimmy Barnes (attendance 11,800: largest concert crowd ever)

03/01/1986 HEART/Autograph

03/08/1986 ALABAMA/Charlie Daniels Band

03/15/1986 JOHN COUGAR MELLENCAMP

03/25/1986 KENNY ROGERS/Sawyer Brown/Lee Greenwood

03/27/1986 HANK WILLIAMS JR/Earl Thomas Conley

04/17/1986 NEW EDITION/Force MDs, Cherelle, Alexander O'Neal

06/08/1986 RUN DMC/BEASTIE BOYS

07/29/1986 OZZY OSBOURNE/Metallica

09/25/1986 MOODY BLUES/The Fixx

10/08/1986 ITZHAK PERLMAN & Chattanooga Symphony

10/29/1986 MONKEES/Herman's Hermits/Grassroots/Gary Puckett

11/26/1986 FRANKIE BEVERLY & MAZE/Midnight Star/SOS Band

01/21/1987 RATT/Queensryche

02/11/1987 FREDDIE JACKSON/Ray, Goodman, and Brown/Najee

02/12/1987 DAVID LEE ROTH/Tesla

02/17/1987 HUEY LEWIS/Robert Cray Band

03/07/1987 SANDI PATTI

03/13/1987 BILLY JOEL

05/06/1987 REO SPEEDWAGON/Joan Jett

05/14/1987 BOB HOPE/Chattanooga Boys Choir

06/06/1987 KOOL & THE GANG/Klymaxx/The System

07/24/1987 CAMEO

08/01/1987 LL COOL J

10/30/1987 TINA TURNER/Go West

11/08/1987 BAR-KAYS, LEVERT, FORCE MD'S

11/21/1987 MOTLEY CRUE /GUNS N' ROSES

12/01/1987 STEVE GREEN

12/14/1987 ANDY WILLIAMS/Chattanooga Boys Choir

02/19/1988 HANK WILLIAMS JR/WAYLON JENNINGS

03/13/1988 WHITESNAKE/Great White (attendance 11,700: 2nd largest concert crowd ever)

03/20/1988 KENNY ROGERS/Forester Sisters

04/12/1988 AEROSMITH/White Lion

05/31/1988 LYNYRD SKYNYRD/Rossington Band

07/06/1988 DOPE JAM-KOOL MOE DEE/ERIC B

08/05/1988 RUN-DMC/JAZZY JEFF/JJ FAD/PUBLIC ENEMY/SALT N PEPA

09/15/1988 DEF LEPPARD/QUEENSRYCHE (sellout)

09/29/1988 SALT-N-PEPA / KEITH SWEAT/Rob Base/DJ EZ Rock

10/19/1988 POISON/Britny Fox/Lita Ford

11/18/1988 SANDI PATTI/Billy Crockett

12/06/1988 JOHN DENVER/Chattanooga Boys Choir

01/28/1989 NEW EDITION/BOBBY BROWN/AL B SURE

02/11/1989 CHICAGO/Tommy Conwell & the Young Rumblers

03/04/1989 HANK WILLIAMS JR/Steve Earle

04/18/1989 KENNY G

05/04/1989 ROD STEWART

05/06/1989 BOBBY WOMACK/Johnnie Taylor

05/25/1989 CINDERELLA/Bullet Boys/Winger

07/05/1989 LL COOL J/SLICK RICK/TOO SHORT

07/14/1989 BON JOVI / Blue Murder

8/15/1989 METALLICA/The Cult

8/23/1989 DOOBIE BROTHERS/Henry Lee Summer

10/5/1989 M C HAMMER/EPMD/2 LIVE CREW

10/11/1989 BEACH BOYS/Southern Pacific

11/02/1989 TESLA/GREAT WHITE

11/03/1989 R.E.M./Pylon

01/31/1990 MOTLEY CRUE/Warrant

03/08/1990 NEW KIDS ON THE BLOCK

03/16/1990 HANK WILLIAMS JR/Sawyer Brown/Kentucky Headhunters

03/24/1990 STATLER BROTHERS/Ricky Skaggs/Suzy Bogguss

04/27/1990 DAVID PEASTON / MIKI HOWARD

05/22/1990 AEROSMITH/Joan Jett

07/19/1990 M C HAMMER/Oaktown 357, Michel'le, Troop, After 7

07/24/1990 RICHARD MARX/Wilson Phillips

10/17/1990 POISON/Warrant

10/20/1990 STEVE GREEN

10/27/1990 RANDY TRAVIS/Shenandoah/Shelby Lynne

12/02/1990 GEORGE JONES/CONWAY TWITTY/MERLE HAGGARD

02/08/1991 BAD COMPANY / Damn Yankees

02/13/1991 VANILLA ICE

02/27/1991 ZZ TOP/Black Crowes

05/25/1991 NELSON / Enuff Z'nuff

06/28/1991 QUEENSRYCHE/Suicidal Tendencies

07/24/1991 CLINT BLACK/Merle Haggard/Billy Dean

08/04/1991 MICHAEL BOLTON / Oleta Adams

09/16/1991 CARMAN

09/28/1991 ANDRE WATTS with Chattanooga Symphony

10/24/1991 SANDI PATTI

11/16/1991 AMY GRANT

12/07/1991 LUTHER VANDROSS/Lisa Fisher/Sinbad

02/12/1992 VAN HALEN/Baby Animals

02/21/1992 CHILL DEAL BOYS / Poison Clan

03/12/1992 METALLICA

03/13/1992 RANDY TRAVIS/Trisha Yearwood

04/05/1992 HANK WILLIAMS JR/Patty Loveless/Doug Stone

04/16/1992 M C HAMMER/Boys II Men/Jodice/Oaktown's 3*5*7

09/11/1992 CHUBB ROCK / Eric B. & Rakim

10/07/1992 KRIS KROSS/MC Lyte

11/13/1992 REBA MCENTIRE/BROOKS & DUNN/Mike Reid

12/04/1992 DEF LEPPARD

3/18-19/1993 TRAVIS TRITT/Trisha Yearwood/Little Texas

03/26/1993 CARMAN

04/17/1993 TOO SHORT/DA LENCH MOB/N2DEEP

04/22/1993 ALAN JACKSON/Billy Dean

04/29/1993 MICHAEL W SMITH/ DC TALK

05/06/1993 LYNYRD SKYNYRD/Drivin N Cryin/ Bad Company

05/14/1993 WYNONNA JUDD / CLINT BLACK/Michael Johnson

11/12/1993 REBA MCENTIRE/John Michael Montgomery

12/09/1993 BILLY RAY CYRUS/Toby Keith

12/16/1993 JUDY COLLINS

02/26/1994 ROD STEWART

02/27/1994 VINCE GILL/Trisha Yearwood/Larry Stewart

04/29/1994 BROOKS AND DUNN/Toby Keith/Aaron Tippin

07/12/1994 MOODY BLUES/Chattanooga Festival Orchestra

07/28/1994 R KELLY /Salt N Pepa

08/01/1994 MICHAEL BOLTON /Celine Dion

10/12/1994 ZZ TOP/Jackyl

10/14/1994 CARMAN

12/08/1994 TRAVIS TRITT/Joe Diffie/Lee Roy Parnell

02/05/1995 REBA MCENTIRE/Tracy Byrd/Rhett Akins

03/31/1995 JOHN MICHAEL MONTGOMERY/Hal Ketchum

04/01/1995 AMY GRANT/Gary Chapman

04/07/1995 BOYZ II MEN

04/20/1995 TIM MCGRAW/Little Texas/Blackhawk

04/28/1995 LYNYRD SKYNYRD / HANK WILLIAMS JR/Billy Joe Shaver

09/19/1995 BON JOVI/Dokken

10/19/1995 BEACH BOYS

11/08/1995 ALLMAN BROTHERS/Gov't Mule

03/14/1996 CARMAN

03/23/1996 VINCE GILL/Patty Loveless

04/21/1996 TIM MCGRAW/FAITH HILL

05/08/1996 R KELLY/LL COOL J/XScape

08/09/1996 REBA MCENTIRE/Linda Davis/Billy Dean

10/11/1996 TRAVIS TRITT/Marty Stuart/Paul Brandt

11/14/1996 STEVEN CURTIS CHAPMAN/Audio Adrenaline/Carolyn Arends

03/28/1997 VINCE GILL\Bryan White

08/14/1997 LYNYRD SKYNYRD/Paul Rodgers/Kenny Wayne Shepherd

10/25/1997 BILL GAITHER & FRIENDS

06/17/1998 SOUL ASYLUM/Freddy Jones Band

10/24/1998 GAITHER FAMILY

11/06/1998 SHANIA TWAIN/The Leahy Family

01/06/1999 AEROSMITH/Candlebox

02/20/1999 ELTON JOHN

04/11/1999 DC TALK/The W's

04/12/2000 RED HOT CHILI PEPPERS/Foo Fighters/Muse

04/24/2000 KISS/Ted Nugent/Skid Row

07/22/2000 MOTLEY CRUE/MEGADETH/Anthrax

01/20/2001 NEWSONG/JANUARY JAM

02/13/2001 CARMAN

07/10/2001 MYSTICAL

08/25/2001 ALABAMA

10/14/2001 DISTURBED/Drowning Pool/Stereomud/Systematic

11/15/2001 MARK LOWRY/Anthony Burger

11/21/2001 WIDESPREAD PANIC

11/24/2001 KENNY CHESNEY/Rascal Flatts/Sara Evans

01/31/2002 LUDACRIS

02/28/2003 GAITHER FAMILY/Vestal Goodman/Eva Mae LeFevre

04/27/2003 MICHAEL W SMITH

05/16/2003 ALAN JACKSON/Joe Nichols

10/05/2003 RASCAL FLATTS/Chris Cagle/Brian McComas

12/04/2003 MARTINA MCBRIDE

01/17/2004 NEWSONG/Audio Adrenaline

01/27/2004 3 DOORS DOWN/Shinedown

02/12/2004 KID ROCK/Gov't Mule

03/27/2004 KENNY CHESNEY, Keith Urban/Dierks Bentley

09/13/2004 CHER/Tommy Drake

10/23/2004 RASCAL FLATTS/Chris Cagle/Julie Roberts

11/12/2004 THIRD DAY/Toby Mac

01/21/2005 NEWSONG, Rachel Lampa, Toby Mac

04/19/2005 STEVEN CURTIS CHAPMAN

11/08/2005 3 DOORS DOWN/Shinedown/Silvertide

11/13/2005 TRANS-SIBERIAN ORCHESTRA

11/17/2005 BRAD PAISLEY/Sara Evans/Sugarland

01/14/2006 NEWSBOYS, NewSong, Toby Mac, Michael Tait

01/26/2006 GRETCHEN WILSON/Blaine Larsen/Van Zant

09/22/2006 STAIND/Hinder/Three Days Grace/Black Stone Cherry

10/20/2006 LIL WAYNE/T-Pain

11/12/2006 CARRIE UNDERWOOD/Rocky Lynne

12/10/2006 BOW WOW/DJ Unk

02/08/2007 TOBY KEITH/Miranda Lambert/Flynnville Train

03/16/2007 STEVEN CURTIS CHAPMAN/NewSong/Hawk Nelson

04/26/2007 BRAD PAISLEY/Kellie Pickler/Jack Ingram/Taylor Swift

11/02/2007 GAITHER FAMILY

11/04/2007 THREE DAYS GRACE/Breaking Benjamin/Seether/Red

01/11/2008 NEWSONG/MercyMe/BarlowGirl/Mandisa

04/18/2008 CASTING CROWNS/Leeland/John Waller

10/18/2008 TAYLOR SWIFT/Love and Theft

12/08/2008 CARRIE UNDERWOOD/Little Big Town

01/09/2009 TOBY MAC/Brandon Heath/Newsong/Hawk Nelson

03/27/2009 JEFF DUNHAM

05/13/2009 SHINEDOWN/Halestorm/10 Years/Saving Abel

07/15/2009 SLIM THUG/ Trina

09/19/2009 JEREMIH/Whild Peach

10/10/2009 CASTING CROWNS/Matt Redman

01/08/2010 FIREFLIGHT/Red/Tenth Avenue North/Third Day

08/26/2010 MAROON 5/VV Brown/Kris Allen

11/19/2010 ELTON JOHN /Leon Russell

11/20/2010 GAITHER FAMILY

01/07/2011 NEWSBOYS/Red/Chris August

02/01/2011 JASON ALDEAN/ Eric Church/JaneDear Girls

02/12/2012 Winter Jam: Skillet/We As Human/Newsong/Kari Jobe/Building 429

03/10/2012 GAITHER FAMILY

04/06/2012 CASTING CROWNS

01/06/2013 Winter Jam/Toby Mac

02/16/2013 BRANTLEY GILBERT/Kip Moore

Cher dazzled a sold-out audience at UTC Arena in 2003. (Dave Weinthal)

03/23/2013 ELTON JOHN

01/12/2014 Newsboys/NewSong

03/20/2014 ZAC BROWN/AJ Ghent Band/Levi Lowrey

03/21/2014 ANDY GRAMMER/The Ready Set

Just one year after opening for Brad Paisley, Taylor Swift headlined her own show at UTC Arena in 2008. She is pictured with Ricky Crook.

03/15/2015 Winter Jam

01/10/2016 Winter Jam/For King & Country/Matthew West/Crowder/Red/NewSong

02/10/2016 Newsboys/Jeremy Camp/Mandisa

03/12/2016 ELTON JOHN

04/23/2016 JAMES TAYLOR

With a home in nearby Atlanta, Elton John became a regular headliner at UTC Arena in the 2010s. (Dave Weinthal)

03/26/2017 Winter Jam (Crowder, Britt Nicole, Tenth Avenue North, Colton Dixon, NewSong)

02/25/2018 Winter Jam (Featuring Skillet, Kari Jobe, Building 429, John Crist, KB, NewSong, Jordan Feliz, Dan Bremnes, Mallary Hope, Westover, and Nick Hall)

03/10/19 Winter Jam (Featuring Newsboys United, Danny Gokey, Mandisa, Rend Collective, NewSong, Ledger, Manic Drive, and Hollyn)

11/23/2019 FIVE FINGER DEATH PUNCH/Three Days Grace, Bad Wolves/ Fire From the Gods

02/15/20 BRANTLEY GILBERT, Dylan Scott, Brandon Lay

Brantley Gilbert headlined the final concert before UTC Arena and other venues had to shut down due to the Coronavirus pandemic in 2020. (Don Luzynski Photography)

CHAPTER 5

High Schools, Colleges, Stadiums, Ball Fields and Gyms

Beginning in the 1920s, Chattanooga High School on East 3ʳᵈ Street hosted musical shows in its auditorium. It is now the site of Chattanooga School for Arts and Sciences. (Chattanooga High moved to its current location on Dallas Road in north Chattanooga in 1963).

The Chattanooga High stage even hosted a Bob Hope NBC network radio show in 1947 (see Chapter 11). Beverly Sills, who would become an operatic superstar performed there in 1955, at the age of 25.

In the 1960s, the McCallie School featured some of the top names in top-40 and soul music.

Johnny Cash frequently spoke of his 1967 drug arrest in Walker County, Georgia, calling it among the low points in his life. He credited Sheriff Ralph Jones with helping him turn his life around. In 1970, he showed his appreciation by bringing the cast of his ABC prime time show to Lafayette High School to hold a fund-raising concert for new athletic facilities. A crowd of 12,000 attended, creating perhaps the largest single gathering in the county's history.

In a great "before they were stars" moment, Baylor School of Chattanooga hosted the rock band Lynyrd Skynyrd in 1973, a year before "Sweet Home Alabama" catapulted them into stardom. Two decades later, Widespread Panic played at McCallie School, well ahead of their rise to national fame.

Area colleges, including UTC (before the Arena or Finley Stadium were built), Southern Missionary College in Collegedale, and Cleveland State also hosted concerts. UTC's Chamberlain Field, built in 1908 for football, was also used for shows ranging from the pop flavored Osmond family, to southern rockers Stillwater.

When Finley Stadium opened on the city's southside in 1997, promoters had a new 20,000 seat outdoor venue. Primarily the home of the UTC football Mocs, it has also served as a popular soccer venue. In the facility's early years, a few concerts were held with varying amounts of success.

Johnny Cash with Walker County (GA) Sheriff Ralph Jones prior to his 1970 benefit concert at Lafayette High School. (Origin unknown)

10/28/1922 John Phillip Sousa and band at Wyatt Auditorium at Chattanooga High School on East 3rd Street.

4/13/1923 St. Louis Symphony at Wyatt Auditorium at Chattanooga High School.

10/8/1923 Oscar Seagle (baritone) at Wyatt Auditorium at Chattanooga High School.

2/4/1924 Lucy Gates (soprano) at Wyatt Auditorium at Chattanooga High School.

3/10/1924 Mischa Elman (Russian violinist) at Wyatt Auditorium at Chattanooga High School.

1/25-27/1955 Beverly Sills (age 25) in "Don Giovanni" at Chattanooga High School

12/8/60 The Brothers Four at Chattanooga High School auditorium.

11/15/62 Woody Herman and the Herd at Brainerd High School

12/7/62 Porter Wagoner, Mother Maybelle and the Carter Sisters, Norma Jean, and Buck Trent performed at Chattanooga High School

5/16/63 Stan Kenton and orchestra at Central High School on Dodds Avenue in Chattanooga.

5/29/65 Otis Redding performed at McCallie School

11/7/63 Woody Herman and the Swingin' Herd performed at Brainerd High School

5/28/66 Major Lance performed at McCallie School

5/27/67 Maurice Williams and the Zodiacs performed at McCallie School

3/17/68 Norman Luboff Choir performed at Southern Missionary College in Collegedale

5/28/69 Clarence Carter performed at McCallie School

6/6/69 Kitty Wells and Johnny Wright performed at Red Bank High School

4/10/70 Swinging Medallions perfromed at Girls Preparatory School

5/29/70 Major Lance performed at McCallie School

8/13/70 Johnny Cash performed at Lafayette High for athletics facilities fundraiser, with June Carter Cash, the Statler Brothers, Carl Perkins, the Carter Family and the Tennessee Three. There were 12,000 fans in attendance.

7/12/72 The Osmonds, Bo Donaldson and the Heywoods at Chamberlain Field at UTC

2/3/73 Van Cliburn (pianist) at Southern Missionary College in Collegedale, TN

6/1/73 Lynyrd Skynyrd at Baylor School

4/26/74 Jerry Clower at Ringgold High School

9/5/74 Jerry Clower at the new UTC Student Center (football kickoff dinner for Chattanooga Quarterback Club)

11/14/74 Actor Anthony Quayle performed at UTC Theater Arts Center

3/6/76 Jeanne Pruett, Jerry Clower at Ringgold High gym

11/10/76 Frank Sinatra Jr. at UTC Student Center

4/29/78 Stillwater at Chamberlain Field at UTC

10/27/79 Hank Williams Jr. at Cleveland State Community College

4/17/80 Marshall Chapman, Louisiana's LeRoux at UTC Spring Fest on campus

11/14/81 Jerry Clower at Ooltewah High School

2/27/82 Leon Russell at Dalton Jr. High

10/26/82 Jerry Reed at Central High School (Lamar Alexander for Governor campaign rally)

5/17/83 Lee Greenwood at Soddy-Daisy High School

11/17/83 Lee Greenwood, Danny Shirley and Crossroads Band at Soddy-Daisy High School

3/16/84 Tom T. Hall and Con Hunley at Rhea County High School

11/3/84 Jerry Clower at Southern College, Collegedale, TN

10/17/85 Lewis Grizzard spoke at Dalton GA Jr. High Auditorium

10/8/87 Don McLean at Southern College, Collegedale, TN

4/30/90 Maynard Ferguson (trumpeter) at Tyner High School

9/19/92 Fabulous Thunderbirds at City Lights, Kirkman football field

1/23/93 Widespread Panic at McCallie School

11/6/93 Radney Foster, Lee Roy Parnell, Dalton Roberts, Roger Alan Wade Fabulous at City Lights, Kirkman football field

1/19/94 Odetta at Girls Preparatory School

9/10/94 Gibson/Miller Band at City Lights, Kirkman football field

5/16/97 Dennis Weaver at Chattanooga State (one man show *"Irreverent Shakespeare"*)

5/2/98 Keith Harling, JoDee Messina, Lorrie Morgan, Ricochet at Finley Stadium

5/30/98 Michael Bolton and Wynonna at Finley Stadium

7/12/98 Lynyrd Skynyrd, .38 Special, Drivin' n' Cryin' at Finley Stadium

10/22/02 Anthony Burger at Lee University Conn Center in Cleveland, TN

10/28/03 Lynyrd Skynyrd, .38 Special at Finley Stadium

9/4/04 Frankie Beverly & Maze, Gap Band, Impressions, Lakeside, Midnight Star at Finley Stadium

7/20/12 Aaron Tippin at Redoubt Soccer Field in Chattanooga

9/9/16 Usher at Dalewood Middle School (outdoor concert)

Country singer-songwriter Tom T. Hall performs at Rhea County High School in 1984. (Cindy Lowery)

Maclellan Gym, built in 1961 on the University of Chattanooga campus (the school became the University of Tennessee at Chattanooga in 1969)

Maclellan Gym was a frequently used stage for music shows in the 1960s and 1970s. Still used today for some UTC sports, the gym's capacity of 4,177 made it a popular venue for rock and roll shows, including the school's annual homecoming concerts.

Chattanooga native Usher poses with police officers after his 2016 concert at Dalewood Middle School. (WDEF)

The Student Government Association aggressively booked and promoted shows during the 1970s. The Allman Brothers Band had not yet made it to headline status when they opened for Country Joe McDonald in May 1971. The students also booked Rufus featuring Chaka Khan a year before the single "Tell Me Something Good" began its ride up the charts.

One of the more bizarre moments in Chattanooga concert history occurred on the night of November 12, 1977, when soul star Marvin Gaye, who was described as "very relaxed" prior to the show, gave a "mediocre" performance. Gaye was scheduled to perform at 11:00 p.m., but didn't take the stage until 1:15 a.m. The 38-year-old singer, who had recently topped the charts with his single "Got to Give It Up," later attributed his illness to exhaustion due to a heavy travel schedule. He spent several days recovering at Chattanooga's Memorial Hospital.

Dionne Warwick with WGOW radio morning deejay Chickamauga Charlie at UTC Homecoming concert at Maclellan Gym in 1970. (Bob Todd)

10/19/67 The Association

10/17/69 Box Tops, Spiral Starecase, Peggy Scott & JoJo Benson

10/18/69 Percy Sledge

11/6/70 Dionne Warwick (estimated 5,000 fans)

11/7/70 Pacific Gas & Electric

5/7/71 Country Joe McDonald, Allman Brothers

10/15/71 B. B. King

10/27/72 Black Oak Arkansas

4/7/73 Ike and Tina Turner (estimated 5,000 fans)

10/5/73 Rufus featuring Chaka Khan

3/14/75 Dave Loggins/ Pure Prairie League

9/29/77 Atlanta Rhythm Section/Overland

11/12/77 Marvin Gaye (Gaye became ill the day of the show, began his performance several hours late, starting at 1:15 a.m., and was treated for exhaustion at Memorial Hospital for several days)

3/10/78 Dan Hill

9/13/78 Exile/Prism

2/14/80 Sha Na Na/Sam and Dave

3/28/81 Gallagher

Engel Stadium (3ʳᵈ Street at Oneal, opened 4/15/30)

Chattanooga's historic baseball stadium occasionally did double duty as a venue for concerts, evangelical meetings, and circus performances. The stadium's capacity was listed at 12,000, and a 1950 appearance by Rev. Billy Graham resulted in an overflow crowd. In the 1950s, Engel hosted several gospel shows. By the 1970s, rock and roll promoters, riding the wave of popular outdoor concerts, booked acts into the stadium, often with great success.

In 1974, Leon Russell drew a large crowd, and up-and-coming acts like Blue Oyster Cult and Nazareth played Engel long before their music found a mass audience.

Alabama, which had labored for years as a club band, finally found commercial success in 1980, and Engel was one of their first large venue shows before they became a country music powerhouse.

In 1982, the stadium hosted three summer concerts that served as a precursor to the Riverbend Festival, which premiered later that year at Ross's Landing. Rick Springfield, the Commodores, and the Beach Boys proved that Chattanooga audiences would support outdoor shows.

Poster for Leon Russell's 1974 concert at Engel Stadium. Several local entertainers opened for the rock superstar.

A July 1990 Jimmy Buffett show drew a big crowd, but became somewhat infamous for the field's sloppy conditions. Rains prior to the show created a mud bowl. The field's poor drainage created standing water near the stage, and fans sloshed through ankle-deep mud, further damaging the field in the middle of the Lookouts' baseball season. Buffett never played Chattanooga again, although it is unknown if the less than ideal conditions at Engel Stadium played any part in that.

10/22/50 Rev. Billy Graham (estimated 20,000 spectators)

7/1/53 Wally Fowler/Chuck Wagon Gang, Martha Carson, LeFevres

8/15/53 Wally Fowler, LeFevres, Blackwood Brothers, Statesmen

9/7/53 Wally Fowler, LeFeveres, Blackwood Brothers, Statesmen, Harmoneers, Speer Family

5/28/55 Fess Parker (Davy Crockett) personal appearance

6/1/74 Leon Russell, Gap Band, Jimmy Tawater, James Rogers

7/6/74 Blue Oyster Cult/Rare Earth/Nazareth

7/6/79 Earl Scruggs Revue/ Barefoot Jerry

6/15/80 Ray, Goodman, and Brown/Skyy

10/5/80 Alabama, James Rogers, Overland Express, Sylvia, Leon Everette

5/29/82 Rick Springfield

6/24/82 Beach Boys/Franke & the Knockouts

7/4/82 Commodores

8/1/82 B.B. King/Bobby Blue Bland

8/8/82 Louise Mandrell, RC Bannon, Ferlin Husky

8/13/82 Alabama (featuring Randy Owen & Teddy Gentry) vs. KZ-106 Foul Tips in charity softball game for Orange Grove Center and Speech and Hearing Center)

9/19/82 Lee Greenwood, Waylon Jennings, Jessi Colter, Sandy Croft, John Conlee

7/10/86 Three Dog Night

9/5/87 Fat Boys, Salt n Pepa

10/17/87 Marshall Tucker Band/ Billy Joe Royal

7/14/90 Jimmy Buffett, Little Feat

8/1/93 Michael Bolton's Bombers softball team vs. Chattanooga media team (prior to Bolton's concert at UTC Arena)

5/2/13 Charlie Daniels Band/Overland Express

5/1/15 Corey Smith

4/22/17 Yacht Rock Revue/Jason D. Williams

AT&T Field (downtown Chattanooga, first known as BellSouth Park from 2000 until 2007)

When it became apparent that long overdue repairs to the Engel Stadium were cost-prohibitive, Lookouts owner Frank Burke decided to build a new stadium on the site of the former Kirkman High School football field. "Hawk Hill" as it was known, was located just south of the Olgiati Bridge between Highway 27 and Chestnut Street. It was a tight fit, but Burke found just enough space to build the 6,100 seat stadium for $10 million dollars.

After a one-year construction period, the park opened on April 1, 2000 with an exhibition game between the Cincinnati Reds (parent club of the Lookouts) and the Baltimore Orioles. Former president George H.W. Bush and his first lady Barbara Bush provided star power by throwing out the first pitch.

Like Engel, the new Bellsouth Park proved to be a functional venue for rock and country concerts. An early highlight was the pairing of two music legends. On June 1, 2005 Willie Nelson and Bob Dylan continued their American Ball Parks tour, performing on a rainy night before 5,500 fans.

9/20/02 Mark Chesnutt, Joe Diffie, Craig Morgan

5/17/03 Survivor, Eddie Money

9/9/03 Montgomery Gentry, Marty Stuart

6/1/05 Willie Nelson, Bob Dylan

10/6/06 Dierks Bentley, Miranda Lambert

5/3/18 Nelly, Juvenile, Bone Thugs & Harmony

5/18/18 Chris Janson, Jordan Davis

6/28/18 Jake Owen, Chris Janson, Ashley McBryde

11/14/20 Blackberry Smoke

CHAPTER 6

Riverbend Festival and Bessie Smith Strut

Although most Chattanoogans consider the Riverbend Festival at Ross's Landing (established in 1982) as the city's premier festival, it was not the first. From approximately 1896 to 1906, the downtown Chattanooga Spring Festival's street fair and midway were located on 11th Street. It featured a flower parade, bicycle races, and exotic animals, among other attractions.

For the next seventy years, the word "festival" was used to promote many Chattanooga area public events, from the National Folk Festival in 1935, to various arts and crafts festivals that also featured musical performances.

What we have known as Riverbend can trace its beginnings to the early 1980s. Sid Hetzler and Mayor Pat Rose had attended the Spoleto Charleston Festival in Charleston, South Carolina. They liked what they saw.

They shared their enthusiasm and ideas with other Chattanoogans, including Bruce Storey, a partner in Variety Services. Storey had successfully booked entertainers and speakers into the Chattanooga market. He recruited Walker Breland to be the first president of the festival's board of directors. Breland successfully solicited financial help from the Lyndhurst Foundation, American National Bank president Scotty Probasco and Provident Insurance CEO Carey Hanlin. With the seed money in place, the planning began.

Mickey Robbins, Fred Behringer, Nelson Irvine, Rody Davenport, Hugh Moore, Betsy Bramlett, Margaret Culpepper, Hicks Armor, Howard Roddy, Moses Freeman, and Sally Robinson were among those who soon joined the Festival leadership, offering ideas on how best to celebrate the city through the performing arts.

Storey, along with his Variety Services partner Richard Brewer were the first executive directors of the Riverbend Festival. Chip Baker, and Mickey McCamish followed, ushering the festival into the 21st century and beyond. Bob Payne, Jeff Styles, and Joe "Dixie" Fuller are among those who have booked much of the talent, with help from several local radio station personalities.

The Kirkman High School football field, the street outside the Tivoli Theater, and Vine Street all hosted early forays into what would later morph into Riverbend. The downtown block of ML King Boulevard at Broad Street was the site of a 1981 series of big-name concerts called "Five Nights in Chattanooga." Don McLean, Sarah Vaughan, Hank Williams Jr., BB King, and Bill Monroe covered most of the musical bases, drawing a wide range of demographics to a downtown area that had been mostly deserted after dark.

That led to three Engel Stadium summer concerts in 1982, featuring Rick Springfield, the Commodores, and the Beach Boys. In late August of 1982, several acts performed at Ross's Landing over a five-night period in what is now considered the first Riverbend Festival.

Each year since then (except for the pandemic year of 2020), the streets of downtown Chattanooga have been filled with music fans, numbering into the tens of thousands. Although the festival was held in August during its earliest years, it has been held primarily in June. In most years, the event was held over a nine-day period (including the free Bessie Smith Strut on M.L. King Boulevard). In 2019, the festival was shortened to four consecutive nights in late May.

Riverbend has weathered a few storms, literally and figuratively. Actual thunderstorms have wreaked havoc with several shows, chasing crowds (and entertainers) away on nights when Gloria Estefan and Alabama played. Estefan's show ended abruptly, while Alabama took a two-hour break and returned to the stage, playing to the hardy souls who waited out the storm.

Occasional acts of violence also put a damper on the annual street party, usually after the shows ended.

In 1986, the Oak Ridge Boys were called in as a last-minute replacement for Willie Nelson, who cited a broken thumb. This rankled some fans, who noted that Nelson had played the Alabama June Jam in Fort Payne a week earlier, with that same broken thumb. All was later forgiven, as Nelson returned to play Riverbend in 2009, along with other Chattanooga stages many times over the course of his long career.

Also in 1986, big band era clarinetist Benny Goodman passed away one week before his scheduled appearance on the Coca Cola stage. Goodman's longtime friend, bandleader Lionel Hampton stepped in with a show that pleased Goodman's fans and honored his memory.

On June 25, 1989 festival organizers got late word that Coca Cola Stage headliner Jerry Lee Lewis had a leg injury, and would not be able to perform. In a stroke of luck, another talented singer, Ronnie McDowell had just wrapped up his shows at Lake Winnie, about twenty minutes away. McDowell rushed to Ross's Landing while Suzy Bogguss entertained the crowd, and together, they saved the day.

Cee Lo Green rocked the Riverbend boat in 2013 with a profanity-laced show, and a memorable photo op in which he "mooned" the audience. He later apologized, but as of this writing, he has not been invited back to the festival. Officially, the word was, Cee Lo was not banned, but he is also "not welcome to come back."

Country star Luke Combs suddenly lost his voice on the day before his scheduled 2018 performance, and bookers scrambled to find a replacement just hours before showtime. Thankfully, Brett Young was available, and the show went on.

The famed Coca Cola stage, an iconic floating barge, was a Riverbend trademark. However, it weathered criticism as well, from entertainers who felt they were too far removed from their fans, and fans who felt likewise about their distance from the stage. The barge was retired after the 2019 festival, with plans for a new festival layout that would place a stage underneath the Olgiati Bridge.

The festival's annual music lineup was always a lightning rod for debate. Although festival producers did their best to provide "something for everyone," some segments of the music-loving public always felt their particular genre was shortchanged.

However, it was generally agreed that the smaller side stages provided a variety of niche performers and rising stars. One can look at the lineup for a random year, (2012 and 2013 are good examples) and see what appears to be a superstar lineup, viewed through today's eyes. However in most years, many of those acts were relatively unknown, giving music fans a chance to see a future superstar in the making.

In late 2020, Friends of the Festival, the organization that long produced Riverbend and some smaller events, announced a reduction of staff, releasing five of its seven employees. Board chair Mary Kilbride also announced plans to "streamline our operations," including the sale of assets including staging, fencing, and a warehouse.

The organization was surely hurt by the coronavirus pandemic, which hampered similar music festivals worldwide. However, some critics had complained that Riverbend "shot itself in the foot" with a slow response to changing audience tastes, and the unpopular decision to shorten the festival to four nights in 2019.

Riverbend officials left the door open for a renewed festival experience after social distancing rules are relaxed, but indicated that future events would likely be staged on a smaller scale.

The Generosity of Bret Michaels

Here's a Riverbend story from Chris Varnell:

When Bret Michaels was at Riverbend in 2017, my grandson Kyle was invited to meet with him prior to the show. Bret invited us to Nashville a month later when Poison performed with Cheap Trick. Kyle was able to hand deliver a thank you note to Bret after Kyle had attended the camp for diabetic children. It was through Bret's generosity that Kyle was able to take ownership of his diabetes and is now able to give himself injections and monitor his blood sugar as a result of attending camp.

So, not only did a famous rock star come to Chattanooga, but he made a life-changing difference for my grandson. To this day, we remain in touch with Bret. This man has a big heart, and I am honored to share this with your readers.

*Bret Michaels, former lead singer of Poison poses with fans at the 2018
Riverbend Festival. (Friends of the Festival)*

Country star Brett Young at Riverbend 2017. (Friends of the Festival)

The following is a list of well-known acts that played Riverbend, and the Bessie Smith Strut, during the first thirty-eight years of their existence.

1981 (Five Nights in Chattanooga, downtown) Don McLean, B. B. King, Hank Williams Jr., Bill Monroe, Sarah Vaughan

1982 Count Basie, Andre Crouch, Roberta Flack, John Hartford, Bobby Blue Bland, Overland, Dukes of Dixieland

1983 Cab Calloway, Gary Morris, Lacy J. Dalton, Kingston Trio, John Hartford, Atlanta Rhythm Section, Odetta, Ramsey Lewis Trio

1984 Crystal Gayle, Exile, Dizzy Gillespie, James Rogers, Queen Ida

1985 Ray Charles, Three Dog Night, James Rogers, Fabulous Thunderbirds, Ricky Skaggs, Lou Rawls, Nicolette Larson, Confederate Railroad, Pointer Sisters

Lionel Richie on the Coca Cola Stage at Riverbend 2019. (Friends of the Festival)

1986 Oak Ridge Boys (substituting for Willie Nelson, who had broken his thumb), Sweethearts of the Rodeo, Nitty Gritty Dirt Band, Lionel Hampton (substituting for Benny Goodman, who had recently died), Dionne Warwick, Patti LaBelle

1987 Reba McEntire, Buckwheat Zydeco, Bobby Vinton, The Judds, The Spinners, Sarah Vaughan, Chicago, Al Hirt, Arlo Guthrie, Pete Seeger, Alex Chilton, Sonny Geraci, Dennis Yost, Gary Lewis, Blood, Sweat and Tears, O'Kanes, Jason and the Scorchers

Keith Urban was among the headliners in 2019 at the Riverbend Festival.
(Friends of the Festival)

1988 Gloria Estefan and Miami Sound Machine, Gatlin Brothers, Lyle Lovett, Smokey Robinson, Chuck Berry, Gladys Knight, Mel Torme

1989 Ronnie McDowell (who was rushed to Ross's Landing from Lake Winnie, as last minute substitute for the ailing Jerry Lee Lewis), Suzy Bogguss (also a Lewis fill-in), Jimmy Hall, Restless Heart, Barbara Mandrell, Georgia Satellites, George Benson, B. B. King, Judy Collins, The Kinsey Report, Etta James

1990 Bill Cosby, B.J. Thomas, Lettermen, Bobby Goldsboro, Travis Tritt, Tanya Tucker, Michael McDonald, Tracy Chapman, Ricky

Van Shelton, Jason D. Williams, Dixie Hummingbirds, Mary Chapin Carpenter, Marcia Ball, 1964 (Beatles tribute)

1991 LaToya Jackson, Jason D. Williams, Laura Branigan, Four Tops, K.T. Oslin, Natalie Cole, Oak Ridge Boys, Julio Iglesias

1992 Gatlin Brothers, Bebe & CeceWinans, Vince Gill, Kenny Loggins, Queen Latifah, Patti Austin (a substitution for Woody Harrelson, who was making a movie), Bernadette Peters, Remingtons, Blind Boys of Alabama

1993 Glenn Frey, Joe Walsh, PM Dawn, Shai, Little Richard, Trisha Yearwood, REO Speedwagon, Joe Diffie, Jon Secada, John Gorka, Jason D. Williams, Subdudes, Ricky Lynn Gregg, Webb Wilder, Buckwheat Zydeco, Pat Upton, Cub Koda, Al Wilson, Len Barry, Sonny Geraci, Billy Childs, Preston Reed, Jennifer Daniels

1994 Neville Brothers, Crosby, Stills and Nash, Al Green, Peabo Bryson, Faith Hill, Luther "Guitar Jr."Johnson, Kathy Mattea, Indigo Girls, AJ Croce, Janis Ian, Richie Havens, Spyro Gyra, John Sebastian, Boy Howdy, The Impressions, Classic Rock All- Stars, Brewer and Shipley

1995 Confederate Railroad, Earth, Wind and Fire, Mary Chapin Carpenter, Mark Lindsay, Alison Krauss and Union Station, Gillian Welch and David Rawlings, All-4-One, Crickets, Chely Wright, Dion, Santana, Gary Puckett, Chubby Checker, Roger McGuinn, Beau Jocque, David Wilcox

1996 Brooks and Dunn, Temptations, Emmylou Harris, Four Tops, Shawn Colvin, Freddy Cole Trio, Dr. John, David Gates, Grassroots, T.S. Monk, Martha Reeves, Guess Who, Pam Tillis, Bodeans, Tommy James, Todd Snider, Rhonda Vincent, Glenn Yarbrough, Jerry Jeff Walker, BR-549, James McMurtry

1997 Charlie Daniels Band, Kool and the Gang, Don McLean, Paul Brandt, Taylor Dayne, Patty Loveless, James Brown, Richie Havens, Chaka Khan, Righteous Brothers, Fabulous Thunderbirds, Jason and the Scorchers, Marshall Chapman, Edgar Winter, Mila Mason, Guy Davis

1998 Doobie Brothers, Tinsley Ellis, Frankie Valli, Oak Ridge Boys, Maze with Frankie Beverly, Spencer Davis Group, Soul Asylum, LeAnn Rimes, KC & the Sunshine Band, Stephen Bishop, Black Oak Arkansas, Classic Rock All-Stars, Richard Marx, Roger McGuinn, Greg Kihn Band, Dee Dee Bridgewater

1999 Blue Oyster Cult, Aaron Tippin, Amazing Rhythm Aces, Bruce Hornsby, Jennifer Daniels, Johnny Rivers, Uncle Lightnin', Leon Russell, Isley Brothers, Peter Frampton, Donna Summer, Sawyer Brown, TS Monk, Jason D. Williams, Buckinghams, Susan Werner, John McEuen

2000 Alabama, Chicago, Morris Day and the Time, War, Jethro Tull, Rebecca Lynn Howard, Grassroots, Atlanta Rhythm Section, Impressions, Brad Paisley, Edwin McCain, Keith Harling, Letty and Georgia, Jason D. Williams

2001 Kenny Wayne Shepherd, Al Jarreau, Collective Soul, The Fixx, Karla Bonoff, Montell Jordan, EG Kight, Carman, Travis Tritt, JoDee Messina, Rascal Flatts, Leo Kottke, Goose Creek Symphony, Starship, Roger Alan Wade, Mothers Finest

2002 Lynyrd Skynyrd, The Gap Band, Art Garfunkel, Kirk Franklin, Blues Traveler, Montgomery Gentry, Lone Star, Delbert McClinton, Jason D. Williams, Little River Band, Dickey Betts, Mallary Hope, Norman Blake, The Cumberland Trio, Mother's Finest, Chubby Carrier, Jimmy Tawater, Nickel Creek, Pat Green, The Turtles (Flo and Eddie)

2003 Leon Redbone, Martina McBride, Blind Boys of Alabama, Molly Hatchet, The Tams, Dr. Hook, Goose Creek Symphony, John Michael Montgomery, Kim Richey, John Anderson, Joe Cocker, The Temptations (with Chattanooga Symphony Orchestra), Rebecca St. James, New Edition, Billy Preston, Everclear, Gary Wright, Edgar Winter, Al Stewart, Ambrosia, Firefall, Jennifer Daniels, James Rogers

2004 Keith Urban, Jason D. Williams, Little Big Town, Michelle Branch, Toby Mac, Randy Newman, John Lee Hooker Jr, LL Cool

J, Little Feat, Pat Green, Sara Evans, Todd Snider, Guy Clark, Keb Mo', Lee Roy Parnell, Michael W. Smith, Poco, Styx, The Impressions, Wet Willie

2005 Boys II Men, Kid Rock, The Newsboys, Cheap Trick, Rodney Crowell, Roger Alan Wade, Big & Rich, Pat Benatar, Jennifer Daniels, Colin Hay, Here Come the Mummies, Michael McDonald, Uncle Lightnin', Trace Adkins, Rhonda Vincent, Pure Prairie League, Spyro Gyra, Goose Creek Symphony

2006 Kenny Rogers (with Chattanooga Symphony Orchestra), Allman Brothers, Eric Church, Suzy Bogguss, Sam Bush, Al Di Meola, Jack Ingram, Sugarland, Trisha Yearwood, Hank Williams Jr., Audio Adrenaline, Los Lonely Boys, Gretchen Peters, Spinners, Yo Mama's Big Fat Booty Band, Angie Stones, Derek Trucks Band, Mustang Sally

2007 Ricky Skaggs, Blake Shelton, Steve Miller Band, Tim Wilson, The Bar-Kays, Dalton Roberts, Craig Morgan, Jars of Clay, Earth Wind and Fire, Avett Brothers, Alan Parsons, Chris Daughtry, Vince Gill, Allman Brothers, Roger Alan Wade, Randall Bramlett, Ten Years After

2008 Black Crowes, Josh Turner, ZZ Top, Mercy Me, Rodney Atkins, Burton Cummings, Anthony Hamilton, Little Big Town, Mark Farner, Ohio Players, Joe Bonamassa, America (with Chattanooga Symphony Orchestra), Bachman-Cummings Band, Alex Chilton Trio

2009 Willie Nelson, Montgomery Gentry, Steven Curtis Chapman, Midnight Star, Train, Commodores, Little Richard, Three Dog Night (with Chattanooga Symphony Orchestra), B-52s, Jake Owen, Angie Aparo, The Outlaws, Bernard Allison

2010 Sheryl Crow, Darius Rucker, Billy Currington, George Clinton (P-Funk), Overland Express, Alison Krauss, Joan Osborne (with Chattanooga Symphony Orchestra), David Nail, Bad Company, Charlie Daniels Band, Chris Hillman, Dan Baird, T. Graham Brown, Third Day, Jimmy Webb, Drivin' 'n Cryin', Grace Potter

2011 Alan Jackson, Starship featuring Mickey Thomas, Dirty Guv'nahs, Kellie Pickler, John Lee Hooker Jr., Secret Sisters, Uriah Heep, Huey Lewis and the News, Casting Crowns, Beach Boys, Miranda Lambert, The Machine (with Chattanooga Symphony Orchestra), Brian McKnight, Mitch Rossell, Maurice Williams and the Zodiacs

2012 Eric Church, Foreigner, Turtles (Flo & Eddie), Grassroots, Micky Dolenz, Gary Puckett, Buckinghams, Charlie Wilson, Cody McCarver, Commander Cody, Foghat, Chris Tomlin, Goo Goo Dolls, Roger Alan Wade, Here Comes the Mummies, Junior Brown, The Band Perry, Lauren Alaina, Gov't Mule, Blackberry Smoke

2013 Jake Owen, Newsboys, Gavin DeGraw (substituting for Weezer), The Malemen, James Rogers, Cody McCarver, Psychedelic Furs, CeeLo Green, Dierks Bentley, OAR, Moon Taxi, Tim Wilson, Hot Chelle Rae, Brandy, Lynyrd Skynyrd, Florida Georgia Line, 10,000 Maniacs, Strung Like a Horse, Larry Carlton Trio, The Beaters

2014 Corey Smith, Boston, Young the Giant, Widespread Panic, The Family Stone, Gary Allan, Joan Jett and the Blackhearts, Buddy Guy, Toby Mac, Justin Moore, Allen Stone, Dan & Shay

2015 Martina McBride, St. Paul and the Broken Bones, Matthew West, Little River Band, Gregg Allman, 3 Doors Down, Yacht Rock Revue, Leon Russell, Doug E. Fresh and Slick Rick, Hunter Hayes, Here Come the Mummies, Sam Hunt, Suzy Bogguss, War, Merle Haggard, Melissa Etheridge, Cole Swindell, Stone Temple Pilots, Molly Hatchet, Juice Newton, Exile

2016 Thomas Rhett, Heart, Latimore, For King and Country, Salt n Pepa, REO Speedwagon, Firefall, Ambrosia, Voices of Lee, Blood Sweat and Tears (featuring Bo Bice), Chris Young, Kane Brown, Here Come the Mummies, Brett Eldredge, Shovels and Rope, .38 Special, Trampled by Turtles, Chris Lane

2017 Toby Keith, Billy Joe Shaver, Corey Smith, Boz Scaggs, Ludacris, Brett Young, The Producers, Flaming Lips, Morris Day and the Time,

Don Felder, Old Dominion, George Thorogood and the Destroyers, James Rogers, Jason D. Williams, Kathy Tugman, Crowder, Yardbirds

2018 Hank Williams Jr., Wallflowers, Brett Young (substituting for Luke Combs, who had lost his voice), Flo Rida, Switchfoot, Third Eye Blind, Kelley Lovelace and Rivers Rutherford, Dustin Lynch, Bret Michaels, Tower of Power, Delbert McClinton, Mitch Rossell, Mitch Ryder, Convertibull

2019 Lionel Richie, Weezer, Macklemore, Keith Urban, Larkin Poe, Old Crow Medicine Show, Jimmie Allen, Mitch Rossell

The 2020 festival was canceled due to the COVID-19 pandemic.

Bessie Smith Strut headliners (ML King Blvd.)

8/25/83 Ramsey Lewis Trio, Odetta

6/17/85 Willie Dixon

6/16/86 Albert King

6/21/87 Lonnie Brooks

6/20/88 Rockin' Dopsie & the Zydeco Twisters

6/19/89 Clarence "Gatemouth" Brown

6/18/90 Koko Taylor, John Hammond, Dirty Dozen Brass Band

6/23/91 Johnny Winter

6/22/92 Johnny "Clyde" Copeland

6/21/93 Walter "Wolfman" Washington

6/20/94 Junior Wells

6/19/95 Buddy Guy

6/24/96 Luther Allison, EG Kight

6/16/97 Anson Funderburgh and the Rockets, Shirley Lewis

6/15/98 Charlie Musselwhite

6/14/99 Bernard Allison, Roger "Hurricane" Wilson

6/12/00 Lonnie Brooks

6/11/01 Kenny Neal

6/10/02 Liz Melendez

6/9/03 Roger "Hurricane" Wilson

6/14/04 Joan Baby

6/13/05 Tinsley Ellis

6/12/06 Walter "Wolfman" Washington

6/11/07 Watermelon Slim, Deacon Bluz & Holy Smoke Band

6/6/08 Trombone Shorty Andrews

6/8/09 Randy Pavlock

6/14/10 Kenny Neal

6/13/11 John Lee Hooker Jr.

6/11/12 Lionel Young Band

6/10/13 Pimps of Joytown

6/9/14 Bobby Rush

6/8/15 Theodis Ealey

6/13/16 Latimore

6/12/17 Wilson Meadows

6/11/18 Christone Kingfish Ingram

In 2019, the Strut was moved to October as part of the Riverbend Festival's new 4-night format.

10/5/19 B. Slade

The 2020 Strut was canceled due to the COVID-19 pandemic.

CHAPTER 7

More Outdoor Shows

Block Parties, Street Concerts, Outdoor Shows, Fairs, Festivals, and Nightfall

In addition to the outdoor shows at the Riverbend Festival, Lake Winnie, and the various ball parks, the Tennessee Valley kept open-air music fans happy at race tracks, ranches, fairgrounds, drive-in theaters, amphitheaters, closed-off city streets, parks, farms, pavilions, and even a miniature golf course.

These venues provided plenty of memorable moments. The Hamilton County fair (once known as the Interstate Fair) hosted several major country stars, as did the annual Fall Color Cruise in Marion County.

In early 1977, in the midst of a career lull, Kenny Rogers signed a contract to perform a summer show at the Blue Sky Drive-In Theater in Lafayette, Georgia. By the time his August show date arrived, Rogers had scored a surprise comeback with the number-one record, "Lucille." Rogers was suddenly besieged with offers from larger venues, but being a man of his word, he kept his commitment to the small town theater. Many of those in attendance in Lafayette couldn't believe that a star of Rogers' caliber was at their local drive-in.

Beginning in the early 1980s, radio station WSKZ (KZ-106) established a popular tradition by hosting various River Roasts, Raft Races, and other outdoor events, usually at Ross's Landing. The shows featured current and classic hit makers, and often included two headliners, playing on Friday and Saturday nights.

The band Alabama created another long-running annual event, the June Jam in Fort Payne, Alabama, which began in 1982 and continued through 1997. Most of the proceeds benefited Fort Payne area schools and charities. Each year the lineup included the biggest names in country music. Band members Randy Owen, Jeff Cook, and Teddy Gentry were all Fort Payne natives (and residents), and along with drummer Mark Herndon, they were responsible for donating hundreds of thousands of dollars to help their northeast Alabama neighbors.

Among the most frequent "outdoor" performers were southern rockers Charlie Daniels, the Marshall Tucker Band, 38 Special, Wet Willie, and Confederate Railroad. Traditional country stars like Ricky Skaggs, George Jones, and Merle Haggard also performed regularly under the stars.

Among the more unusual sightings were Brooke Hogan (and her famous dad, Hulk Hogan) at Sir Goony's Golf Center in Chattanooga, country star Johnny Paycheck at Boyd's Speedway, E Street sax star Clarence Clemons at the Hunter Museum, superstar George Jones at a "backyard jam" at a Soddy-Daisy restaurant, Grateful Dead founder Bob Weir at Cherokee Farms in Lafayette, Georgia, and flamboyant rock and roll pioneer Little Richard in the usually conservative confines of Cleveland, Tennessee.

One of the largest outdoor crowds for a single artist gathered at Chattanooga's Coolidge Park in 2011 to give a hero's welcome to north Georgia's own Lauren Alaina, returning home after a sensational run on TV's "American Idol."

Ross's Landing provided a great backdrop to several events beyond the Riverbend Festival, including the annual Three Sisters Bluegrass Festival, and the annual Southern Brewers Festival (1994-2017), each attracting top musical talent.

Coolidge Park became a fall hotspot in 2018 and 2019 with the Moon River Festival, a two-day musical event with a strong lineup of current and rising stars. Like most live shows, it was canceled in 2020 due to the coronavirus pandemic, but is expected to bounce back strong when social distancing is no longer required.

Nightfall, a Friday night tradition at Miller Plaza in downtown Chattanooga, is one of the city's most durable events. Beginning in

1988, the artists make up an eclectic mix of past, present, and future stars from genres including rock, soul, folk, and country music. The format allows local musicians to open for more widely known acts. Admission is free, and diversity is celebrated among the performing artists and the audience members.

Radio station J103 has had great success promoting Jfest, which they call "The Tennessee Valley's largest Christian music festival." The annual event has often been held at Camp Jordan Park in East Ridge (and more recently at the Tennessee Riverpark on Amnicola Highway), and has hosted the top recording artists in Contemporary Christian music. Station officials say the purpose is two-fold: "To provide wholesome entertainment for the entire family, and to evangelize those seeking hope."

Here are some of the highlights of Tennessee Valley outdoor shows:

5/1/38 Jack Savage and his Cowboys at Texas Ranch in Ringgold, GA

1940 Grandpa Jones at Texas Ranch in Ringgold, GA

9/24/67 Dolly Parton appeared with WMOC at Chattanooga-Hamilton County Interstate Fair at Warner Park

10/29/72 Chet Atkins, Grandpa Jones at Fall Color Cruise in Marion County, TN

9/17/73 Archie Campbell at Chattanooga-Hamilton County Interstate Fair (Bonny Oaks Drive)

9/18/73 Stringbean at Chattanooga-Hamilton County Interstate Fair

9/19/73 Lester Flatt at Chattanooga-Hamilton County Interstate Fair

10/28/73 Grandpa Jones, and Bonnie Lou and Buster at Fall Color Cruise in Marion County, TN

10/25/75 Roni Stoneman at Fall Color Cruise in Marion County, TN

7/28/77 Dr. Hook at Blue Sky Drive-In Theater in LaFayette, GA

8/11/77 Kenny Rogers, Stella Parton at Blue Sky Drive-In Theater in Lafayette, GA

5/29/78 Marshall Chapman at WSIM concert at Lake Chickamauga

7/4/78 Gene Cotton concert outside WFLI studio

6/2/79 Stillwater at Blue Sky Drive In, Lafayette, GA

9/6/79 Jeannie C. Riley at Hamilton County Fair (Amnicola Highway)

6/18/82 Pure Prairie League at Jaycee Fairgrounds (KZ-106 River Raft Race)

5/28/83 George Jones, Terri Gibbs, Vern Gosdin, Melba Montgomery, Sandy Croft, and Marti Brown at Dunlap Country Roundup

7/9/83 David Allan Coe, Danny Shirley, Con Hunley at July Jam at Powell's Crossroads in Marion County, TN

9/18/83 Ronnie McDowell and Steve Wariner in Dunlap, TN

7/3/84 Forester Sisters and Asleep at the Wheel at Downtown Block Party at Miller Park

7/3/85 Atlanta Rhythm Section at Downtown Block Party

10/4/85 Jim Ed Brown at Hamilton County Fair

6/14/86 Minnie Pearl, Jerry Clower, Ed Bruce, Gov. Lamar Alexander, Alex Haley at Tennessee Homecoming '86 program at Johnston Park, Cleveland, TN

7/3/86 Pure Prairie League at Downtown Block Party

9/1/86 Johnny Paycheck at Boyd's Speedway

7/3/87 Charlie Daniels Band, Asleep at the Wheel at Downtown Block Party

9/5/87 Jerry Lee Lewis, Jim Glaser, Ace Cannon at Raccoon Mountain Music Festival

7/3/88 Henry Lee Summer at Downtown Block Party

7/15/88 Roger Miller, Tanya Tucker, and Lyle Lovett taped a TNN special on the Mississippi Queen visiting Chattanooga

7/2/89 Edgar Winter, Leon Russell, Michael Damian at Downtown Block Party

7/14-15/89 Greg Volz and Fred "Rerun" Berry at Summer Jam at Eastgate parking lot

6/30/90 Foghat at Downtown Block Party

7/3/91 B. B. King at Downtown Block Party

7/23/91 Bill Monroe, Albert King, Don McLean, Bobby Blue Bland at 900 Market Street for 10th anniversary of Chattanooga's Five Nights Festival

5/16//92 Four Tops at Heritage Landing, Chattanooga for Children's Hospital

9/5/92 Wet Willie at Bluff Bash, Hunter Museum

5/1/93 Elvin Bishop at opening of Walnut Street Bridge

9/1/93 Confederate Railroad at Sale Creek Mountain

9/1/93 John Hartford at Chattanooga Nature Center

9/18/93 Clarence Clemons at Bluff Bash, Hunter Museum

5/19/94 Marty Stuart at Strawberry Festival in Dayton, TN

9/10/94 Impressions at Bluff Bash, Hunter Museum

9/9/94 Kevn Kinney of Drivin' and Cryin' at Ringgold Rocks flood relief concert at old L&N Depot

October 1994 Deana Carter at Fall Color Cruise in Marion County, TN

5/21/95 Aaron Tippin, Martina McBride at Frazier Farm in Ooltewah, TN

6/27/95 Sammy Kershaw and Forester Sisters at Lamar Alexander for President event at Thunder Farms in Ooltewah

9/2-3/1995 Lee Greenwood, Ronna Reeves, Paul Overstreet, J.D. Sumner and Stamps, Ricky Skaggs at Glory Days Country Music Festival at Bradley Industrial Park, Cleveland, TN

5/4/96 George "Goober" Lindsey at Down Home Days in Chickamauga, GA

7/4/97 Jim Ed Brown at Camp Jordan in East Ridge

9/20/97 George Jones at Charlie's in Soddy Daisy "Backyard Jam"

4/25/98 Marshall Tucker Band and .38 Special at the Kudzu Cook-off outside Whitfield County Courthouse in Dalton, GA

9/12/98 Steppenwolf at Camp Jordan in East Ridge

9/13/98 Ricky Skaggs at Camp Jordan

9/19/98 Keith Harling at Charlie's in Soddy-Daisy "Backyard Jam"

10/25/98 Eric Heatherly at Fall Color Cruise in Marion County, TN

4/24/99 Three Dog Night, Lovin Spoonful and the Association at Kudzu Festival in Dalton, GA

5/21/99 Blackhawk at Cricket Pavilion

5/22/99 Drivin 'n Cryin' at Cricket Pavilion

5/23/99 Collective Soul, Train at Cricket Pavilion

4/22/00 Steppenwolf at Kudzu Festival at Dalton Fairgrounds

5/6/00 Montgomery Gentry at Down Home Days in Chickamauga

10/15/00 Jason D. Williams at Cricket Pavilion

5/5/01 Clark Family Experience at Down Home Days in Chickamauga

5/19/01 Angie Winans, Ray J at WJTT Spring Jam at Cricket Pavilion

5/4/02 Ricky Skaggs at Down Home Days in Chickamauga

10/4/02 Joan Osborne, Derek Trucks at Cricket Pavilion

10/19/02 Charlie Louvin at Fall Color Cruise in Marion County, TN

5/3/03 Chris Cagle, Rebecca Lynn Howard at Down Home Days in Chickamauga

9/27/03 Sam Bush, John Prine and Gillian Welch at Cherokee Farms, Lafayette, GA

9/28/03 Merle Haggard, Confederate Railroad at Stage at South Cumberland, Monteagle, TN

10/19/03 Don Williams at Stage at South Cumberland

5/1/04 Charlie Daniels Band at Down Home Days in Chickamauga

5/8/04 Joe Nichols at Stage at South Cumberland

5/25/04 Beach Boys at Stage at South Cumberland

6/13/04 John Anderson, Confederate Railroad at Stage at South Cumberland

7/25/04 George Jones at Stage at South Cumberland

8/21/04 John Michael Montgomery at Stage at South Cumberland

9/5/04 Merle Haggard at Stage at South Cumberland

9/25/04 Kentucky Headhunters at Stage at South Cumberland

925/04 Bob Weir at Cherokee Farms, Lafayette, GA

9/25/04 Josh Gracin, Little Big Town at Whitewater Center, Ocoee, Cherokee National Forest

10/16/04 Rhonda Vincent at Stage at South Cumberland

10/16/04 Hulk Hogan, Brooke Hogan at Sir Goony's on Brainerd Road

5/7/05 Ronnie Milsap at Down Home Days in Chickamauga

5/22/05 Slim Thug, Nappy Roots at First Tennessee Pavilion

8/11/05 Jars of Clay at Rossville, GA Centennial

8/12/05 John Michael Montgomery at Rossville, GA Centennial

8/13/05 Montgomery Gentry at Rossville, GA Centennial

9/3/05 Marshall Tucker Band at Kimball, TN Fireworks Festival

10/31/05 Little Richard at Cleveland TN Block Party

5/6/06 Josh Gracin at Down Home Days in Chickamauga

5/5/07 Luke Bryan, Andy Griggs, Cody McCarver at Chickamauga GA Down Home Days

5/12/07 Mike Jones, Trey Songz at WJTT Spring Jam at First Tennessee Pavilion

9/1/07 David Lee Murphy, Tony Joe White at First Tennessee Pavilion

5/3/08 James Otto at Down Home Days in Chickamauga

5/30/08 Goose Creek Symphony at Evening Shade at Johnston Park in Cleveland, TN

5/1/09 Randy Houser at Down Home Days in Chickamauga

5/1/09 Henry Gross at Evening Shade at Johnston Park in Cleveland, TN

5/29/09 Leon Redbone at Evening Shade at Johnston Park in Cleveland, TN

7/18/09 Mark Wills, Jeff Bates and Trent Willmon at First Tennessee Pavilion

5/4/10 Kyle Petty (stock car driver) with singers Mark Collie and Kip Moore at Miller Plaza

5/7/10 Craig Fuller at Evening Shade at Johnston Park in Cleveland, TN

5/14/10 Jay and the Techniques at Evening Shade at Johnston Park in Cleveland, TN

5/28/10 Gregg Allman at First Tennessee Pavilion

8/17/10 Colbie Caillat at Northwest Georgia Bank Amphitheater in Ringgold, GA

5/6/11 Grascals at Boxcar Pinion Festival at Raccoon Mountain Campgrounds

5/12/11 Peter Rivera (Rare Earth) at Evening Shade at Johnston Park in Cleveland, TN

5/14/11 Lauren Alaina at Coolidge Park

5/21/11 Mother's Finest at Thunder Creek Harley Davidson on Lee Highway

5/21/11 Mallary Hope and Jacob Lyda, tornado relief concert at Tennessee Aquarium

7/14/11 Josh Turner tornado relief concert at Davis Cattle Co. Rodeo in Ringgold, GA

9/2/11 Eric Heatherly at Riverfront Nights, Ross's Landing

10/1/11 Charlie Daniels Band at Northwest Georgia Bank Amphitheater in Ringgold, GA

5/4/12 EG Kight at Evening Shade at Johnston Park in Cleveland, TN

5/25/12 Dennis Tufano (Buckinghams) at Evening Shade at Johnston Park in Cleveland, TN

6/28/12 Confederate Railroad at Northwest Georgia Bank Amphitheater in Ringgold, GA

5/30/13 Ron Dante (The Archies) at Evening Shade at Johnston Park in Cleveland, TN

6/29/13 Atlanta Rhythm Section at Camp Jordan in East Ridge

8/24/13 St. Paul and the Broken Bones at Southern Brewers Festival at Ross's Landing

9/29/13 Amazing Rhythm Aces at Hamilton County Fair

Dolly Parton and Carl Dean got married in Ringgold, Georgia on May 30, 1966.
(Origin unknown)

10/12/13 Booker T. Jones, Radney Foster at River Rocks Festival Block Party outside Tennessee Aquarium

9/13/14 Mike Snider of "Hee Haw" at Cowpea Festival in Charleston, TN

7/3/15 Tinsley Ellis on lawn of Bessie Smith Hall

4/24/16 Ricky Skaggs at South Pittsburg Cornbread Festival

5/14/16 Chris Janson at Boyd's Speedway

9/24/16 Arlo Guthrie at WTCI benefit, 8th and Chestnut Street

7/4/18 John Schneider, Cody McCarver at Harris Park in Dunlap, TN

9/8/18 Drew Holcomb, Trampled By Turtles, I'm With Her, Secret Sisters at Moon River Festival at Coolidge Park

9/9/18 Avett Brothers, Margo Price, Dirty Guv'nahs, Mavis Staples, Judah and the Lion at Moon River Festival at Coolidge Park

9/30/18 Charlie Daniels Band at Jasper Highlands

10/6/18 Luke Bryan, Chase Rice at Doug Yates Farm in Ringgold, GA

9/7-8/19 Jason Isbell, Brandi Carlile, St. Paul and Broken Bones, Moon Taxi, Josh Ritter, Drew and Ellie Holcomb at Moon River Festival at Coolidge Park

8/15/20 Jason D. Williams at Tennessee Riverpark

10/17/20 Here Come the Mummies at AT&T Field

10/25/20 For King and Country at Tennessee Riverpark

Everybody Loves Dolly

Did you know Dolly Parton was once a regular performer on Chattanooga TV? In the mid-1960s, she made the weekly trip from Nashville to the Channel 3 studio for "The Porter Wagoner Show." Before the videotape era, Porter took his busload of pickers and singers around the south for weekly shows on local TV stations. Monday night they might be in Birmingham, Tuesday in Chattanooga, Wednesday in Knoxville, and so on.

When I've spoken with Channel 3 employees of that era, they recalled Porter's bus pulling up to 1214 McCallie Avenue to unload their gear. There were tiny little dressing rooms in the building, used by newsmen, wrestlers, and country music stars. They tell me that Dolly, barely five feet tall, would "carry a box about as big as she was," which contained her gigantic wig. She would later emerge in full Dolly mode to sing her her solo number, usually followed by a duet with Porter.

She has another strong connection to the Chattanooga area. It's a popular myth that Dolly and Carl Dean were married at the Ringgold Wedding Chapel, or the Catoosa County Courthouse. Actually they exchanged vows at Ringgold Baptist Church on May 30, 1966. A historical marking tablet written by Randall Franks sits near there today. Carl was familiar with the area from having spent part of his youth on Missionary Ridge, and Dolly learned that couples could get

their marriage license and get married the same day in Ringgold. Plus, she said, it sounded good: Ring-gold was a good place to get hitched.

ROSS'S LANDING

River Jam, Tennessee River Roast:

6/7/86 Gregg Allman, Danny Shirley, Roger Alan Wade

6/6/87 Rare Earth, Ozark Mountain Daredevils

5/19/90 Delbert McClinton

6/2/90 Henry Lee Summer, Alethea, Beaters

5/17/91 Cornelius Brothers and Sister Rose

5/18/91 Steppenwolf

Leon Redbone plays an Evening Shade show at Johnston Park in Cleveland, Tennessee in 2009. (Allen Mincey)

6/1/91 Poco, Wet Willie, Outlaws

5/15/92 The Impressions

5/16/92 Mitch Ryder

Jason D. Williams (left, with Joel Beaver) has played many of Chattanooga's outdoor venues during his long career. (Joel Beaver)

6/6/92 Marshall Tucker Band, Molly Hatchet, Webb Wilder

6/5/93 Foreigner, Foghat

5/20/94 Clovers

6/3/94 Eddie Money

6/4/94 Starship, Dr. Hook

5/19/95 Jonathan Butler

5/20/95 Juice Newton, Goose Creek Symphony

6/2/95 Ricky Van Shelton

6/3/95 Atlanta Rhythm Section, Little River Band

Harry Connick Jr paid tribute to the five victims of the military terrorist attack in Chattanooga at a benefit concert in 2015 at Ross's Landing. (Jackie Griffey)

5/16/96 Steppenwolf, Amazing Rhythm Aces

5/31/96 Gary Puckett

6/1/96 ELO with Chattanooga Symphony Orchestra

5/17/97 Guess Who

8/2/97 Georgia Satellites, Molly Hatchet

5/20/00 .38 Special

5/4/02 Mark Farner

5/20/06 Kansas

(Other miscellaneous Ross's Landing Shows)

8/31/96 Montell Jordan, CeCe Penniston

8/30/97 Warren G, Usher

8/1/97 Georgia Satellites

8/2/97 Molly Hatchet, Overland

10/24/98 Lil Jon, Destiny's Child

8/24/02 Keith Sweat, Boys II Men

8/27/05 Sister Hazel at HOG rally

8/28/05 Steppenwolf at HOG rally

9/4/05 En Vogue, Tempations, Parliament/Funkadelic

8/13/06 Violent Femmes

9/2/11 Eric Heatherly at Riverfront Nights

10/5/12 Dailey & Vincent

9/16/15 Brantley Gilbert, Harry Connick Jr, and Samuel L. Jackson (Chattanooga Unite, a Tribute on the River, for the five servicemen killed in terrorist attack on July 16, 2015)

8/27/16 Jason D. Williams at Riverfront Nights

On August 18, 1965, then Chattanooga Free Press reporter Hugh Moore was assigned to cover the Beatles visit to Atlanta. It was one of thousands of concerts Moore has attended, spanning more than six decades. From left to right are Hugh Moore, Paul McCartney, Mayor Ivan Allen, Ringo Starr, George Harrison, and John Lennon. (Hugh Moore)

The Man of a Thousand Concerts

First, let me apologize for a slightly misleading headline. Hugh Moore has actually attended closer to two thousand concerts. That just sounded snazzier to me.

Hugh is a Chattanooga attorney who graduated from the McCallie School, Vanderbilt University, and Yale Law School. His personal music resume' includes playing clarinet in the McCallie band. He has practiced law for almost fifty years. He and his wife Jean have raised two adult daughters. Jean, he says, has attended "about ninety percent of the concerts with me."

Even with that impressive resume, Hugh's crowning achievement is his devotion to live entertainment. As Johnny Cash would say, "He's been everywhere man, he's been everywhere." Of course, that includes several Johnny Cash concerts.

Growing up in Chattanooga, Hugh's mom would take him to community symphony concerts at the Soldiers and Sailors

Memorial Auditorium. That began a lifetime love affair with musical performances of every genre. You name it, he's seen it. He finally began keeping a list of shows he attended in 1984, so he can only estimate the number he attended in the quarter-century prior to that. His best guess is around fifteen-hundred total, and many of those were at festivals with multiple acts and stages, like the Riverbend Festival.

He remembers the 1950s, when black and white artists could not perform together on the same stage in southern cities like Chattanooga, Birmingham, and Memphis. He recalls a 1957 show at Chattanooga's Memorial Auditorium when Fats Domino, Chuck Berry and the Drifters were allowed to appear, while Paul Anka, Buddy Holly and the Everly Brothers had to sit it out, literally, waiting outside in the bus.

He said, "I remember sitting in a car outside the Auditorium one hot night in the late 50s with my parents and brother, and seeing Fats Domino walk from his bus into the Auditorium. You could hear everything outside because the large windows were all open. This was before air conditioning."

As a ninth-grader, he got to see Louis "Satchmo" Armstrong, the legendary bandleader and trumpeter, at the University of the South in Sewanee, Tennessee. "This was really a treat because he led a racially mixed band, and they were not allowed to play in Chattanooga," Hugh said.

Much like today, the Chattanooga concert scene was not limited to only the Auditorium and the Tivoli Theater. In 1960, he saw the folk group the Brothers Four ("Greenfields") at the old Chattanooga High School on 3rd Street, now the Chattanooga School for Arts and Sciences.

Later in the 1960s, he spent summers and school breaks as a reporter for the Chattanooga News Free Press. He was assigned to cover and review several concerts for the paper, including an appearance by the Beatles at the new Atlanta Stadium on August 18, 1965. He attended the press conference that afternoon, even managing to squeeze into a photo with the Fab Four and Atlanta Mayor Ivan Allen.

While working for the newspaper, he also interviewed stars like Peter Noone of Herman's Hermits, and Peter and Gordon, among others. He also covered multi-star shows like the Motortown Revue, starring Marvin Gaye.

Since then, he and his wife have traveled thousands of miles to attend concerts, checking almost every big name off his list. Leonard Bernstein? Yep. The Rolling Stones? "Several times." Elvis? "Sure did, in Murfreesboro. We left about the time they announced 'Elvis has left the building.' We were heading to our car, and we see this big limousine, and there's Elvis, in the back seat, waving at us."

He considers Paul McCartney the best performer he has ever seen. "I've seen five or six of his shows," Hugh said, "and he never disappoints. He plays for about three hours, with no intermission, and the entire audience knows every single song."

There are so many indelible memories, of music stars at their best, and worst. He saw the Mamas and the Papas at the north Georgia amusement park Lake Winnie. "They had this look on their face, like, who booked us here?" he said with a laugh.

There was Eddie Money, who refused to perform his big hit, "Baby Hold On." Hugh recalls, "That was about the only one of his songs anyone knew, so that was weird." The same thing happened with the O'Jays in Chattanooga. "Everybody came to hear Love Train, and they didn't sing it."

He remembers Waylon Jennings performing with his back turned to the audience. There was the night fellow "outlaw" singer Jerry Jeff Walker was supposed to open for Willie Nelson, but didn't show.

Willie's band came out early to fill the time, and Jerry Jeff finally wandered on stage in the middle of Willie's set. "He was obviously drunk, waving his backpack around, and getting on Willie's nerves A few minutes later, two big guys dragged him off the stage. Willie was not pleased."

He has seen "both" Bob Dylans. He said, "I've seen him on various Chattanooga stages, inside and outside, and in Dalton too. You never know what you're going to get. Sometimes he just hangs his head and mumbles, but other times, he puts on a great show. That's just Bob."

However, most of his concert experiences have been well worth the price of admission. "I saw Peter Frampton in 2019 at the Tivoli in Chattanooga," Hugh said. "He played like there was no place in the world he would rather be."

"I've seen the Beach Boys, in their various incarnations, about fourteen times from 1965 to 2018," he said. "I would happily go again."

He also has high praise for some of the lesser known names on his list. "Delbert McClinton puts on a great show," he said." I can't leave out John Prine, and I love The Old Crow Medicine Show. Some of these acts are not necessarily superstars, but they are great live performers," he said.

When time permits, Hugh and Jean will hop on a plane to see a show, but it has to be special. "We've seen the reunion of Cream, and the reunion of the Rascals, both in New York City," he said.

He missed out on a few shows, and still has regrets. "Otis Redding and Joe Tex played Chattanooga in 1965, and for some reason or other I didn't go. Otis died two years later, and now Joe is gone too. I never did get to see them," he said.

He does have one pet peeve about attending live music shows, and it doesn't involve any of the performers. "It's these people who pay good money for a concert, and then they'll sit there and talk throughout the show, like they're watching TV," he said. "I don't understand that."

"I just love live music, all kinds of it, from concerts to plays," Hugh said. "I admire the creativity, and the energy."

With a smile, he recalls a reading from "King Lear" at the Tivoli Theater with Sir Michael Redgrave performing "Shakespeare's People." He said, "He was getting up in years, and at one point he obviously forgot his lines. He paused for a few seconds, and totally in character he said, "I know not what to say." Eventually someone prompted him, and he went on, but he never went out of character."

Hugh and Jean almost never miss a Chattanooga Symphony and Opera performance, but they're just as likely to be seen in the audience for Neko Case, ZZ Top, or Train. He has long been a Riverbend Festival board member, and he supports the area's outdoor concerts like the Nightfall series.

He concluded, "Sometimes younger people look at my wife and me, like aren't y'all too old to be here? We just laugh about it. We're still looking for more great shows. It has been time well spent."

3 Sisters Bluegrass Festival at Ross's Landing

10/5/07 Norman and Nancy Blake

10/3/08 Rhonda Vincent, Steep Canyon Rangers

10/4/08 Dan Tyminski

10/2/09 Grascals

10/3/09 Del McCoury Band

10/1/10 Ricky Skaggs

10/2/10 Cherryholmes

9/30/11 Hot Rize

10/1/11 Travelin' McCourys

Jean and Hugh Moore in 2020.

10/5/12 Yonder Mountain String Band, Dailey and Vincent

10/6/12 Steep Canyon Rangers, Travelin' McCourys

10/4/13 Sam Bush

10/5/13 Travelin' McCourys

10/3/14 Del McCoury

10/4/14 Devil Makes Three, Rhonda Vincent

10/2/15 Travelin' McCourys

10/1/16 Greensky Bluegrass, Bela Fleck and Angela Washburn, and Keller Williams

10/6/17 Del McCoury

10/7/17 Sam Bush

10/5/18 Infamous Stringdusters

10/6/18 Noam Pikelny

10/5/19 Steep Canyon Rangers, Dan Tyminski Bluegrass Band

Southern Brewers Festival (Original location was on Broad Street in front of Aquarium, moved to Ross's Landing in 2000)

8/27/94 Chubby Carrier

8/26/95 NRBQ

8/24/96 Anders Osborne

8/23/97 V-Roys

8/22/98 Kingsized

8/28/99 Trish Murphy

8/26/00 Leona Naess

8/25/01 The Derailers

8/24/02 Goose Creek Symphony

8/23/03 C. J. Chenier

8/28/04 Radiators

9/10/05 BoDeans, Uncle Lightnin'

8/26/06 Last Waltz Ensemble, Randall Bramblett Band

8/25/07 Randall Bramblett Band, Pat McLaughlin

8/23/08 Stratoblasters, Cherry Poppin' Daddies, Pat McLaughlin Band

8/22/09 Trombone Shorty

8/28/10 Big Head Todd and the Monsters

8/27/11 Los Lobos

8/25/12 Drive By Truckers, Chuck Leavell

8/24/13 Galactic, St. Paul and the Broken Bones

8/30/14 Big Something

8/22/15 Flow Tribe

8/20/16 Nick Lutsko

8/25/17 Magpie Salute

Nightfall (at Miller Plaza)

6/10/88 Karla Bonoff

8/26/88 Dave Mason

6/2/89 Taj Mahal

7/7/89 Anson Funderburgh and the Rockets

5/4/90 Christine Lavin, Livingston Taylor

5/12/90 T.G. Shepard with Chattanooga Symphony Orchestra

5/28/90 Leon Redbone

5/29/90 John Prine

8/31/90 Clarence "Gatemouth" Brown

9/14/90 Dave Brubeck

7/12/91 John Prine

8/30/91 Bela Fleck & Flecktones

9/10/91 Glenn Miller Orchestra

7/10/92 Lucinda Williams

7/17/92 Leo Kottke

8/21/92 NRBQ

8/28/92 Loudon Wainwright III

10/2/92 Confederate Railroad

5/28/93 Steve Forbert

7/9/93 Alison Krauss & Union Station

7/17/93 Joe Ely

9/10/93 Tuck and Patti

9/17/93 Charles Brown

9/24/93 Beth Neilson Chapman

7/15/94 Robert Earl Keen

7/29/94 Jr. Walker and the All Stars

8/12/94 Mac Gayden

8/19/94 Dan Hicks

9/21/94 Livingston Taylor

9/30/94 Hugh Masekela

6/2/95 Jr. Walker and the All Stars

6/20/95 Nelson

7/7/95 The Roches

7/14/95 Dave Hole

9/15/95 Charles Brown

8/2/96 Irma Thomas

8/9/96 Mitch Ryder

8/23/96 Keb Mo', Jim Wann

8/30/96 Rosie Flores

5/30/97 Barenaked Ladies

6/6/97 Kelly Willis, Bruce Robinson

7/25/97 Laura Love

7/27/97 Christine Lavin

5/30/98 Susan Tedeschi

7/17/98 Richard Thompson

8/14/98 Todd Snider

9/25/98 Norman Blake, Tony Rice

6/4/99 Maria Muldaur

7/23/99 A.J. Croce

7/30/99 Bela Fleck and the Flecktones

8/13/99 R.L. Burnside

9/24/99 Chubby Carrier

7/21/00 Doc Watson

8/4/00 Eric Heatherly, Uncle Lightnin'

9/15/00 Derek Trucks Band

6/1/01 Jesse Colin Young

7/6/01 Persuasion

7/13/01 Nickel Creek

8/10/01 Eddie Floyd

8/31/01 Steve Earle

5/31/02 Graham Parker

7/5/02 Brothers Johnson

9/6/02 Jesse Winchester

9/20/02 Leon Redbone

5/23/03 The Impressions

5/30/03 Here Come The Mummies

8/8/03 Terence Martin

8/29/03 NRBQ

9/26/03 Del McCoury Band

5/28/04 Billy Joe Shaver

7/30/04 Larry Carlton

9/3/04 Janis Ian

5/27/05 Buckwheat Zydeco

7/8/05 Marcia Ball

7/22/05 Ladysmith Black Mambazo

8/5/05 Marshall Crenshaw

9/2/05 Black Keys

9/23/05 Adrian Belew

6/23/06 Junior Brown

6/30/06 Susan Cowsill

9/29/06 Bettye LaVette

5/12/07 Mike Jones, Trey Songz

5/25/07 Chris Thile

6/22/07 Cadillac Sky

9/28/07 Howard Jones

5/30/08 Karla Bonoff

8/8/08 Michelle Shocked

8/22/08 Robben Ford

8/29/08 Hal Ketchum

7/10/09 Dan Baird

9/11/09 Carlene Carter, Roger Alan Wade

9/2/10 Bo Bice

8/3/12 Strung Like a Horse

6/28/13 Lake Street

7/19/13 Allen Stone

8/9/13 Aaron Brown

8/7/15 David Mayfield

9/3/15 Malpass Brothers

6/3/16 Nick Lutsko

7/7/17 Shawn Mullins

7/21/17 Fastball

7/27/17 The Greyhounds

6/20/19 Jessy Wilson

Jfest (Camp Jordan, East Ridge 1999-2008, 2010-18)

1999

Michael W Smith, Russ Taff, Bob Carlisle, Cheri Keaggy, Crystal Lewis, Natalie Grant, Heather Miller (Friday's Promise, Scott Tatum, Church Alive Band)

2000

4Him, Out of the Grey, Layton Howerton, The Darins, Watermark, Ginny Owens

2001

Salvador, Sonic Flood, Tammy Trent, The Darins, Watermark, Jake

2002

Avalon, The Katinas, Greg Long, Cheri Keaggy, Clay Crosse, Erin O'Donnell

2003

Newsong, Big Daddy Weave, Ronnie Free3man, The Darins, Paul Coleman Trio, Whisperloud

2004

Audio Adrenaline, Casting Crowns, Zoegirl, Warren Barfield, (Megan Roberson, Sammy Ward)

2005

Casting Crowns, Big Daddy Weave, Building 429, Erin O'Donnell, Overflow, Jaime, Fusebox, Tree63

2006

Chris Tomlin, Caedmons Call, Natalie Grant, Building 429, Matthew West, Joel Engle, Joanna Martino, Warren Barfield

2007

Mercy Me, David Crowder Band, Newsong, Apologetix, Warren Barfield, Cheri Keaggy, 33Miles, David Klinkenberg, Cheri Keaggy, (Vince Stalling, The Turning) (Will Graham-Evangelist)

2008

Big Daddy Weave, Newsong, Matthew West, Building 429, Steve Fee, Scott Krippayne, Vicki Beeching, Nate Huss, (Metro Praise, Haley McGuire, Sound Method, Tabernacle, Team Impact-Jeff Neal)

2009 (Abba's House)

Salvador, Building 429, FFH, Mark Harris, John Waller, Francesca Battistelli, (Tabernacle, Chelsie Boyd, The Birdsongs, Eight Days After, 22 Visionz, They Came Running, Team Impact-Jeff Neal)

2010

Lincoln Brewster, Barlow Girl, Matthew West, Natalie Grant, 33Miles, Aaron Shust, Britt Nicole, Matt Maher, Jonny Diaz, Sidewalk Prophets,

Among the Thirsty, (Blue City Band, Calling Glory, Too Many Drummers, Comedian Thor Ramsey)

2011

Big Daddy Weave, Salvador, Francesca Battistelli, Bebo Norman, Addison Road, The Museum, Among the Thirsty, New World Son (Team Impact, Tom Coverly-Illusionist, Jeff Bodley, Battle for Christ Local Band Competition Finalist)

2012

Kutless, Building 429, Sidewalk Prophets, Dara Maclean, Chris August

2013

Jeremy Camp, Sanctus Real, Royal Tailor, Kerrie Roberts, Jason Gray, Luminate, City Harbor, Adam Cappa, Calling Glory

2014

Mandisa, Building 429, Thett Walker Band, Chris August, Finding Favour, Calling Glory, Unspoken, Love & The Outcome, (They Came Running)

2015

For King and Country, Sanctus Real, Royal Tailor, Finding Favour, Tim Timmons, I Am They, Moriah Peters, Blanca, Capital Kings

2016

Crowder, Jamie Grace, Chris August, 7th Time Down, Jason Gray, Hollyn, Zealand Worship (Mending Wall)

2017

Jeremy Camp, Sanctus Real, Family Force Five, Ryan Stevenson, Zach Williams, Hollyn, Micah Tyler, Gawvi

2018

Tenth Avenue North, Britt Nicole, Unspoken, Calling Glory, Finding Favour, The Color, Mallary Hope, The Young Escape, Aaron Cole

2019 (Tennessee Riverpark)

Lecrae, Matthew West, Building 429, Riley Clemmons, Ryan Stevenson, Tauren Wells, The Young Escape

Calhoun GA Musicland

5/14/82 Ronnie Milsap

5/21/82 Louise Mandrell

6/5/82 Marty Robbins

6/12/82 T. G. Sheppard

6/26/82 Ray Stevens, Whitewater Junction

7/10/82 Loretta Lynn

8/21/82 Roy Clark, Whitewater Junction

8/28/82 Ronnie McDowell, Lee Greenwood

9/4/82 Con Hunley, Gail Davies

9/18/82 Brenda Lee, Gene Watson

9/25/82 Merle Haggard, Leona Williams

10/9/82 Alabama

10/23/82 Hank Williams Jr.

10/30/82 Tom T. Hall

4/23/83 Lee Greenwood, Ricky Skaggs

5/14/83 Marshall Tucker Band, Bobby Bare

5/21/83 Merle Haggard, Leona Williams

6/25/83 Mel Tillis

7/1/83 Ronnie Milsap

7/16/83 Don Williams, New Grass Revival

7/29/83 Emmylou Harris, Con Hunley

8/6/83 T. G. Sheppard, Steve Wariner

8/13/83 George Jones

8/20/83 Johnny Rivers, Atlanta

9/3/83 Charley Pride, Whitewater Junction

10/8/83 Beach Boys

10/29/83 Jerry Lee Lewis

6/8/84 Beach Boys

7/21/84 Drifters, Coasters

8/4/84 George Jones

5/4/85 Emmylou Harris, Vern Gosdin

8/24/85 Merle Haggard

Concerts in the Country, Calhoun GA
5/3/86 Conway Twitty, Jerry Clower

6/7/86 Oak Ridge Boys, Williams & Ree

7/26/86 Charley Pride, Dan Seals

8/23/86 Waylon Jennings, Jessi Colter, Vern Gosdin

9/6/86 Ray Stevens, Sawyer Brown

9/26/86 Merle Haggard, Reba McEntire

10/4/86 Johnny Cash, June Carter Cash, Billy Joe Royal

10/18/86 Alabama, Kathy Mattea

4/25/87 Lee Greenwood, Forester Sisters

5/23/87 Randy Travis, Gene Watson

6/20/87 Conway Twitty, Holly Dunn

7/18/87 Sawyer Brown, John Schneider

7/25/87 Ricky Skaggs, T. Graham Brown

8/8/87 Judds, Southern Pacific

8/15/87 George Jones, Sweethearts of the Rodeo

10/3/87 Alabama, Pake McEntire

10/10/87 Oak Ridge Boys, Kathy Mattea

5/28/88 Randy Travis, Kyle Petty

7/9/88 Reba McEntire

7/23/88 Waylon Jennings, Exile

8/27/88 Dan Seals, Ronnie McDowell

9/10/88 Nitty Gritty Dirt Band, Highway 101

9/24/88 Ronnie Milsap, KT Oslin

10/15/88 Bill Gaither Trio, Gaither Vocal Band

10/22/88 Ray Stevens, Jerry Clower

5/12/90 Kenny Rogers, Skip Ewing

6/2/90 Ray Stevens, Patty Loveless

6/30/90 Statler Brothers, Suzy Bogguss

7/21/90 Merle Haggard, Vern Gosdin

8/18/90 Charlie Daniels Band, Billy Joe Royal

9/15/90 Earl Thomas Conley, William Lee Golden

10/6/90 Sawyer Brown, Eddy Raven

4/27/91 Judds, Pirates of the Mississippi

5/25/91 Vern Gosdin, Gene Watson

6/29/91 Travis Tritt, Holly Dunn

7/13/91 Lee Greenwood, Diamond Rio

8/3/91 Conway Twitty, Loretta Lynn

9/28/91 Reba McEntire, Vince Gill

10/5/91 Waylon Jennings, Charlie Daniels Band

7/11/92 Kathy Mattea, Paul Overstreet

7/18/92 Sawyer Brown, Mark Collie

7/26/92 Wayne Newton

8/15/92 Conway Twitty, George Jones

9/12/92 Kitty Wells, Grandpa Jones, Jett Williams, Pee Wee King, Bill Monroe, Ralph Emery

10/16/92 Ricky Van Shelton, Collin Raye

10/30/92 Billy Ray Cyrus, Mark Collie

5/8/93 Doug Stone, John Michael Montgomery

6/12/93 Wynonna Judd, Collin Raye

7/10/93 George Jones, Tracy Lawrence

7/16/93 Vince Gill, Radney Foster

8/14/93 Kathy Mattea, Hal Ketchum

9/25/93 Charlie Daniels Band, Restless Heart

10/16/93 Tanya Tucker, Aaron Tippin

5/7/94 Marty Stuart, T. Graham Brown

6/3/94 Diamond Rio, Patty Loveless

7/23/94 Aaron Tippin/John Berry

9/30/94 Confederate Railroad, Marshall Tucker Band

10/8/94 John Anderson, Little Texas

10/16/94 Doug Stone, Doug Supernaw

7/2/95 Clay Walker

June Jam, Fort Payne, Alabama

6/4/82 Alabama, Janie Fricke, Louise Mandrell, RC Bannon, Oak Ridge Boys

6/11/83 Alabama, Janie Fricke, Lee Greenwood, William Lee Golden

6/9/84 Alabama, Janie Fricke, Lee Greenwood, Ed Bruce, Bill Medley, Ralph Emery

6/15/85 Alabama, Judds, Eddy Raven, Ralph Emery, Bill Medley, Charlie Daniels Band, Glen Campbell, Bellamy Brothers

6/14/86 Alabama, Willie Nelson, Gary Morris, Forester Sisters, Charlie Daniels, Mark Gray, Mel Tillis

6/13/87 Alabama, John Schneider, Oak Ridge Boys, Restless Heart, Percy Sledge, Sawyer Brown, The Shooters, Carl Perkins, Michael Johnson

6/11/88 Alabama, Restless Heart, Charlie Daniels Band, Exile, Carl Perkins, Travis Tritt, Steve Earle, KT Oslin, Eddy Raven, Sawyer Brown, Mel McDaniel, Sweethearts of the Rodeo, The Shooters, Dan Seals, Ricky Van Shelton, Bellamy Brothers

6/10/89 Alabama, Ricky Van Shelton, Southern Pacific, Eddie Rabbitt, Nitty Gritty Dirt Band, Buck Owens, Charley Pride, Skip Ewing, Gatlin Brothers, Bellamy Brothers, Charlie Daniels Band

6/9/90 Alabama, Dolly Parton, Clint Black, Lorrie Morgan, Alan Jackson, Travis Tritt, Asleep at the Wheel, Baillie and the Boys, Holly Dunn

6/15/91 Alabama, Garth Brooks, Baillie and the Boys, Doug Stone, Mark Chesnutt, Aaron Tippin, Joe Diffie, Clint Black, Neal McCoy,

Alan Jackson, Trisha Yearwood, Ricky Van Shelton, Vince Gill, Ray Kennedy

6/13/92 Alabama, Travis Tritt, Wet Willie, Vince Gill, Ricky Van Shelton, Billy Ray Cyrus

6/12/93 Alabama, Alan Jackson, Sawyer Brown, Confederate Railroad, Vince Gill, Diamond Rio, Tracy Lawrence, Pam Tillis, Collin Raye, Michelle Wright, John Anderson, Neal McCoy, Clinton Gregory, Confederate Railroad

6/11/94 Alabama, Vince Gill, John Berry, Aaron Tippin, Diamond Rio, Patty Loveless, Michelle Wright, Confederate Railroad, Neal McCoy, Lee Roy Parnell, Steve Wariner, Clinton Gregory, Mark Collie.

6/10/95 Alabama, Vince Gill, Toby Keith, Ty England, Neal McCoy, Shelby Lynne, Doug Supernaw, Confederate Railroad, Chely Wright, George "Goober" Lindsey

6/15/96 Alabama, Oak Ridge Boys, Neal McCoy, Brooks and Dunn, Vince Gill

6/21/97 Alabama, Tracy Lawrence, Cledus T. Judd, Dennis Haskins, Neal McCoy, Billy Ray Cyrus, Daron Norwood, Heartland

CHAPTER 8

Convention Centers

Chattanooga Convention Center

The long discussed, long delayed "civic center" Chattanooga leaders had wanted finally became a reality on April 18, 1985 on Carter Street in the downtown area. Almost immediately, events that had long been held at Soldiers and Sailors Memorial Auditorium (including car shows, boat shows, and the Home Show) made use of the roomy exhibit halls at the new facility.

A 1979 feasibility study was dismissed by some critics, who said the city already had sufficient exhibition hall space, and more than enough performance stages. But the tide began to turn in 1982, when political and business leaders determined such a facility would benefit the city.

Soon after the center opened, large banquets that had outgrown the Read House, the Sheraton Hotel, and the Chattanooga Choo Choo ballroom switched to the Convention Center, which was first referred to as the "Convention and Trade Center." A popular annual event was Siskin Children's Institute's fundraiser "StarNight," usually held in August or September.

Many visiting speakers and musical acts have played the Convention Center, often in conjunction with charity fund-raising luncheons and dinners.

An expansion completed in 2003 tripled the original size of the facility. Here is a partial listing of the entertainers who have appeared at the Chattanooga Convention Center:

4/23/85 Forester Sisters at Lung Association Gala

8/29/87 Tony Bennett/Henny Youngman

9/16/89 Rich Little

2/23/90 Peabo Bryson, Four Tops

9/8/90 Melissa Manchester

3/1/91 Gladys Knight, Impressions

9/7/91 Ben Vereen

9/12/92 Marilyn McCoo

12/31/92 Joe Diffie

3/12/93 Whispers, Sinbad

9/18/93 Mary Wilson

3/18/94 Peabo Bryson, Roberta Flack

4/27/94 George Duke, Rachelle Ferrell with Chattanooga Symphony Orchestra

9/10/94 Spinners

4/14/95 Four Tops, Phyllis Hyman, George Wallace

9/9/95 Lou Rawls

3/15/96 Jerry Butler, Patti Austin

7/16/96 Ted Nugent, Bad Company

8/17/96 Susan Anton, Jason D. Williams

4/11/97 Peabo Bryson, O'Jays

9/13/97 Crystal Gayle

8/29/98 Suzanne Somers

4/23/99 Ashford and Simpson, Temptations

8/28/99 Gary Morris

3/24/00 Smokey Robinson, The Emotions

9/9/00 Lorrie Morgan

4/27/01 Jeffrey Osborne, Regina Belle, The Manhattans

9/8/01 Four Tops

3/22/02 Teddy Pendergrass, Stylistics

9/14/02 Spinners

12/5/02 Roberta Flack

4/5/03 Smothers Brothers with Chattanooga Symphony Orchestra

9/19/03 Three Mo Tenors

12/4/03 Nancy Wilson

8/28/04 Kenny Rogers

3/26/04 Gerald & Eddie Levert

4/3/04 Patti LuPone and Chattanooga Symphony Orchestra

11/20/04 Clarence Carter, Shirley Brown, Latimore

12/31/04 Wet Willie

4/24/05 Patti LaBelle

9/10/05 Emmylou Harris

4/21/06 En Vogue

8/26/06 LeAnn Rimes

4/27/07 Jeffrey Osborne, Stephanie Mills

8/10/07 B. J. Thomas and Billy Joe Royal at Shriner's Convention

9/1/07 Hootie and the Blowfish

10/20/07 Brick

12/14/07 Jennifer Holliday

4/18/08 Angie Stone, Joe

8/16/08 Sugarland

4/17/09 Fantasia

4/19/09 Phil Stacey

7/8/09 David Cook

8/22/09 Boys II Men

3/19/10 Babyface Edmonds

8/28/10 Trisha Yearwood

9/13/11 Kenny Rogers

5/19/12 Isley Brothers, Morris Day and the Time

7/21/12 Nicholas Sparks, Bill & Giuliani Rancic

7/22/12 Cheryl Burke and Mark Ballas

8/25/12 Josh Turner

5/11/13 Kool and the Gang, Monica

9/7/13 Wilson Phillips

4/12/14 Charlie Wilson

5/15/14 Kelley Lovelace, Craig Morgan

8/6/14 Colbie Caillat

4/25/15 Ledisi

8/22/15 The Band Perry

8/20/16 Kevin Costner with band Modern West

4/8/17 Eddie Levert, Impressions

4/27/17 Chris Janson, Kelley Lovelace

8/26/17 Sheila E.

8/25/18 LOCASH

8/24/19 Plain White T's

Actor Kevin Costner has an enjoyable "side gig" playing music with his band Modern West. He's shown here after a Siskin StarNight show in 2016 with Tennille and Gator Harrison.

Chattanooga Choo Choo Convention Center, 1400 Market Street

Chattanooga's old Terminal Station, no longer a railroad hub, was in danger of being demolished in 1973, when a group of investors decided to capitalize on the "Chattanooga Choo Choo" song, popularized in the 1940s by the Glenn Miller Orchestra. The newly refurbished Chattanooga Choo Choo Hilton and Entertainment Complex featured live music from local entertainers almost nightly, with occasional visits by nationally known performers. In fact, the baggage room was converted into the Station House, with singing waiters and waitresses. The Station House also served as the launching pad for singer-songwriter James Rogers, a north Georgia native who would go on to national fame, and a close association with Dolly Parton.

In 1989, the facility was upgraded again, and renamed the Chattanooga Choo Choo Hotel.

Country music duo LOCASH headlined Siskin StarNight in 2018.
(Don Luzynski Photography)

James Rogers, a hometown guy who has never forgotten his roots.

James Rogers, our local treasure

Talk about an unsung hero: how about James Rogers!

He's a yes man if there ever was one, and I mean that in a good way. James says yes each and every time he is asked to raise funds for his hometown, and other places near and far. If the funds raised will benefit children, he will say yes even quicker.

During a career that has spanned more than forty years, he has picked up his guitar and sang to millions of satisfied listeners. Never a frown, and no sign of any ego trips or temper tantrums.

My friendship with James goes back many years. I didn't know him when he was a kid, but he has often told the story of how that first guitar under the Christmas tree changed his life. He was 11 years old, and there has been a guitar by his side ever since.

While working at filling stations, drug stores, factories, supermarkets, and construction sites, James would sneak away during breaks teaching himself to "finger-pick," classical style. After high school and college, he planned to go to law school. Several well-meaning adults had told him he needed a real career. He could still fool around with music on weekends, they said. He was accepted by three schools of law.

We will never know what a great attorney he might have been. As is so often the case, fate intervened and put him where he was supposed to be. A Chattanooga nightclub needed a fill-in act for a couple of weeks, and James just happened to be available. The "fill-in" guy became permanent, at least until the National Guard called.

After his service was over, James talked his way into an audition at the Chattanooga Choo Choo Station House, where he became a local legend. As the featured attraction at the Station House, James did what we all aspire to do: he embarked on a career that allows him to say, "I've never worked a day in my life." You can say that if you're fortunate enough to do something you love.

Along the way, he married his beautiful wife Debbie, and they raised two great children, Heather and Justin. James gives Debbie much of the credit, because a performer's life is spent on the road. For many years he shared America's stages with the biggest names in music, most notably Dolly Parton.

It was Dolly who saw such potential in James that she made him the marquee name at the Music Mansion in Pigeon Forge during much of the 1990s. When I went to see his show, I was lucky to get a seat. It was another in a long string of nightly sellouts. I said to the lady at the box office, "I'm an old friend of James, but do the rest of these folks even know who he is?" She said, "No, not when they get here. But they do when they leave." She added, "When people ask about his show, we tell them if they're not totally satisfied, they can get their money back on the way out." I said, "Does that ever happen?" She said, "Never. Not once. They keep coming back for more."

12/9/73 Jerry Reed hosts NBC's "Music Country USA" from the Choo Choo.

11/14/75 Frank Sinatra Jr.

9/16-17, 1976 Jimmy Buffett

12/31/79 Dr. Hook, Overland Express

11/30/84 Jerry Clower (benefit for Boyd Buchanan School)

5/10/87 MDA concert featuring Forester Sisters, Gary Morris, Rockin' Sydney, James Rogers, Bellamy Brothers, Nicolette Larson, Asleep at the Wheel

9/11/87 Gary Morris

9/25/87 Ronnie Milsap

10/2/87 Ray Stevens

10/9/87 Mickey Gilley

10/16/87 Sawyer Brown

10/30/87 Temptations

11/6/87 Eddie Rabbitt

11/17/87 Coasters, Drifters, Platters

12/7-8, 1997 Forester Sisters

4/15/88 Keith Sweat, Melissa Morgan

10/29/88 Woody Herman Orchestra at Siskin Star Night at Choo Choo

12/3/95 The Beaters

8/22/96 Eddie Money

9/6/96 Three Dog Night

11/1/97 Goose Creek Symphony

5/6/03 Fannie Flagg

12/31/03 Wet Willie

12/31/04 Wet Willie

9/6/09 Eric Church

9/11/10 Luke Bryan

12/2/11 Jars of Clay

12/30/11 Avett Brothers

12/31/11 Dirty Guv'nahs

10/3/13 Natalie Stovall

Dalton (Georgia) Convention Center

The "Carpet Capital of the World," Dalton, Georgia proved worthy of its own convention center, which opened in 1991. The first manager was Clyde Hawkins, who had left Chattanooga's Soldiers and Sailors

Memorial Auditorium in 1988 after eighteen years on the job. His challenge was to build what was then known as the "Northwest Georgia Trade and Convention Center" from the ground up. In addition to entertainment show, the Convention Center is home to the Georgia Athletic High School Coaches Hall of Fame, and has hosted basketball and arena football games. The facility is located at 2211 Dug Gap Battle Road in Dalton. Here are some of the Convention Center's best-attended shows:

9/19/91 Lewis Grizzard

8/3/92 Billy Ray Cyrus, Roger Alan Wade

12/4/92 Drivin 'n Cryin'

10/17/93 Sawyer Brown, Mark Chesnutt

6/9/94 Hank Williams Jr./Roger Alan Wade

3/18/95 Danny Davis & the Nashville Brass

5/8/99 Willie Nelson

1999 Charlie Daniels Band

9/22/99 B B King, Tower of Power, Kenny Wayne Shepherd

11/17/00 Kenny Rogers

Jan 4, 2001 Jeff Foxworthy/Third Day

4/27/01 Bill Cosby

5/2/01 Bob Dylan

11/23/01 Oak Ridge Boys

3/23/02 Brad Paisley, Neal McCoy, Lee Roy Parnell

9/20/02 Eric Heatherly

1/26/02 George Jones

11/30/02 Lee Greenwood

2003 (date unknown) Marshall Tucker Band

10/2/04 Ronnie Milsap

9/20/08 Casting Crowns (SELLOUT)

10/7/11 James Gregory

10/5/12 Lauren Alaina

6/22/19 Jason Crabb

CHAPTER 9

Sports Celebrities

C hattanooga is not a major league city but has become a popular stop for the biggest names in sports.

In fact, although Chattanooga's sports programs are not in the Southeastern Conference, the giants of the SEC have spent many a day in the city. Whether they're recruiting, speaking, playing for charity, or just meeting with fans and alumni, our short drive, or quick plane hop from many SEC schools make us a frequent destination.

The reasons for Chattanooga's importance in the sports world are many and varied. The city has a long history with baseball, led by Joe Engel, one of the greatest minor league owners (and promoters) in the sport's history. It has produced a number of star high school players in every major sport. From the city's prestigious private schools to its storied public schools, scholarship athletes have made their way to successful college and professional careers.

Many wealthy business owners and civic leaders have helped build championship level golf courses and tennis facilities, attracting the superstars of those sports for business endorsements, exhibition matches, and charity tournaments.

Chattanooga's proximity to nearby major league cities has encouraged players and coaches from Atlanta and Nashville to visit regularly for fan-oriented events. (Check out some of the Atlanta Braves caravan lists from the 1960s and 1970s: they brought all the big names.)

It may be hard for current-day fans to believe, but from the 1930s through the 1950s, Chattanooga's Engel Stadium attracted major league teams each year for spring training exhibition games. In some cases, two big league teams played each other, and on other dates, a major league team would play against the minor league Lookouts. Chattanooga was a convenient stop between the teams' Florida spring training sites and their home ballparks, so an exhibition game or two at Engel served as a way to stay loose after spending long stretches on the road. As a result, most of the legendary stars of the mid-century took the mound or swung a bat in Chattanooga. The New York Yankees, one of the top teams of that era (or pretty much any other), were among the most frequent visitors.

In 1931, a teenage girl pitching phenom famously struck out Yankee stars Babe Ruth and Lou Gehrig in an Engel Stadium exhibition game. About fifteen years later, Red Sox great Ted Williams sent a baseball sailing over the right field wall. In the 1950s, future home run king Henry Aaron would make his Engel Stadium debut. Around the same time, Jackie Robinson, the first player of color to play in the big leagues would become a regular visitor to Engel, both as a member of the Dodgers, and his own traveling "colored" team. (In the 2010s, Robinson's legacy came full circle when the movie about his life, "42" was partially filmed in Engel Stadium.)

Long before he gained fame for challenging Billie Jean King to a "battle of the sexes" tennis match in 1973, Bobby Riggs was a frequent visitor to Chattanooga, playing exhibition matches from 1940 to 1958.

In the 1940s and 1950s, promising high school and college football stars like Frank Sinkwich, Johnny Unitas, and Paul Hornung played on local fields. Steve Spurrier played here too, but his sport was baseball at the time.

A 15-year-old kid named Willie Mays got his professional start playing on a Negro League team in Chattanooga in 1945. He became one of the best players to ever wear a major league uniform.

Throughout the 1960s, Chattanooga was practically a second home for the most famous golfer in the world, Arnold Palmer. He owned the company which manufactured golf clubs bearing his name, and it was located in Chattanooga. Needless to say, he usually played a few rounds of golf during his local visits, and often brought along famous friends.

Although Chattanooga rarely hosted big-name professional boxing bouts, our Soldiers and Sailors Memorial Auditorium welcomed many former heavyweight champs as guest "referees" for pro wrestling matches. One such champ, Evander Holyfield visited numerous times in a different capacity, as the guest of youth boxing coach Joe Smith.

For sheer longevity, Leroy "Satchel" Paige deserves special mention. His pitching appearances span a 33-year period, from his days with the "Black Lookouts" in 1926 to an exhibition game at Engel Stadium in 1959, at the age of 53.

Along the way, practically every head coach of every sport at the University of Tennessee stopped in to either recruit players, speak to civic groups, or greet avid Vols fans. Despite Chattanooga having its own fine college teams, the city has always shown strong support for "the big brother" school in Knoxville.

The Fellowship of Christian Athletes has strong local chapters as well, and has brought in many of sports' biggest names to speak at its annual gatherings. Fran Tarkenton, Bart Starr, and Tom Landry are just a few household names who visited with FCA students.

Just as the Pat Boone Bethel Bible Village concert series brought in Hollywood stars and top-selling musical acts, the Boone golf tournament hosted some of the biggest names in sports each May. It was one of many charity tournaments, like the ones hosted by hometown baseball hero Rick Honeycutt, that attracted famous athletes.

Chattanooga's premier golf and tennis facilities have attracted young athletes who went on to phenomenal careers, including Tiger Woods, Chris Evert, and Jimmy Connors, all of whom played the city's courses and courts in their teens.

Peyton Manning has a home in the Chattanooga area, and fellow football superstars like Reggie White, Terrell Owens, Bill Curry, and Ray Oldham either attended school or resided in Chattanooga. Manning, White and Owens are in the Pro Football Hall of Fame, Curry played ten seasons in the NFL, and Oldham earned a Super Bowl ring as part of the Pittsburgh Steelers defense in 1978. Since 2016, Ridgeland High standout Vonn Bell has become a mainstay of the New Orleans Saints secondary. Many others are listed below.

In the 21st century, the Chattanooga Times Free Press sports department has hosted superstar athletes and coaches each year at its

Best of Preps banquet, honoring top high school stars. In prior years, the annual Scrappy Moore Awards banquet also brought in big-name speakers.

Of course, star athletes are human too, so not every superstar has pleasant memories of their time spent in Chattanooga. While a Dodgers minor league hopeful in 2013, Lookouts outfielder Yasiel Puig was ticketed for speeding (97 mph) in front of the Chattanooga Police Department on Amnicola Highway. He was soon called up to the big league team, but had to make a return visit to Chattanooga for a court appearance. The prosecutor dropped charges after Puig produced proof of twelve hours of community service he had performed in Los Angeles.

Here are highlights of Chattanooga's sports history, beginning with the years prior to 1930:

Apr. 11, 1885 the Chicago White Stockings played the Chattanooga Lookouts, with future Hall of Famers Cap Anson and King Kelly in the lineup.

In 1904 Ty Cobb played at Andrews Field (site of the future Engel Stadium)

July 6-10, 1920 golfer Bobby Jones won Southern Amateur championship at Chattanooga Golf and Country Club.

9/26/1922 Pro golfer Walter Hagen plays an exhibition at Chattanooga Golf and Country Club. He played a course record 66.

2/22/1923 Baseball Commissioner Judge Kenesaw Mountain Landis spoke to a combined meeting of the Rotary Club and the American Legion at the Hotel Patten. He said his first visit to the area was in 1888, when he joined his father, who was a Union soldier in the Civil War, at a 25 year reunion of the Battle of Chickamauga.

4/5/1925 Babe Ruth and NY Yankees played an exhibition game at Andrews Field, in front of 8,000 fans. "The Sultan of Swing" hit two home runs. He was in Chattanooga five times between 1925 and 1934.

Lou Gehrig, Jackie Mitchell, Joe Engel, and Babe Ruth at Engel Stadium in 1931.
(Chattanooga Lookouts)

In 1926, Satchel Paige played at Andrews Field as part of the Chattanooga White Sox (of the Negro Southern League).

5/27/1928 Pro golfer Bobby Jones played an exhibition at Chattanooga Golf and Country Club.

10/17/1928 Pro golfers Johnny Farrell and Gene Sarazen played an exhibition at Chattanooga Golf and Country Club.

The 1930s

From 1930 to 1933 Arch McDonald was the radio announcer for the Chattanooga Lookouts on WDOD. Starting in 1934, he began calling major league games for the Washington Senators, and for one year, the New York Yankees. He also called pro football games for the Washington Redskins. He was a graduate of Chattanooga's McCallie School, and in 1999, he was posthumously honored with the Ford Frick Award, enshrining him into the broadcasters' wing of the Baseball Hall of Fame.

4/10/30 Babe Ruth, Lou Gehrig & New York Yankees were among the players in a baseball exhibition game at the new Engel Stadium vs. The Chattanooga Lookouts

4/2/31 Babe Ruth and Lou Gehrig famously struck out against 18-year-old female pitcher Jackie Mitchell in an exhibition game between the Chattanooga Lookouts and New York Yankees at Engel Stadium.

4/5/31 Pro golfer Walter Hagen played an exhibition at Chattanooga Golf and Country Club.

4/3/32 Washington Senators (managed by Walter Johnson) played Chattanooga Lookouts in exhibition game at Engel Stadium. Carl Reynolds was the Senators' hitting star.

4/5/32 The St. Louis Browns played the Chattanooga Lookouts in an exhibition game at Engel Stadium. Rick Ferrell and Goose Goslin were among the standouts for the Browns.

4/7 and **4/8, 1932** the Cleveland Indians played the Chattanooga Lookouts in an exhibition game at Engel Stadium. Indians' stars included Wes Ferrell and Earl Averill.

4/3/33 Washington Senators played Chattanooga Lookouts in exhibition game at Engel Stadium. Senators' stars included Joe Cronin and Goose Goslin.

4/4/33 Detroit Tigers played Chattanooga Lookouts in exhibition game at Engel Stadium. Tigers' stars included Charlie Gehringer, Whitlow Wyatt, Jo Jo White, and Pete Fox.

4/9 and **4/10, 1934** New York Yankees play Chattanooga Lookouts in two exhibition games at Engel Stadium. Yankees stars include Babe Ruth, Lou Gehrig, Tony Lazzeri, and Bill Dickey.

4/4 and **4/5, 1936** Washington Senators play Chattanooga Lookouts in exhibition game at Engel Stadium. Buddy Myer and Buck Newsome were among the Senators' stars.

4/12/37 New York Yankees (1936 World Series champions) played Chattanooga Lookouts in exhibition game at Engel Stadium. It was called the "greatest array of talent" ever to play at the stadium by a local newspaper columnist. Yankees stars included rookie outfielder Joe DiMaggio, Bill Dickey, Lou Gehrig and Tony Lazzeri.

4/15/37 St. Louis Cardinals played Chattanooga Lookouts in exhibition game at Engel Stadium. Cardinals stars included Joe "Ducky" Medwick, Pepper Martin, Leo Durocher, and Frankie Frisch.

In 1938, Baseball Hall of Famer Rogers Hornsby was player/manager of the Lookouts at Engel Stadium.

4/10/38 Philadelphia Phillies played the Chattanooga Lookouts at Engel Stadium in an exhibition game. Phillies stars included Gene Corbett and Frank Morehouse.

In 1939, Baseball Hall of Famer Kiki Cuyler became player/manager of the Lookouts.

4/7/39 and **4/8/39**, Philadelphia Phillies played Chattanooga Lookouts in exhibition games at Engel Stadium. Chuck Klein, Al Hollingsworth, and Dick Lanahan were among the Phillies standouts.

5/10/39 Pro golfers Sam Snead and Gene Sarazen played at Chattanooga Golf and Country Club and appeared at Martin-Thompson Sporting Goods on Cherry Street

The 1940s

4/6/40 Detroit Tigers played Brooklyn Dodgers in exhibition game at Engel Stadium. Tigers stars included Hank Greenberg, Birdie Tibbetts, Dodgers stars included Pee Wee Reese, Luke Hamlin, and Charley Gilbert.

4/10/40 Philadelphia Athletics played Chattanooga Lookouts in exhibition game at Engel Stadium. Athletics stars included Wally Moses and Sam Chapman, and manager Connie Mack.

5/12/40 Archie Henderson defeated Bobby Riggs in Tennessee Valley Invitational tennis at Chattanooga Tennis Club. Riggs and Alice Marble won a doubles match.

4/30/41 Bobby Jones played at Chattanooga Golf and Country Club

5/1/41 Golfer Bobby Jones played in Rotary Golf Tournament, and spoke to Rotary Club at Chattanooga Golf and Country Club

5/3/41 Bobby Riggs defeated Billy Talbert in Tennessee Valley Invitational tennis at Chattanooga Tennis Club

Nov. 1942 Frank Sinkwich, who would go on to win the Heisman Trophy, played for the University of Georgia vs. University of Chattanooga at Chamberlain Field

12/4/44 Jimmy Conzelman, coach of the Chicago Cardinals of the NFL, spoke to Quarterback Club

In parts of 1945 and 1946, future Baseball Hall of Fame member Willie Mays, at the age of 15 and 16, played for the Chattanooga Choo Choos of the Negro Southern League at Engel Stadium.

11/19/45 Major League Baseball commissioner A. B. "Happy" Chandler spoke to the Rotary Club at the Hotel Patten.

12/4/45 Georgia Tech football coach Bobby Dodd spoke to Quarterback Club at Chattanooga Golf and Country Club

4/7/46 Detroit Tigers played the Boston Braves in an exhibition game at Engel Stadium before a crowd of 9,300 fans. Braves players included Al Dark, Billy Herman, Warren Spahn, and Johnny Sain. Tigers players included Dizzy Trout, Paul Richards, Billy Hitchcock, and George Kell.

4/11/46 Pro golfers Byron Nelson and Lawson Little played an exhibition at Chattanooga Golf and Country Club, and were also guests of the Rotary Club

6/5-9/46 Bobby Riggs, Fred Perry, Bill Tilden, and Frank Kovacs at Chattanooga Tennis Club pro tennis tournament on First Street

New York Giants outfielder Willie Mays and Brooklyn Dodgers pitcher Don Newcombe were part of a "colored" All-Star troupe that toured the country in the mid-1950s, including exhibition games at Engel Stadium. (Origin unknown)

4/7/47 Boston Red Sox played the Cincinnati Reds in an exhibition game at Engel Stadium. Red Sox star Ted Williams cleared the right field wall with a massive home run. Other Red Sox stars included Johnny Pesky, Bobby Doerr, and Dom DiMaggio. Reds players included Grady Hatton and Bert Haas.

4/9/47 Washington Senators played the Philadelphia Phillies in an exhibition game at Engel Stadium. Phillies stars included Andy Seminick, Frank McCormick, and Del Ennis. Senators stars included Earl Wooten, Mickey Vernon, and Luman Harris.

8/22/47 Future actor Chuck Connors, then a player for the Mobile Bears of the Southern League, hit a home run against the Chattanooga Lookouts at Engel Stadium

From 1947-50, former University of Chattanooga running back Gene "Choo Choo" Roberts played in the NFL.

The 1950s

4/7/50 Pittsburgh Pirates played Chattanooga Lookouts in exhibition game at Engel Stadium. Pirates stars included Wally Westlake, Danny Murtaugh, and Clyde McCullough.

4/21/50 Pro golfers Sam Snead and Cary Middlecoff played an exhibition at Chattanooga Golf and Country Club

5/3/50 Bobby Riggs, Jack Kramer, and Pancho Gonzales at new McCallie School gym in tennis exhibition

7/28/50 Arnold Palmer, a student at Wake Forest University plays in Tennessee Valley Invitational amateur tournament at Chattanooga Golf and Country Club

7/8/51 Pro golfer Ben Hogan played at Chattanooga Golf and Country Club

10/17/51 Jackie Robinson, Sam Jethroe, Minnie Minoso, Larry Doby, and other "Negro major leaguers" play an exhibition (against the Indianapolis Clowns) before 8,000 fans at Engel Stadium

4/6/52 Boston Braves vs. Brooklyn Dodgers exhibition game at Engel Stadium. Braves pitchers Warren Spahn and Ernie Johnson combined to pitch a no-hitter. Preacher Roe was the starting pitcher for the Dodgers. Other Dodgers standouts included Pee Wee Reese, Duke Snider, Jackie Robinson, and Roy Campanella. Braves stars included Sam Jethroe, Earl Torgeson, Eddie Matthews, and Walker Cooper. The Lookouts' single season attendance record was set in 1952 with 252,703 fans. Cal Ermer was Lookouts manager.

10/30/52 Paul Hornung (future Heisman Trophy winner) played at Chamberlain Field for Louisville's Flaget High School vs. Chattanooga Central High School. The game ended in a 7-7 tie.

10/31/52 Johnny Unitas (future NFL superstar quarterback) played for the University of Louisville vs. University of Chattanooga at Chamberlain Field. UC won 47-17.

1/21/53 Georgia football coach Wally Butts spoke to Dalton Quarterback Club

4/4/53 Brooklyn vs. Milwaukee exhibition baseball at Engel Stadium. Dodger players included Jackie Robinson, Duke Snider, Pee Wee Reese, George Shuba, and Don Zimmer. Braves players included Eddie Matthews, Ernie Johnson, Ebba St Claire, and Ben Thorpe.

10/14/53 Roy Campanella and an "all colored" team played an exhibition game at Engel Stadium.

10/17/53 Jackie Robinson, Gil Hodges, Al Rosen, Ralph Branca and other stars in exhibition game vs. Indianapolis Clowns at Engel Stadium

4/5/54 Brooklyn Dodgers and Milwaukee Braves played an exhibition game at Engel Stadium. Braves players included Lew Burdette, Eddie Matthews, and the "touted Negro star from Jacksonville, Henry Aaron." Dodgers players included Jackie Robinson, Duke Snider, Rube Walker, and Junior Gilliam.

4/6/54 Boston Red Sox and Milwaukee Braves played an exhibition game at Engel Stadium. Braves players included Ernie Johnson and Henry Aaron. Red Sox players included Willard Nixon and Joe Dobson. The Braves were managed by Charley Grimm, and the Red Sox were managed by Lou Boudreau.

8/18/54 NFL Exhibition game featuring Chicago Cardinals vs. Chicago Bears at Chamberalin Field, playing before 10,000 fans. Among the players were quarterback Zeke Bratkowski (who played at Georgia) of the Bears. and fellow Georgia standout Charley Trippi of the Cardinals, who spoke to Georgia fans at a luncheon earlier in the day.

9/17/54 Bobby Dodd, Georgia Tech football coach, spoke to Rotary Club at Hotel Patten

1/12/55 Georgia head football coach Wally Butts spoke to Bulldog Alumni Club at Hotel Patten

4/3/55 Milwaukee Braves vs. Brooklyn Dodgers in exhibition baseball game at Engel Stadium. Braves players included Chuck Tanner, Joe Adcock, Andy Pafko, Del Crandall, and Johnny Logan. Dodgers stars included Pee Wee Reese, Duke Snider, Roy Campanella, Gil Hodges, Jackie Robinson, and Carl Furillo.

4/4/55 New York Yankees vs. Chattanooga Lookouts in exhibition baseball game at Engel Stadium.. Yankees stars included Mickey Mantle, Yogi Berra, Hank Bauer, Ed Lopat, and Johnny Sain,

10/13/55 Frank Leahy, former Notre Dame football coach, spoke to Rotary Club

10/17/55 National League baseball "colored" all-stars (including Henry Aaron, Ernie Banks, Willie Mays, Don Newcombe) managed by Roy Campanella) vs American League "colored" all-stars (including Larry Doby) at Engel Stadium

4/9/56 Washington Senators vs. Cincinnati Redlegs exhibition baseball at Engel Stadium: Senators players include Clint Courtney, Roy Sievers,

Jim Lemon, and Eddie Yost. Redleg stars include Gus Bell, Smokey Burgess, Ted Kluszewski, Art Fowler, and Joe Nuxhall.

8/5/56 Mason Rudolph wins Tennessee Amateur Open at Chattanooga Golf and Country Club.

4/6/57 Exhibition baseball game at Engel Stadium: Washington Senators vs. Cincinnati Reds. Senators players included Jim Lemon, Dean Stone, Ted Abernathy, Eddie Yost, and Pete Runnels. Reds stars included Frank Robinson, Ted Kluszewski, Art Fowler, Gus Bell, and Wally Post.

6/11/57 Longtime major league baseball player and manager Chuck Dressen visited Engel Stadium

8/16/57 Tennessee football coach Bowden Wyatt speaks to Civitan Club at Hotel Patten

3/29/58 Pro golfer Tommy Bolt played at Chattanooga Golf and Country Club

4/10/58 Boston Red Sox played Chattanooga Lookouts in exhibition game at Engel Stadium. Red Sox players included Ted Williams, Willard Nixon, Pete Runnels, Jimmy Piersall, and Ken Aspromonte.

8/17/58 Bobby Riggs plays tennis exhibition at Castle in the Clouds, Lookout Mountain, GA

9/18/58 Georgia Tech football coach Bobby Dodd speaks to Rotary Club at Hotel Patten

7/30/59 Tennessee football coach Bowden Wyatt speaks to Rotary Club at Hotel Patten

From 1959-65 former University of Chattanooga football player Bill Butler was a safety in the NFL.

9/10/59 Leroy "Satchel" Paige, 53-year-old pitcher, played in exhibition game at Engel Stadium: Detroit Stars vs. Kansas City Monarchs. Paige, who pitched in the majors, got his start with the Chattanooga White Sox of the Negro Southern League in 1926.

10/28/59 Pro golfers Miller Barber and Dave Ragan visited First Flight Golf in Chattanooga.

The 1960s

3/22/60 Wally Butts, Georgia head football coach, spoke at banquet for University of Chattanooga athletes at First Cumberland Presbyterian Church

5/18/60 Golf pro Dave Ragan played exhibition at Rivermont Golf Club.

From 1960-63, former University of Chattanooga quarterback Johnny Green played in the American Football League.

4/13/61 Pro golfer Gary Player visited First Flight in Chattanooga.

In 1961, Steve Sloan graduated from Bradley County High School. He played football for the University of Alabama, and was a quarterback for two years in the NFL.

2/17/62 Army football coach Paul Dietzel, Arkansas football coach Frank Broyles, and players Raymond Berry, Steve Sloan, Fran Tarkenton, Bill Wade, Bill Krisher and others spoke at FCA rally at various churches

3/18/62 Golf pro Gene Littler played exhibition at Rivermont Golf Club.

7/26/62 Former heavyweight boxing champ Ezzard Charles referees pro wrestling at Memorial Auditorium

9/20/62 Former heavyweight boxing champ "Jersey Joe" Walcott referees pro wrestling at Memorial Auditorium

1963-66 Jimmy Connors and Brian Gottfried, future tennis greats, played at Manker Patten from ages 11-14, winning several national doubles and junior championships.

From 1963-67 former University of Chattanooga safety Jim Bradshaw played in the NFL.

5/13/63 Pro golfers Arnold Palmer and Gary Player visited First Flight in Chattanooga.

6/4/63 Science Hill High School (Johnson City) right-hander Steve Spurrier pitches in state baseball championship at Engel Stadium (Spurrier was a three-sport athletic star)

9/26/63 Former heavyweight boxing champion Archie Moore referees wrestling at Memorial Auditorium

11/18/63 Golfer Arnold Palmer spoke at All-Sports banquet at the Read House.

3/8/64 Newly hired Tennessee football coach Doug Dickey spoke to Quarterback Club members at the Hotel Patten

4/10/64 Philadelphia Phillies (managed by Gene Mauch) played the Pittsburgh Pirates (Danny Murtaugh) in an exhibition game at Engel Stadium. Pirates players included Bob Veale, Wilbur Wood, Vern Law, Bob Priddy, Elroy Face, Bill Mazeroski, Roberto Clemente, Bill Virdon, and Willie Stargell. Phillies players included Richie Allen, Jim Bunning, Dallas Green, Bobby Wine, Johnny Callison, Cookie Rojas, and Pat Corrales.

8/11/64 Pro golfer Arnold Palmer played an exhibition game at Valleybrook Golf Club in Hixson (5,000 fans attended), and later that night, he presented a $1,000 check to the United Fund at the Pan O Ram Club on Lookout Mountain.

11/24/64 Dick Sisler, manager of Cincinnati Reds, spoke at All-Sports banquet at the Read House.

3/15/65 Jasper TN native, and former Vanderbilt quarterback Bill Spears, a member of the College Football Hall of Fame spoke to Quarterback Club

Arnold Palmer played "regularly" at Chattanooga Golf and Country Club in the 1960s, including **3/26/65**, according to longtime employees

12/14/65 Atlanta Braves manager Bobby Bragan, shortstop Denis Menke, and broadcaster Ernie Johnson Sr. spoke at All-Sports banquet at Hotel Patten

2/2/66 Bobby Bragan (manager), Joe Torre, Mack Jones, Mike de La Hoz, Dixie Walker (scout) and Milo Hamilton (broadcaster) at Braves caravan at Dupont plant, Siskin Memorial Foundation, Combustion Engineering, Lookout Sporting Goods, Martin-Thompson Sporting Goods.

12/1/66 Bud Wilkinson, ABC-TV football analyst and former Oklahoma football coach, spoke to All-Sports awards banquet at Hotel Patten

1/24/67 Ray Mears, Tennessee basketball coach, spoke to Chattanooga Jaycees at Hotel Patten

2/16/67 Dallas Cowboys football coach Tom Landry spoke to FCA members at Provident Cafeteria.

2/16/67 Atlanta Falcons owner Rankin Smith spoke to Rotary Club at Hotel Patten

3/10/67 Arnold Palmer plays at Chattanooga Golf and Country Club (and visited city often in later years due to his partnership in the Arnold Palmer Golf Co. in Ooltewah)

5/4/67 NY Giants quarterback Fran Tarkenton spoke to FCA annual banquet at Provident Cafeteria.

In 1967, Bobby Scott graduated from Rossville (GA) High School. He played quarterback for the Tennessee Volunteers from 1968 to 1971, and then played ten years in the NFL as a quarterback for the New Orleans Saints.

In 1967, Bob Johnson graduated from Bradley County High School. He then played football for the University of Tennessee Vols, and went on to a 12-year career in the NFL as an offensive lineman.

In 1967, David Roller graduated from Rhea County High School. He played football at the University of Kentucky, and played defensive tackle for seven years in the NFL.

In 1967 and 1968, John Hannah played football at Chattanooga's Baylor School. He later was a star player at the University of Alabama, and later played for the New England Patriots from 1973 to 1985.

10/5/67 Former NY Yankee 2nd baseman Bobby Richardson spoke to FCA members at Provident Cafeteria.

2/5/68 Clete Boyer (Atlanta Braves) speaks to Quarterback Club

2/9/68 Braves Caravan at Read House, Chattanooga Coca Cola and Boys Club on Highland Park Avenue, featuring Clay Carroll, Pat Jarvis, Bob Uecker, and Phil Niekro

7/27/68 Chris Evert (age 13) wins National 14s tennis championship at Manker Patten Tennis Courts

8/10/68 National wrestling champion Lou Thesz wrestles at Memorial Auditorium

11/21/68 Tennessee sports broadcaster John Ward spoke at Chattanooga Advertising Club at Read House

12/5/68 Former heavyweight boxing champion Joe Louis referees wrestling at Memorial Auditorium

1/27/69 Milo Hamilton (announcer), Bob Uecker (announcer), and players Pat Jarvis and Ron Reed speak to Quarterback Club as part of Braves Caravan

5/1/69 Dallas Cowboys football star Don Perkins spoke to FCA annual banquet at Provident Cafeteria.

5/3/69 O.J. Simpson spoke at Maclellan Gym and to University of Chattanooga Mocs football players in a locker room talk. His visit was sponsored by the Mental Health Association

Heavyweight boxing champion Muhammad Ali "spars" with WRCB sports director Jerry Wilson during a 1976 interview at Club Lakeshore in Chattanooga. (Jerry Wilson)

6/11-12/69 Mickey Mantle appeared at grand opening of Mickey Mantle Men's Shop at Eastgate Mall

8/14/69 Tennessee football coach Doug Dickey spoke to Rotary Club at Read House, and to Tennessee fans at Provident Cafeteria

10/25/69 Quarterback Terry Bradshaw, later a Pittsburgh Steeler Super Bowl champion, led Louisiana Tech to a 55-7 victory over the University of Chattanooga Mocs at Chamberlain Field.

12/17/69 Harmon Killebrew of Minnesota Twins, and former Chattanooga Lookout, spoke at All-Sports Banquet at Tivoli Theater

The 1970s

Dave Bristol, Baylor school alumnus, and longtime manager of Cincinnati Reds, Milwaukee Brewers and Atlanta Braves spoke frequently to Chattanooga Quarterback Club in 1970s and 1980s

The longtime radio voice of University of Tennessee Volunteers football and basketball, John Ward (right) is pictured with WDEF radio general manager Ben Cagle in 1979. (Ben Cagle)

Eddie Brown, a Marion County High 1970 graduate, played football for the University of Tennessee, and from 1974 to 1979 he played in the NFL for the Los Angeles Rams, Washington Redskins, and Cleveland Browns.

5/11/70 Atlanta Falcons coach and Philadelphia Eagles quarterback Norm Van Brocklin spoke to Quarterback Club

8/6/70 Pro golfer (and 3-time Masters champion) Jimmy Demaret spoke to Rotary Club at Hotel Patten

8/13/70 Alabama football coach Paul "Bear" Bryant, former Georgia football coach Wally Butts, Tennessee football coach Bill

Battle, and Clemson football coach Frank Howard attended the retirement dinner for UTC football coach A.C. "Scrappy" Moore at the Parliament Club.

10/15/70 Former NY Yankee 2nd baseman Bobby Richardson spoke to FCA members at Provident Cafeteria.

1/12/71 Phil Niekro, Ron Reed, Sonny Jackson, Hoyt Wilhelm, Bob Didier, and Cecil Upshaw at Braves caravan at Read House and Orange Grove Center

2/4/71 Tennessee football coach Bill Battle spoke to FCA members at Provident Cafeteria.

3/10/71 Soviet Union wrestling team vs. USA wrestling team, featuring future Olympian Dan Gable at UTC's Maclellan Gym in exhibition, with 4,500 fans in attendance. "Strongest man in the world" Paul Anderson also performed.

3/22/71 Georgia Tech football coach Bud Carson spoke to Quarterback Club at the Downtowner

4/28/71 Tennessee basketball coach Ray Mears spoke to Quarterback Club at thd Downtowner

From 1971 to 2012, former University of Chattanooga football player Joe Lee Dunn coached numerous college football teams.

2/12/72 Jesse Owens, American track and field star, and 4-time Gold Medalist, spoke at All-Sports Banquet at Read House

9/9/72 Pro Football Hall of Famer Sam Huff at Quarterback Club event at UTC Maclellan Gym and to the Rotary Club at Hotel Patten

Feb. 1973 Darrell Evans and Milo Hamilton (broadcaster) at Braves caravan

3/31/73 Bethel Bible School golf tournament with Vanderbilt Coach Steve Sloan, Herman Weaver, Chicago Bears coach Abe Gibron, Ray Oldham, and Bobby Majors at Creeks Bend Golf Club

From 1973 to 1979, longtime New York Giants running back Joe Morrison was head coach of the UTC Mocs football team.

In 1973, Charles Hannah graduated from Baylor School. He later played football at the University of Alabama, and was an offensive lineman for 12 years in the NFL.

11/24/73 Ed "Too Tall" Jones (future Dallas Cowboy) played defensive tackle for Tennessee State in their 44-7 win over UTC at Chamberlain Field

Feb. 1974 Eddie Matthews (manager) Braves Caravan

May 1974 Bethel Bible School golf tournament, with Steve Sloan, Kyle Rote Sr., Kyle Rote Jr., Jimmy Piersall, Luke Appling, Ray Oldham, John Hannah.

8/15/74 Former Washington Redskins star Charlie "Choo Choo" Justice played at Chattanooga Golf and Country Club

9/26/74 Professional wrestler (and sometime actor) Andre the Giant made his first appearance at Memorial Auditorium. He would perform at the Auditorium a total of eight times between 1974 and 1989.

1/23/75 Clyde King (manager), Marty Perez, Joe Niekro, Phil Niekro, Buzz Capra, Mike Lum, and Darrell Evans at Braves caravan at Choo Choo Hilton and Lookout Sporting Goods

1975-1982 Mickey Mantle played in golf tournament that bears his name at Battlefield Golf Club in Fort Oglethorpe, with Sam Huff, Ray Oldham, and Joe Morrison

5/23/75 Tom T. Hall golf tournament for Bethel Bible School, with Hall, Chet Atkins, Johnny Unitas, Jerry Reed, Luke Appling, and Bill Battle at Creeks Bend Golf Club.

6/29/75 Texas Tech head football coach Steve Sloan played in Archie Campbell Invitational Golf Tournament at Rolling Hills in Cleveland, TN.

9/11/75 Former NY Yankee 2nd baseman Bobby Richardson spoke to FCA members at Hungry Fisherman in East Ridge

10/16/75 NBA exhibition game: Atlanta Hawks (Connie Hawkins, Lou Hudson, Tom Van Arsdale, Herm Gilliam) vs. New Orleans Jazz (Pete Maravich, Louie Nelson, Nate Williams) at UTC's Maclellan Gym, with more than 4,000 fans packing the gym.

1/2/76 Tennis stars Roscoe Tanner, Bob Lutz, Bill Martin, and Dennis Ralston were among those competing in the Commerce Union Bank-Junior League Tennis Classic at Memorial Auditorium.

1/28/76 Braves caravan with Dave Bristol (manager)

2/23/76 Vanderbilt football coach Fred Pancoast spoke to Quarterback Club at Admiral Benbow Inn.

5/13/76 Dallas Cowboys football coach Tom Landry spoke to FCA annual banquet at Provident Cafeteria.

5/15/76 Tom T. Hall golf tournament for Bethel Bible School with Hall, Tommy Nobis, Darrell Royal, John Hannah, Bill Battle, and singer Ronnie Dove at Creeks Bend

6/3/76 Muhammad Ali dined at Club Lakeshore while discussing buying prayer rugs from Salem Carpets

6/26/76 Texas Tech head football coach Steve Sloan played in Archie Campbell Invitational Golf Tournament at Rolling Hills in Cleveland, TN.

1/17/77 Dave Bristol (manager), Phil Niekro, Buzz Capra, Rowland Office, and Jerry Royster at Braves caravan

2/10/77 Atlanta Braves manager Dave Bristol spoke at Cleveland Old Timers Hall of Fame banquet at Holiday Inn of Cleveland.

4/13/77 UT Vols football coach Johnny Majors spoke to Quarterback Club

4/18/77 Johnny Majors, University of Tennessee football coach spoke at Scrappy Moore awards dinner at Downtown Sheraton

5/13/77 Alabama football coach Bear Bryant, Texas coach Darrell Royal, Auburn coach Doug Barfield, Atlanta Falcons star Tommy Nobis, and former Arkansas coach Frank Broyles played golf in Tom T. Hall Bethel Bible School tournament

6/1/77 Former Yankees Whitey Ford and Mickey Mantle played golf at Mantle's charity tournament in Fort Oglethorpe, GA

7/7/77 Baseball home run king Henry Aaron, broadcaster Ernie Johnson Sr, and former Braves pitching star Johnny Sain appeared at Engel Stadium for Southern League All Star game

9/19/77 Former Auburn football coach (1951-75) Ralph "Shug" Jordan spoke to Auburn Alumni club at the Chattanooga Choo Choo

1/25/78 Bobby Cox (manager) at Braves Caravan

1/30/78 Ray Oldham, NFL defensive back (and Chattanooga resident) spoke to Quarterback Club at Town and Country Restaurant

4/17/78 Georgia Tech football coach Bobby Dodd spoke at Scrappy Awards banquet at UTC Student Center

5/8/78 Florida State football coach Bobby Bowden spoke to FCA annual banquet at Provident Cafeteria.

6/15/78 Former Clemson football coach Frank Howard spoke at UTC Athletics fund raising kickoff.

In 1978, Mike Jones graduated from Chattanooga's Riverside High. He went on to play football at Tennessee State University, and was a wide receiver for seven years in the NFL.

Jan. 1979 University of North Carolina basketball coach Dean Smith at Baylor School

1/15/79 Former Atlanta Falcons coach and Philadelphia Eagles quarterback Norm Van Brocklin spoke to Quarterback Club

1/18/79 Former NY Yankee 2nd baseman Bobby Richardson spoke to FCA annual banquet at First Baptist Church in downtown Chattanooga

1/30/79 Bobby Cox (manager) and several players at Braves Caravan at Northgate Mall

2/12/79 Georgia football coach Vince Dooley spoke to Quarterback Club at the Downtowner

2/19/79 Tennessee football coach Johnny Majors spoke to Quarterback Club at the Downtowner.

3/19/79 Georgia Tech football coach Pepper Rodgers spoke to Quarterback Club

4/16/79 Alabama head football coach Paul "Bear" Bryant spoke at Scrappy Awards banquet at Maclellan Gym.

5/18/79 Various celebritites played golf or tennis for Pat Boone Bethel Bible School charity weekend, including Fred MacMurray, James Franciscus, Ron Masak, James Hampton, Debby Boone, actor Tom Hallick, NBA legend Gail Goodrich, football stars Ray Oldham, Bobby Majors, Herman Weaver and Steve Sloan, Virgil Trucks, Bob Turley.

7/17/79 Pro golfer Arnold Palmer was at Creek's Bend Golf Course where he met the winner of the Ladies Invitational, 19-year-old Debbie Walker, and rewarded her with a kiss.

Starting in October 1979, pro golfer Chi Chi Rodriguez participated in exhibitions at Chattanooga Golf and Country Club and Rivermont Golf Club.

The 1980s

1/24/80 Bobby Cox (manager), Phil Niekro, Gene Garber, Dale Murphy, Gary Matthews, Al Hrabosky, Jerry Royster, Bob Horner, Chris Chambliss, Ernie Johnson Sr., and Pete Van Wieren at Braves Caravan at Northgate Mall

3/24/80 Former Clemson football coach Frank Howard spoke at Quarterback Club at the Downtowner Hotel.

4/22/80 Georgia football coach Vince Dooley spoke at the Scrappy Moore Awards banquet at UTC Student Center.

From 1980-87 former UTC Moc Greg Cater was a punter in the NFL.

1/15/81 Bobby Cox (manager) Bob Horner, Phil Niekro, Gary Matthews, Bruce Benedict, Rick Camp, Glenn Hubbard, Dale Murphy, Jerry Royster, Ernie Johnson Sr., Pete Van Wieren and Darrell Chaney at Braves caravan at Northgate Mall

2/9/81 Atlanta Braves manager Bobby Cox spoke to Cleveland Old Timers annual banquet at Elks Lodge in Cleveland. Cox was one of many Braves stars invited each year by Lou Fitzgerald, a Braves scout and Cleveland resident.

In 1981, Donnie Elder graduated from Brainerd High School, and played football for the University of Memphis State. He went on to play as a defensive back for eight years in the NFL.

7/16/81 Hank Aaron, former Atlanta Brave, and baseball's home run king, appeared at grand opening of American National Bank on East Third St. in Chattanooga (He also told reporter Mark McCarter that he frequently went fishing with his wife at Chickamauga Dam, and was rarely recognized)

7/31/81 Tennessee sports broadcaster John Ward spoke at Big Orange Barbecue at Chester Frost Park

9/5/81 University of Tennessee basketball coach Don DeVoe spoke to UT Alumni chapter at Downtown Sheraton

10/13/81 NBA exhibition game at Maclellan Gym Kansas City Kings (with Ernie Grunfeld) vs. Utah Jazz (Adrian Dantley)

1/13/82 Joe Torre (manager), Phil Niekro, Dale Murphy, Bob Horner, Bruce Benedict, Rick Camp, at Braves Caravan at Children's Hospital and Northgate Mall

4/22/82 Auburn head football coach Pat Dye spoke at Scrappy Awards banquet at UTC Student Center

5/22/82 Atlanta Falcons stars Steve Bartkowski and William Andrews play in Bethel Bible School celebrity softball game at Engel Stadium. Also playing were NY Jets quarterback Pat Ryan, punter Chuck Ramsey, and kicker Pat Leahy

5/27/82 Former NY Yankee 2nd baseman Bobby Richardson spoke to FCA annual banquet at Provident Cafeteria.

7/31/82 Hall of Fame pitcher Bob Feller appeared an Engel Stadium, holding youth clinic and broadcasting a Lookouts game

From 1982-87 former UTC Moc football player Curtis Rouse was an offensive lineman in the NFL

From 1982-85 Longtime NBA star Gerald Wilkins played for UTC Mocs basketball team

From 1982 to 1989, former UTC basketball player Russ Schoene played in the NBA.

11/16/82 John McEnroe vs. Guillermo Vilas tennis exhibition at UTC Arena

12/1/82 The University of Tennessee Vols, the men's basketball team, defeated the UTC Mocs 55-49 in the first game played at UTC Arena. Among the Vols players was future NBA star Dale Ellis. UTC's Gerald Wilkins would also go on to be an NBA star from 1985 to 1999 with the New York Knicks.

12/21/82 Michael Jordan plays basketball at UTC Arena (North Carolina vs. UTC). Former Baylor School star Jimmy Braddock also played for the Tarheels, coached by Dean Smith. North Carolina defeated UTC 73-66.

1/17/83 Joe Torre (manager), Dale Murphy, Rick Camp, Steve Bedrosian, Terry Harper, and Glenn Hubbard at Braves Caravan at Northgate Mall

2/3/83 Roscoe Tanner vs. Bjorn Borg tennis exhibition at UTC Arena

2/14/83 Atlanta Braves pitcher Phil Niekro spoke to Cleveland Old-Timers annual banquet at Holiday Inn in Cleveland, TN

3/23/83 Former major leaguer Tony Cloninger, Braves mascot Chief Noc-a-homa, NFL stars Ray Oldham and Bobby Scott, and UT football star Reggie White were among the athletes who participated in the Catoosa County Special Olympics in Ringgold, Ga. Scott and Oldham began attending the annual event in 1979. Cloninger's first appearance was in 1981.

4/19/83 Vanderbilt basketball coach C.M. Newton spoke at Scrappy Awards Banquet at UTC Student Center

5/10/83 University of Alabama football coach Ray Perkins spoke to Alabama Alumni Association at Dalton GA Golf and Country Club

5/19/83 Vanderbilt football coach George MacIntyre spoke to FCA annual banquet at Provident Cafeteria.

6/2/83 John Thompson, Georgetown University basketball coach speaks to Boys Club at Chattanooga Choo Choo

6/5/83 Golf exhibition with Lee Trevino, Gibby Gilbert, and Ray Oldham at Chattanooga Golf and Country Club.

10/19/83 Philadelphia 76ers (Moses Malone, Julius Erving, Andrew Toney, Bobby Jones, coach Billy Cunningham) played Boston Celtics (Larry Bird, Danny Ainge, Robert Parish, Cedric Maxwell, Kevin McHale, coach K.C. Jones) in exhibition basketball game at UTC Arena

10/29/83 Braves second baseman Glenn Hubbard signs autographs at The Leader clothing store in Brainerd Village

12/7/83 Dale Murphy appears on WDEF-TV Morning Show, speaks to Chattanooga Church of Latter-Day Saints

1/26/84 Chris Chambliss, Joe Torre (manager), Rick Camp, Glenn Hubbard, Len Barker, Terry Forster at Braves caravan at Northgate Mall

3/20/84 Sharon Fanning, UTC women's basketball coach, appeared on the WDEF-TV Morning Show. She later coached several major college women's basketball teams.

4/23/84 Auburn basketball coach Sonny Smith spoke at Scrappy Moore Awards banquet at the UTC Arena.

12/21/84 College football coach Lou Holtz (Arkansas, Minnesota) spoke at kickoff of Krystal Classic Tip Off at Downtown Sheraton

From 1984 to 1992, Buddy Nix was UTC Mocs head football coach. He later became general manager of the Buffalo Bills in the NFL.

1/23/85 Eddie Haas (manager) Brad Komminsk, Gerald Perry, and Pete Van Wieren at Northgate Mall

2/11/85 Baseball home run king Henry Aaron spoke to Cleveland Old-Timers annual banquet at Bradley County High School

5/7/85 Ga. Tech football coach Bill Curry speaks at Scrappy Moore Awards at UTC Student Center

In 1985 Venus Lacy, future US Olympic star and WNBA basketball player, graduated from Brainerd High School.

5/18/85 Baseball Hall of Fame 3rd baseman Brooks Robinson (Baltimore Orioles) and country singer Charly McClain appeared at Engel Stadium as part of Red Food Cancer Control drive

5/23/85 Buddy Curry, Stacey Bailey, Eric Sanders, Billy Johnson, and William Andrews at Atlanta Falcons caravan at the Loft restaurant on Cherokee Boulevard, and Northgate Mall

9/5/85 UT Lady Vols coach Pat Summitt spoke to Rotary Club at Read House

11/27/85 John Ward, University of Tenn. Football/basketball announcer on WDEF-TV Morning Show

1/24/86 John McEnroe vs. Mats Wilander tennis exhibition at UTC Arena

2/5/86 Grambling University football coach Eddie Robinson at Centra City Complex

3/25/86 Former major leaguers Bob Turley, Denver Lemaster, Virgil Trucks, Whitlow Wyatt, and Bobby Dews were among the players at Catoosa County Special Olympics old-timers game at Engel Stadium.

4/18/86 Indiana basketball coach Bobby Knight conducted a basketball clinic at the UTC Arena.

4/29/86 Atlanta Falcons running back William Andrews spoke at Scrappy Moore Awards Banquet at UTC Arena

5/9/86 Chicago Bulls star Michael Jordan, Atlanta Falcons star Billy "White Shoes" Johnson and former Boston Bruins hockey star Bobby Orr tour Red Food Stores for Cancer Control drive

7/26/86 Multi-sport superstar Bo Jackson at Engel Stadium playing for Memphis Chicks

8/15/86 Mercury Morris speaks at Crossroads Drug Treatment Center on Brainerd Road, and to UTC football players

12/29/86 Kyle Rote Jr., soccer star on WDEF-TV Morning Show

1/15/87 Atlanta Braves manager Chuck Tanner spoke to the annual Cleveland Old Timers Club dinner at the Cleveland Golf and Country Club

3/20/87 Philadephia Eagles defensive end (and Howard High graduate) Reggie White was on WDEF Morning Show (White also frequently appeared at charity events and hosted sports camps in Chattanooga area for young athletes. A portion of Carter Street was named in his honor on March 1, 1997, with a huge parade attended by 5,000 people.

3/30/87 Former major leaguers Hillis Layne, Johnny Mize, Billy Hitchcock, Roy Hawes, Ron Reed, Cecil Upshaw and George Archie at Catoosa County Special Olympics in Ringgold, GA. On **3/31/87** an Old Timers game was held at Engel Stadium.

4/23/87 New York Knicks star Gerald Wilkins (former UTC Moc) spoke to Scrappy Awards at UTC Student Center

5/8/87 Duke football coach Steve Spurrier joins Reggie White, coach June Jones and others at Pat Boone Golf Tournament

5/16-17, 1987 Atlanta Falcons star Billy "White Shoes" Johnson, singers Lynn Anderson and Gary Morris and former Miami Dolphins running back Larry Csonka visited several Red Food Stores for Cancer Control Drive.

5/27/87 Ga. Tech basketball coach Bobby Cremins spoke at Chattanooga Choo Choo Boys Club event

9/21/87 Ralph "Shug" Jordan, former Auburn football coach, spoke to Chattanooga Auburn Club at the Choo Choo.

11/31/87 Mercury Morris, former Miami Dolphins running back films anti-drug announcements at Video Masters on McCallie Avenue

2/2/88 Bobby Cox (GM), Ernie Johnson Sr., Dale Murphy, Ken Oberkfell, and Charlie Puleo at Children's Hospital for Braves Caravan

3/23/88 CBS sportscaster, Baseball Hall of Fame broadcaster (and Tennessee native) Lindsey Nelson spoke at Orange Grove Breakfast of Champions. His daughter Sharon later became an Orange Grove resident.

4/13/88 NBC sportscaster Bob Costas attended Chattanooga Lookouts game at Engel Stadium and spoke at Chattanooga Regional History Museum. He took batting practice and caught fly balls after the game.

5/20/88 Bill Bates of the Dallas Cowboys and former Tennessee Volunteer, spoke at Scrappy Awards at the UTC Student Center.

5/27/88 Former Atlanta Braves pitcher Phil Niekro, former Atlanta Falcons star Tommy Nobis, ABC Good Morning America weatherman Spencer Christian, signer Irlene Mandrell, former NFL quarterback Archie Manning, NBA Hall of Famer Bob Cousy, baseball Hall of

Famer Willie Stargell, singers Jim Ed Brown and Helen Cornelius visited several Red Food Stores for Cancer Control Drive.

10/27/88 Los Angeles Dodger stars Orel Hershiser and Brett Butler "roast" Oakland Athletics pitcher (and Fort Oglethorpe native) Rick Honeycutt at MS Dinner of Champions at Choo Choo Convention Center

2/2/89 Bobby Cox (GM), Ernie Johnson Sr., Gerald Perry, Paul Assenmacher, and Mark Lemke at Signal Center and Quality Inn East Ridge for Braves Caravan

2/23/89 Former NFL star Ray Oldham spoke at Old Timers Hall of Fame banquet at UTC Student Center

4/27/89 Johnny Majors, head football coach at Tennessee, spoke to Rotary Club at Read House

5/6/89 Former major leaguers Jim Nash, Jim Turner, and Harry "The Hat" Walker at Engel Stadium for Catoosa County Special Olympics fundraiser game

5/11/89 Former NY Jets wide receiver Don Maynard, Greg Cater, Buddy Nix, Wade Houston, singer Dickey Lee at Pat Boone Bethel Bible School golf tournament at Rivermont Golf and Country Club

5/16/89 Tennessee basketball coach Wade Houston spoke at Scrappy Awards banquet at UTC Student Center

8/30/89 Tennessee Vols broadcaster John Ward spoke to Big Orange Club at Chattanooga Choo Choo

The 1990s

1/18/90 Russ Nixon (manager), Don Sutton (broadcaster) Jeff Treadway, Derek Lilliquist, Nick Esasky, and Mark Lemke at Braves Caravan at Orange Grove Center

5/10/90 Former Alabama football star John Croyle spoke to Scrappy Awards banquet at UTC Student Center

8/6/90 UT Vols basketball coach Wade Houston became the first Black member of the Honors Golf Course in Ooltewah

12/9/90 UT Vols football coach Johnny Majors spoke to Orange Grove Breakfast of Champions.

From 1990 to 2001 golfer Chi Chi Rodriguez participated in the Capital Toyota March of Dimes classic, at the invitation of Bob McKamey

In the 1990s, Reggie White, football star at Howard High, University of Tennessee and Green Bay Packers would speak frequently for FCA at Chattanooga area high schools.

1/16/91 Glenn Hubbard, Tom Glavine, Ron Gant, and John Schuerholz at Braves caravan at Hamilton Place mall

4/4/91 University of Alabama Athletic Director "Hootie" Ingram spoke to Alabama Alumni Association at Chattanooga Golf and Country Club

5/14/91 Alabama football coach Gene Stallings spoke at Scrappy Awards dinner at Comfort Inn.

7/21/91 John Daly, Brad Faxon, Lance Ten Broeck, and others played at Chattanooga Classic at Valleybrook Golf Club. The tournament was won by Dillard Pruitt.

8/20/91 US Amateur Golf Championship at Honors Golf Course, with Tiger Woods (age 15), and defending champion Phil Mickelson (age 21). Woods and his dad Eldrick also played at Moccasin Bend Golf Course after exiting the tournament. Jack Nicklaus attended the tournament in support of his son Gary.

10/11/91 NFL (and Alabama) quarterback Joe Namath spoke at Memorial Hospital and Baylor School while visiting Chattem, where he was a commercial spokesperson for FlexAll.

1/21/92 John Smoltz and Greg Olson at Braves Caravan at Children's Hospital and UTC Student Center

2/7/92 Alabama football coach Gene Stallings spoke at Orange Grove Breakfast of Champions

5/15/92 Frank Gifford, Bruce Jenner, and Kris Jenner on Celebrity Cruise on Southern Belle for Red Food Cancer Control Drive

5/24/92 Dave Dravecky at Lee Highway Church of God for adopting fundraiser

7/30-31 and **8/30-9/2/94** Michael Jordan plays baseball at Engel Stadium for Birmingham Barons. Jordan has also played golf occasionally at the Honors Course in Ooltewah

1993-96 Terrell Owens played football and basketball at UTC

1/27/93 Bobby Cox (manager), Ernie Johnson Sr. (broadcaster), Rafael Belliard and Francisco Cabrera at Braves Caravan at Children's Hospital and UTC Mocs basketball game

2/15/93 Former UT Vol and NFL great Reggie White spoke at Chattanooga Sports Hall of Fame banquet at UTC Student Center

2/19/93 Soccer star and ABC "Superstars" champion Kyle Rote Jr. spoke at Lee College in Cleveland

2/26/93 Tennessee football coach Philip Fulmer spoke at Orange Grove Center Breakfast of Champions

3/19/93 Former UT Vol and NFL great Reggie White, along with fellow pro football players Keith Jackson and Tony Page, spoke at Dalton Ga. Mayor's Prayer Breakfast, Dalton High School, and the Tivoli Theater in Chattanooga.

5/4/93 Dallas Cowboys coach Tom Landry spoke to FCA at The Farm golf club in Dalton, GA

In 1993, Johnny Taylor, future NBA star, graduated from Howard School, and he graduated from UTC in 1997.

6/15/93 Pittsburgh Steelers star "Mean" Joe Greene visited Chattem, where he served as commercial spokesperson for FlexAll.

2/11/94 Tony Tarasco, Terry Pendleton, Greg McMichael, and Pete Van Wieren at Braves Caravan at Children's Hospital

In 1994, Tawambi Settles, future NFL star, graduated from McCallie School.

1994-2003 Golfer Chi Chi Rodriguez held exhibitions at Council Fire Golf Course

9/10/94 Steve McNair, then QB of Alcorn State led his team to a 54-28 win over UTC at Chamberlain Field

1/16/95 Oakland A's pitcher Rick Honeycutt spoke at Quarterback Club at Town and Country restaurant

1/19/95 Oakland A's pitcher Rick Honeycutt spoke at Sequatchie County athletic banquet in Dunlap, TN

4/28/95 Former Cincinnati Reds reliever Rob Dibble, with Birmingham of the Southern League, pitched at Engel Stadium vs. Chattanooga Lookouts

5/2/95 Mike McCoy, former defensive tackle for Green Bay Packers, spoke to FCA Dinner of Champions at Provident Cafeteria

6/22/95 Tennessee football coach Phillip Fulmer spoke at Best of Preps banquet at Chattanooga Convention Center

7/27/95 NBA (and former Auburn) star Charles Barkley appeared and spoke at Mack McCarthy basketball camp at Baylor School. Barkley also played golf at the Honors Course.

9/14/95 UT Lady Vols coach Pat Summitt spoke to Rotary Club at Read House.

4/2/96 Former Cincinnati Reds and Detroit Tigers manager Sparky Anderson threw out the first pitch at Chattanooga Lookouts exhibition game with the Portland Sea Dogs at Engel Stadium

4/11/96 Duke basketball coach Mike *Krzyzewski ("Coach K") spoke at Chattem and the Chattanooga Convention Center.*

5/3/96 Dick "Night Train" Lane, former Detroit Lions NFL star, played at Pat Boone Bethel Bible Village golf tournament at Rivermont Golf Club.

5/20/96 Tennessee basketball coach Kevin O'Neill was guest speaker at the Scrappy Awards banquet at the Clarion Hotel

6/1/96 Tiger Woods (age 20) wins NCAA Golf Championship at Honors Course

6/20/96 Former Tennessee Volunteer and NFL quarterback Heath Shuler spoke at Best of Preps banquet at Chattanooga Convention Center

7/7/96 Gold medal contender Lilia Podkopayeva was part of a Ukrainian gymnasts' exhibition at Maclellan Gym.

7/17/96 Former Vanderbilt women's basketball star Heidi Gillingham and Washington Bullets point guard Brent Price spoke to Calvary Baptist Church in Red Bank. Gillingham also participated in a "Hoop Dreams Camp at Grace Academy.

1/30/97 World famous trick shot artist Mike Massey appeared at Chattanooga Billiard Club East

2/3/97 St. Louis Cardinals pitcher Rick Honeycutt spoke to Quarterback Club at Town and Country Restaurant

2/9/97 Baseball Negro League legend Buck O'Neill at Chattanooga Regional History Museum

2/13/97 MLB star Brett Butler and Falcons quarterback Steve Bartkowski spoke to FCA at Chattanooga Convention and Trade Center

4/27/97 Former Pittsburgh Pirates outfielder Willie Stargell and Atlanta Falcons head coach Dan Reeves appeared at Red Food fair at Chattanooga Convention and Trade Center

5/7/97 UT Lady Vols coach Pat Summitt spoke at Women of Distinction lunch at Chattanooga Convention Center

In 1997, Alabama head football coach Mike DuBose spoke at Best of Preps banquet at Chattanooga Convention Center

In 1997, Terdell Sands, future NFL star graduated from Howard High School, and he graduated from UTC in 2001

From 1997 to 2000, 2nd baseman Eric Young Sr. (Colorado Rockies, Los Angeles Dodgers, Chicago Cubs and Milwaukee Brewers) lived in Chattanooga. His then-wife Malika is from Chattanooga, and is the daughter of Yusuf Hakeem, a former city council member and a state representative. Their wedding was on December 5, 1998 at First Cumberland Presbyterian Church. Among the baseball stars in attendance were Barry Bonds, Gary Sheffield, Charlie Hayes, Bobby Bonilla, Dante Bichette, Ellis Burks, Jacob Brumfield, and Otis Nixon. The reception was at the Chattanooga Convention Center.

7/26/97 Tennessee Oilers and Atlanta Falcons played an exhibition game at UTC's Chamberlain Field. 7,000 fans attended. Oilers were coached by Jeff Fisher, and the Falcons were led by Dan Reeves. Falcons players included Chris Chandler, Jamal Anderson, Michael Haynes and Morten Andersen. Oilers included Steve McNair, Eddie George, Frank Wycheck, and Al Del Greco.

9/4/97 Former Alabama football coach Gene Stallings spoke to United Way at Chattanooga Convention Center

2/24/98 Quarterback Danny Wuerffel and Atlanta Falcons quarterback Steve Bartkowski spoke to FCA at Chattanooga Convention and Trade Center. Musician Phil Driscoll performed.

In 1998, Jason Davis, future major league baseball pitcher, graduated from Charleston High School in Bradley County. He pitched for several big league teams, most notably the Cleveland Indians, from 2002 to 2008.

6/10/98 Pro Golfer Nancy Lopez visited employees at Arnold Palmer Golf Co. in Ooltewah

6/11/98 UT Lady Vols coach Pat Summitt spoke to Rotary Club at Read House, and signed autographs at Waldenbooks at Northgate Mall.

6/25/98 Former Brainerd High, Louisiana Tech and US Olympics basketball star Venus Lacy spoke at Best of Preps banquet at Chattanooga Trade Center

8/22/98 Georgia Bulldogs broadcaster Larry Munson spoke to Northwest Georgia Bulldog Club at Walker County Civic Center in Rock Spring, Ga.

9/1/98 UT Lady Vols coach Pat Summitt spoke at Chattanooga United Way kickoff at UTC Arena

In 1999, longtime Charleston TN and Bradley Central TN girls basketball coach Jim Smiddy was posthumously elected to the Women's Basketball Hall of Fame. During his 45-year career, he compiled a record of 1,217 wins and only 206 losses. He is considered the winningest basketball coach in any level of the sport.

2/11/99 Tennessee Vol kicker Jeff Hall fills in for "snowed-in" former Nebraska football coach Tom Osborne as speaker at FCA annual banquet at Chattanooga Convention Center

5/6/99 Frank Wycheck and broadcaster Mike Keith at O'Charley's Shallowford Village for Titans Caravan.

6/22/99 Former Marion County High and current Tennessee Volunteer linebacker (and future NFL player) Eric Westmoreland spoke at Best of Preps banquet at Chattanooga Convention Center

8/2/99 Former Green Bay Packers quarterback Bart Starr spoke to Boyd Buchanan football players at practice

8/3/99 Bob Kesling, Tennessee sports broadcaster, spoke at Orange Grove Breakfast of Champions

10/15/99 Baseball star Gary Carter was one of many celebrities who played in both the Blood Assurance Sam Woolwine Benefit tournament at Valleybrook and the Rick Honeycutt Youth Benefit at Battlefield Golf and Country Club. A concert featured Confederate Railroad in the Imperial Ballroom of the Chattanooga Choo-Choo. Among those in attendance were Tom Browning, Joe Rudi, Scott Sanderson, Gibby Gilbert, Dave Bristol, David Palmer, Bobby Thigpen, Ron Reed, Rick Mahler, and Todd Helton. Helton, a Colorado Rockies first baseman, is married to the former Christy Bollman, a Chattanooga native and Notre Dame High School graduate.

In the late 1990s, San Francisco quarterback Joe Montana was an occasional visitor to Chattem where he served as a commercial spokesperson for FlexAll.

The 2000s

3/7/00 Former Green Bay quarterback Bart Starr speaks to FCA at Chattanooga Convention and Trade Center

3/13/00 Tennessee football coach Phillip Fulmer spoke to FCA at Northwest Georgia Convention and Trade Center in Dalton, GA

4/1/00 Future Hall of Famers Barry Larkin, Cal Ripken Jr., Mike Mussina and Ken Griffey Jr. played in Cincinnati Reds vs. Baltimore Orioles exhibition game to open BellSouth Park in Chattanooga. Other players included Brady Anderson, Albert Belle, Will Clark, Pokey Reese, Jeff Conine, Aaron Boone, and Sean Casey. Managers were Mike Hargrove (Orioles) and Jack McKeon (Reds). Ken Griffey Sr. was also at the game.

4/4/00 Steve McNair, Fred Miller, broadcasters Mike Keith and Larry Stone Titans Caravan at Hamilton Place Mall.

4/11/00 Alabama football coach Mike DuBose spoke to Alabama Alumni Club at Provident Cafeteria

4/20/00 Indianapolis Colts quarterback (and former Tennessee star) Peyton Manning spoke to Rotary Club at the Read House

6/19/00 Tennessee Titans defensive coordinator (and soon-to-be Buffalo Bills head coach) Gregg Williams spoke at Best of Preps banquet at Chattanooga Convention Center

10/7/00 Atlanta Hawks (Dikembe Mutombo) scrimmage at UTC Arena (Coach Lon Kruger)

10/15/00 Harmon Killebrew, Brooks Robinson, Ferguson Jenkins, and Todd Helton attended autograph show at Camp Jordan in East Ridge. Helton, along with Joe Rudi, Jay Howell, Ron Reed, Scott Sanderson, Ed Bailey, Dave Bristol, Rick Mahler, Kevin Bass, Tom Browning, Al Hrabosky, and Mudcat Grant played at Rick Honeycutt and Blood Assurance charity golf tournaments at Council Fire in Chattanooga and Battlefield in Fort Oglethorpe.

In 2001, future NFL players Daniel and Josh Bullocks graduated from Hixson High School.

2/26/01 Tennessee football coach Phillip Fulmer spoke to FCA at Chattanooga Convention and Trade Center

4/24/01 Brad Hopkins and Joe Nedney at Titans Caravan at Hamilton Place Mall.

From 2001 to 2004, former Marion County High and University of Tennessee football star Eric Westmoreland played in the NFL.

10/17/01 Colorado Rockies first baseman Todd Helton, former Montreal Expos catcher Gary Carter. Cleveland Indians/Minnesota Twins pitcher Jim "Mudcat" Grant, Gaylord Perry, Rick Honeycutt, Al Hrabosky, Dave Bristol, Jay Howell, Joe Rudi, Kevin Bass, Tom Paciorek and Tug McGraw at Swing with the Legends event at Battlefield Golf and Country Club.

2/11/02 Former Nebraska football coach Tom Osborne spoke to FCA annual banquet at Chattanooga Convention and Trade Center

3/29/02 Cincinnati Reds played Minnesota Twins in exhibition at BellSouth Park. Players included Jose Rijo, Bob Boone, Aaron

Boone, Brady Clark, Barry Larkin, Adam Dunn, Ken Griffey Jr., A.J. Pierzynski, Doug Mientkiewicz, and Jose Rijo. Mike Eruzione, captain of the 1980 US Olympics hockey team was a guest at the game.

4/10/02 Randall Godfrey and Mike Green at Titans Caravan at Hamilton Place Mall.

6/25/02 Steve Sloan, former quarterback for Alabama and the Atlanta Falcons, spoke at Best of Preps banquet at Chattanooga Convention Center.

8/16/02 Former Atlanta Braves star Dale Murphy was at BellSouth Park for First Things First

10/22/02 Major leaguers Tug McGraw, Bobby Thigpen, Pete Smith, Jay Howell, Gary Carter, and Harmon Killebrew played in Rick Honeycutt golf tournaments at Council Fire in Chattanooga, and Battlefield Golf and Country Club in Fort Oglethorpe.

12/8/02 Wrestlers Ric Flair, Stacy Keibler, Chris Jericho and Kane performed at the UTC Arena

2/5/03 Joe Simpson (broadcaster), Terry Pendleton, Gary Sheffield, and John Schuerholz at Hamilton Place Mall and Children's Hospital for Braves Caravan

2/24/03 Tennessee football star Anthony Munoz spoke to FCA annual banquet at Chattanooga Convention and Trade Center

4/28/03 Zach Piller and Benji Olson at Titans Caravan at Hamilton Place Mall.

In 2003, golfer Luke List graduated from Chattanooga's Baylor School. He has been on the PGA tour since 2007.

6/17/03 UTC (and future Auburn) basketball coach Jeff Lebo spoke at Best of Preps banquet at Chattanooga Convention Center

10/21/03 Todd Helton (Colorado Rockies) at Blood Assurance golf tournament at Council Fire and Rick Honeycutt Golf Tournament at Battlefield Golf and Country Club

3/2/04 Former NY Yankee 2nd baseman Bobby Richardson spoke to FCA annual banquet at Chattanooga Convention and Trade Center

4/3/04 Baltimore Orioles played Cincinnati Reds at BellSouth Park exhibition game. Among the players were Javier Lopez, Miguel Tejada, BJ Surhoff, and Rafael Palmiero.

4/19/04 Chris Brown and Drew Bennett at Titans Caravan at Hamilton Place Mall.

5/6/04 NFL kicker Morten Anderson, Sawyer Brown lead singer Mark Miller, football star Steve Sloan and pitcher Rick Honeycutt played in Celebrity Skins charity golf tournament at Black Creek golf club in Chattanooga.

5/20/04 Peyton Manning spoke at Steak and Stake dinner for Boys and Girls Club at Northwest Georgia Trade Center in Dalton, GA

In 2004, future major league pitcher Cory Gearrin graduated from Rhea County High School, pitching against various Chattanooga area school teams.

6/22/04 Philadelphia Eagles tight end Keith Jackson at Best of Preps at Chattanooga Convention and Trade Center

6/23/04 Ed Jasper, Terrance Melton, and Will Overstreet at Falcons caravan at Children's Hospital

Oct. 2004 NFL quarterbacks Jim McMahon and Steve DeBerg, and baseball stars Will Clark, Rick Honeycutt, and Graig Nettles played in Blood Assurance golf tournament at Council Fire.

2/4/05 Former NY Yankee World Series MVP Bobby Richardson spoke at Bayside Baptist Church wild game dinner on Highway 58

3/8/05 NFL coach Tony Dungy spoke to FCA annual banquet at Chattanooga Convention and Trade Center

4/8/05 Dave Dravecky, former major league pitcher, spoke at fundraiser at Silverdale Baptist Academy.

4/11/05 Frank Wycheck, tight end Ben Troupe and broadcasters Mike Keith and Larry Stone at Titans Caravan at Rock Creek Outfitters near Hamilton Place.

5/13/05 Peyton Manning at Chattanoogan Hotel for Boyd Buchanan School fundraising dinner.

6/3/05 Ike Reese, Frank Omiyale, and Mookie Moore at Atlanta Falcons caravan at Boys and Girls Club of Chattanooga

6/21/05 South Carolina football coach Steve Spurrier spoke at Best of Preps at Chattanooga Convention and Trade Center

Oct. 2005 Tracy Stallard (Boston Red Sox) and Phil Gordon (World Poker Tour champ) at Rick Honeycutt Golf Tournament at Battlefield Golf and Country Club

10/27/05 Atlanta Hawks (Joe Johnson) vs. Memphis Grizzlies (Shane Battier) exhibition game at UTC Arena

1/30/06 Former Braves pitcher John Smoltz spoke to FCA annual banquet at Chattanooga Convention and Trade Center

2/7/06 Pete Van Wieren, John Schuerholz (GM) and Pat Corrales at Braves Caravan, Hamilton Place

4/15/06 Jack Nicklaus at Steak and Stake dinner for Boys and Girls Club at Northwest Georgia Trade Center in Dalton, GA

4/20/06 Green Bay Packers quarterback Brett Favre spoke at UTC football fundraiser at Finley Stadium.

5/10/06 Troy Fleming and Tyrone Calico at Titans Caravan

6/20/06 Coach David Cutcliffe at Best of Preps at Chattanooga Convention and Trade Center

6/22/06 Former Dallas Cowboys quarterback Roger Staubach at Blue Cross Blue Shield headquarters

12/14/06 Former Alabama quarterback Jay Barker spoke at FCA Championship Breakfast at Chattanooga Convention Center

1/11/07 Former Georgia football coach Vince Dooley signed books at Gateway Bank and Trust in Ringgold, GA.

1/27/07 Matt Diaz and Pete Van Wieren (broadcaster) at Braves Caravan, Hamilton Place

2/27/07 Clemson coach Tommy Bowden spoke to FCA annual banquet at Chattanooga Convention and Trade Center

4/9/07 John Croyle, former Alabama football star, spoke to FCA at Colonnade in Ringgold, GA

4/25/07 Ahmard Hall and Stephen Tulloch at Titans Caravan, Boys and Girls Clubs of Cleveland, TN and Bi Lo on Brainerd Road in Chattanooga

5/1/07 Tennessee football coach Philip Fulmer and basketball coach Bruce Pearl greeted fans at the Big Orange Caravan at the Chattanooga Choo Choo

5/5/07 Former NFL coach Sam Rutigliano at Chattanooga State commencement

5/9/07 Bill Curry speaks at Law Day Celebration for Chattanooga Bar Association

5/18/07 Rudy Ruettiger, subject of the movie "Rudy" talked about his persistence to play football at the University of Notre Dame, at the "Dream Big and Never Quit" banquet benefiting David Brainerd Christian School at the Chattanooga Convention Center.

5/21/07 Former Georgia football coach Vince Dooley spoke at the Better Business Bureau annual luncheon at the Chattanooga Convention Center

In 2007, Harris English, future professional golfer, graduated from Baylor School in Chattanooga.

6/12/07 University of Alabama athletic director Mal Moore spoke to Alabama Alumni Club at Chattanooga Golf and Country Club

6/19/07 Coach Bill Curry spoke at Best of Preps at Chattanooga Convention and Trade Center.

From 2007 to 2010, Buster Skrine played football for the UTC Mocs. Starting in 2011, he started a long, successful career in the NFL as a cornerback for several teams.

12/13/07 Former NFL player and college football coach Bill Curry spoke at Chattanooga Convention and Trade Center. He was also leadership director at Baylor School from 2008 to 2010.

2/19/08 Former NFL running back Sherman Smith spoke to FCA annual banquet at Chattanooga Convention and Trade Center

3/29/08 University of Alabama athletic director Mal Moore and Clemson assistant football coach Dabo Swinney spoke at the funeral of Victor Ellis at Lookout Mountain Presbyterian Church. Swinney recruited Ellis to play at Alabama while he was a coach at that school. Ellis played for Red Bank High School, and was a star linebacker for Alabama from 1998 to 2001. He died at the age of 28 after a bout with cancer.

4/14/08 UT Vols basketball coach Bruce Pearl spoke at Better Business Bureau luncheon at Chattanooga Convention and Trade Center

4/16/08 Roger Staubach, former Cowboys quarterback spoke at Chattanooga Spirit of Innovation Awards

4/18/08 UT Vols basketball coach Bruce Pearl spoke at Breakfast of Champions for Orange Grove Center

4/22/08 Tony Brown, Al Del Greco and Roydell Williams at Titans Caravan at Sportsman Warehouse

5/10/08 UT Lady Vols coach Pat Summitt spoke at commencement exercises at Tennessee Wesleyan College in Athens, Tennessee

5/30/08 Evander Holyfield spoke at banquet at Chattanooga Convention Center for YCAP program, headed by Joe Smith

6/8/08 Professional tennis star Ivan Lendl played at Windstone Golf Club in Chattanooga. He often accompanied his daughter Isabelle to tournaments at the club, serving as her caddy.

6/17/08 Coach Phil Fulmer spoke at Best of Preps banquet at Chattanooga Convention and Trade Center

In August 2008 Flintstone, Georgia native Ashley Harkleroad, a professional tennis player, was the subject of a cover story and eight-page pictorial in Playboy magazine. She had attended Chattanooga Christian School, and was very successful on the pro tennis circuit from 2002 to 2012. She later became a commentator for the Tennis Channel.

10/19/08 Two-sport athlete Brian Jordan (Braves, Cardinals, Falcons) played in Blood Assurance/Rick Honeycutt golf tournament)

1/28/09 Stephen Curry (now an NBA star) played for Davidson against UTC at the UTC Arena

Two University of Tennessee coaching legends, Pat Summitt and Phillip Fulmer dance "The Tennessee Waltz" at Jasper Highlands in 2012. Owner John "Thunder" Thornton had the peak of a mountain named in her honor "Pat's Summitt." She had recently stepped down from her basketball coaching post after being diagnosed with Alzheimer's Disease. (Jasper Highlands)

In 2014, UTC women's basketball coach Jim Foster (right) sits for a post-game interview with broadcaster Larry Ward. Foster had been inducted into the National Women's Basketball Hall of Fame in 2013.

3/2/09 Gold medal Olympic swimmer Josh Davis spoke to FCA annual banquet at Chattanooga Convention amd Trade Center

4/21/09 Tennessee football coach Lane Kiffin and basketball coach Bruce Pearl greeted fans at Big Orange Caravan at Chattanooga Choo Choo

5/10/09 Siran Stacy, former Alabama running back, spoke at Abba's House in Hixson

5/11/09 Siran Stacy, former Alabama running back, spoke to Alabama Alumni Association at Bessie Smith Hall

5/18/09 Olympic Gold Medalist swimmer Michael Phelps at Best of Preps at Chattanooga Convention and Trade Center

7/1/09 Tommy Lasorda (former Dodgers manager) visits A T &T Field

10/8/09 Basketball legend Magic Johnson visited Normal Park Upper School.

Future Los Angeles Dodgers superstar shortstop Corey Seager played for the Chattanooga Lookouts at AT&T Field in 2014. (Chattanooga Lookouts)

The 2010s and Beyond

2/9/10 Otis Nixon and Mike Minor at Atlanta Braves caravan at Hamilton Place mall

3/2/10 Former Florida State football coach Bobby Bowden spoke at FCA banquet at the Colonnade in Ringgold, GA

3/12/10 Colt McCoy, Cleveland Browns QB at the Chattanoogan Hotel for Boyd Buchanan School

Former heavyweight boxing champion Evander Holyfield (right) has been a frequent visitor to Chattanooga, supporting amateur boxing. He is pictured with youth coach Joe Smith and Zach Trainor in 2014. (Joe Smith)

4/21/10 Sen'Derrick Marks, Kenny Britt, and broadcaster Mike Keith at Tennessee Titans Caravan Academy Sports, Hamilton Place.

5/4/10 Stock car driver Kyle Petty visited Children's Hospital

5/6/10 Tennessee football coach Derek Dooley greeted fans at the Big Orange Caravan at the Chattanoogan.

6/10/10 Tennis stars Venus and Serena Williams visited Children's Hospital while in Chattanooga for Best of Preps at Convention and Trade Center

8/7/10 Former Georgia football coach Vince Dooley and his wife Barbara spoke at Bradley Sunrise Rotary benefit auction at Museum Center

9/17/10 Former Georgia football coach Vince Dooley at WRCB studio

1/17/11 Former Georgia Tech basketball coach Bobby Cremins spoke to Quarterback Club at Finley Stadium

2/1/11 Frank Wren (GM) Eddie Perez and Cory Gearrin at Braves Caravan at Academy Sports, Hamilton Place

3/1/11 Former NFL Quarterback Jim Kelly and his wife Jill, an author spoke to FCA annual banquet at Chattanooga Convention and Trade Center

4/28/11 Rudy Ruettiger, the University of Notre Dame football player immortalized in the 1993 film "Rudy" spoke to Boys and Girls Club of Dalton fundraising dinner.

5/24/11 New Orleans Saints quarterback Drew Brees at Best of Preps at Chattanooga Convention and Trade Center

In May 2011, Ryan "Blue Chip" Martin graduated from Central High School in Chattanooga. He would go on to become a champion junior welterweight boxer with a record of 24-1, with 14 knockouts.

6/18/11 Tennessee football coach Derek Dooley spoke at Bradley Sunrise Rotary benefit auction in Cleveland, TN

7/15/11 Tommy Lasorda (former Dodgers manager) visits A T &T Field

11/3/11 Magic Johnson speaks at Chattanoogan Hotel for cancer benefit

11/7/11 Alabama football broadcaster Eli Gold spoke to Quarterback Club at Finley Stadium

2/9/12 Freddie Freeman, Jason Heyward, and Cory Gearrin (from Rhea County) at Braves Caravan at Taco Mac in Chattanooga

3/31/12 Tennis stars Dick Stockton and Brian Gottfried dedicated new Baylor School tennis courts

In 2012, future Atlanta Braves catcher Evan Gattis played left field for the Mississippi Braves at AT&T Field.

5/4/12 Kenny Britt and Jake Locker at Tennessee Titans Caravan Academy Sports, Hamilton Place.

5/5/12 Former Tennessee Lady Vols basketball coach Pat Summitt and former Vols football coach Phillip Fulmer visited the pavilion at Jasper Highlands to receive the dedication of "Pat's Summitt,"including the pavilion and the ten acres it sits on.

In 2012, Keionta Davis graduated from Red Bank High School. He would go on to be a defensive lineman for UTC, and played for the New England Patriots from 2017-19.

6/7/12 New York Giants quarterback Eli Manning at Best of Preps at Chattanooga Convention and Trade Center

8/15/12 Former Braves pitcher John Smoltz at Lee University in Cleveland for United Way

1/28/13 Brian Snitker, Craig Kimbrel, and Frank Wren (GM) at Braves Caravan at Academy Sports in Dalton, Ga

2/25/13 Former Atlanta Falcons All Pro running back Gerald Riggs spoke to Quarterback Club at Finley Stadium

2/28/13 Georgia football coach Mark Richt spoke to FCA at the Colonnade in Ringgold, GA

3/1/13 Tamika Catchings, WNBA player, spoke to FCA at Chattanooga Convention Center

4/10/13 Shaquille O'Neal visited Chattem

4/28/13 Yasiel Puig played for Lookouts at AT&T Field, and was also arrested by Chattanooga Police for speeding (97 mph on Amnicola Highway)

4/29/13 Vanderbilt University football coach James Franklin spoke to Quarterback Club at Finley Stadium

5/8/13 Colin McCarthy, Zach Brown, Marc Mariani and broadcaster Mike Keith at Tennessee Titans Caravan Academy Sports, Hamilton Place

5/16/13 Tennessee football coach Butch Jones, men's basketball coach Cuonzo Martin, and women's basketball coach Holly Warlick greeted fans at the Big Orange Caravan at the Chattanoogan.

In 2013, future major league pitcher Dakota Hudson graduated from Sequatchie County High School, pitching against various Chattanooga area school teams.

In 2013, Vonn Bell, future NFL safety graduated from Ridgeland High School. He would go on to play for several years with Ohio State, and the New Orleans Saints and Cincinnati Bengals.

From 2013 to 2018 Jim Foster was head coach of the UTC Lady Mocs basketball team. He was inducted into the Women's Basketball Hall of Fame in 2013, after his previous coaching assignments at St. Joseph's, Vanderbilt, and Ohio State.

5/23/13 Former Atlanta Falcons and former coach Leeman Bennett conducted a "Locker Room Conversation" at Blue Water Grill. William Andrews, Bobby Butler, Billy "White Shoes" Johnson and Gerald Riggs Sr. joined linebacker Buddy Curry to help raise money for Curry's "Kids and Pros" organization

6/3/13 Atlanta Braves pitcher Brandon Beachy pitched in a rehabilitation assignment for the Mississippi Braves against the Chattanooga Lookouts at AT&T Field.

6/7/13 Tennessee football coach Butch Jones spoke at Bradley Sunrise Rotary benefit auction at Bradley Central High School in Cleveland, TN

6/17/13 Atlanta Braves 3rd baseman Chipper Jones at Best of Preps at Chattanooga Convention and Trade Center

8/21/13 Tommy Lasorda (former Dodgers manager) visits A T &T Field

11/11/13 Former Boyd Buchanan High School quarterback, then-UTC assistant coach, and now UNC head football coach Will Healy spoke to Quarterback Club at Finley Stadium

1/30/14 Fredi Gonzalez, Don Sutton (Hall of Fame) and Kris Medlen at Braves Caravan at Academy Sports in Hixson

2/11/14 Alabama cornerback Jeremiah Castille spoke to Alabama Alumni Association at Stadium Club at Finley Stadium

2/20/14 University of Tenn. Lady Vols and WNBA star Chamique Holdsclaw was featured speaker at Bradley County Youth All Stars tournament at Ocoee Middle School

3/6/14 Kids and Pros football camp at Finley Stadium, featuring Bill Curry, Buddy Curry, Gerald Riggs, and Chuck Ramsey

4/30/14 Clayton Kershaw (Dodgers) pitches for Lookouts at A T & T Field (on rehab assignment)

5/16/14 Kendall Wright, Justin Hunter, and broadcaster Mike Keith at Tennessee Titans caravan at Academy Sports, Hamilton Place.

5/19/14 Tennessee basketball coach Donnie Tyndall and football coach Butch Jones greeted fans at Big Orange Caravan at the Chattanoogan.

5/29/14 NASCAR driver Dale Earnhardt Jr. at Best of Preps at Chattanooga Convention and Trade Center

6/14/14 South Carolina football coach Steve Spurrier spoke at Bradley Sunrise Rotary benefit auction at Museum Center at Five Points in Cleveland, TN

6/28/14 ESPN/ABC college football commentator Kirk Herbstreit appeared at the Man Xpo at Finley Stadium

9/9/14 Former Alabama and NFL quarterback John Parker Wilson spoke to Alabama Alumni Club at Finley Stadium

12/3/14 Former heavyweight boxing champion Evander Holyfield visited USA Boxing Team trials at Chattanooga Convention Center

1/29/15 Charlie Leibrandt, Marquis Grissom, and Javier Lopez at Braves Caravan at Academy Sports near Hamilton Place

2/17/15 Former University of Alabama and Seattle Seahawks running back Shaun Alexander spoke to FCA annual banquet at Chattanooga Convention and Trade Center

4/23/15 Former Tennessee football coach Phil Fulmer speaks to Rotary Club at Read House

5/9/15 Broadcaster Mike Keith, players Chance Warmack and Karl Klug at Tennessee Titans Caravan at Academy Sports, Hamilton Place

5/13/15 University of Tennessee coaches Butch Jones and Rick Barnes, and broadcaster Bob Kesling at Big Orange Caravan at the Chattanoogan Hotel.

5/17/15 Phil Fulmer hosts Pat Summitt Foundation golf tournament at Lookout Mountain Golf Club

6/1/15 Former Atlanta Braves pitcher John Smoltz spoke at Best of Preps at Chattanooga Convention and Trade Center

6/6/15 Former Atlanta Braves pitcher Tom Glavine spoke at Bradley Sunrise Rotary benefit auction at Cleveland, TN Golf and Country Club

6/22/15 Former Tenn. Football coach Phil Fulmer spoke at expansion of Erlanger East Hospital (his granddaughter was born there)

9/10/15 University of Georgia and NFL star Herschel Walker visited Signal Mountain Middle/High School in fundraiser for Mountain Education Fund

In 2016-17 Bryan Carvalho and his wife Hayleigh Hampton-Carvalho of Bravo TV's "My Giant Life" were volleyball coaches at Lee University in Cleveland, TN

2/4/16 Former Chicago Bulls star Bob Love (1968-77) spoke at Southern Adventist University in Collegedale

2/25/16 Sportscaster Ernie Johnson Jr spoke at Mountain View Luncheon at McCallie School

4/4/16 Former Chicago Bulls star Dickey Simpkins, now a Chattanooga resident, played basketball at the East Lake Youth and Family Development Center as part of Mayor Andy Berke's Get Fit challenge. Simpkins played for the Bulls from 1994-2000.

5/5/16 Tennessee football coach Butch Jones and basketball coach Rick Barnes greeted fans at Big Orange Caravan at the Chattanoogan.

5/7/16 Jurrell Casey, Rishard Matthews and Justin Hunter at Tennessee Titans Caravan at Academy Sports, Hamilton Place

6/9/16 Eric Berry of the Kansas City Chiefs at Best of Preps at Chattanooga Convention and Trade Center

10/10/16 Mike Keith, voice of the Tennessee Titans spoke to Quarterback Club at Finley Stadium

11/23/16 Tenn. Football coach Butch Jones and players Derek Barnett, Jalen Reeves-Maybin and Alvin Kamara visited injured victims of the Woodmore Elementary School bus crash at Children's Hospital.

2/28/17 Tennessee football coach and athletic director Phillip Fulmer spoke to FCA annual banquet at Colonnade in Ringgold, GA

5/2/17 UT Lady Vols coach Holly Warlick was Tenn. Woman of Distinction at Chattanooga Convention Center

5/7/17 Jack Conklin and Quinton Spain and defensive lineman Austin Johnson at Tennessee Titans Caravan at Academy Sports, Hamilton Place.

6/3/17 Tennessee basketball coaches Rick Barnes and Holly Warlick, and football coach Butch Jones greeted fans at the Big Orange Caravan at First Tennessee Pavilion.

6/27/17 Vic Beasley of the Atlanta Falcons at Best of Preps at Chattanooga Convention and Trade Center

7/27/17 Former UT Vol football coach Phillip Fulmer spoke at Red Bank Baptist Church dinner of champions

8/4/17 Former Atlanta Braves outfielder David Justice threw the first pitch at Chattanooga Lookouts game at AT&T Field

1/30/18 Former major league pitcher R. A. Dickey spoke to FCA annual banquet at Colonnade in Ringgold, GA

2/2/18 Former NFL quarterback Ryan Leaf spoke at Dr. Pepper luncheon at McCallie School

2/20/18 Philip Fulmer and Bill Battle speak at Classic 150 roast of John "Thunder" Thornton at Chattanooga Convention and Trade Center

4/29/18 Corey Davis and Jayon Brown at Tennessee Titans Caravan at Academy Sports, Hamilton Place.

5/10/18 Tennessee Vols athletic director Phillip Fulmer and newly-hired head football coach Jeremy Pruitt visited fans at First Tennessee Pavilion with Big Orange Caravan. Women's basketball coach Holly Warlick also attended.

6/14/18 Tennessee Titans quarterback Marcus Mariota at Best of Preps at Chattanooga Convention and Trade Center

7/20/18 Former UT Vol and NFL quarterback Josh Dobbs spoke at Red Bank Baptist Church dinner of champions

8/4/18 Terrell Owens made his Pro Football Hall of Fame induction speech at UTC Arena

8/31/18 ESPN/ABC college football commentator Kirk Herbstreit was at McCallie School watching his twin sons play football for Nashville's Montgomery Bell Academy. Herbstreit, a Nashville resident, said he was in Chattanooga often watching his sons play against local schools.

11/16/18 US Olympic softball pitcher Jennie Finch spoke at Gordon Lee High School

1/14/19 Los Angeles Dodgers pitching coach (and Lakeview native) Rick Honeycutt spoke to Quarterback Club at Chattanooga Convention Center.

1/24/19 LSU soccer star Mo Isom spoke at FCA Girls Night Out at Grace Baptist Academy

2/1/19 Blake Leeper, Paralympic athlete, spoke to Dr. Pepper Luncheon at McCallie School

2/27/19 LSU soccer star Mo Isom speaks at FCA leadership breakfast at Ridgedale Baptist Church

5/15/19 Former UTC Moc Corey Levin, Dee Liner and Jonnu Smith at Tennessee Titans Caravan at Academy Sports, Hamilton Place.

6/11/19 Tennessee Vols basketball star Admiral Schofield at Best of Preps at Chattanooga Convention and Trade Center

6/14/19 Kelley Harper, UT women's basketball coach speaking for CSLA at Southern Adventist University in Collegedale

7/26/19 Former Auburn quarterback Patrick Nix and former Alabama quarterback Greg McElroy spoke at Red Bank Baptist Church dinner of champions

8/19/19 University of Alabama football announcer Eli Gold at Car Barn for Alabama Alumni Association. He also broadcast several Birmingham Barons baseball games at Engel Stadium from 1983 to 1986.

10/24/19 Peyton Manning spoke at Chattanooga Preparatory School

1/21/20 Classic 150 roast of Rick Honeycutt, with Orel Hershiser and Dave Bristol at Chattanooga Convention Center.

Former University of Alabama and Seattle Seahawks running back Shaun Alexander poses with Angie Shumaker at FCA banquet in 2015. (Angie Shumaker)

Former UTC Mocs wide receiver Terrell Owens, who went on to a Hall of Fame career in the NFL, always enjoys visiting with fans at Mocs games.

1/31/20 Former Indianapolis Colts linebacker Gary Brackett spoke at Dr. Pepper luncheon at McCallie School

2/5/20 Derrick Coleman, who was a fullback in the NFL from 2012-17 spoke at Rise luncheon for Partnership for Families, Children and Adults at the Westin Hotel. He was the first deaf offensive player in NFL history.

*Former Atlanta Braves outfielder David Justice threw out the first pitch at a 2017
Lookouts game at AT&T Field. (Alex Tainsh/Chattanooga Lookouts)*

3/3/20 Will Healy, Boyd Buchanan graduate and UNC-Charlotte football coach, speaks at FCA banquet at Colonnade in Ringgold, GA

11/15/20 Former Florida and NFL quarterback Tim Tebow spoke at First Baptist Church in Cleveland, TN

Former NFL fullback Derrick Coleman, the first deaf offensive player in pro football history, is pictured with Betty Proctor at the RISE luncheon in 2020. (Betty Proctor)

Other sports notables:

Baseball Hall of Famers who played, coached or managed at Engel Stadium (including exhibition games) include Burleigh Grimes (Andrews Field, 1913), Lou Gehrig (various, 1930s), Babe Ruth (various, 1930s), Casey Stengel (1931), Walter Johnson (1932), Joe Cronin (1933), Hank Greenberg (1934, 1940), Bill Dickey (1936), Joe DiMaggio (1936), Frankie Frisch (1937), Joe "Ducky" Medwick (1937), Rogers Hornsby (1938), Kiki Cuyler (1939), Connie Mack (1940), Pee Wee Reese (1940, 1952), Willie Mays (1947 & 1955), Jackie Robinson (1951 & 1953), Warren Spahn (1952), Luke Appling (manager of Memphis Chicks, 1952) Henry Aaron (1953-55), Harmon Killebrew (1957-58), Ted Williams (1958), Ferguson Jenkins (1964), Eddie Murray (1976), Alan Trammell (1976-77), Tim Raines (1979), Cal Ripken Jr. (1979-80), Edgar Martinez (1985-86), Tom Glavine (1986) Larry Walker (1987), Randy Johnson (1987), Willie Stargell (as Braves minor league hitting instuctor in the 1990s), Chipper Jones (1992),Trevor Hoffman (1992).

Among other major leaguers who played or managed at Engel Stadium: Cecil Travis (1931-33), Hillis Layne (1941, 1946), Gil Coan (1945), Bobo Newsom (1949-50), Robin Roberts (1950), Cal Ermer (manager 1952-57), Jim Lemon (1955), Bob Allison (1957-58), Jim Kaat, Jimmie Hall (1959), Tim McCarver (1960), Frank Lucchesi (manager in 1961), Grant Jackson (1964), Mike Marshall (1964-65), Al Raffo (1965), Matt Keough, Brian Kingman, Dwayne Murphy (1976) Steve McCatty (1976-77), Jim Bouton (1978), Joe Charboneau (1979), Kelly Gruber (1982), Mario Diaz (1983-85), Ivan Calderon, Jim Presley, Danny Tartabull, Robert Long, Mark Langston, Darnell Coles, Alvin Davis (1983), Donell Nixon, Mickey Brantley (1984), Jose Canseco (1985), Mark McGwire (1986), Sal Rende (1978-82 as player, 1987 as manager, later became Philadelphia Phillies hitting coach), Ron Oester, Keith Lockhart, Chris Hammond, Joe Oliver, Scott Scudder, Keith Brown (1988) Tom Runnells (manager in 1988), Freddie Benavides (1989-90), Bo Jackson (1991), Jim Tracy (manager 1991), Reggie Sanders (1991,

1997), Tim Costo (1991-92), Willie Greene (1992), Steve Gibralter (1993),Pokey Reese, Scott Sullivan (1994), CJ Nitkowski (1994-95), Chad Mottola (1994-97), Aaron Boone, Brendan Donnelly (1996), Mark Wohlers (1991, 1999), Jason LaRue and Scott Williamson (1998), Brady Clark (1998-99), Jayhawk Owens (1999).

Major leaguers who have played or managed at Bell South Park/ AT&T Field include Corky Miller (2000-01), Adam Dunn (2001), Austin Kearns (2001-03), Edwin Encarnacion (2003-04), Chris Denorfa (2004-05), Brian McCann (2005), Jeff Francoeur (2005), Ryan Hanigan (2005-07), Joey Votto (2006), Jay Bruce, Johnny Cueto (2007), Justin Turner, Drew Stubbs (2008), Jason Heyward (2009), Freddie Freeman (2009), Javy Guerra (2009-11), Dee Gordon (2010), Kenley Jansen (2010), Scott Van Slyke (2010-11), Evan Gattis (2012), Yasiel Puig (2013), Joc Pederson (2013), Pedro Baez (2013-14), Corey Seager (2014), Max Kepler, Jorge Polanco, Byron Buxton, Miguel Sano, Jose Berrios, Josh Hader (2015), Max Kepler (2015), Doug Mientkiewicz (manager 2015-16), Ozzie Albies (2016), Ervin Santana (2018), Cristian Pache (2019), and Ian Anderson (2019). Hall of Famer Ryne Sandberg made several visits as manager of the Tennessee Smokies in 2009.

Former Lakeview High School baseball star Rick Honeycutt became a top major leaguer for the Oakland Athletics and pitching coach for World Series champions Los Angeles Dodgers until his retirement in 2019.

Cal Ermer, Minnesota Twins manager (1967-68) and Chattanooga Lookouts manager (1952-57), lived in Chattanooga for 57 years.

Paul "Showtime" Gaffney, a former standout at Tennessee Wesleyan College in Athens, played from 1992 to 2008 with the Harlem Globetrotters in the role of primary showman. He is a resident of the Chattanooga area.

C. L. "Gibby" Gilbert II, a Chattanooga native, graduated from the University of Chattanooga, and became a professional golfer in 1965.

For more than three decades he won several titles on the PGA and Senior PGA tour. His son Gibby III is also a professional golfer.

Benny Hull, Rossville, GA native is longtime national TV and radio fishing show host, with longest-running outdoor show.

Grant Adcox of Chattanooga was a top stock car driver who died in an auto racing accident in 1989 at the age of 39.

NASCAR driver Austin Dillon married UTC graduate Whitney Ward in 2016, and they visit Chattanooga often. Whitney starred in "Racing Wives," a reality show on CMT.

2020 Former UTC Mocs tight end Faysal Shafaat appears on Big Brother and The Challenge: Total Madness on MTV

Peyton Manning frequently plays at the Honors Golf Course, of which he is a member. He said he has brought fellow quarterbacks John Elway, Tom Brady, Matt Ryan, Sam Bradford, and his brother Eli along with his dad Archie and his brother Cooper.

Internationally renowned golf course designer Pete Dye designed the Honors Golf Course.

Jack Nicklaus designed the Bear Trace golf course at Harrison Bay

CHAPTER 10

Political and Military Leaders

Political and government leaders from the United States and around the world have visited the Chattanooga area (presidents who visited before, during and after their terms are listed in the article that accompanies this chapter, and other political figures are included in the listings for Memorial Auditorium and Tivoli Theater). In many cases they spoke to local civic clubs, or appeared at fundraisers for themselves, or for local or state candidates.

Several Chattanooga and Tennessee political figures have gone on to national prominence. Republican Newell Sanders, who owned a farm equipment company in Chattanooga, was appointed to the US Senate in 1912 to fill an unexpired term. He only served for one year. Estes Kefauver was a member of the US House of Representatives, a US Senator, and a Democratic vice-presidential candidate in 1956. Cordell Hull was Secretary of State in the Franklin D. Roosevelt administration from 1933 to 1944. Bill Brock was a member of the United States House of Representatives, a United States Senator, US Trade Representative and Secretary of Labor in the Reagan administration. Howard Baker Jr. was a US Senator who also served as President Reagan's Chief of Staff. Fred Thompson was an attorney who served on the Senate Watergate Committee, an actor, and a United States Senator. Lamar Alexander was governor of Tennessee, president of the University of Tennessee, and US Secretary of Education before serving three terms as a US Senator. Albert Gore Jr., the son of a US Senator, was a journalist who was later elected to the Senate, and served two terms as Vice President under Bill Clinton. He narrowly lost the 2000 presidential election to George W. Bush. Bob Corker was a builder and mayor of Chattanooga before serving two terms in the US Senate.

Many Georgia political leaders have also been frequent visitors to the Chattanooga area. Chattanooga's proximity to North Georgia has given many Georgia political candidates and office holders an outlet for public speaking engagements and media appearances.

The annual Armed Forces Day parade, held each year in May, has provided a forum for political and military leaders.

Many future national leaders attended Chattanooga's prestigious private schools, and frequently returned to speak at their alma mater.

Not unlike some of the prominent sports figures listed in the previous chapter, Chattanooga's "money people" have attracted (or invited) some of the nation's top elected officials, and those who aspired to become one.

There are undoubtedly many who are not listed here because they made private, unpublicized visits to the homes or businesses of potential campaign donors.

Here is a listing of some of the famous political, government, and military leaders who have visited the Chattanooga area, beginning with the years prior to 1960:

In 1922 (exact date unknown) former Secretary of State and two-time presidential candidate William Jennings Bryan spoke to the Rotary Club.

Tennessee 3rd District Representative, US Senator and 1956 vice presidential candidate Estes Kefauver (D) practiced law in Chattanooga from 1927 to 1939.

2/24/32 "British statesman, soldier and author" Winston Churchill visited Chickamauga battlefield, stayed overnight in the Mary Garden suite of the Read House in downtown Chattanooga. He refused to speak to "newspaper men," slamming the door on a reporter, and warning the hotel manager that he was not to be interrupted.

11/16/39 US Rep. Estes Kefauver (D-Chattanooga) spoke to Rotary Club at Hotel Patten

6/4/43 1940 Republican presidential nominee Wendell Wilkie spoke to reporters at the Mountain City Club. He said he was in Chattanooga to visit a friend, and was "not here to talk politics." (Although he later sought the 1944 nomination, he dropped out of the race early, and died of heart failure in August 1944.)

4/2/45 US Rep. Albert Gore (D-Carthage) spoke to Rotary Club at Hotel Patten

5/7/47 Mexican President Miguel Aleman, visited Chattanooga's TVA's projects to help Mexico build up its industry and economy. After he flew into Lovell Field aboard President Harry Truman's personal plane, the Sacred Cow C-54, thousands lined the parade route as his car made its way to the Read House, where he was staying in the Mary Garden Suite.

8/16/48 Former Georgia Gov. Ellis Arnall spoke to Chattanooga Jaycees

4/9/50 Georgia Gov. Herman Talmadge spoke to 10,000 supporters at the former military base in Fort Oglethorpe

10/10/50 Sen. Estes Kefauver (D-TN) spoke to Kiwanis convention at Hotel Patten

11/12/51 US Rep. Franklin D. Roosevelt Jr. spoke at the Bonds for Israel dinner at Hotel Patten

2/17/53 Former South Carolina Gov. (and 1948 Dixiecrat presidential candidate) Strom Thurmond spoke to Cleveland, Tenn. Chamber of Commerce

9/17/54 Sen. Everett Dirksen (R-Illinois) spoke at a Mickey Spence for US House rally at the Hamilton County Courthouse

9/29/55 US Sen. Albert Gore Sr. (D-Tenn) spoke to Rotary Club at Hotel Patten

6/7/56 Georgia Democratic US Senate candidate Herman Talmadge spoke to Rotary Club at Hotel Patten

8/17/56 Georgia Democratic US Senate candidate Herman Talmadge spoke to 5,000 supporters at the former military base in Fort Oglethorpe

9/23/58 U.S. Sen. Herman Talmadge (D-Ga) spoke to Electric League at Hotel Patten

The 1960s

5/19/60 Former Ga. Gov. Marvin Griffin spoke at Armed Forces Day luncheon

3/21/63 US Rep. Bill Brock (R-Chattanooga) spoke at Rotary Club at Hotel Patten

5/17/63 Sen. Thomas Dodd (D-Conn) spoke at Armed Forces Day luncheon

Oct 1963 Ga. Gov. Carl Sanders spoke to Ringgold Rotary Club

7/8/64 Tenn. Gov. Frank Clement campaigned for US Senate at Read House and Patten Hotel

10/17/64 Vice President Hubert H. Humphrey spoke at Lovell Field airport

10/20/64 Sen. Everett Dirksen (R-Illinois) spoke at Howard Baker for Senate luncheon at Read House

1/13/66 US Rep. Bill Brock (R-Chattanooga) spoke to Rotary Club at Hotel Patten

5/2/67 US Sen. Strom Thurmond spoke as part of American Forum series at Tivoli Theater

6/12/67 Ga. Gov. Lester Maddox visited site of Peerless Mills fire in Rossville

7/15/67 Ga. Gov. Lester Maddox spoke at Welcome Center on I-75 in Ringgold, GA

10/21/67 US Rep. Bill Brock (R-Chattanooga) spoke at dedication of new Red Bank City Hall

12/14/67 Sen. Howard Baker (R-TN) spoke to Rotary Club at Hotel Patten

2/27/68 Richmond Flowers, former Alabama attorney general spoke at Brotherhood Week program at Notre Dame High School

6/12/68 Presidential candidate George Wallace of Alabama campaigned at Memorial Auditorium

9/19/68 Muriel Humphrey, wife of Vice President Hubert Humphrey, visited Lovell Field to speak to Democratic women on behalf of her husband's presidential campaign

11/7/68 US Rep. Bill Brock (R-Chattanooga) spoke to Rotary Club at Hotel Patten

3/22/69 Sen. Barry Goldwater (R-Arizona) spoke to Metropolitan Dinner Club at Hotel Patten

Sen. Barry Goldwater with Chattanooga Times reporter Michael Loftin in 1969

4/4/69 Ga. Gov. Lester Maddox spoke at groundbreaking of Ga. Highway 2-A which would connect Fort Oglethorpe to Ringgold

10/22/69 Former Ga. Gov. Carl Sanders spoke to Ringgold Rotary Club

The 1970s

1970 Ga. Gov. Lester Maddox appeared on WDEF-TV Morning Show

4/11/70 US Sen. Albert Gore Sr. (D-TN) spoke at McCallie School

6/13/70 Former Georgia Gov. Carl Sanders spoke to Chattanooga Valley Kiwanis Club

10/1/70 US Rep. Bill Brock (R-Chattanooga) spoke to Rotary Club at Read House

10/29/70 Sen. Albert Gore Sr (D-TN) and Republican challenger US Rep. Bill Brock debated at Engel Stadium in "Meet The Candidates" event

3/29/71 Tenn. Gov. Winfield Dunn spoke to Chattanooga Engineers Club at Hotel Patten

8/20/71 Ga. Lt. Gov. Lester Maddox spoke to Civitan Club at Hotel Patten

8/26/71 US Sen. Bill Brock (R-TN) spoke to Rotary Club at Read House

2/3/72 Sen. Howard Baker Jr. (R-TN) spoke to Rotary Club at Read House

4/28/72 Presidential candidate George Wallace spoke at a dinner in his honor at the Hotel Patten

4/1/73 Ga. Lt. Gov. Lester Maddox spoke at Tri-County Hospital expansion in Fort Oglethorpe, GA

9/17/73 Sen. Bill Brock (R-TN) spoke at UTC Student Methodist Center, and to the Tennessee Consumer Credit Association at the Choo Choo.

Zell Miller visited Chattanooga many times during his terms as Georgia Lt. Governor (1975-91) Governor (1991-99) and US Senator (2000-05)

4/2/75 US Sen. Lloyd Bentsen (D-TX), a candidate for the 1976 Democratic presidential nomination, campaigned during a brief stop at Lovell Field.

4/24/75 James Neal, associate prosecutor in the Watergate Hearings, spoke to Rotary Club at the Sheraton Hotel

5/16/75 Howard "Bo" Callaway, Secretary of the Army, and former US Rep. from Georgia, spoke at Armed Forces Day luncheon

12/5/75 Sen. Frank Church (D-Idaho) spoke at the annual Kefauver dinner for Hamilton County Democrats at Chattanooga Choo Choo Convention Center. Former US Sen. Albert Gore Sr. also attended.

Pre-1976 Ga. Gov. Jimmy Carter appeared on WDEF-TV Morning Show

2/12/76 US Sen. Bill Brock (R-TN) spoke to Rotary Club at Read House

2/13/76 US Sen. Bill Brock (R-TN) spoke to students at Tennessee Temple University

5/12/76 Former US Secretary of State Dean Rusk spoke at re-dedication of Freedom Shrine at Walker County Courthouse in Lafayette, GA

5/15/76 Sen. Jesse Helms (R-NC) campaigned for presidential candidate Ronald Reagan at Chattanooga airport

5/21/76 Future First Lady Nancy Reagan accompanied her husband Ronald Reagan when he visited Tennessee Temple University

10/22/76 Sen. Robert Byrd (D-West Virginia) spoke at reception for US Senate candidate Jim Sasser at Downtown Sheraton

2/22/78 Charles Colson, a figure in the Nixon Watergate scandal who later became a Christian minister, spoke at Chattanooga Prayer Breakfast at Chattanooga Choo Choo

4/27/79 Sen. Lawton Chiles (D-Florida) spoke at Kefauver dinner for Hamilton County Democrats at Chattanooga Downtown Sheraton

5/18/79 Veterans Administration director Max Cleland spoke at Armed Forces Day luncheon

8/9/79 National Republican party chairman Bill Brock spoke to Rotary Club at Read House

9/9/79 Alabama Gov. Fob James, a Baylor School graduate, spoke to Rotary Club at Read House

The 1980s

1/3/80 US Sen. Jim Sasser (D-TN) spoke to Rotary Club at the Read House

2/17/81 Georgia State Sen. Julian Bond spoke during Black Awareness Week at UTC's Patten Chapel

4/2/81 Former US Senator and then-US Trade Representative Bill Brock (R-TN) spoke to Rotary Club at the Read House

5/16/81 Sen. John Warner (R-Va) spoke at Armed Forces Day luncheon

5/14/82 Rep. Sonny Montgomery (D-Miss), a McCallie School graduate, spoke at Armed Forces Day luncheon

7/10/82 Rep. Jack Kemp (R-NY) spoke at fundraiser at the home of Gordon Davenport

8/11/83 Former US Senator and US Trade Representative Bill Brock (R-TN) spoke to Rotary Club at the Read House

1/23/84 US Trade Representative (and former Congressman and US Senator) Bill Brock, Chattanooga native appeared on the WDEF-TV Morning Show, and he spoke to the Better Business Bureau annual meeting at the Read House

6/23/84 Barbara Bush (wife of Vice President George H.W. Bush) and Sen. Howard Baker (R-TN) spoke at "Reagan Roundup" political event at Red Bank Jr. High Auditorium

8/7/84 Gen. William Westmoreland, commander of US military forces during a portion of the Vietnam war, spoke to Rotary Club at Read House.

10/10/84 First Lady Nancy Reagan spoke to Teen Challenge residents at the Christian Business Men's Committee Building on McCallie Avenue as part of her Just Say No anti-drug campaign.

5/28/85 Ga. Secretary of State Max Cleland spoke to Catoosa County Schools Academic Awards Banquet at Chattanooga Choo Choo

7/30/85 Tenn. Lt. Gov. Ned McWherter appeared on WDEF-TV Morning Show

9/26/85 Ga. Governor Joe Frank Harris spoke at John Ross Festival in Rossville, GA

4/28/86 US Rep. Jim Wright (D-Texas) spoke at a campaign event for TN 3rd Dist. Rep. Marilyn Lloyd

5/17/86 Former US Rep. Shirley Chisholm spoke at UTC Women's Conference

6/24/86 Gen. Alexander Haig, former Secretary Of State, appeared on WDEF-TV Morning Show, dined at Mount Vernon restaurant, and spoke to Kiwanis Club at Read House, as he embarked on a campaign for the 1988 Republican presidential nomination.

11/15/86 Ga. State Senator Julian Bond spoke at Central City Complex in Chattanooga for MLK Community Development Corporation

12/3/86 US Sen. Al Gore (D-TN) appeared on WDEF-TV Morning Show

1/29/87 Ga. Secretary of State Max Cleland spoke to Catoosa County Chamber of Commerce at Chattanooga Convention and Trade Center

2/27/87 Ga. Secretary of State Max Cleland appeared on WDEF-TV Morning Show

3/23/87 Ga. US Senator Wyche Fowler appeared on WDEF-TV Morning Show

5/15/87 Former NATO ambassador David Abshire spoke at Arts and Education lecture at Choo Choo

9/25/87 Ga Secretary of State Max Cleland spoke at Rossville Civic Center

9/15/88 Barbara Bush, wife of Vice President (and presidential candidate) George H. W. Bush campaigned for Republican candidates on Madonna Avenue in East Ridge, and visited Chattanooga School for Arts and Sciences, Oak Grove Elementary in Cleveland, and Project READ in Chattanooga.

10/7/88 Republican vice-presidential candidate Dan Quayle spoke at Chattanooga State

The 1990s

6/14/90 Former Interior Secretary Stewart Udall spoke at Arts and Education lecture at UTC Fine Arts Center

2/28/92 Former US Senator and White House Chief of Staff Howard Baker spoke at Lincoln Day Republican event at Chattanooga Convention Center

3/2/92 House Minority Whip Rep. Newt Gingrich campaigned for President George H.W. Bush at Lovell Field airport in Chattanooga

5/7/92 Former Senator Howard Baker spoke at Arts and Education lecture at Tennessee Aquarium

11/2/92 Vice President Dan Quayle campaigned at Krystal Aviation South in Chattanooga.

In the 1994 US Senate campaign, Fred Thompson (Republican) and Jim Cooper (Democrat) made several visits to Chattanooga. Thompson won the election.

5/9/94 Senator Robert Dole (R-Kansas) appeared on behalf of US Senate candidate Fred Thompson at the home of George Pettway, and at a Lovell Field airport news conference.

6/16/94 Former Tenn. Gov. Winfield Dunn spoke to Rotary Club at Read House

1/12/95 US Energy Secretary Hazel O'Leary spoke to Rotary Club at Read House

4/1/95 and **4/24/99** Sen. Fred Thompson (R-TN) spoke at Lincoln Day events at Chattanooga Convention Center

6/1/95 US Sen. Bill Frist (R-TN) spoke to Rotary Club at Read House

8/17/95 US Sen. Fred Thompson (R-TN) spoke to Rotary Club at Read House

12/1/95 Sen. Trent Lott (R-Miss) spoke in support of Rep. Zach Wamp at Chattanooga Convention Center

12/14/95 Former Tenn. Gov. Lamar Alexander campaigned for president at the Creative Discovery Museum. He visited Chattanooga numerous times during his two terms as governor (1979-1987) and his tenure as US Senator (2003-2021)

2/23/96 Tenn. Gov. Don Sundquist spoke at Orange Grove Breakfast of Champions

10/16/96 Republican Vice Presidential candidate Jack Kemp spoke at Kirkman field in downtown Chattanooga

3/20/97 Former Sen. Bill Brock (R-TN) spoke at Lincoln Day event at Bryan College in Dayton, TN

5/1/97 Dr. David Abshire, Chattanooga native and former NATO ambassador spoke to Rotary Club at Read House

5/16/97 US Sen. Max Cleland (D-Ga) was featured speaker at Armed Forces Day luncheon at Read House

4/9/98 US Sen. Bill Frist (R-TN) spoke to Rotary Club at Read House

The 2000s

5/7/00 US Sen. Bill Frist (R-TN) spoke at UTC Commencement

10/18/00 Elizabeth Dole campaigned for George W. Bush's presidential bid at UTC Arena

10/23/00 Tipper Gore, wife of presidential candidate Al Gore, appeared at Miller Park with Sen. Max Cleland (D-Ga)

10/25/00 Barbara Mandrell campaigned for US Sen. Bill Frist (R-TN) at his re-election rally at Miller Park in downtown Chattanooga

US Sen. Bob Corker (2007-19), a Chattanooga native and mayor from 2001 to 2005, spoke several times to the Rotary Club of Downtown Chattanooga throughout his career

10/30/01 Former Vice President Al Gore spoke at Kefauver dinner for Hamilton County Democrats at Chattanooga Convention Center

2/8/02 Former First Lady Barbara Bush spoke at a fundraiser for Boyd Buchanan School at the Chattanoogan Hotel

6/20/03 First Lady Laura Bush spoke at Bicentennial Library and Creative Discovery Museum

11/10/03 Sen. John McCain spoke at Chattanoogan Hotel at a fundraiser for Rep. Zach Wamp

12/18/03 US Sen. Bill Frist (R-TN) spoke to Rotary Club at Read House

2/20/04 Sen. Bill Frist (R-TN) spoke at Lincoln Day event at Chattanooga Convention Center

4/1/05 Sen. Lindsey Graham (R-SC) spoke at Lincoln Day event at Chattanooga Convention Center

4/16/05 US Sen. Bill Frist (R-TN), also Senate Majority Leader spoke to Cleveland Rotary Club

5/10/05 Andrew Young, former UN ambassador and Atlanta mayor spoke at Community Choice banquet at Chattanooga Convention Center

7/14/05 Former Sen. Bill Brock (R-TN) spoke to Rotary Club at Read House

7/21/05 Former Sen. Howard Baker Jr. (R-TN) spoke to Rotary Club at Read House

11/8/05 Former US Sen Max Cleland (D-Ga) spoke at Kefauver dinner for Hamilton County Democrats at Chattanooga Convention Center

11/3/05 Dr. David Abshire, Chattanooga native and former NATO ambassador, spoke to Rotary Club at Read House

3/29/07 Former First Lady Barbara Bush spoke at Helene DiStefano Fund (cancer charity) luncheon at Chattanooga Convention Center

9/1/07 Former UN ambassador Andrew Young attended premiere of "Rwanda Rising" at UTC's Benwood Center

4/2/08 Dr. David Abshire, Chattanooga native and former NATO ambassador spoke to Rotary Club at Read House, and at UTC University Center

4/16/08 Former US Sen. Bill Frist (R-TN) spoke to Rotary Club at Read House

7/15/08 Tenn. Gov. Phil Bredesen, Sen. Bob Corker and Sen. Lamar Alexander appeared at press conference to announce Volkswagen's selection of Chattanooga for its next American manufacturing plant. The event was held at Hunter Museum.

9/19/08 Vice President Dick Cheney attended the 145th anniversary of the Battle of Chickamauga

The 2010s and Beyond

4/29/10 Former presidential candidate Rev. Jesse Jackson spoke at Howard High School and Olivet Baptist Church, and was also interviewed by Brewer Media.

5/10/10 US Sen. Bob Corker (R-TN) spoke at Better Business Bureau annual luncheon

6/17/10 Political strategist Donna Brazile spoke to Tennessee Multicultural Chamber of Commerce at Chattanooga Choo Choo

US Rep. John Lewis in Chattanooga in 2012 (Hugh Moore)

11/18/10 Newark NJ Mayor Cory Booker spoke at UTC Fine Arts Center

2/18/12 US Rep. John Lewis (D-GA) spoke to Hamilton County Democratic Party at Olivet Baptist Church. He also spoke to St. Paul AME Church

2/25/12 Former US Sen. Rick Santorum (R-PA) candidate for president, spoke at Abba's House in Chattanooga.

2/28/12 Former US House Speaker Newt Gingrich spoke at a fundraiser at the Chattanooga Choo Choo for his presidential campaign

3/5/12 Former US House Speaker Newt Gingrich and Herman Cain spoke at Chattanooga airport. Gingrich was a candidate for the Republican presidential nomination, and Cain had been until a few months earlier.

3/26/12 Country singer John Rich performed at a campaign event for Congressional candidate Weston Wamp at the Lindsay Street Music Hall.

5/28/13 US Sen. Lamar Alexander (R-TN) spoke at Better Business Bureau annual luncheon at Chattanoogan hotel.

3/18/14 US Rep. John Lewis (D-GA) spoke to students at McCallie School

9/9/14 US Education Secretary Arne Duncan spoke at Chambliss Center for Children

6/10/15 Former Sen. Rick Santorum (R-PA) spoke at Lincoln Day fundraiser for Hamilton County Republican party at the Chattanoogan, during his presidential campaign.

8/10/15 US Sen. Ted Cruz (R-TX) campaigned for president at Hamilton County Republican party headquarters on Chestnut Street

9/3/15 US Sen. Marco Rubio (R-FL) campaigned for president at Lindsay Street Hall, and at the home of former Rep. Zach Wamp

10/11/15 Dr. Ben Carson, a Republican presidential candidate, signed books at Barnes and Noble at Hamilton Place Mall.

8/30/16 Andrew Young, former UN ambassador and Atlanta Mayor spoke at McCallie School.

9/13/16 US Education Secretary Arne King spoke at Battle Academy

4/27/18 Corey Lewandowski, Former campaign manager for President Trump spoke at Lincoln Day at Chattanoogan Hotel

7/21/18 Vice President Mike Pence spoke at Lee University in Cleveland, TN

Garry Mac with former Tenn. Gov. Phil Bredesen in 2018

10/1/18 Former Tenn. Governor (and 2018 Democratic senatorial candidate) Phil Bredesen spoke at Bessie Smith Hall

11/1/18 Vice President Mike Pence and Georgia Republican gubernatorial candidate Brian Kemp campaigned at Dalton Convention Center

11/4/18 Former Tenn. Governor (and Democratic senatorial candidate) Phil Bredesen spoke at Bessie Smith Hall

11/4/18 Vice President Mike Pence spoke at campaign rally with President Trump at the UTC Arena in Chattanooga.

11/13/19 Tennessee Gov. Bill Lee spoke at ceremony to rename a portion of Chattanooga's National Guard Armory for retired US Army Brig. Gen. Carl Levi

2/12/20 Democratic presidential candidate Michael Bloomberg spoke at Bessie Smith Hall

2020 US Senator Marsha Blackburn (R-TN) and Republican US Senate candidate Bill Hagerty visited Chattanooga several times to campaign. Hagerty was elected to the Senate in November 2020.

11/20/20 US Labor Secretary Eugene Scalia visited Volkswagen of Chattanooga

11/24/20 US Sen. Lamar Alexander (R-TN) visited Chickamauga Lock, as he ended his third term in the Senate.

11/28/20 US Sen. Kelly Loeffler (R-GA), US Rep. Marjorie Taylor Greene (R-GA) and US Rep. Chuck Fleischmann (R-TN) spoke at Spring Hill Suites in Ringgold, GA for Loeffler's Senate campaign

12/14/20 US Sen. David Perdue (R-GA) and his cousin, former Ga. Gov. Sonny Perdue visited Dalton Airport for Senate campaign

12/15/20 US Sen. Kelly Loeffler (R-GA) spoke at Park Place restaurant in Fort Oglethorpe as part of her campaign for Senate

12/19/20 Donald Trump Jr. spoke at the Colonnade in Ringgold, GA in support of US Sen. David Perdue (R-GA), who was also in attendance

US Sen. Lamar Alexander at Chickamauga Lock in 2020

Among notable graduates of McCallie School: US Sen. Howard Baker (1943) US Sen. Bill Brock (1949) and US Rep. Zach Wamp (1976)

Rep. Wamp's service in Congress (1995-2011) ended a consecutive and continuous 48-year run in which five McCallie grads served in Congress: Howard Baker, Bill Brock, Carroll Campbell (US House then Governor of SC), Sonny Montgomery (MS) and Wamp. Wamp said few other secondary schools (if any) can match that record from 1963-2011.

Visits from Presidents of the United States (before, during, and after their terms)

By my count, 27 presidents to visit the Chattanooga area, going back almost 200 years. A few of them visited before or after their terms, but around 15 stopped in while serving as president.

The first was our nation's fifth president **James Monroe**, who visited the Brainerd Mission on the banks of the South Chickamauga Creek in 1820. **Andrew Jackson** was our next presidential guest, visiting a number of times prior to the Civil War. Tennessee native **James Polk** was also a frequent visitor during that era. Fellow Tennessean **Andrew Johnson** also stopped in Chattanooga several times before and after the war.

Our 18th president, **Ulysses S. Grant**, was headquartered in Chattanooga when he served as a general of the Union Forces during the Civil War. This was certainly not a presidential visit, but he did occupy the White House about five years later. The man who became president a few years after Grant, **James Garfield**, was also stationed in Chattanooga during the war, serving on the staff of Union General William Rosecrans.

President **Rutherford Hayes** made a stop in the city on September 20, 1877. Hayes had recently appointed U. S. Senator David Key to be his Postmaster General. Key, a Chattanooga-based attorney, was the first Southerner, first Confederate officer, and first Democrat appointed to the Presidential cabinet since the Civil War. President Hayes' visit to Chattanooga was part of a goodwill tour after a contested 1876 presidential election.

(President Garfield had planned a trip to Chattanooga in 1881 for a memorial service that was to be held by Union and Confederate veterans. There was to be a celebration around the community of the battles of Chickamauga and Missionary Ridge. However, he was shot by a gunman in July of that year, and he died two months later. At Cameron Hill four Confederate and four Union veterans raised a flag and then lowered it half-staff in his honor.)

President Theodore Roosevelt on Lookout Mountain in 1902
(Chattanooga Public Library)

Presidents **Grover Cleveland** and **Benjamin Harrison** each visited in the latter part of the 19th century. Cleveland greeted a cheering crowd on October 17, 1887, while Harrison greeted citizens at Ninth and Broad Streets in Chattanooga on April 15, 1891.

President #25, President **William McKinley** had visited once in 1895 while serving as governor of Ohio, and after he was elected president he opened Chickamauga Park on June 13, 1897.

Theodore "Teddy" Roosevelt was another presidential visitor. During TR's seven-year stint in the White House, he made one trip to Chattanooga, and another shortly after his second term ended. The first was on September 7-8, 1902, to speak to the Brotherhood of Locomotive Firemen at the City Auditorium on Ninth Street at Georgia Avenue. During his visit he also rode the Incline, walked to Point Park, attend First Baptist Church in downtown Chattanooga, and speak at the city auditorium and the courthouse lawn. No doubt he used his "bully pulpit." (Note: At the time, "bully" was a positive word, meaning "grand" or "excellent.") He also visited the area in the fall of 1907 ("an impromptu reception of 20,000 people at the train shed") and made a brief stop at the train station on October 9, 1910.

Woodrow Wilson spoke to the American Bar Association convention in Chattanooga on August 31, 1910, while he was president of Princeton University. On that date, he also visited the Chattanooga Golf and Country Club. He was elected president in 1912.

During his single term as president, **William Howard Taft** was in the city on November 11, 1911 at the University of Chattanooga (he had also made a campaign stop in 1908, and visited the city in 1906 while he was Secretary of War). Then-Senator **Warren G. Harding** visited Chattanooga on October 13, 1920 as the Republican presidential nominee, and stayed at the Signal Mountain Inn (now the site of Alexian Village). He also spoke at the Hotel Patten downtown and the Billy Sunday Tabernacle that evening.

President Franklin D. Roosevelt at Chickamauga Dam construction site in 1938.
(Jimmy Mooney)

President **Franklin D. Roosevelt** made three stops in the area. On November 21, 1938, he visited Chickamauga Dam while it was under construction. He and first lady Eleanor Roosevelt also visited Point Park on Lookout Mountain. Along with numerous Washington dignitaries, he returned for the dedication of Chickamauga Dam on September 2, 1940. During both his 1938 and 1940 visits, he and the First Lady spent the night at Judge Will Cummings' farm in the Lookout Valley area at the foot of Lookout Mountain. Cummings was a long-serving county judge, and a top local Democratic official. He helped convince his friend the president to support the dam project to ease flooding, and to provide electricity and jobs. During World War

II, FDR inspected the Women's Army Center in Fort Oglethorpe on April 17, 1943.

On January 28, 1939, six years before **Harry S Truman** became president upon Roosevelt's death, he attended the funeral of former US Senator Newell Sanders at First Baptist Church in Chattanooga. Truman was a Senator from Missouri at the time.

Although **Dwight D. Eisenhower** did not visit during his presidency in the 1950s, he was stationed in Fort Oglethorpe for a time during the first World War in 1918.

While in his first year as a Senator from Massachusetts, **John F. Kennedy** spoke to the Downtown Rotary Club and toured TVA facilities on December 10, 1953. A former Chattanooga newspaper reporter, then working in Washington, knew Kennedy was interested in a presidential run, and told him he should start making appearances

President Lyndon B. Johnson at Chattanooga airport in 1964
(Chattanooga Public Library)

in the south. JFK was a newlywed, having married Jacqueline Bouvier just three months earlier. He would be elected president in 1960.

Lyndon Johnson made an airport campaign stop during his successful 1964 campaign for a full term, on October 24th of that year. (While campaigning for the vice presidency, then Sen. Johnson spoke to a crowd of about 2,000 at Memorial Auditorium on Sept. 30, 1960)

His successor, **Richard Nixon** visited Chickamauga Dam, and made a campaign appearance at Memorial Auditorium on September 27, 1968, speaking to an overflow crowd. Twenty years earlier, on January 21, 1948 while a California Congressman, Nixon was at the Read House accepting an award from the Chattanooga Jaycees. Nixon also spoke at Memorial Auditorium on October 10, 1964 at a rally for Republican presidential candidate Barry Goldwater.

Former Vice President Richard Nixon and US Rep. Bill Brock in Chattanooga in 1964 (Howard H. Baker Jr.)

Then-House Minority Leader **Gerald Ford** spoke in support of Rep. Bill Brock in Chattanooga on May 6, 1966. As vice-president, Ford spoke at the Chattanooga Choo-Choo on February 18, 1974 and also attended a Republican fund-raising reception in the Riverview area. He returned on October 6, 1988 to help Republican Congressional candidate Harold Coker at a fund-raiser at the Read House. He did not visit Chattanooga during his time as president from 1974 to 1977.

Although **Jimmy Carter** didn't stop in during his single term in office (1977-81), he was frequently in the Chattanooga area before and after his presidency. While governor of Georgia, he attended the funeral of Mort Lloyd, the news anchor-turned Congressional candidate who died in a plane crash in August 1974. The funeral was held at Brainerd Church of Christ in Chattanooga. As Carter was beginning his run for the presidency he spoke to the local Democratic party's Kefauver dinner on August 22, 1974 at the Tivoli Theater. On June 20, 1975 he made a campaign appearance at the Downtown Sheraton, and a horse farm in Wildwood, Georgia. After his presidency, on May 28, 1985, he spoke to several Chattanooga foundation leaders at the Mountain City Club, seeking funding for his presidential library and the Carter Center. He attended the Bass Masters Classic fishing tournament weighing-in ceremony at the UTC Arena on August 15, 1986. He and his extended family vacationed at the Chattanooga Choo Choo on August 23, 1991. He and his wife Rosalynn spoke to Hamilton County Democrats at the Kefauver dinner at the Chattanooga Convention Center on October 18, 2014.

The Day I Interrupted Jimmy Carter's Vacation

It was Friday, August 23, 1991. I was in the Channel 3 newsroom waiting for something to happen. Suddenly, the phone rang. Was it a heavenly voice on the other end, granting my wish for a little nugget of news? No. It was just my old radio buddy Dex (Bill Poindexter).

At the time, he was managing the Gardens restaurant at the Chattanooga Choo Choo. "Dave, you'll never guess who's eating a cheeseburger about twenty feet away from me," Dex said. "You're right," I said. "Who is it?"

"It's President Jimmy Carter, with his wife Rosalynn, and their grandkids. They're having lunch, and then they're gonna get on the box cars," Dex said. He capped it off with, "And you're the only person I'm telling." I yelled to my photographer Glen Wagner, "Let's go, we've got a president at the Choo Choo!" Glen grabbed the camera, and we took off. As we got in the car, I told him about Dex's confidential tip. "Does President Carter know we're coming?" he asked. "I don't think so," I said. "I guess we'll surprise him."

When we got to the Choo Choo, there was nothing out of the ordinary. "Gee, I hope we didn't miss him," Glen said. There was no limo, and no Secret Service agents staring us down. A few scattered tourists were roaming the grounds. We headed to the restaurant area. We didn't want to barge in, so we took a quick look through the window. There they were! The First Family, ten years removed from the White House, enjoying a quiet lunch with the grandkids. "Glen!" I said. "Go ahead and set up your camera, this may be all we get!" He dutifully aimed through the glass, and Mrs. Carter spotted us. I'm not a lip-reader, but she said something to her husband, like, "How nice! A couple of delightful local news people found out we're here on vacation! What a pleasant surprise!" Or maybe that's not exactly what she said. Anyway, Mr. Carter turned around, looked through the window, and looked me right in the eye.

He quickly turned back to his wife with that "busted" look on his face. Sensing his disappointment, I said, "I'll tell you what, Glen. Let's give them time to eat, and do their sightseeing, and then I'll ask him to do an interview." It turns out there were a couple of Secret Service guys who politely requested we give the President "a little space." Fearing a headline of "Alleged news guy ruins Presidential vacation," I gladly consented.

Glen and I waited, and our persistence was rewarded. About a half-hour after finishing their meal, the Carter family had apparently wrapped up their tour of the complex. The cute grandchildren had hopped on and off every box car in sight, so I said to Glen, "Here's our chance!" I walked up to Mr. Carter, shook his hand, and introduced myself. "Mr. President," I said, "I really hate to bother folks when they're on vacation…" He stopped me in mid-sentence, flashed that famous grin, and said, "It must not bother you too much." I laughed awkwardly. (Was he kidding? Or did I just play Fail to the Chief?), I plodded on. "If you can spare a minute for a quick interview…" He stopped me again. "Make it quick, we're about to leave." I can take a subtle hint. Fortunately, Glen worked fast, and we were ready to roll.

After that rough start, he couldn't have been any nicer. I had my questions ready. Could there be a female presidential candidate in 1992? Absolutely, he said. There were several qualified women. Did he expect a big-name politician to win the '92 Democratic nomination (Al Gore, Jerry Brown and Mario Cuomo were front-runners), or would it be a relative unknown, as he had been in 1976? He said the election was still 15 months away, and there was plenty of time for a lesser-known candidate to emerge (It turned out to be an obscure southern governor named Bill Clinton. Whatever happened to him?)

He also commented on his knowledge of downtown Chattanooga, the railroads, and even the quality of his lunch. He didn't seem too annoyed as we parted company, and I had my exclusive interview for the evening news.

The next day, I called Dex. "I just wanted to thank you again for tipping me off about this," I said. "Yeah, that was really something," Dex said. "I told the staff to take good care of him and his family, and after a while, I went to the bathroom. There was somebody in the next stall, and I later realized it was him. That was the first time I met a sitting president."

President Ronald Reagan and Red Bank High School senior (and Tennessee Jr. Miss)
Deanna Duncan at UTC Arena in 1987

President **Ronald Reagan**'s appearance in Chattanooga on May 19, 1987 was among the most memorable presidential visits. The main event was at the UTC Arena. The first item on the agenda was lunch with some of the county's top students. Most of his speech centered around the theme of "Excellence in Education." The event was filled with pomp and circumstance, literally, because it served as the commencement exercise for three thousand high school seniors.

Reagan had previously visited Chattanooga twice. On May 21, 1976, he spoke to 4,000 people at Tennessee Temple during his unsuccessful campaign for the Republican presidential nomination. And on April 1, 1959, long before he entered politics, he spoke at the Hotel Patten during a public relations tour for General Electric, for whom he acted as spokesman. Reagan's visit was co-sponsored by the Chattanooga Jaycees and the Ad Club.

The Day President Reagan Came To Town

President Ronald Reagan's visit to Chattanooga on May 19, 1987 was quite memorable. Upon landing at the airport, he made brief remarks, with some shout-outs to Chattanoogans Tom Griscom (then his Director of Communications) and Bill Brock (former US Senator, then Secretary of Labor) and Howard Baker (McCallie School graduate, former US Senator, then Reagan's Chief of Staff). Then it was off to the main event, at the UTC Arena. The first item on the agenda was lunch with some of the county's top students. Many of them described him as friendly and talkative, saying he really didn't have time to eat very much before the graduation program. Most of his speech centered around the theme of "Excellence in Education."

The event was filled with pomp and circumstance, literally, because it served as the commencement exercise for about 3,000 Hamilton County high school seniors. The class of 1987 was represented most prominently by Deanna Duncan of Red Bank High School, who introduced the president.

Several presidents had visited Chattanooga in the past, but the Reagan visit was the first in the "live TV" era. By the mid-1980s, all three local stations had the capability of doing remote broadcasts from the immediate viewing area. In fact, WRCB Channel 3 did a handful of live shows from remote locations in the early 1960s, but due to the bulky equipment and elaborate set-up, they were few and far between. By May of 1987, it was far less cumbersome, so the presidential visit was a "must-do" live event for local stations.

Before the president spoke to the high school seniors, he made time for a visit with some of the county's top teachers and a session with newspaper reporters. The questions ranged from concerns over the Persian Gulf to textile layoffs in Rhea County, but "The Great Communicator" offered polite responses, and said he was ready for another round after each reporter had asked their allotted single question.

Then-White House communications director Tom Griscom, a native Chattanoogan, remembers how the trip was arranged, and recalls a fun fact about a local fast food favorite.

Griscom said, "The White House was looking for a graduation event. It was a surprise to learn that my hometown was chosen. This was a few months after Sen. Howard Baker had become chief of staff to President Reagan. Sen. Baker, a longtime Krystal hamburgers fan, felt it would be a great addition to the trip to serve Krystals on Air Force One. The Krystal Company set up grills in the hangar, adjacent to the presidential aircraft. As the hamburgers were being brought aboard Air Force One, the White House physician questioned whether they could be served to the President since there had not been a food test. Sen. Baker quickly interceded, and the burgers were served on the aircraft as it lifted off from Lovell Field for the return trip to Washington."

George H. W. Bush was in Chattanooga during the 1980 presidential election campaign, before he was chosen as Reagan's running mate. He later appeared at a Chattanooga fundraiser in 1986, hinting at his run for the presidency in 1988. He returned just before election day 1992 for an airport rally (accompanied by singers Ricky Skaggs and Naomi Judd), and in on April 3, 2000, he and his wife Barbara helped open the Chattanooga Lookouts new baseball stadium, then known as BellSouth Park. On April 2, 2003, "Bush 41" visited Chattanooga for a fishing and golf trip (at the Honors Course) and dined at J. Alexander's near Hamilton Place.

The elder Bush's son **George W. Bush** held an airport rally with running mate Dick Cheney just before the 2000 presidential election, and returned for a health care summit at the Chattanooga Convention and Trade Center in February 2007, also visiting Erlanger Medical Center and Porker's Bar-B-Q. He also visited with Chattanooga accountant Joe Decosimo, who handled some of the family's financial dealings.

President George W. Bush dines with patrons at Porker's Bar-B-Q in Chattanooga in 2007. (White House/Paul Morse)

Barack Obama visited Chattanooga while in office, touring the Amazon Fulfillment Center in Chattanooga, and speaking to Amazon employees on July 30, 2013.

Long before being elected president, **Donald Trump** was at the Chattanooga airport, Lovell Field with then-girlfriend Marla Maples on Christmas Eve 1990. He also visited Northwest Whitfield High School's homecoming football game in Tunnel Hill, Georgia with Maples (the school's 1981 homecoming queen) on October 21, 1991, and at an Alzheimer's fund-raising reception (hosted by Maples) at the Dalton, GA Golf and Country Club on March 21, 1992.

President Barack Obama speaks to Amazon employees in Chattanooga in 2013.

During his term, he spoke at a political rally for Republican US Senate candidate Marsha Blackburn at the UTC Arena on November 4, 2018, and at Dalton GA airport on Jan. 4, 2021 in support of US Senators David Perdue and Kelly Loeffler.

On November 4, 1977, the man who would become our 46th president in 2021, **Joe Biden**, then a 35-year-old Democratic Senator from Delaware, spoke at the Kefauver dinner for Hamilton County Democrats at the Downtown Sheraton.

Biden returned to Chattanooga as Vice President, on August 15, 2015, speaking at the Fallen Five Memorial Service at the UTC McKenzie Arena. The event honored the four Marines and one Sailor who died in the Navy Operational Support Center Chattanooga shooting on July 16, 2015.

From military service, vacationing, campaigning, to dedicating government facilities, the Chattanooga area has proven to be a popular destination for our commanders-in-chief

Vice President Joe Biden speaking at Fallen Five Memorial Service in Chattanooga in 2015. (U.S. Navy photo: Mass Communication Specialist 2nd Class Justin Wolpert)

CHAPTER 11

Miscellaneous Celebrity Appearances and Visits

This may be my favorite chapter in the book.

Although I originally intended only to document the performing artists who played Chattanooga's big stages, I quickly realized I would be ignoring a lot of history if I stopped there. There are many great stories about famous people who stopped by, passed through, or in some way made a personal connection to Chattanooga.

As you'll read below, "Buffalo Bill" had family in the Chattanooga area. Helen Keller "saw" our beautiful scenery. Winston Churchill angrily lashed out at a prying newspaper reporter from the door of his hotel room.

Everybody who was anybody spoke to the Rotary Club, or played golf at the Chattanooga Golf and Country Club. Aviation heroes Charles Lindbergh and Amelia Earhart were in our town, not to mention countless war heroes.

The iconic names of our childhood: Billy Graham, Bob Hope, Roy Rogers and Dale Evans, Gene Autry, Bing Crosby, Betty White, Red Skelton, Regis Philbin, "The Fonz," "The Cisco Kid" and "Daniel Boone" all made stops here.

We've hosted the stars of the Metropolitan Opera and the stars of the Grand Ole Opry. The Prince of Prussia has visited, as have the Dukes of Hazzard.

Elvis Presley never played a show in Chattanooga, but he stopped in to visit a few times.

Rev. Martin Luther King Jr wanted to work in Chattanooga early in his career, and when that didn't work out, he moved on to other endeavors.

"Gomer Pyle" worked, acted, and sang in Chattanooga before he dazzled everyone else with his talent.

Aretha Franklin sang on one of our stages, but only as a preacher's daughter. Diane Sawyer also attracted local attention while she was a teenager.

During the 1970s, you might see Tiny Tim, Andy Warhol, or the Sheriff from "Walking Tall" on our streets.

We have hosted beauty queens, astronauts, world leaders, evangelists, famous journalists, billionaires, and best-selling authors. Even a US Supreme Court Justice was just another tourist, making a fuss over our Tennessee Aquarium.

On the other side of the coin, many of our locals, born and raised here, spread their wings and shared their talents with the world. Thankfully, they still come back home now and then. They're documented here too.

Here is a listing of some of the well known people who spent a little, or a lot of time in Chattanooga, beginning with the years prior to 1940:

Buffalo Bill Cody visited Chattanooga with his Wild West show seven times between 1895 and 1911. His first appearance was October 26, 1895. His daughter Erma and son-in-law. 2nd Lt. Clarence Stott, lived in Fort Oglethorpe where Stott was stationed. Cody made annual visits (usually at Christmas time) to visit them in the early 1900s.

3/2/1902 Prince Henry of Prussia took a ride on the Incline Railway.

3/16/1906 Sarah Bernhardt in "Camille" in old Auditorium at East 9th St. (burned 1916)

11/8/1910, Ethel Barrymore starred in "Mid Channel" at the Lyric Theater in downtown Chattanooga.

3/14/1911 Sarah Bernhardt, actress appeared at the Bijou Theater

Bessie Smith ("Empress of the Blues") born in Chattanooga April 15, 1894, performed in the city as part of a vaudeville troupe in 1912

2/22/1916 Helen Keller, deaf-blind activist, author, and lecturer at Bijou Theater (she said she had visited Chattanooga several times before, and had enjoyed "seeing" the beauty of the scenery)

3/19/1919 Internationally known Scottish comedian Harry Lauder spoke to Rotary Club of Chattanooga

5/29/19 Sgt. Alvin C. York, Tenn. Native and World War I hero, speaks to Rotary Club at Hotel Patten

11/9/1919 and **12/21/1919** Rev. Billy Sunday at makeshift tabernacle at 9th and Broad (site of old City Auditorium)

2/19/1920 Gen. John J. Pershing, World War I hero, visited Chickamauga Battlefield, McCallie School, the Hotel Patten, the Billy Sunday Tabernacle, and the Chattanooga Golf and Country Club. His aide was Col. George Marshall, who went on to become Army Chief of Staff during World War II Secretary of State, and Secretary of Defense.

5/19/22 Adolph S. Ochs, publisher of Chattanooga Times and New York Times spoke to Rotary Club at Chattanooga High School

10/16/1924 Conductor and composer John Phillip Sousa speaks to Rotary Club at Hotel Patten

July 1925 Scopes trial in Dayton, TN. Clarence Darrow and William Jennings Bryan spent a considerable amount of time in the Chattanooga area, and Bryan spent his last night at the Hotel Ross on Patten Parkway. Journalist H.L. Mencken's commentaries were syndicated nationally, and he stayed on Lookout Mountain during the trial. Darrow lectured at the Tivoli Theater, and attended a dinner party at the Fairyland Club on Lookout Mountain.

"Gone With The Wind" author Margaret Mitchell visited friends in Chattanooga and Dalton, GA often, beginning in 1927. She visited local Civil War battlefields.

10/5/1927 Charles Lindbergh at Marr Field, then downtown at 11th and Broad St.

1928 Helen Keller and Anne Sullivan visited Ringgold, GA High School

7/2/28 Admiral Richard E. Byrd, polar explorer, visited Adolph J. Ochs 50 year celebration as publisher of the Chattanooga Times, at the Lookout Mountain Hotel

11/29/28 Adolph Ochs, publisher of New York Times and Chattanooga Times, spoke to Rotary Club at Hotel Patten

2/24/32 Winston Churchill, described by the Chattanooga Times as a British soldier, statesman, and author, chased a Times reporter away from his Read House hotel room door after the reporter had arrived unannounced and uninvited. He was staying for the night in the Mary Garden Suite of the Read House en route from from Atlanta to Grand Rapids, Michigan with his daughter Diana. Churchill, who had visited the Chickamauga Battlefield earlier in the day, was wearing a "brown dressing gown," according to the reporter. Churchill called the hotel manage, and demanded a guard for the remainder of his stay.

2/6/34 Amelia Earhart, aviation pioneer, and the first woman to fly solo across the Atlantic Ocean, spent the night at the Hotel Patten en route from Rome, Georgia to Washington D.C. and then to her home in New York. A newspaper report says she was driving solo as well, in an "enormous Lincoln." She said she wished she had more time to see Chattanooga's attractions, and hoped to return in the future. Sadly, she and her navigator are thought to have disappeared in the central Pacific Ocean on July 2, 1937. She was 39 years old.

4/27- 5/19, 1935 Rev. Billy Sunday at First Baptist Church in Chattanooga (he became ill, and died several months later)

In 1936, Billy Graham attended Bob Jones College (now Bob Jones University) when it was in Cleveland, Tennessee. He delivered his first sermon at Charleston Methodist Church, and his second at Antioch Baptist Church, both in Bradley County, Tennessee.

1938 George "Little Georgie" Gobel appeared at WDOD Playhouse in downtown Chattanooga at age 18. He later starred in various CBS and NBC television shows.

6/2/38 Roy Rogers promoted his new movie "Under Western Stars" at the Rialto Theater, E.7th at Market Street

2/9/39 Actress Ethel Barrymore at the Bijou Theater (almost thirty years after her first Chattanooga visit)

7/16/39 Singing Cowboy Gene Autry at the Bijou Theater

Bing Crosby in Fort Oglethorpe, Georgia in 1943. (National Park Service)

The 1940s

10/2/41 Actress Susan Hayward rode the Incline Railway and visited Warner Park while in Chattanooga for the Cotton Ball. She stayed at the Fairyland Club during her visit, and also attended a Rotary Club dinner. She had been invited by Tivoli Theater manager Emmett Rogers.

9/1/42 Actress Greer Garson and World War I hero Alvin C. York spoke at the Read House for War Bonds promotion.

6/1/43 Bing Crosby at Fort Oglethorpe Women's Army Auxiliary Corps Training Site, performed at the open air theater, spent the night at Read House.... Did the show on 24 hours notice, after being asked to make a stop on his way from Birmingham to Nashville. Crowd estimated at 6,000. Other visitors to the training center included: Sgt Alvin York, World War I US Army Medal of Honor recipient, actor Walter Pidgeon, Sir Winston Churchill's daughter Mary Churchill, actor John Payne, entertainer Al Jolson, and opera star Marian Anderson.

In 1943, future Israeli Prime Minister Golda Meir visited Chattanooga.

In 1946, Pat Robertson, evangelist, future Republican presidential candidate (1988), and 700 Club TV host, graduated from McCallie School

6/2/47 Bob Hope played golf at the Chattanooga Golf and Country Club

6/3/47 Bob Hope played golf at the Fairyland Golf Club on Lookout Mountain

6/3/47 Bob Hope broadcast his weekly NBC radio show from Chattanooga High School auditorium with Van Heflin, Desi Arnaz, Jerry Colonna, and Georgia Gibbs

In the 1940s, Bob Hope and Doris Day appeared at Engel Stadium

5/14/48 Cowboy movie star Gabby Hayes signed autographs at Lookouts game at Engel Stadium. He also visited the News-Free Press to meet with 11-year-old Charles Cronan, whom he was sponsoring in the Soap Box Derby

5/24/48 Ralph McGill, Atlanta Constitution editor and McCallie School alumnus, spoke at McCallie commencement.

From 1949 to 1955 pro wrestler Gorgeous George appeared several times at Memorial Auditorium. Wrestler Buddy Rogers, a national champion, appeared on March 16, 1953.

The 1950s

1950s (exact date unknown) Artist Edward Hopper stayed at the Park Hotel in Chattanooga. He was passing through Chattanooga when his car broke down, and he had to stay at the hotel for several days.

On **3/8/50** and **12/5/52** Cowboy actor/singer Gene Autry visited T.C. Thompson Children's Hospital, and the Mountain City Club.

5/15/50 World War I hero Alvin C. York and World War II hero Charles Coolidge rode in the first Armed Forces Day parade in downtown Chattanooga.

1953 Rev. Martin Luther King Jr. applies for the pastor's position at First Baptist Church on East 8th Street. At age 24, the church deacons thought he was too young.

3/15-4/12, 1953 Rev. Billy Graham at Warner Park Fieldhouse

3/25/53 Rev. Billy Graham speaks to combined meeting of Kiwanis, Rotary and Civitan Clubs at Read House

4/5/53 Rev. Billy Graham spoke at Chamberlain Field at University of Chattanooga (attendance 12,500)

5/2/53 Roy Rogers and wife Dale Evans rode the Incline

Russ Ward, who was an NBC News correspondent from 1953-1987 was born and raised in Chattanooga, and graduated from Chattanooga High School

5/28/55 Fess Parker appeared at Engel Stadium

In 1956, Tommy Charles (whose real name was Charles Epperson) appeared in the movie "Shake, Rattle and Rock." Charles was a Chattanooga native who went on to a successful radio and recording career. As Charles Epperson, he sang on WDEF-TV from 1954 to 1956, and was signed to Decca Records. In 1953, he performed on the Horace Heidt national radio show on the CBS network. He was a graduate of McCallie School and the University of Chattanooga.

7/4/56 Elvis Presley has breakfast at Chattanooga Choo Choo terminal while en route from New York to Memphis

1957 Don Everly (Everly Brothers) gets married at Ringgold, GA Wedding Chapel

In parts of 1957 and 1958, Jim Nabors, who would later become famous as "Gomer Pyle" worked as a film cutter at WRGP (now WRCB) Channel 3, and also appeared in several Chattanooga Little Theater plays.

6/7/57 Dave Garroway and Helen O'Connell broadcast the NBC Today Show live from Lookout Mountain. O'Connell also broadcast her weekly evening show from Rock City that night.

7/17/57 Actor Fess Parker met with fellow Pi Kappa Alpha fraternity members at the University of Chattanooga on Oak Street.

7/19/57 Actor James MacArthur signed autographs at the State Theater and Brainerd Theater while in town filming "Light in the Forest," a Disney movie.

7/19/57 Actor Fess Parker signed autographs at Capitol Theater, while in town filming "Light in the Forest," a Disney movie.

4/13/58 Esther Williams (actress) at Fairyland Club and grand opening of Bill Penney Tire & Marine

5/16/58 Miss America Marilyn Van Derbur performed at Miss Chattanooga pageant at Tivoli Theater

6/11/58 Duncan Renaldo (TV's Cisco Kid) appears at gun safety "western show" at Engel Stadium

2/20/59 Minnie Pearl speaks to Chattanooga Civitan Club

5/13/59 Miss America Mary Ann Mobley performs at Miss Chattanooga pageant at Tivoli Theater

In 1963, America's Junior Miss, 17-year-old Diane Sawyer of Kentucky made several appearances in Chattanooga, including a visit with Channel 3 host Roy Morris. Sawyer would go on to a long broadcast journalism career at CBS and ABC.
(Irv Prevou family/WRCB)

5/15/59 Medal of Honor recipients Desmond Doss and Charles Coolidge are grand marshals of Armed Forces Day parade in downtown Chattanooga

In the late 1950s, Lester Flatt and Earl Scruggs would do their weekly TV show live in Chattanooga TV studios.

The 1960s

In early 1960, country star Bill Anderson hosted a live Saturday morning show on WRGP-TV (now WRCB) Channel 3

From 1960 to 1963, Rev. C. T. Vivian, a civil rights leader, was pastor of the Cosmopolitan Community Church in Chattanooga

Jay Garner, Broadway and TV actor, was a Chattanooga native who worked at WDEF-TV in the early 1960s.

In the 1960s and 1970s, actors Eddie Albert ("Green Acres"), Denver Pyle ("The Dukes of Hazzard") and Burl Ives ("Rudolph the Red Nosed Reindeer") visited with psychic Doc Anderson at his home in Rossville, GA.

4/4/60 Aretha Franklin (age 18) sang at Howard High School during the appearance by her father Rev. C. L. Franklin.

4/27/60 Miss America Lynda Lee Mead performs at Miss Chattanooga pageant at Tivoli Theater

11/2/60 Russ Carlyle Orchestra at Pan-O-Ram on Lookout Mountain

11/26/60 Johnny Long and his band at Pan-O-Ram on Lookout Mountain

3/2/61 Ink Spots at Pan-O-Ram on Lookout Mountain

3/7-8/61 Woody Herman and his Orchestra at Pan-O-Ram on Lookout Mountain

4/24/61 Count Basie and his Orchestra at Pan-O-Ram on Lookout Mountain

9/25/61 Dr. Wernher Von Braun, director of Marshall Space Flight Center in Huntsville, Alabama spoke to Tennessee Valley Medical Assembly at the Read House.

11/29/61 Shep Fields and his Orchestra at Pan-O-Ram on Lookout Mountain

2/13/62 Lester Lanin and his Traveling Orchestra at Pan-O-Ram on Lookout Mountain

3/13/62 Woody Herman and his Orchestra at Pan-O-Ram on Lookout Mountain

6/26/62 Chuck Cabot Orchestra at Pan-O-Ram on Lookout Mountain

10/31/62 Tony Pastor, saxophonist at Pan-O-Ram on Lookout Mountain

7/15-16, 1963 Diane Sawyer, 17-year-old America's Jr. Miss from Kentucky, appears at Tivoli Theater for Style Show, a luncheon at the Read House, and on Channel 3's "Roy Morris Show." She visited Siskin Memorial Foundation, Lookout Mountain, Lake Chickamauga, and the Chattanooga Coca Cola Bottling Company. She would go on to become an anchor/host for CBS and ABC.

1/25/64 Cumberland Trio featuring Jerre Haskew of Chattanooga appears on ABC's "Hootenanny" TV show

Jan. 20 thru March 12, 1964 Former Teamsters President Jimmy Hoffa was in federal court on charges of jury tampering. He returned for court proceedings in 1967 and 1969.

2/13/64 Jimmy Hoffa took time out from his jury tampering trial to attend a 51st birthday party in his honor at the Pan-O-Ram club on Lookout Mountain. He then returned to the Hotel Patten.

7/15/64 Ed White (astronaut) speaks at dedication of Lovell Field airport

Mid 1960s Porter Wagoner (with Dolly Parton) would do his TV show in the Channel 3 studio at 1214 McCallie Avenue.

6/26/65 Miss America Vonda Kay Van Dyke performed at Miss Chattanooga pageant at the Tivoli Theater.

3/16/66 Dr. Norman Vincent Peale spoke to Metropolitan Dinner Club at Hotel Patten

5/30/66 Dolly Parton marries Carl Dean at Ringgold Baptist Church in Ringgold, GA

9/20/66 Cowboy actor/singer Roy Rogers at skeet tournament at Moccasin Bend Gun Club

1967 Tammy Wynette married Don Chapel at Ringgold, GA Wedding Chapel

Minnie Pearl is pictured with WDOD announcer Earl Freudenberg at the radio station's Talkathon for Cancer in 1970. (Earl Freudenberg)

5/2/67 Columnist Drew Pearson spoke to Metropolitan Dinner Club at Hotel Patten

Ben Haden, nationally known "Changed Lives" host, was pastor of First Presbyterian Church from 1968 to 1999.

Jim Nabors and his friend Farol Seretean, a Chattanoogan who helped launch his career. Nabors would often visit the Seretean family in Chattanooga. (Bert Morgan)

4/2/68 Johnny Weismuller ("Tarzan" actor, swimmer) appeared at Home Show at Memorial Auditorium

1/24/69 "Society bandleader" Lester Lanin and his orchestra played for the March of Dimes benefit at the Read House

2/16/69 George Jones marries Tammy Wynette at Ringgold, GA Wedding Chapel

2/22/69 Actor Vincent Price spoke to Metropolitan Dinner Club at Hotel Patten

5/17/69 Wilma Dykeman at Fairyland Club

5/17/69 Miss Universe Martha Vasconcellos of Brazil, was guest of Chattanooga Jaycees at Hotel Patten

5/31/69 Russ Ward, NBC news reporter and University of Chattanooga 1950 graduate, spoke to UC Alumni

6/28/69 Sir Edmund Hillary (among the first climbers to reach the summit of Mt. Everest in 1953) spoke at Read House in Chattanooga

The 1970s

In the 1970s, actor Dean Jones visited his uncle, Rev. Elton Jones of Wesley Memorial UMC in Chattanooga

In the 1970s and 1980s, TV personalities Dennis James and Art Linkletter were in Chattanooga frequently to do commercials and appearances on behalf of local financial institutions. James was spokesperson for First Federal and Linkletter did commercials for Chattanooga Federal. Both spoke to local civic clubs and charity groups during their visits.

7/25/70 Minnie Pearl visits WDOD Talkathon for Cancer

1971-72 Actor Lloyd Bridges is at Lake Chickamauga to film clips for his TV series "Lloyd Bridges Water World."

10/31/71 Leif Erickson of NBC's "High Chaparral" appears at Fall Color Cruise in Marion County

11/29/72 Gloria Steinem (feminist journalist, political activist) spoke at UTC Student Center

In 1973. Steve Allen frequently visited WRCB-TV and WDXB studios to tape commercials.

Madeleine L'Engle, author "A Wrinkle in Time" at Baylor School **9/28/73, 11/26/79**, and **1/16/86**

5/3/73 Jimmy Dean promoted his sausage brand on WDEF radio and TV

6/5/73 Buford Pusser appeared at Showcase Cinema on Brainerd Road to promote the movie about his time as Sheriff of McNairy County, Tennessee, "Walking Tall"

3/7/74 Jerry Clower spoke to Rotary Club at Read House

4/4-6, 1974 Ginger Rogers appeared at Chattanooga JC Penney stores

4/21/74 Civil rights activist Stokely Carmichael spoke at Cosmopolitan Community Church on E. 3rd Street in Chattanooga.

4/24/74 Author Wilma Dykeman spoke at Baylor School

5/18/74 Several celebrities attended Bud Seretean's surprise 50th birthday party, aboard the Julia Belle Swain riverboat, and at the Chattanooga Choo Choo. Guests included Minnie Pearl, Charo, Marguerite Piazza, Phyllis Diller, Tennessee Gov. Winfield Dunn, Kay Starr, and Jim Nabors. Bud's wife Farol Seretean had many friends in show business.

7/22/74 Former McNairy Co TN Sheriff Buford Pusser ("Walking Tall" movie) opens Ray Blanton gubernatorial campaign headquarters on Brainerd Road. Pusser died in an auto accident 29 days later.

2/25/75 Consumer advocate Ralph Nader spoke at UTC Maclellan Gym

3/5/75 Ossie Davis and Ruby Dee spoke at UTC University Center

6/4/75 Clint Walker (TV's "Cheyenne") playing in Mickey Mantle golf tournament at Battlefield Golf Club, and visiting with "Doc" Anderson, who offered psychic advice to several celebrities

1/16/76 William Manchester, author of "Death of a President," was in Chattanooga doing research for a biography on Gen. Douglas MacArthur. The general's father, Arthur, had received a Medal of Honor for heroism on Missionary Ridge during the Civil War

1/27/76 "World's Strongest Man" Paul Anderson performed at FCA banquet at Read House.

2/22/76 Burt Ward (Robin from the Batman TV series) signed autographs at the Rod and Custom Autorama at Memorial Auditorium. During his Chattanooga visit, he also appeared at Hixson Elementary School.

1976, probably summertime, Elvis Presley paid a surprise visit to the Read House, where he briefly talked to WDXB announcers in their studio in the building's basement. Various Read House staff members say Presley stayed at the Read House (secretly) a handful of times over the years.

4/2/75 TV game show host Dennis James spoke to Rotary Club at Read House

6/29/75 Archie Campbell hosted a charity golf tournament at Rolling Hills Club in Cleveland for Bachman Home

4/7/76 TV game show host Dennis James spoke to Kiwanis Club

6/26/76 Archie Campbell hosted a charity golf tournament at Rolling Hills Club in Cleveland for Bachman Home

10/27/76 Richard Adams (author, Watership Down) spoke at Baylor School

1/22/77 Tiny Tim sang at Tenn. Jr. Miss pageant at Tivoli Theater

March 1977 Apollo 15 astronaut James Irwin spoke at Lee College in Cleveland, TN

3/19/77 Artist Andy Warhol visited sculptor Andre Harvey's exhibition at the Hunter Museum, at the invitation of art dealer Frank Fowler. Warhol also visited Gay and Frank Fowler in 1980

Alabama lead singer Randy Owen is set to run the bases at a charity softball game at Engel Stadium in 1982. (Alan Vandergriff)

5/28/77 Helen Wagner ("Nancy Hughes" on CBS soap opera As the World Turns) appeared at Crown Craft Mills Store, Highland Plaza in Hixson

Artist Jamie Wyeth visited the Frank Fowler family in 1977 and 1978

Artist Andre Harvey visited the Frank Fowler family in 1978

3/3/78 Archie Campbell spoke to Chattanooga Advertising Federation

George Takei (right) of Star Trek signs autographs at a WDSI promotion in 1986. He is pictured with Gary Fisher of WDSI. (Gary Fisher)

10/16/78 "Morgana the Kissing Bandit," famous for kissing baseball players on the field, appeared at Classic Cat on East Main Street

12/4/78 George Takei of "Star Trek" appeared at CARTA's new headquarters on Wilcox Boulevard

3/29/79 Political activist Eldridge Cleaver spoke at Greater Chattanooga Area Prayer Breakfast at Chattanooga Choo Choo Convention Center

11/1/79 Rev. Jesse Jackson spoke at Orchard Knob Jr. High

The 1980s

Dr. John Ankerberg, minister and author, broadcast worldwide from his Chattanooga headquarters since 1980.

4/29/80 Rev. Jerry Falwell spoke at Trinity Baptist Church on Bonny Oaks Drive

5/16/80 Retired Maj. Gen. John K. Singlaub spoke at Armed Forces Day luncheon at Read House

7/26/80 Rev. Jesse Jackson visits Chattanooga to calm residents after three nights of violence that followed a Ku Klux Klan involved shooting.

Bertie Higgins recorded hit song "Key Largo" at Pyramid's Eye Recording Studio on Lookout Mountain in 1981. Also recorded there: Allman Brothers album "Reach for the Sky," Dickey Betts' solo album, and projects by Wet Willie, Alabama, Melissa Manchester, and "The Night The Lights Went Out in Georgia" movie soundtrack with Dennis Quaid and Kristy McNichol. Producers included Scott McClellan and Sonny Limbo, and the studio was very active from the late 1970s into the 1980s.

Alabama drummer Mark Herndon visited the Chattanooga Speech and Hearing Center often in the 1980s and 1990s. Herndon served as the agency's celebrity spokesperson.

1/24/81 Alex Haley ("Roots" author) at Southern College in Collegedale, TN

1/28/82 Minnie Pearl visited the News Free Press to promote her autobiography

3/24/82 Author Dr. Roderick Nash spoke at Baylor School

7/20/82 Alabama band members Randy Owen and Teddy Gentry headed a softball team that played the KZ-106 Foul Tips at Engel Stadium. Proceeds went to Chattanooga Hamilton County Speech and Hearing Center and Orange Grove Center. Owen and Gentry sang the National Anthem.

7/22/82 Retired astronaut James Irwin (Apollo 15 in 1971) spoke to Rotary Club at Read House

10/7/82 Rev. Jerry Falwell spoke to Rotary Club at Read House

1/29/83 Ken Kercheval ("Dallas" signed autographs at National Knife Show at Chattanooga Choo Choo

6/28/83 Humorist Lewis Grizzard spoke at Chattanooga Choo Choo

8/13/83 Willard Scott appeared at Riverbend Festival, visited WRCB-TV studio

12/13/83 Lewis Grizzard spoke to Chattanooga Advertising Federation at Chattanooga Golf and Country Club

1/31/84 Deborah Allen and Rafe Van Hoy appeared at Blood Assurance

2/27/84 Kathy Mattea, singer, appeared on WDEF-TV Morning Show

3/6/84 Lewis Grizzard appeared at B. Dalton bookstore at Northgate Mall

4/5/84 Consumer advocate Ralph Nader spoke at UTC University Center

6/8/84 Actress Dale Evans and singer Debby Boone appeared at Bethel Bible School fundraiser at Quality Inn South

8/24/84 John Hartford, singer-songwriter was a guest on WDEF-TV Morning Show

9/24/84 Amy Grant was a guest on WDEF-TV Morning Show

1/11/85 Jerry Clower, comedian was a guest on WDEF-TV Morning Show

2/7/85 Clara Peller (Where's The Beef" lady) appeared at new Wendy's I-24 at 4th Avenue, and on WDEF-TV Morning Show

2/19/85 Singer Cristy Lane appeared on WDEF-TV Morning Show

2/24/85 Gary Morris and Forester Sisters appeared at Blood Assurance

3/12/85 Author/Historian Wilma Dykeman spoke at Baylor School

4/23/85 Marguerite Piazza, soprano appeared at Lung Association banquet at Chattanooga Convention Center

5/17/85 Rhea Seddon (astronaut) spoke at Armed Forces Day luncheon at Choo Choo Imperial Ballroom

6/14/85 Actor Ernest Borgnine and his wife Tova spoke at the United Scleroderma Foundation annual banquet at the Choo Choo Hilton.

8/14/85 Tipper Gore (Parents Music Resource Center) was a guest on WDEF-TV Morning Show

11/19/85 Millard Fuller, founder of Habitat for Humanity, spoke at Chattanooga Hamilton County Bicentennial Library.

Michael Houser, a graduate of Hixson High School, was a member of Widespread Panic from 1986 until his death in 2002. The band performed frequently in Chattanooga.

Todd Nance, a graduate of Central High School was a member of Widespread Panic from 1986 to 2016. He died in 2020.

1/24/86 Tatum O'Neal accompanied John McEnroe at tennis exhibition, UTC Arena

3/17/86 Alex Haley ("Roots" author) at Chattanooga Convention and Trade Center

3/20/86 The Osmond brothers visited Children's Hospital and WDEF-TV Morning Show

4/18/86 The Judds and Forester Sisters appeared at Blood Assurance

4/28/86 Rev. Jerry Falwell was at B Dalton Booksellers in East Ridge to sign copies of his new book "If I Should Die Before I Wake"

5/1/86 Mel Tillis and Ralph Emery were at the Litchfield Cinema, Northgate Crossing for the premiere of the movie "Uphill All The Way," which starred Tillis and Roy Clark. Proceeds from the event went to Chattanooga Hamilton County Speech and Hearing Center.

5/2/86 Singer Ty Herndon appeared on WDEF-TV Morning Show

5/9-10, 1986 T. G. Sheppard and Tom T. Hall appeared at Chattanooga Convention and Trade Center for Red Food fair.

5/15/86 UPI White House reporter Helen Thomas spoke at Arts & Education Lecture at Read House

5/16/86 Author Betty Friedan spoke at UTC Women's Conference

7/4/86 George Takei, Nichelle Nichols, James Doohan (Star Trek) at Chattanooga Convention Center for Trek-a-thon Convention (sponsored by WDSI) and at Engel Stadium for Lookouts baseball game

8/15/86 Gen. Chuck Yeager, the first pilot to exceed the speed of sound, attended the weighing-in ceremony of the Bass Masters Classic fishing tournament at the UTC Arena.

9/1/86 "MASH" stars McLean Stevenson, Jamie Farr, and Larry Linville signed autographs during "MASH-a-thon" (sponsored by WDSI) at Jaycee Fairgrounds on Amnicola Highway

10/15/86 Tamilee Webb ("Buns of Steel" fitness author and video star) appeared on WDEF-TV Morning Show

10/29/86 Actress Morgan Fairchild visited UTC Arena, with boyfriend Gary Puckett

3/6/87 Tom Wopat appeared at Blood Assurance (US-101 Vein Drain)

3/13/87 Christie Brinkley (and daughter Alexa) accompanied Billy Joel at his UTC Arena concert

4/25/87 DeForest Kelley and Walter Koenig (Star Trek) appeared at "Trek-a-Thon" (sponsored by WDSI) at Chattanooga Convention and Trade Center

5/11/87 Forester Sisters MDA charity concert and golf tournament at Chattanooga Choo Choo and Chattanooga Golf and Country Club with guests Leslie Nielsen (Naked Gun, Airplane) Gary Morris, Chet Atkins, Sweethearts of the Rodeo, Rockin' Sidney, Boots Randolph, and Vince Gill.

5/19/87 During President Reagan's visit to the UTC Arena, the traveling press corps included ABC's Sam Donaldson and CBS's Bill Plante, both White House correspondents and by then, celebrities in their own right.

8/2/87 Rev. Jerry Falwell spoke at Trinity Baptist Church in Chattanooga

8/25/87 Lewis Grizzard spoke at Sheraton City Center Hotel

9/17/87 Author/Historian Wilma Dykeman at Baylor School

10/15/87 Miss America 1987 Kellye Cash of Tennessee was guest speaker at Chattanooga Realtors 75th anniversary celebration at Choo Choo Imperial Ballroom

5/12/88 Anthony Lewis, 2-time Pulitzer Prize winning columnist for the New York Times, spoke at Arts and Education lecture at Choo Choo

6/9/88 Evangelist Jimmy Swaggart spoke at opening of Bible Teaching Center on Brainerd Road

6/23/88 NBC Today weatherman Willard Scott did a live broadcast from Riverbend Festival

10/3/88 Poet Maya Angelou speaks to 2,000 students at Howard High School

10/29/88 Marguerite Piazza, soprano, appeared at Siskin Star Night at Choo Choo

April 6-8, 1989 Southern Literature Conference at Tivoli Theater and UTC, with authors William Styron, Walker Percy, Louis Rubin, Horton Foote, Shelby Foote, Cleanth Brooks, C. Vann Woodward, Larry Brown, Clyde Edgerton, Gail Godwin, and Josephine Humphreys.

4/30/89 Alex Haley ("Roots" author) spoke at UTC commencement, UTC Arena (with US Education Secretary Lamar Alexander)

5/18/89 Former Federal Budget Director Bert Lance spoke at Arts & Education council at Chattanooga Convention Center

5/19/89 Singers Jeannie C. Riley, Sylvia, T. Graham Brown, and Lynn Anderson visited several Red Food stores for Cancer Control Drive. They were accompanied by NFL stars Bill Bates and Alex Webster, and radio/TV host Wolfman Jack.

NBC's Today Show weatherman Willard Scott (3rd from left) broadcasting live from the Share Your Christmas Food Drive with (from left) WRCB's Cindy Sexton, David Glenn, and Bill Markham. (WRCB)

11/16/89 Actor Dennis Haskins of "Saved by the Bell," a Notre Dame High School graduate, spoke to students at his alma mater.

Lisa Robertson, a graduate of Southern College in Collegedale was Miss Tennessee 1989, and became a popular host on QVC.

Chattanooga native Dennis Haskins (left) with one of his many local fans, Jon Coppinger. Haskins played "Mr. Belding" on NBC's "Saved By The Bell" and visited his hometown often. (Jon Coppinger)

Hey Hey Hey, it's Mr. Belding!

Every now and then, you'll hear someone say, "If you ever make it to Hollywood, don't forget your friends!" Well, Dennis Haskins made it to Hollywood in a big way, and he sure hasn't forgotten his friends. The Chattanooga native, a proud alumnus of Notre Dame High School and UTC, is a frequent visitor to his hometown, and he always makes us smile.

Prior to his acting career, Dennis managed and promoted several acts back in the 1970s, including Overland Express.

Dennis first got national attention as "King of the Don't Blinks," as in, don't blink or you'll miss him. He was often cast in bit parts, including the first episode of "Dukes of Hazzard," playing a long-haired, mouthy rascal who got a little too close to Daisy Duke. Soon he was turning up in various sitcoms and dramas, but rarely for more than a minute or so. That all changed in 1988 when he was hired to play the principal in a Saturday morning sitcom called "Good Morning Miss Bliss," which soon morphed into "Saved By The Bell." NBC picked up the show, and it's been on TV ever since it premiered on August 20, 1989. You can bet that somewhere in the world, right now, one of those reruns is on the air.

As principal Richard Belding, Dennis played the well-meaning, but often befuddled authority figure at Bayside High School. Zack, Slater, Screech, Jessie, Lisa and Kelly were always up to something, and Mr. Belding was there to smooth things out. On more than one occasion, the gang would try to sneak something past him, usually resulting in Mr. Belding exclaiming, "Hey, hey, hey, hey, hey....WHAT is going ON here?" Things usually worked out fine, and kids across America wished they had a principal who was that cool.

I got to know Dennis pretty well while he was filming the show, and have a lot of great memories from those years. Each Christmas he would come back home to visit his family (in fact, he had a framed picture of them in his TV principal's office). He would always ask me to line up a visit to Children's Hospital. The kids were thrilled to see a genuine TV star, and he was even happier to pose for pictures and sign autographs.

In 1992, I somehow talked my boss into flying a news photographer and me to Los Angeles to do some behind-the-scenes stories on Dennis and his show, and we had a great time. The cast members and producers couldn't have been nicer, despite the fact they were cranking out shows one after another, with little time to socialize. We had a lot of laughs doing these stories, and they are among the most viewed videos on my YouTube channel.

After the original cast "graduated," there were several sequels: The College Years, The New Class and others. New cast members floated in and out, but Mr. Belding was the one constant.

During his visits to Chattanooga, Dennis never disappoints his fans. He's always approachable, and is genuinely grateful for the fame and friendships he's gained over the years.

Dennis is a huge fans of the UTC Mocs, often showing up at games, or tweeting about their big wins. For many years, he has returned home for the holidays to reunite with his old friends from radio, TV, music and sports.

Dennis will always be part of our family in Chattanooga. Thanks for always making us smile, Dennis.

Rev. Billy Graham Visits Baylor School

It was September 24, 1991. Rev. Billy Graham visited Chattanooga's Baylor School to dedicate the new Alumni Chapel. He arrived by helicopter, on a rainy day with students lining Baylor's parking lot. He only had about 15 minutes to preach. He was introduced by Rev. Ben Haden, with music provided by Dr. Glenn Draper and the Chattanooga Singers.

Graham's message was aimed primarily at teens. "Sex outside of marriage is wrong, and you know that," he said. "And it's becoming very dangerous."

A couple of times during his message, he mistakenly referred to being at "McCallie School" instead of Baylor. The mention of the rival school elicited a few groans from the Baylor audience, but his error was understandable. He was close friends with the McCallie family, who had helped arrange his visit.

After the chapel program and a lunch with local dignitaries, a select group of Baylor patrons enjoyed an autograph and photo session, before he was whisked away in a waiting helicopter. He had just flown in from New York, and was due in France the next day.

This was not Graham's first visit to Chattanooga. In 1950, he preached at Engel Stadium. In 1953, he made history at the Warner Park Fieldhouse. His crusades had long been segregated, but he had decided to end that practice. According to Earl Freudenberg, Graham personally moved the rope, allowing all races to join together. "It made one usher very upset," Freudenberg said, "but it needed to happen, and that's a big part of the history of Billy Graham."

As Graham told his Baylor audience, "I just determined this is how it was going to be. I never again spoke to a segregated crowd." Although Billy Graham was able to personally meet only a fraction of his Chattanooga area followers, those who were in attendance at Baylor that day say they'll never forget his passion, his charisma, and his inspiring message.

The 1990s

In the 1990s, actress Dixie Carter ("Designing Women"), a Tennessee native, and her husband Hal Holbrook ("Mark Twain") owned a vacation home in the Harrison area, and Dixie appeared in several commercials for the BellSouth Yellow Pages, filmed at her home.

During the 1990 college basketball season, 12-year old Usher Raymond sang the national anthem and performed at halftime during UTC games. The Dalewood Middle School student also was part of a vocal group called The Happy Clowns managed by Daryl Wheeler, before moving to Atlanta to pursue a solo career.

1/3/90 Wrestlers Hulk Hogan and Dusty Rhodes performed at the UTC Arena

2/17/90 TV personality and radio disc jockey Wolfman Jack appeared at the Adult Toy Show at Chattanooga Convention Center

2/19/90 Nina Totenberg of NPR spoke at Baylor School

5/25/90 Robin Leach, Mickey Gilley, and Janie Fricke were on Celebrity Cruise on Southern Belle for Red Food Cancer Control Drive

7/10/90 Desmond Doss, Medal of Honor winner spoke at dedication of highway in his honor in Walker County, GA. He was a longtime Chattanooga area resident, primarily in Lookout Mountain, GA. He was the subject of the movie "Hacksaw Ridge" in 2016.

8/19/90 Actress Dixie Carter, longtime University of Georgia football coach Vince Dooley, GA Gov. Joe Frank Harris, TN Gov. Ned McWherter, US Interior Secretary Manuel Lujan, TN US Rep. Marilyn Lloyd, and GA US Rep. Buddy Darden were at Chickamauga and Chattanooga National Military Park Centennial celebration

10/14/90 Lt. Col. Oliver North spoke at Chattanooga Choo Choo

12/4/90 Historian Taylor Branch spoke at Baylor School

1/8/91 Wrestlers Hulk Hogan, Randy Savage, and Sgt. Slaughter performed at UTC Arena

1/21/91 Truett Cathy, founder of Chick-fil-A, spoke at McCallie School.

4/4-6, 1991 Southern Literature Conference at Tivoli Theater, UTC and the Read House, with authors Shelby Foote, Eudora Welty, Alfred Uhry, Tina McElroy Ansa, Madison Smartt Bell, John Hope Franklin, Jill McCorkle, Elizabeth Spencer, Peter Taylor, Andrew Lytle, C. Vann Woodward, Cleanth Brooks, Louis Rubin, Horton Foote, Ernest Gaines, George Garrett, George Core, Fred Chappell, Wendell Berry, Blyden Jackson, Walter Sullivan, and Lewis Simpson.

4/12/91 NBC News anchor Deborah Norville spoke at Girls Preparatory School

8/2/91 Evangelist Jimmy Swaggart spoke at Bible Teaching Center on Brainerd Road

9/24/91 Rev. Billy Graham spoke at Baylor School chapel dedication

11/14/91 ABC's "Good Morning America" broadcast live from the UTC campus and Point Park, with anchors Charles Gibson, Joan Lunden, and Spencer Christian

12/11/91 NBC "Today Show" personality Willard Scott did a live broadcast from WRCB Share Your Christmas Food Drive at Ross's Landing

1992 The Stray Cats recorded their album "Choo Choo Hot Fish" at Pyramid Studio on Lookout Mountain

1/22/92 Truett Cathy, founder of Chick-fil-A, spoke at UTC University Center.

5/9/92 Jerry Clower was commencement speaker at Cleveland State Community College

From 1993 to 1995 Lara Spencer of ABC's Good Morning America worked as a reporter at WDEF-TV

1/14/93 Ted Turner spoke at his alma mater, McCallie School

5/11/93 Dr. June Scobee Rodgers, widow of Challenger Space Shuttle Commander Richard "Dick" *Scobee*, spoke at Women of Distinction luncheon. Dr. Rodgers is a Chattanooga resident who has dedicated her life to writing, speaking, and education. She serves as a Founding Chairman for the Challenger Center for Space Science Education, where each year over 500,000 students participate in space programs.

8/11/93 Ed McMahon of "Star Search" appeared at Choo Choo for American Red Cross

11/16/93 Sir Edmund Hillary spoke at Baylor School

11/30/93 Lewis Grizzard signed autographs at Barrett and Company Booksellers in Riverview

5/18/94 Kenny Chesney signed autographs at Turtles record store in Chattanooga

6/26/94 Rev. Jerry Falwell spoke at Heritage Baptist Church in Chattanooga

8/1/94 Michael Bolton's softball team "Bolton's Bombers" played a Chattanooga media team at Engel Stadium.

9/8/94 Actress Brenda Vaccaro took a break from filming in Nashville to dine at the River Inn and visit the Tennessee Aquarium

10/28/94 Singer Barbara Mandrell spoke at Girls Preparatory School

12/18/94 Actress Marla Maples Trump and her daughter Tiffany Trump visited Hamilton Place Mall for a photo with Santa Claus.

From 1995 to 1997, Kirsten Gum, Travel Channel host, worked at WRCB-TV.

5/18/95 Comedian/activist Dick Gregory spoke at mental health workshop at Chattanooga Choo Choo

5/26/95 Willard Scott appeared at the opening day of Creative Discovery Museum

2/22/96 Dennis Weaver visited CARTA to see electric buses

4/4/96 Frank and Kathie Lee Gifford attended Chattanooga Lookouts game at Engel Stadium

4/22/96 Rev. Franklin Graham spoke at Baylor School

5/7/96 Gordon Jump ("lonely" Maytag repairman) visited Maytag employees in Cleveland, TN

10/15/96 Charlton Heston spoke at the Chattanooga Choo Choo on behalf of U.S. Senator Fred Thompson's re-election campaign.

Rocker Adam Ant (real name Stuart Goddard) lived in Bledsoe County, Tennessee "for a couple of years" he said. His daughter Lily Goddard was born in Tennessee in 1998. Rhea County Executive Billy Ray Patton performed Ant's wedding to Lorraine Gibson at the Rhea County Courthouse in 1997. They divorced the following year.

2/16/97 "Stone Cold" Steve Austin, Vader, the Undertaker and Bret "Hit Man" Hart at WWF wrestling at UTC Arena

5/2/97 Henry "The Fonz" Winkler at Chattanooga Convention and Trade Center (dyslexia conference)

9/27/97 Dr. Ruth Westheimer, sex therapist and TV talk show host, spoke to Jewish Federation at Chattanooga Theatre Center

10/16/97 Actor Dennis Weaver spoke at Chattanooga State (environmental speech)

Kathie Lee Gifford (left) is pictured with WTVC news anchor MaryEllen Locher at a Chattanooga Lookouts game in 1996. (WTVC)

In 1998 and 1999, Ryan Owens of ABC News worked at WRCB-TV

4/4/98 Truett Cathy, founder of Chick-fil-A, spoke at 25th anniversary of Brainerd Baptist School at Downtown Marriott in Chattanooga.

5/25/98 Pro wrestlers The Rock (Dwayne Johnson), "Stone Cold" Steve Austin, the Undertaker, and Triple H at UTC Arena for WWF Raw

Singer Aaliyah visited radio personality Eric Foster at the WJTT Power 94 studio in Chattanooga in 1996. (Eric Foster)

9/1/98 Gordon Jump, Maytag commercial "lonely" repair man, spoke to United Way of Cleveland, TN

9/4/98 Richard Simmons appeared at Hamilton Place Mall and WRCB-TV studio

11/19/98 Dixie Carter speaks at Celebrity Luncheon for the Junior League at the Chattanooga Convention Center

1/15/99 Truett Cathy, founder of Chick-fil-A, spoke to Catoosa County Chamber of Commerce awards banquet at Northwest Georgia Convention and Trade Center in Dalton, GA.

Fitness instructor and TV personality Richard Simmons visited Cindy Sexton and David Carroll at WRCB during a series of appearances in Chattanooga in 1998.

1/17/99 Henry Winkler spoke at UTC (dyslexia speech)

2/16/99 "Stone Cold" Steve Austin and the Undertaker at WWF Raw wrestling at UTC Arena

3/30/99 Wilma Dykeman spoke at Baylor School

6/26/99 "Gilligan's Island" stars Bob Denver and Dawn Wells were on Southern Belle for Blood Assurance fundraiser, and at Hamilton Place Mall

11/19/99 Dr. Ben Carson spoke to Chattanooga-Hamilton County Medical Society at Chattanooga Convention and Trade Center

---

The Joy of Richard Simmons

During the 1980s and 90s Richard Simmons was a constant presence on TV. He had his own daily show for a while, and later was a frequent guest with David Letterman, Jay Leno and Regis Philbin. Attired in a sparkly tank top and short shorts, he shared his own weight loss story, and encouraged millions of Americans to sweat to the oldies.

In September 1998, he visited Chattanooga. He held a Friday workout at the YMCA, and hosted a Saturday public appearance at Hamilton Place Mall.

We were fortunate to have him on Channel 3's "Live at 5:30" program on that Friday evening. Cindy Sexton and I, along with our entire crew, have fond memories of that day. Richard was in top form, bubbling over with enthusiasm, throwing our scripts in the air, massaging our feet, and spreading his special brand of joy.

The 2000s

Rachel Boston, a Signal Mountain resident who graduated from GPS in 2000, has starred in several TV shows and movies. She was Miss Tennessee Teen USA 1999.

5/20/00 Actress Mary Costa was honored as Tenn. Woman of Distinction at Chattanooga Convention Center

6/24/00 "Munsters" stars Butch Patrick and Al Lewis were on Southern Belle for Blood Assurance fundraiser, and at Hamilton Place Mall

10/20/00 Syndicated columnist Walter Williams spoke at Burkett Miller Lecture Series at UTC Fine Arts Center

10/28/00 Jared Fogle, Subway sandwich spokesperson spoke at Coolidge Park

12/22/00 Pro wrestlers Chris Benoit, Kurt Angle, The Rock (Dwayne Johnson), "Stone Cold" Steve Austin, Kane (now Knox County Mayor Glenn Jacobs), and the Undertaker at UTC Arena

April 2001 Actress Mimi Kennedy spoke at Howard Elementary School, Chattanooga High School for Performing Arts, and Baylor School

5/1/01 Actress Patricia Neal was honored as Tenn. Woman of Distinction at Chattanooga Choo Choo

9/29/01 Patti Davis, daughter of former President Ronald Reagan and First Lady Nancy Reagan, spoke at Retirement Living Expo at Hamilton Place Mall

10/16/01 "Survivor" Season 2 champion Tina Wesson signed autographs at Bi-Lo supermarket on East Brainerd Road

1/16/02 Truett Cathy, founder of Chick-fil-A, spoke at Covenant College on Lookout Mountain.

Feb. 2002 Actress/model Kathy Ireland visited Roan School in Dalton. She was representing Shaw Industries.

5/1/02 US Olympic basketball player (and Brainerd High graduate) Venus Lacy was honored as Tenn. Woman of Distinction at Chattanooga Choo Choo

5/17/02 Gordon Jump ("lonely" Maytag repair man, and star of WKRP in Cincinnati) visits Maytag in Cleveland, TN, and Make A Wish Foundation on Willow Street in Chattanooga

10/10/02 Truett Cathy, founder of Chick-fil-A, spoke at Lee University in Cleveland, TN.

10/18/02 TV personality Art Linkletter spoke at Hamilton Place Mall

12/29/02 Evangelist Jimmy Swaggart spoke at the funeral for Clyde Fuller, City Church of Chattanooga

4/18/03 Jim Fowler of NBC's "Wild Kingdom" appeared at Chattanooga Nature Center

May 2003 Billionaire Warren Buffett spoke to Boys and Girls Club of Dalton annual dinner, and made generous donations to the organization for many years.

10/11/03 Jared Fogle, Subway sandwich spokesperson was a guest at the Hamilton County Heart Walk

12/9/03 Actress and model Kathy Ireland spoke at the Big Brothers Big Sisters annual luncheon at the Chattanooga Convention Center

In 2004 Actress Dawn Wells spoke to acting students at Chattanooga High School and Chattanooga Theatre Center

3/6/04 Actress Mimi Kennedy spoke at Theater Conference at Chattanooga Theatre Center

August 2004 "Leave it to Beaver" stars Tony Dow and Ken Osmond, along with comedian Sinbad appeared at Allan Jones' home in Cleveland, where he surprised his daughter Abby with a Back To School party.

11/11/04 Truett Cathy, founder of Chick-fil-A, spoke at Peerless Road Church in Cleveland, TN for Tennessee Christian Academy fundraiser

2/6/05 Fitness expert and TV host Jack LaLanne, age 90, spoke (and worked out) at Hamilton Place Mall with his wife Elaine

10/5/05 Author Arthur Golden ("Memoirs of a Geisha") spoke at Baylor School

10/6/05 Rev. Jerry Falwell spoke at Highland Park Baptist Church in Chattanooga

5/5/06 Actress/author Carrie Fisher spoke at Chattanoogan Hotel for AIM Center

9/10/06 Actor Henry Winkler appeared at Hamilton Place Mall

12/20/06 Author Arthur Golden signed autographs at Rock Point Books

Will Carr of ABC News (and formerly Fox News) worked at WRCB (2006-2009) and WTVC in Chattanooga 2009-10)

1/15/07 Rev. C.T. Vivian spoke to Baylor School students and the ML King Day observance at the Tivoli Theater

9/15/07 Erik Estrada visited Dalton, GA for a car seat safety demonstration, and at WRCB studio

10/8/07 Novelist Pat Conroy spoke at Baylor School

11/17/07 Jim Lehrer of PBS dedicated new WTCI-TV studio on Bonny Oaks Drive in Chattanooga

11/27/07 Jared Fogle, Subway sandwich spokesperson, spoke at Bess T. Shepherd and Allen Elementary Schools

1/8/08 Gloria Steinem appeared at Chattanooga Convention Center, speaking to Womens Leadership Institute

1/24/08 Ted Turner spoke at McCallie School

1/24/08 "Inside Edition" host Deborah Norville (a native of Dalton, GA) spoke at the Northwest Georgia Convention Center in Dalton.

5/31/08 Actor-wrestler Tiny Lister visited Chattanooga inner city neighborhoods and spoke at Olivet Baptist Church.

9/22/08 Leonard Pitts (syndicated columnist, author) spoke at Girls Preparatory School

12/4/08 Author Jon Meacham (McCallie School graduate) signed books at Rock Point Books in downtown Chattanooga

In 2009 Maci Bookout and Ryan Edwards, Chattanooga natives, began appearing on MTV's long-running "Teen Mom," reality show.

1/14/09 Historian Doris Kearns Goodwin spoke at UTC University Center

1/19/09 Morris Dees, founder of Southern Poverty Law Center at MLK Day, Tivoli Theater

6/17/09 Rev. Jesse Jackson spoke to Volkswagen executives about minority hiring

In 2008 actor-wrestler Tiny Lister, pictured with Louis Lee, visited Chattanooga's inner city neighborhoods. (Louis Lee)

7/11/09 Paula Deen, TV cooking star and author spoke at the She Expo at Chattanooga Convention and Trade Center

10/3/09 Vern Yip of HGTV's "Deserving Design" appeared at the Home Show at Chattanooga Convention and Trade Center.

10/12/09 Marlee Matlin, the first deaf actress to win an Academy Award, spoke as part of a disability awareness campaign at the UTC Fine Arts Center

10/13/09 TV personality Jack Hanna, a zookeeper and wildlife conservationist appeared at Banana Ball at Chattanooga Zoo

11/22/09 Maci Bookout, a Chattanooga resident on MTV's "Teen Mom" reality show, spoke to students at Notre Dame High School.

Marlee Matlin, the first deaf actress to win an Academy Award, spoke at the UTC Fine Arts Center in 2009. (Wes Schultz)

Our Quiet Hero

For many years, Desmond Doss's story wasn't widely known outside a handful of Chattanooga area veterans, but that finally changed in 2016.

The movie "Hacksaw Ridge" was directed by Mel Gibson, and starred Andrew Garfield as Doss. Among the producers was Terry Benedict, a Chattanooga area resident. He befriended Doss in the early 2000's, and produced a documentary on his life, which inspired the movie.

For many years until his death in 2006, Doss lived in Walker County on Lookout Mountain. I met him at the Medal of Honor Museum in Chattanooga in the 1980s. I found him to be a quiet and humble man, very appreciative of the honors bestowed on him decades after his heroism in World War II. His then-wife Dorothy was a vocal cheerleader on his behalf, beaming with pride when a north Georgia highway was named in his honor in 1990.

The movie depicts Doss as a quiet participant in the war effort, though firmly against using a weapon. A devout Seventh Day Adventist, Doss looked for other ways to serve his country. Although Doss didn't talk much about it later in life, he was subjected to taunts from his fellow soldiers for his refusal to carry a gun.

He also faced harassment for his devotion to prayer. At one point an officer sought to have him discharged on the ground of mental illness.

He became a medic, the only way he could follow the Sixth Commandment (Thou shalt not kill), as well as the Fourth Commandment (to honor the Sabbath). Seventh-day Adventists consider Saturday the Sabbath, but Doss felt he could serve as a medic every day because he said, "Christ healed on the Sabbath."

In late April and early May of 1945, Doss's skills were put to the test in Okinawa, on the jagged Hacksaw Ridge, some 400 feet high. The conscientious objector became an active participant, saving the lives of many of his fellow soldiers in the US Army's 77th Infantry Division.

His Medal of Honor proclamation reads in part, "As troops gained the summit, a heavy concentration of artillery, mortar and machine gun fire crashed into them, inflicting approximately 75 casualties and driving others back. Private First Class Doss refused to seek cover and remained in the fire-swept area with the stricken, carrying them one-by-one to the edge of the escarpment and lowering them on a rope-support down the face of a cliff to friendly hands.

He was exposed to heavy rifle and mortar fire in rescuing a wounded man 200 yards forward. Two days later he treated four men who had been cut down while assaulting a strongly defended cave, advancing through a shower of grenades to within eight yards of enemy forces in a cave's mouth, where he dressed his comrades' wounds before making four separate trips under fire to evacuate them to safety.

He braved enemy shelling to assist an artillery officer. He applied bandages, moved his patient to a spot that offered protection from small arms fire and, while mortar shells fell close by, painstakingly administered plasma. When an American was severely wounded by fire from a cave, he crawled to him, rendered aid, and carried him 100 yards to safety while continually exposed to enemy fire."

His heroics didn't end there. "On May 21st, in a night attack, he remained in exposed territory while the rest of his company took cover, aiding the injured until he was himself seriously wounded in the legs by the explosion of a grenade. He cared for his own injuries and waited five hours before two rescuers could come to his aid. The trio was caught in an enemy tank attack and Private First Class Doss, seeing a more critically wounded man nearby, directed his bearers to aid the other man. Awaiting their return, he was again struck, this time suffering a compound fracture of one arm. With magnificent fortitude he bound a rifle stock to his shattered arm as a splint and then crawled 300 yards over rough terrain to the aid station. Through his outstanding bravery, he saved the lives of many soldiers. His name

On October 12, 1945 President Harry S Truman awards the Congressional Medal of Honor to Corporal Desmond Doss on the White House lawn.
(National Medal of Honor Museum)

became a symbol for outstanding gallantry far above and beyond the call of duty."

President Harry S Truman presented Desmond Doss with the Medal of Honor on October 12, 1945 calling him "one of the few objectors who was on the level." After the war, he was diagnosed with tuberculosis. This resulted in years of treatment and the loss of one lung. An overdose of antibiotic damaged his hearing, which was partially restored in 1991 with a cochlear implant. In later years, he became more interested in sharing his story, especially with younger people who could not imagine the horrors he endured.

"Hacksaw Ridge" producers said the movie showed the graphic, disturbing reality of war. It finally put Desmond Doss's name into the forefront of war heroes who have become household names.

The 2010s and Beyond

Legendary actress Betty White is pictured with WRCB's Greg Glover and Callie Starnes during her 2010 appearance at the Chattanooga Convention Center. (Callie Starnes)

During the 2010s decade, Remote Area Medical clinics founder Stan Brock, a philanthropist and TV host ("Wild Kingdom") visited the Chattanooga and Cleveland areas on numerous occasions to promote and supervise the free health and dental clinics.

Rock and Roll Hall of Fame members Fred Cash and Sam Gooden meet one of their fans,
Sam Blevins at UTC in 2016. (Sam Blevins)

In 2010, actress Mimi Kennedy spoke at Chattanooga High School
(Creative Arts School)

Actor Tom Wopat (Luke Duke from "Dukes of Hazzard") was married
to a woman from Rhea County, Tennessee. His son Walker Wopat
graduated from Rhea County High School in 2014. He later attended
UTC. His daughter Taylor graduated from Rhea County High in 2010.

2/19/10 Leonard Pitts Jr. (author, columnist) spoke at Baylor School

3/3/10 Judy Woodruff of PBS spoke at WTCI fundraiser, at
Chattanoogan hotel

WDEF radio's Luther Masingill, with Vince Carroll, celebrating the renaming of a portion of Broad Street in his honor, commemorating his world record broadcasting career.

3/28/10 Duane Chapman ("Dog the Bounty Hunter") signed autographs at Books a Million in Hixson

4/22/10 "Biggest Loser" and "Days of Our Lives" star Alison Sweeney spoke at Girls Night Out event at Northwest Georgia Trade Center in Dalton

6/26/10 Maksim Chmerkovskiy ("Dancing with the Stars") visited Children's Hospital

Henry Winkler, who became famous as Fonzie on TV's "Happy Days" with Signal Mountain High School cheerleaders during a fundraiser for the Mountain Education Fund in 2012. (Laura Davey Willingham)

7/10/10 Jillian Michaels, fitness expert, spoke at the She Expo at Chattanooga Convention & Trade Center

7/11/10 Pat and Gina Neely (Food Network) appeared at the She Expo at Chattanooga Convention Center.

8/15/10 Betty White, actress appeared at Senior Expo at Chattanooga Convention and Trade Center

9/17/10 Sam Gooden and Fred Cash (The Impressions) spoke at Tyner Academy

10/5/10 Malcolm Gladwell (author) spoke at UTC University Center

10/8/10 Jack Hanna appeared at Banana Ball at Chattanooga Zoo

12/17/10 Lionel Richie visited Chattanooga-Hamilton County Bicentennial Library and Pleasant Garden Cemetery for filming of

NBC series "Who Do You Think You Are" (aired March 2011). Richie's great grandfather John Louis Brown is buried at the cemetery. Richie had lunch at the Chattanoogan hotel.

Feb. 14-20, 2011 Ty Pennington and the crew of "Extreme Home Makeover" filmed an episode in Catoosa County, GA while renovating the home of Patrick Sharrock, a 9-year-old boy with brittle bone disease. Among those who visited were Leigh Ann Tuohy ("The Blind Side"), Xhibit, Ed Sanders, and Eduardo Xol.

3/9/11 Gwen Ifill of PBS spoke at Chattanooga Convention Center for WTCI fundraiser

April 2011 actress Jennifer O'Neill spoke at Boys and Girls Club fundraiser at Cleveland, TN Golf and Country Club

4/11/11 Miss America 1958 Marilyn Van Derbur spoke for Children's Advocacy Center banquet at the Read House.

4/25/11 Ted Turner spoke at McCallie School

May 2011 American Idol runner-up Lauren Alaina (Suddeth) graduated from Lakeview Fort Oglethorpe High School

7/16/11 Bethenny Frankel ("Real Housewives of New York") appeared at the She Expo at Chattanooga Convention Center

7/17/11 Chattanooga natives Lakeeda "Lake" Kelley and Lakeisha "Mariah" Huq, the entrepreneur sisters behind the bedding line *Jewel and Jem*, appeared at She Expo at the Chattanooga Convention Center. Huq later created and starred in "Married to Medicine" on the Bravo network.

7/17/11 Martha Stewart ("lifestyle guru") spoke at the She Expo at Chattanooga Convention and Trade Center

8/27/11 Vicki Lawrence, actress, performed at the Life Expo at Chattanooga Convention and Trade Center

9/13/11 Andrew Zimmern, Travel Channel chef, visited 212 Market restaurant in Chattanooga

10/25/11 Astrophysicist and author Neil deGrasse Tyson spoke at Chattanooga State

1/7/12 Actor, motivational speaker and "Dancing with the Stars" dancer JR Martinez (a Dalton High graduate who was seriously injured in the Iraq war) was honored with a parade, and gave a speech in Dalton at the Northwest Georgia Convention Center.

2/1/12 Matt Taibbi, contributing editor at Rolling Stone, spoke at UTC University Center

2/23/12 Stacy Allison, the first American woman to climb Mt. Everest, appeared at Chattanooga Convention Center, speaking to Womens Leadership Institute

3/22/12 JR Martinez spoke at Boys and Girls Club annual dinner in Dalton, and at Southeast Whitfield High School

4/21/12 Victoria Justice ("Victorious" TV show) appeared at Chattanooga Convention and Trade Center for Kidz Expo, and also visited Children's Hospital

April 2012 Jenna Bush Hager, daughter of former President and Mrs. George W. Bush spoke at Boys and Girls Club fundraiser at Cleveland, TN Golf and Country Club

July 2012 CBS News correspondent Steve Hartman visited WDEF radio to do a story about local radio legend Luther Masingill, who was in his 72nd year at the station, a world record for broadcasters. He worked into his 74th year until his death in 2014, at the age of 92.

7/21/12 Reality TV stars Bill and Giuliana Rancic, and author Nicholas Sparks appeared at the She Expo at Chattanooga Convention Center.

7/22/12 "Dancing with the Stars" dancers Mark Ballas and Cheryl Burke performed at the She Expo at Chattanooga Convention Center.

9/5/12 Henry Winkler spoke at Signal Mountain Middle High (benefit for the Mountain Education Foundation)

9/25/12 Sean Astin speaks at First Things First banquet at Chattanooga Convention Center

10/6/12 Doris Roberts ("Everybody Loves Raymond") appeared at the Senior Expo at Chattanooga Convention & Trade Center

10/13/12 Jack Hanna appeared at the Banana Ball at Chattanooga Zoo

11/20/12 Author/writer/Newsweek editor Jon Meacham, a Chattanooga native and McCallie School graduate, who began his career as a reporter for the Chattanooga Times, spoke at Lindsay Street Hall

2/28/13 Mae Jemison, astronaut at Chattanooga Convention Center, spoke to Women's Leadership Institute

3/12/13 Sheryl Crow visited US-101 to promote her first country album

4/12/13 Dr. Ben Carson presents Carson Scholarship awards to high school seniors at UTC

4/20/13 Ross Lynch and Laura Marano (Austin and Ally on Disney Channel) appeared at the Kids Expo at Trade Center

7/27/13 "Miss Kay" Robertson ("Duck Dynasty") at the Chattanooga Convention and Trade Center

7/28/13 Deirdre Hall ("Days of Our Lives"), Dr. Travis Stork ("The Doctors") and Caroline Manzo ("Real Housewives of New Jersey") appeared at the She Expo at Chattanooga Convention Center

8/23/13 Rick Bragg, journalist and author, spoke at McCallie School.

8/24/13 Actress Florence Henderson ("The Brady Bunch") appeared at the Life, Boomer and Senior Expo at Chattanooga Convention Center

8/24/13 Bob Eubanks, game show host, spoke at the Bradley Sunrise Rotary benefit auction in Cleveland, TN

10/10/13 Lisa Ling (journalist) spoke at Girls Preparatory School

12/9/13 Actors Ashton Kutcher and Mila Kunis visited Rock City

In 2014, Chattanooga car enthusiasts Harold and Corky Coker had their own reality show "Backroad Gold" on the Travel Channel.

1/23/14 Michio Kaku (futurist) spoke at Chattanooga State

2/27/14 Connie Chung, former journalist at Chattanooga Convention Center, spoke to Women's Leadership Institute

3/6/14 Naomi Judd appeared at WTCI fundraiser

4/27/14 Debby Ryan ("Jessie" on Disney Channel) appeared at Kids Expo, Trade Center

5/10/14 Musical entertainer Kim Criswell, a Chattanooga native, was honored as Tenn. Woman of Distinction at Chattanooga Convention Center

6/2/14 Dr. Ben Carson signed autographs at Books a Million in Hixson

7/20/14 Ree Drummond ("Pioneer Woman") spoke at Chattanooga Convention and Trade Center

7/26/14 Drew and Jonathan Scott ("Property Brothers") appeared at Chattanooga Convention and Trade Center

9/6/14 Regis Philbin appeared at Life, Boomer and Senior Expo at Chattanooga Convention Center, and visited Children's Hospital

9/11/14 Ree Drummond ("Pioneer Woman") spoke at Bright School

10/10/14 Jack Hanna appeared at the Banana Ball at Chattanooga Zoo

2/7/15 Singer Ray Stevens signed books at Barnes and Noble at Hamilton Place

2/12/15 Usher spoke at Chattanooga Center for Creative Arts, Orange Grove Center, and Dalewood Middle School

3/3/15 Susan Packard, co-founder HGTV at Chattanooga Convention Center, spoke to Women's Leadership Institute

April 16-18, 2015 Celebration of Southern Literature at Tivoli Theater: Jill McCorkle, Lee Smith, Roy Blount Jr., Richard Bausch, Bobbie Ann

Mason, Ron Rash, Rick Bragg, Lila Weaver, Natasha Trethewey, and Jayne Anne Philips

5/5/15 Dr. Ben Carson and his wife Candy presented Carson Scholar awards at UTC

5/7/15 Jane Pauley of CBS News spoke at Chattanoogan Hotel for AIM fundraiser

5/16/15 Debbie McKee-Fowler (of Little Debbie snack cake fame) honored as Tenn. Woman of Distinction at Chattanooga Convention Center

6/14/15 Actors Jon Hamm and Zach Galifinakis had lunch at Tupelo Honey restaurant, after attending the Bonnaroo music festival in Manchester, Tennessee. Hamm gave his Bonnaroo all-access wristband to waitress Abby Swartz, who then attended the festival, calling it "the highlight of my life." By the way, Galifinakis left a whopping 250% tip.

6/20/15 Karina Smirnoff and Louis Van Amstel ("Dancing with the Stars") visited Children's Hospital

7/10/15 Lee Greenwood at Barnes and Noble, Hamilton Place book signing for "Proud to be an American"

7/25/15 Leigh Ann Tuohy ("The Blind Side") spoke at Chattanooga Convention and Trade Center

7/26/15 Tabatha Coffey, Australian hair stylist ("Tabatha's Life Takeover" on Bravo Channel) spoke at Chattanooga Convention and Trade Center.

8/16/15 Singer Charlie Puth entertained first responders after Chattanooga's recent terror attacks at World of Beer.

In 2015, Tim McGraw and Faith Hill were frequent visitors to Baylor and McCallie schools when their daughter was a cheerleader for Ensworth High School.

10/1/15 Eve Plumb (Jan in "The Brady Bunch") displayed her art at Gallery 1401 on Main Street, and at WRCB Studio

10/11/15 Jack Hanna appeared at the Banana Ball at Chattanooga Zoo

10/11/15 Dr. Ben Carson signed autographs at Barnes and Noble Hamilton Place

In 2016, artist Wayne White, a Hixson High school graduate, and Emmy Award winner, created Wayne-O-Rama, an exhibit of his work.

2/18/16 Mika Brzezinski, journalist at Chattanooga Convention Center, spoke to Women's Leadership Institute

3/12/16 Lori Greiner (Shark Tank) spoke at Girls Preparatory School

May 2016 Charlie Daniels performed at Alzheimers benefit honoring Pat Summitt at Jasper Highlands

7/6/16 Aubrey Anderson-Emmons ("Lily" on ABC's "Modern Family") and her father Kent Emmons visited Hamilton County Criminal Court Clerk Vince Dean at the courthouse, and stopped in to see Judge Barry Steelman. They later had lunch at Slick's on Main Street.

9/9/16 William Kamkwmba, Malawian inventor and author spoke at McCallie School.

9/30/16 Sam Gooden and Fred Cash (The Impressions) spoke at Tyner Academy

1/21/17 Jenna Bush Hager of NBC spoke at On Point annual banquet at Chattaanooga Convention and Trade Center

5/15/17 Evangelist Franklin Graham spoke to a crowd of 6,200 at Coolidge Park in Chattanooga.

10/14/17 Jack Hanna appeared at Banana Ball at Chattanooga Zoo

In 2017, Hamilton County teacher Veronica-Pooh Nash Poleate, whose YouTube videos about staying out of the ocean ("It's the shark's house") had gone viral, landed a TLC television show called "She's In Charge"

1/22/18 Chris Lee, McCallie School class of 2013 spoke at McCallie. He was in the Broadway cast of "Hamilton."

4/12/18 Actress/singer Keke Palmer was interviewed live on the radio at WJTT studio

4/29/18 Mason Ramsey, 11-year-old "yodeling boy" performed at Walmart on Gunbarrel Road

5/17/18 Singer Trevor Jackson performed at Hixson High School

10/10/18 Jon Meacham, journalist and author, spoke at McCallie School. He graduated from McCallie in 1987.

11/16/18 Mike Love of the Beach Boys spoke at dedication of Top 40 Radio Museum at WFLI Radio

In 2013, singer-songwriter Sheryl Crow visited US-101 radio in Chattanooga. She is pictured here with US-101's Linda White. (WUSY)

During Regis Philbin's 2014 visit to Chattanooga, the longtime TV host stopped in at the NICU unit at Children's Hospital, meeting (L-R) Samantha Pieper, Shaina Chandler, baby Kellan Chandler, and Kendra Belcher. (Shaina Chandler)

2/21/19 Katty Kay, journalist at Chattanooga Convention Center, spoke to Women's Leadership Institute

Feb. 2019 Samuel L. Jackson was in Chattanooga near his childhood home for a CBS 60 Minutes interview with reporter Steve Kroft.

5/23/19 Bill Gates, philanthropist spoke at Howard School

8/10/19 Henry Cho, comedian spoke to Bradley Sunrise Rotary benefit auction at Cleveland (TN) Country Club

9/28/19 Jack Hanna appeared at the Banana Ball at Chattanooga Zoo

10/28/19 Actor Morgan Freeman visited Champy's Chicken in downtown Chattanooga

10/30/19 Rev. Al Sharpton spoke at NAACP Ruby Hurley Image Awards at the Chattanooga Convention Center

12/19/19 Food Network chef Robert Irvine filmed an episode of his "Restaurant: Impossible" show at Blue Orleans restaurant in Chattanooga.

In 1963, Little Debbie herself, Debbie McKee is handing out the snack cakes named in her honor. She would grow up to become executive vice president of her family's company. (McKee Foods Corporation)

1/24/20 Frankie Valli spoke at the Top 40 Radio Museum at WFLI Radio. Mitch Ryder, a fellow 1960s hit maker, was on hand to greet him.

Among other notable celebrities with Chattanooga connections:

Jules Alexander, a founding member of the 1960s rock group The Association, was born in Chattanooga in 1943.

Hugh Beaumont, the actor who played Ward Cleaver in the 1960s ABC sitcom "Leave it to Beaver" graduated from Chattanooga's Baylor School (1930), and attended the University of Chattanooga.

That same "Little Debbie" from McKee Bakery, Debbie McKee Fowler, is pictured with Lauren Anderson in 2018. (Jenifer Anderson)

During a 2016 visit to Chattanooga, Aubrey Anderson-Emmons ("Lily" on ABC's "Modern Family") visited the Hamilton County Courthouse, meeting Criminal Court Judge Barry Steelman. (Vince Dean)

Kane Brown, who attended several different schools in the Chattanooga and north Georgia area, became one of country music's top stars in 2016, and was soon selling out large venues, and topping the music charts.

Actress Barbara Carrera ("Never Say Never Again," "Centennial") was adopted by a family in East Ridge at the age of 17, lived there for a brief period, and competed in the Miss Chattanooga pageant in the early 1960s.

Fred Cash and Sam Gooden, two Chattanooga natives who were part of the Impressions soul music group for more than fifty years, were inducted into the Rock and Roll Hall of Fame in 2001. Both attended Chattanooga's Howard High School in the 1950s.

Actor Lane Davies, a Dalton, GA native, was a cast member on "General Hospital" and "Days of our Lives" in addition to other stage and film roles.

Rachel Held Evans (1982-2019) best-selling Christian author, and Bryan College alum, was a resident of Dayton, Tennessee

The Forester Sisters of Lookout Mountain in Dade County, Georgia, were among the top country music artists in the nation in the 1980s and 1990s, selling out concerts locally and nationally. Kathy, June, Kim, and Christy are in the Georgia Music Hall of Fame.

Corey Forrester of Chickamauga is a nationally known comedian.

Rapper Warren G has family in Chattanooga, and has often visited.

Damon Gillespie, a 2012 graduate of Chattanooga Center for Creative Arts, starred in NBC's "Rise" and the Netflix series "Tiny Pretty Things."

Montego Glover, a Tony-nominated actress, grew up in Chattanooga, and graduated from Chattanooga School for Arts and Sciences in 1992.

Mark Gray, who was raised on Lookout Mountain near Chattanooga, wrote and recorded several top ten country hits in the 1980s and 1990s. He was also a member of the group Exile.

Ben Haden, pastor of Chattanooga's First Presbyterian Church from 1968 to 1999, became internationally known through the religious broadcast, "Changed Lives."

Samuel L. Jackson, who has starred in dozens of popular motion pictures, grew up in Chattanooga, attending Orchard Knob Elementary School, and graduated from Riverside High School (the current Chattanooga School for Arts and Sciences) in 1966.

Actor Leslie Jordan is a Chattanooga native, and has often visited. He is a 1973 graduate of Brainerd High School, and earned a degree in theater from UTC. He did a one-man show called "An Evening of Tasteful Trash" at the Vine Street Market in 1981 that helped fund his journey to Hollywood, where he has starred in TV shows including "Will and Grace," "The Cool Kids," and "Call Me Kat."

Charlie Louvin, born Charles Loudermilk, was born and raised in Henagar, Alabama, and was a frequent visitor to the Chattanooga area. He and his brother Ira were inducted into the Country Music Hall of Fame. The brothers performed on Chattanooga radio stations early in their career, and were top country-western artists in the 1950s and 1960s. Ira was killed in an auto accident in 1965. Louvin died of pancreatic cancer in 2011.

WDEF radio morning announcer Luther Masingill, who holds the world record for broadcasting longevity (1940-2014) was born and raised in Chattanooga, and is the city's only inductee into the National Radio Hall of Fame (2012).

Debbie McKee Fowler is a member of the founding family of Little Debbie Snack Cakes (McKee Bakery in Collegedale, Tennessee), and is the face that has long graced the packages of Little Debbie products. She is currently executive vice president of the company.

Actress Taaffe O'Connell ("Three's Company," "Galaxy of Terror") grew up in Chattanooga

Actress Lori Petty ("A League of Their Own") was born in 1963 in "a double wide trailer" at the Green Acres trailer park in Chattanooga.

Singer-songwriter Mitch Rossell, who has written hit songs for artists including Garth Brooks is a Chattanooga native and a graduate of Silverdale Baptist Academy and UTC.

Between 1936 and 2013, country music pioneer Tommy Scott, a Toccoa, GA native made several appearances in the Chattanooga area.

Carole Smith (1922-2016) wrote hundreds of songs, including Sonny James number-one country single "Don't Keep Me Hangin' On (1970). The Chattanooga resident was active in the music program at Bayside Baptist Church, and Sonny James visited her occasionally.

Actor Lewis Smith ("North and South" miniseries) is a Chattanooga native who graduated from Lookout Valley High School in 1974.

Ted Turner graduated from Chattanooga's McCallie School in 1956. He was later the owner of Turner Outdoor Advertising, which he inherited from his father. In the 1970s, he owned WGOW and WYNQ radio stations in Chattanooga. He sold the stations in 1976, and bought the Atlanta Braves baseball team that same year. In 1980, he founded the Cable News Network. He regularly donated large sums of money to McCallie School.

Linda Vaughn of Dalton, GA is "the First Lady of Motor Sports" and "Miss Hurst Golden Shifter. She was inducted into the Motorsports Hall of Fame of America in 2019.

Roger Alan Wade, a Chattanooga native, is a nationally known singer and songwriter who has also hosted radio shows for Sirius XM's Outlaw Nation channel.

Pez Whatley, a graduate of Notre Dame High School and UTC, was a professional wrestler from 1973 to 1998.

Wayne White, a 1975 graduate of Hixson High School, is an artist, art director, puppeteer, set designer, animator, cartoonist and illustrator. He has won three Emmy Awards for his work. In November 2016 White created an art installation in Chattanooga called Wayne-O-Rama that includes huge cardboard heads of figures from Chattanooga's history.

According to the Read House website and several online sources: Several celebrity guests have stayed at the Read House including: Sir Winston Churchill, notorious gangster Al Capone, Elvis Presley (1972), Oprah Winfrey, and actors Tallulah Bankhead (1937), Gary

Cooper, and Robert Pattinson. Pattinson stayed while filming "Water for Elephants" in 2010. Churchill spent the night on Feb. 24, 1932. Capone reportedly stayed in 1931 (He also spent a considerable amount of time in Monteagle, TN). Winfrey spent the night on June 5, 2006, along with several members of her production crew.

Actor Leslie Jordan, a Chattanooga native who increased his already considerable fame in 2020 during the pandemic with viral Instagram posts, is pictured with fan Autumn Clark

Tennessee Aquarium visitors (Opened May 1992, dates of visits unknown)

Sir David Attenborough

Alton Brown – first to scuba dive while filming a segment for "Good Eats," and later as the founder of the Aquarium's Serve & Protect sustainable seafood program

Brad Paisley and his wife Kimberly Williams-Paisley

Sheryl Crow (singer) and Scott Hamilton (Sheryl's neighbor and Olympic ice skater)

Peyton Manning

Phil Fulmer

Clay Walker

Lauren Hutton

Jackson Browne

James Taylor

Alison Krauss

Dolly Parton

Shannon Brown (NBA basketball player-LA Lakers)

Monica (R&B singer)

Brian McKnight (R&B singer)

Morris Day (singer)

Kim Fields (actress)

Ricky Smiley (comedian)

Gov. Ned McWherter (D-TN)

Gov. Phil Bredesen (D-TN)

Gov. Bill Haslam (R-TN)

Senator Bob Corker (R-TN)

Senator Howard Baker Jr (R-TN)

Howard Hall (IMAX filmmaker)

Jemma Craig (Australian conservationist, film maker)

Tab Benoit (blues guitarist, singer)

Robert Loggia (actor)

Trace Adkins

Toby Keith

Randy Owen

Sandra Bullock

Dame Jane Goodall

Dr. Eugenie Clark ("The Shark Lady")

Stan Waterman, Rodney Fox, and Nick Caloyianis of Blue Water, White Death (1971 documentary)

James Marsden

Connie Britton

Elijah Wood

Ty Bentli (nationally syndicated radio talk show host) and his wife, actress Corrie English

Adam Green–horror movie director

Joe Lynch-director

Dylan Walsh (actor)

John Carter Cash

Sara Evans

Keith Urban

Supreme Court Justice John Paul Stevens

President Vaclav Klaus of Czech Republic

Ashton Kutcher

Mila Kunis

Kirk Herbstreit (ESPN)

Zeb Hogan (Monster Fish)

Fabien, Alexandria, and Jean-Michel Cousteau

Sylvia Earle (marine biologist)

T-Boz (one of the singers of TLC)

Samuel L. Jackson

Usher (at grand-opening, age 13)

Monifah (from R&B Divas) - got engaged in the Delta

Venus Lacy – Olympian and Chattanooga Native

Rapper Lil' Jon

Ex-NBA Basketball player Christian Laettner

Magician David Copperfield

Georgia Bulldog legend Vince Dooley (ex-head coach)

Medal of Honor recipient Desmond T. Doss

Medal of Honor recipient Charles H. Coolidge

Tipper Gore (Vice President Al Gore's wife)

Dr. Robert Ballard (oceanographer, Titanic expert)

Juliet Eilperin (Washington Post national affairs correspondent)

Joel Sartore (photographer, National Geographic)

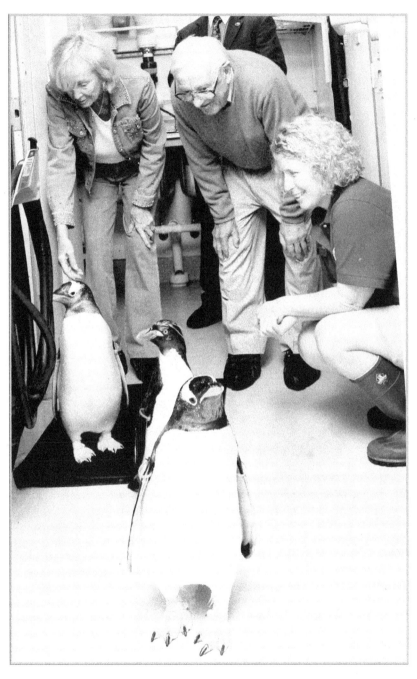

United States Supreme Court Associate Justice John Paul Stevens is pictured during a 2008 visit to the Tennessee Aquarium in Chattanooga. (Tennessee Aquarium)

Singer-songwriter James Taylor (right) enjoys a pre-show visit to the Tennessee Aquarium with band member Arnold McCuller in 2016, prior to their concert at the UTC Arena. (Tennessee Aquarium)

World of Wheels Auto Show

At Memorial Auditorium:

2/21/77 Burt Ward ("Robin" from Batman TV series)

2/25/80 James Best (Dukes of Hazzard)

2/21/81 Steve Kanaly (Dallas)

2/20/82 Lou Ferrigno (The Incredible Hulk)

2/18/84 Michael Nader ("Dynasty")

2/17/85 Sorrell Booke ("Boss Hogg" on "Dukes of Hazzard")

At the 1980 World of Wheels show at Memorial Auditorium, James Best (Sheriff Roscoe P. Coltrane on "Dukes of Hazzard") was excited to meet his fans. (Wayne Murphree)

At Chattanooga Convention Center:

2/16/86 Grant Goodeve (One Life to Live)

1/10/87 Finola Hughes (General Hospital)

1/28/89 Don Diamont (The Young and the Restless)

1/13/90 Jean LeClerc (All My Children)

1/7/94 J. Eddie Peck (The Young and the Restless)

1/8/95 Walter Jones (Mighty Morphin Power Rangers)

1/9/96 Texas Bikini Team

1/11/97 Ricky Van Shelton

1/9/99 Texas Bikini Team

1/9/00 Mankind (wrestler)

1/11/03 Verne Troyer (Mini-Me from the Austin Powers movies)

1/9/05 James Denton (Desperate Housewives)

1/7/06 John Cena (Manhunt) and Ben "Cooter" Jones (Dukes of Hazzard)

1/12/08 Vinnie DiMartino of "Orange County Choppers" and "American Choppers"

1/13/08 Jason Earles of "Hannah Montana"

1/9/09 Sonny Shroyer (Dukes of Hazzard) Ryne Sanborn (High School Musical) Moises Arias (Hannah Montana)

1/11-12, 2013 Henry Winkler, Tim "Mountain Man" Guerady (Duck Dynasty), Danielle Colby-Cushman ("American Pickers")

1/9/16 Laura Marano ("Ally" on Disney Channel "Austin and Ally")

1/10/16 Kevin Nash (actor-wrestler)

1/8/17 Tom Wopat, Catherine Bach ("Dukes of Hazzard")

1/7/18 Dawn Wells ("Gilligan's Island"), Kevin Mack ("Counting Cars" on History Channel) and Daniel Bryan, WWE wrestler

Dawn Wells, who played Mary Ann on Gilligan's Island, signs an autograph for Will Rodgers at the 2018 World of Wheels. (Will Rodgers)

CHAPTER 12

Night Clubs, Bars, and the Comedy Catch

This may have been the most difficult list of all to compile. Chattanooga has always hosted a busy nightlife scene, with talented performers from near and far. It would be impossible to list them all. Most night clubs and bars come and go, and it is not always possible to find the records for those that are long gone. Some advertised their shows, and others did not.

Although many locals have fond memories of seeing a then-unknown band who later went on to worldwide fame, those memories are often fuzzy. Which club? What year? Who knows?

We do know US-101 radio has introduced hundreds of country stars to our city, in many cases on the release of their first recording. The powerful radio station welcomed Garth Brooks and Blake Shelton, among many others, when most fans had no idea who they were.

Also, clubs like the Governor's Lounge and the Hitching Post were like second homes to the biggest names in country music from the 1970s to the turn of the century.

Pop-rock acts including Destiny's Child (featuring 18-year-old Beyonce), John Mayer, Nickelback, Kid Rock, Train, the Red Hot Chili Peppers, Hootie and the Blowfish, and the Dave Matthews Band had to start somewhere, and Chattanooga was among their first stops, often playing to small, but enthusiastic local audiences. The same could be said for comedians Jeff Foxworthy and Brian Regan, who were "openers" at the Comedy Catch before becoming headliners in their own right.

So, here is an admittedly incomplete listing of many of the stars, big and small, who have played night clubs and bars in Chattanooga, followed by some of the famous comedians who have played the Comedy Catch.

The Bay, 238 E. 11th St. (1996-2003)

9/19/97 Marshall Tucker Band

10/16/97 Gran Torino

4/3/98 Drivin' N Cryin'

4/13/98 Nighthawks

8/8/98 Edwin McCain

8/15/98 Jason & the Scorchers

9/1/98 Candlebox

9/24/98 Gran Torino

9/28/98 Better than Ezra, Train

10/15/98 Kid Rock (about 18 people attended)

10/23/98 Drive By Truckers

11/28/98 Cinderella

12/4/98 Derek Trucks Band

3/11/99 Frankie Goes to Hollywood

3/19/99 Vanilla Ice

3/30/99 Salt N Pepa

5/21/99 Smash Mouth

6/6/99 Gran Torino

7/4/99 Henry Rollins

8/7/99 Gran Torino

9/4//99 Wilco

9/12/99 Destiny's Child (including 18-year-old Beyonce Knowles)

12/14/99 GWAR

4/1/00 George Clinton & P-Funk

5/4/00 RUN DMC

9/15/00 Nickelback

7/14/00 Wang Chung, A Flock of Seagulls

9/8/00 Sister Hazel

10/15/00 3 Doors Down

11/4/00 Gran Torino

12/2/00 Drivin' N Cryin'

1/14/01 Slayer

2/2/01 Gran Torino

5/4/01 Edwin McCain

5/25/01 John Mayer

6/14/01 Slayer

6/15/01 Insane Clown Posse

8/10/01 Chris Jerico

8/13/01 Henry Rollins

9/27/01 Nickelback

12/3/01 Robby Krieger (of the Doors)

4/26/02 Quiet Riot

8/16/02 David Allan Coe

9/24/02 Leif Garrett

12/13/02 The Nighthawks

5/3/03 Breaking Benjamin

6/26/03 Sister Hazel

Brass Register (Georgia Avenue)

3/14/85 Forester Sisters

5/31/85 Forester Sisters

Cactus Moon (Eastgate Mall)

Mar. 4, 1993 Mark Chesnutt

3/25/93 Doug Stone

5/17/93 Three Dog Night

4/20/93 Frankie Valli & Four Seasons

9/23/93 Gibson/Miller Band

12/11/92 Steve Wariner

Castaways Club (Brainerd Road)

7/31/70 The O'Kaysions

8/20/70 Archie Bell and the Drells

8/28/70 Swinging Medallions

Charlie's Lounge (Dayton Pike in Soddy-Daisy)

5/9/96 Lonestar

Clancy O'Toole's (Market Street)

10/21/76 Atlanta Rhythm Section

Coat of Arms (Brainerd Road)

7/12/66 Jerry Lee Lewis

12/10/66 Jerry Lee Lewis

2/2/68 Billy Joe Royal

2/24/68 Zombies

Comedy Catch (and Giggles Grill) Brainerd Road (the club occasionally hosted country singers for US-101)

4/23/01 Billy Gilman

4/24/01 Billy Currington (age 12)

2004 Trisha Yearwood

1/30/08 Jake Owen

9/19/08 Randy Houser at Comedy Catch (US-101 High Noon Saloon)

1/30/08 Jake Owen at Comedy Catch (US-101 High Noon Saloon)

The Continental Club (Alton Park)

Trisha Yearwood sings for US-101 at the Comedy Catch in 2004. (John Burks)

10/28/67 Impressions (Sam Gooden and Fred Cash of Chattanooga) and Curtis Mayfield

Funny Page (Brainerd Road)

2/21/-25, 1989 Larry Miller (comedian)

Governor's Lounge (Bonny Oaks Drive)

House band: 90 Proof

The club opened in 1979 (date unknown) Earl Thomas Conley was the first act

12/31/79 J.D. Sumner and Stamps

4/9/82 Gary Morris

5/7/82 Con Hunley

1/19/83 Lee Greenwood

2/27/83 John Anderson

3/13/83 Johnny Paycheck

5/15/83 David Frizzell

6/19/83 Razzy Bailey

7/13/83 Mark Gray

8/14/83 John Anderson/Mark Gray

9/4/83 Con Hunley

9/18/83 Earl Thomas Conley

10/9/83 Gene Watson

10/23/83 Steve Wariner

11/6/83 Lee Greenwood

12/4/83 Vern Gosdin/Mark Gray

12/18/83 Con Hunley

1/15/84 Gus Hardin

2/12/84 Joe Stampley

2/26/84 Exile

4/26/84 Kathy Mattea

5/6/84 George Strait

9/2/84 Con Hunley

10/14/84 Gene Watson

11/4/84 Ronnie McDowell

11/18/84 Mark Gray

1/13/85 Con Hunley

2/17/85 Gene Watson

3/10/85 David Frizzell/Shelley West

8/11/85 Steve Wariner

12/22/85 Con Hunley

3/16/86 Bellamy Brothers

4/13/86 Con Hunley

9/21/86 Steve Wariner

3/29/87 Exile

8/16/87 Alan Pressley

8/23/87 Con Hunley/Billy Joe Royal

11/15/87 T. G. Sheppard

11/29/87 T. Graham Brown

12/6/87 Earl Thomas Conley

12/10/87 The Platters

12/13/87 Con Hunley

12/20/87 David Allen Coe/Danny Shirley

1/24/88 Steve Wariner

2//7/88 Billy Joe Royal

2/21/88 Exile

3/13/88 John Anderson

3/27/88 Percy Sledge/Dr. Hook

4/10/88 Vern Gosdin/Johnny Paycheck/Danny Shirley

4/24/88 William Lee Golden and the Goldens

7/8/88 New Grass Revival

8/14/88 Bill Pinckney & Drifters

8/28/88 David Allan Coe/Danny Shirley

9/18/88 Exile

10/2/88 Keith Whitley/Con Hunley

10/16/88 The Platters

4/2/89 John Hartford/Dismembered Tennesseans

12/28/89 Kentucky Headhunters

4/8/90 Travis Tritt

9/23/90 Travis Tritt

11/11/90 Exile

10/13/91 Exile

12/15/91 Con Hunley

4/26/92 Pirates of the Mississippi

5/31/92 Sammy Kershaw

12/6/92 Sammy Kershaw

2/21/93 Pirates of the Mississippi

3/14/93 Lee Roy Parnell

3/21/93 Confederate Railroad

10/10/93 Ricky Lynn Gregg

10/16/94 Daron Norwood

11/13/94 Kenny Chesney

12/11/94 Confederate Railroad

4/9/95 David Ball

6/12/95 Confederate Railroad

9/21/95 David Lee Murphy

11/5/95 Ty England

11/19/95 Shenandoah

12/17/95 Kenny Chesney

1/14/96 Perfect Stranger

1/21/96 Ken Mellons

3/24/96 Gene Watson

4/7/96 Confederate Railroad

5/12/96 Wade Hayes

10/13/96 Lonestar

10/20/96 Kenny Chesney

12/8/96 Exile

2/16/97 Lee Roy Parnell

2/23/97 Trace Adkins

3/2/97 Gene Watson

4/6/97 Rick Trevino

4/13/97 Richochet

8/10/97 Mark Wills

8/17/97 Gene Watson

9/21/97 Exile

9/28/97 Kenny Chesney

10/1/97 Jack Ingram

10/26/97 David Kersh

11/13/97 River Road

11/23/97 Big House

1/18/98 Crystal Simmons

2/22/98 Rick Trevino

4/26/98 Paul Brandt

9/26/98 Boots Randolph/The Mills Brothers

10/3/98 Fabian, Gary Lewis & Playboys, Shangri-las

10/10/98 Eddy Arnold

10/17/98 Jerry Reed

10/18/98 Wade Hayes

10/24/98 J.D. Sumner and the Stamps

10/31/98 Gold City

11/8/98 T. Graham Brown

12/20/98 Keith Harling

10/28/99 Jerry Kilgore

1/14/00 Yankee Grey

2/13/00 Brad Paisley

5/25/00 Anita Cochran, Craig Morgan

4/19/01 Eric Heatherly

7/19/01 Blake Shelton

Performance dates unknown: Daryl Worley, Vince Gill, Marty Stuart, Garth Brooks

CLOSED MAY 5, 2006

Lee Greenwood meets one of his fans, Elaine Slater at the Governor's Lounge in 1983.

Kenny Chesney at the Governor's Lounge in 1994. (Cindy Lowery)

Blake Shelton finds himself between US-101's afternoon team
(David Earl Hughes and Bill "Dex" Poindexter) in 2001. (US-101)

Grizzly's (3600 Hixson Pike)

6/9/95 Edgar Winter Group

9/14/95 Govt. Mule

9/7/95 Foghat

7/18/95 Marshall Tucker Band

7/3/95 Wet Willie

5/27/95 Molly Hatchet

10/5/95 Peter Frampton

Iron Horse (Brainerd Road)

7/4/69 Drifters

7/25/69 Drifters

8/8/69 Hank Ballard

8/29/69 Charlie Rich

9/19/69 Ace Cannon

7/12/71 Jerry Lee Lewis

8/13/71 Charlie McCoy

JJ's Bohemia (ML King Blvd.)

2/2/08 Justin Townes Earle

3/8/08 The Slits

9/20/08 Moon Taxi

3/8/09 Justin Townes Earle, Roger Alan Wade

2/26/10 T Model Ford

12/11/10 T Model Ford

6/18/11 Bob Dorough

10/15/11 Alabama Shakes

12/16/11 Shovels & Rope

4/9/12 Alabama Shakes

2/8/13 Jonathan Richman

4/24/13 Deerhunter

5/3/13 The Cusses

8/19/13 Diarrhea Planet

10/3/13 Kishi Bashi

11/12/13 Kurt Vile

7/25/14 Bobby Bare Jr.

10/22/15 The Dead Deads

Lamar's (ML King Blvd.)

1/13/06 Jason Isbell

Lions Den (Brainerd Road)

1970-71 Billy Joe Royal, Little Richard, Swinging Medallions, Percy Sledge, Mitch Ryder and Roy Head (dates unknown)

Man 'o War Lounge (Lee Highway)

1/18-22, 1977 Tiny Tim

Market Street Performance Hall (221 Market Street, later became Rhythm and Brews)

1/30/94 Marshall Chapman

4/1/94 Webb Wilder

4/28/94 Steve Forbert

5/26/94 Pat McLaughlin

6/16/94 The Band

6/24/94 Webb Wilder

6/25/94 Todd Snider

7/7/94 Steve Forbert

7/9/94 America

7/28/94 Mark O'Connor

8/5/94 Robin Trower

8/12/94 The Outlaws

8/17/94 Guy Clark

8/20/94 Joe Ely

8/24/94 Guy Clark

8/26/94 Jimmie Dale Gilmore

8/27/94 Webb Wilder

8/29/94 Warren Zevon

9/20/94 Deadeye Dick

10/14-16/94 Goose Creek Symphony

11/20/94 Blackfoot

1/20/95 John Hammond

2/16/95 Leo Kottke

3/3/95 Leon Russell

3/11/95 John Hartford

3/16/95 Jason & the Searchers

3/24/95 Webb Wilder

3/29/95 Tuck & Patti

3/31/95 Guy Clark

5/12/95 Radney Foster

5/19/95 The Band

Market Street Tavern
6/9/12 Commander Cody

Merv's Uptown (Brainerd Road)
10/25/86 Georgia Satellites

Metro (409 Market St.)
5/13/95 Sixpence None the Richer

Michael's (Brainerd Road)

5/1/03 C & C Music Factory and Freedom Williams

5/15/03 Vanilla Ice

7/24/03 Tyrone Smith Revue

Midtown Music Hall (Georgia Avenue)

9/10/05 Todd Snider

10/17/08 Nappy Roots

6/19/09 Brantley Gilbert

10/2/09 Brantley Gilbert

The Night Deposit (Brainerd Road)

8/10/78 Gregg Allman

1/17/80 Exile

1/31/80 Chubby Checker

3/13/80 Smokin' Joe Frazier and the Knockouts

4/27/80 Black Oak Arkansas

9/26/80 Alabama

Nucleus (Main Street)

11/30/85 Red Hot Chili Peppers

2/7/86 Black Flag

Playlate Club (Lee Highway)

5/20/81 Grassroots

6/14/85 Molly Hatchet

10/18/87 Molly Hatchet

(There are also various reports of Chicago, Journey, Triumph, and others playing here, but no dates could be verified)

Playmate Club (Lee Highway)

4/29/70 Stan Hitchcock

Pokey's (Cleveland, TN)

11/26/96 Little River Band

Rhythm & Brews (221 Market Street, 1999-2015)

10/23/99 Jason D. Williams

1/28/00 Leon Russell

2/12/00 The Tams

3/17/00 Clarence Carter

9/1/01 Derek Trucks Band

3/22/02 Angie Aparo

8/2/02 Tinsley Ellis

10/2/02 Drive By Truckers

11/9/02 Drivin' n' Cryin'

11/23/02 BR 549

12/31/02 Hopsing Project

1/30/03 Sister Hazel

2/14/03 Neko Case

5/23/03 Angie Aparo

5/24/03 Graham Parker

6/21/03 Here Come the Mummies

7/19/03 Todd Snider

9/27/03 Old Crow Medicine Show

10/15/03 Dierks Bentley

12/21/03 Eric Heatherly

1/16/04 Rounders/Sugarland with Jennifer Nettles

4/9/04 Derek Trucks Band

5/28/04 Hank Williams III

8/12/04 Edwin McCain

10/8/04 Here Come The Mummies

11/10/04 Vic Chesnutt

11/17/04 Drive By Truckers

11/20/04 Jennifer Daniels

1/29/05 Angie Aparo

3/31/05 Angie Aparo

4/1/05 Drivin' n' Cryin'

3/10/05 Paul Thorn

10/13/05 Drive By Truckers

10/19/05 Paul Thorn

12/1/05 Spin Doctors

2/16/06 Marty Stuart

5/11/06 Angie Aparo

8/23/06 Shooter Jennings (accompanied by actress girlfriend Drea de Matteo of "The Sopranos")

9/23/06 Drivin' n' Cryin'

10/6/06 Dierks Bentley

12/6/06 Gillian Welch

5/26/07 Zac Brown Band

5/30/07 Junior Brown

8/31/07 Jason Isbell

10/29/07 Here Come the Mummies

3/12/08 Blind Melon

3/14/08 Drivin' 'n Cryin'

5/25/08 Pete Best Band

8/7/08 Zac Brown Band

12/11/08 Richie Havens

3/27/09 Black Stone Cherry

4/1/09 Todd Rundgren

5/21/09 Paul Thorn

7/10/09 Drivin' n' Cryin'

7/21/09 Cracker

8/2/09 Marcy Playground

8/5/09 Billy Joe Shaver

10/16/09 Justin Townes Earle

10/21/09 James McMurtry

10/29/09 Here Come The Mummies

11/20/09 Drivin' n' Cryin'

11/27/09 Channing Wilson, Davey Smith

12/3/09 Meat Puppets

2/16/10 Two Fresh, Big Gigantic

3/5/10 Ani DeFranco

3/17/10 Jason Isbell

4/7/10 Moon Taxi

4/22/10 Todd Snider

5t/**13/10** The Verve Pipe

9/13/10 Shelby Lynne

9/22/10 Paul Thorn

10/2/10 Nappy Roots

11/27/10 Drivin' n' Cryin'

12/15/10 Sister Hazel

4/17/11 Todd Snider

5/1/11 Justin Townes Earle

7/17/11 Black Stone Cherry

7/22/11 Velcro Pygmies

7/24/11 Drivin' n' Cryin'

9/18/11 Shawn Mullins

10/12/11 Perpetual Groove

12/30/11 Drivin' n' Cryin'

1/20/12 Paul Thorn, Angie Aparo

2/18/12 James McMurtry

3/2/12 Hank Williams III

4/6/12 Of Montreal

6/1/12 Todd Snider, Justin Townes Earle

7/27/12 Drivin' n' Cryin'

9/21/12 Paul Thorn

12/13/12 St. Paul and the Broken Bones

2/2/13 Drivin n Cryin

5/1/13 James McMurtry

9/5/13 Moon Taxi

10/3/13 Paul Thorn

11/9/13 Birdsmell (Ben Bridwell of Band of Horses)

11/28/13 Hopsing Project

12/7/13 Ryan Beatty (age 17)

1/4/14 Mitch Rossell

4/12/14 Mitch Rossell

4/21/14 Wishbone Ash

7/23/14 Angie Aparo

10/9/14 Jesse McCartney

7/29/15 Chris Janson

8/12/15 Angie Aparo

Rock & Country Club (Airways Boulevard)

5/25/78 Johnny Rodriguez

5/29/78 Stamps Quartet

9/26/78 Stamps Quartet

12/5/78 Sammi Smith

3/6/81 Con Hunley

3/13/81 Bellamy Brothers

Sandbar (Amnicola Highway)

3/1/93 Marcia Ball

6/12/93 Marcia Ball

9/11/93 Leon Russell

9/13/93 The Kinsey Report

9/26/93 Col. Bruce Hampton

3/28/94 Kim Wilson

4/1/94 Dave Matthews Band (This was five months before the debut of their first studio album, which was the beginning of their national success. An estimated thirty people attended.)

4/14/94 Warrant

4/21/94 Lucinda Williams

5/12/94 Tab Benoit

5/21/94 Hootie and Blowfish (this was a month before their album "Cracked Rear View" was released, and three months before their career-making debut on the David Letterman show on CBS)

7/2/94 Derek Trucks

8/7/94 Ace Frehley

8/17/94 311

8/24/94 Dixie Dregs

10/1/94 Wet Willie

11/26/94 Jupiter Coyote

1/12/95 Junior Brown, Dalton Roberts

2/28/95 Al Kooper

3/5/95 Jefferson Starship

3/13/95 Koko Taylor

4/14/95 Warrant

5/6/95 Tinsley Ellis

5/10/95 Blackfoot

5/11/95 Marcia Ball

5/28/95 Drivin' n' Cryin

6/17/95 War

6/24/95 Cake, Tabitha's Secret (later known as Matchbox 20)

7/28/95 Vertical Horizon

9/20/95 Gov't Mule

5/5/96 Lonestar

5/6/96 Anson Funderburgh and the Rockets

1/1/98 Gran Torino

Sing Sing Dueling Pianos (downtown)

9/28/98 Leon Russell

10/6/98 John Entwistle Band

8/30/98 Marshall Tucker Band

9/23/99 Junior Brown

Sound Stage (formerly Hitching Post, Rossville Boulevard)

4/24/78 Rubicon

Urban Cowboy (Lee Highway)

2/27/83 Terri Gibbs

1/10/86 Dan Seals

7/25/86 Lacy J. Dalton

9/26-27/86 Rebecca Holder

10/17-18/86 Billy Joe Royal

10/31/86 Percy Sledge

5/15-16/87 Charly McClain

Vaudeville Cafe (Market Street)

12/6/13 Jim Breuer (comedian)

Vine Street Auditorium

10/16/76 Tom Chapin

2/28/79 Gene Cotton and Overland

3/20/79 Gil Scott-Heron

4/6/80 Sweet Comfort

Warehouse (Market Street)

9/18/11 Stryper

Yesterday's (Patten Parkway, downtown)

8/16/97 Billy Pilgrim (with Kristian Bush, later of Sugarland)

9/12/97 Edwin McCain

The Comedy Catch

Opened in 1985 in Dr. Sages atop the Holiday Inn in downtown Chattanooga. Moved to 3224 Brainerd Road in 1986, then to its current location in the Chattanooga Choo Choo complex in 2015.

Regional favorites including James Gregory, Tim Wilson, Etta May, Killer Beaz and Gary Conrad played the Comedy Catch beginning in the 1980s, and continued each year for many years. Since 2010, David "Mr. Showtime" Scott has been among the most popular acts.

Here are some of the nationally known comedians who have appeared at the Comedy Catch:

1985

11/1-3 Brian Regan (as opening act)

1986

1/9-12 Jeff Foxworthy (as opening act)

11/18-23 Bill Hicks

1987

3/20-22 Jerry Seinfeld

8/16 Jimmie "JJ" Walker

1988

6/10-12 Paula Poundstone

1989

2/22-25 Paula Poundstone

3/27-28 The Amazing Kreskin

1990

11/16-18 Paula Poundstone

1991

9/7-9 Paula Poundstone

9/20-22 Pinkard & Bowden

1992

4/3/4 Jeff Foxworthy

8/14-16 Carrot Top

10/23-24 Pam Stone

1993

1/1-2 Jeff Foxworthy

2/4-6 Larry Miller

3/4-6 Pinkard & Bowden

1995

4/28-30 Ron White

12/6-10 Michael Winslow

1997

3/21-22 Pinkard & Bowden

8/13-15 Billy Gardell

8/29-30 Ralphie May (Chattanooga native)

9/25 Bobcat Goldthwait

12/5-6 Brian Regan

1998

6/5-6 Bobcat Goldthwait

7/20-21 D.L. Hughley

10/9-11 Tommy Davidson

1999

8/6/-7 Larry the Cable Guy

9/12 Rodney Carrington

10/7-9 Henry Cho, Blake Clark

11/17-20 Marc Maron

2000

1/21-22 Bob Saget

2001

6/9-10 Tommy Chong

8/12-13 Bobcat Goldthwait

9/29-30 Dave Attell

2002

2/5 Roy Wood Jr.

5/3-5 Jeff Dunham

8/9-10 Bobcat Goldthwait

8/23-24 Tommy Chong

12/31 Henry Cho

2003

2/28-3/2 Jeff Dunham

4/25-26 Brett Butler

5/15-16 Ralphie May

7/25-26 Ron White

8/17 Pauly Shore

12/31/03 Roy Wood Jr.

2004

2/27-28 Ron White

3/19-21 Tracy Morgan

4/16-17 Jeff Dunham

5/14-16 Paula Poundstone

5/20-23 Ralphie May

7/23-24 Tommy Davidson

11/13-14 Ralphie May

2005

5/6-7 Kevin Pollak

8/19-21 Jeff Dunham

11/29 Henry Cho

2006

1/13-14 Pauly Shore

2/13-14 Ron White

4/6-9 Gallagher

6/23-25 Jeff Dunham

8/18-19 Roy Wood Jr.

10/20-21 Henry Cho

2007

2/16-18 Greg Giraldo

3/2-3 Roy Wood Jr.

2008

4/24-25 Gallagher

2009

8/2 Henry Cho

11/20 Gallagher

2010

2/28 Pauly Shore

7/24-26 Henry Cho

8/6-8 David Alan Grier

8/12-15 Cledus T. Judd

10/7-10 Daniel Tosh

2011

8/12-13 Henry Cho

8/19-20 D.L. Hughley

10/16 Roy Wood Jr.

12/5 Pauly Shore

2012

5/4-6 Henry Cho

2013

6/13 Carlos Mencia

11/29-12/1 D.L. Hughley

12/5 Pauly Shore

2014

1/9-11 Steve-O

3/6-9 Carlos Mencia

5/8-10 Chris Tucker

2015

1/9-10 Rob Schneider

1/12 Chris Redd

4/13 Tom Green

5/16 Tom Segura

10/11 Chris Kattan

11/27-28 Jon Reep

Actor-comedian Kevin Pollak visits with WRCB's Amy Morrow prior to his 2005 appearance at the Comedy Catch.

2016

2/4 Tim Meadows

5/1 Pauly Shore

5/11 Nene Leakes

2017

2/24-26 Fortune Feimster

7/6-9 Carlos Mencia

8/3-6 Chris Redd

10/5 Erik Griffin

10/15-16 Marlon Wayans

Carlos Mencia takes the stage at the Comedy Catch. (Michael Alfano)

2018

4/22 D.L. Hughley

8/16-18 Carlos Mencia

2019

5/7 T. J. Miller

8/15-17 Rod Man

2020

3/12-14 Erik Griffin

D. L. Hughley has watched Danielle and Evan Alfano grow up. Their family owns and operates the Comedy Catch. (Michael Alfano)

CHAPTER 13

Various Venues

Although Chattanooga's Soldiers and Sailors Memorial Auditorium and Tivoli Theater got the bulk of the star bookings during the one-hundred year period covered by this book, some other area stages also brought in some great entertainers.

Church auditoriums of all sizes hosted shows, not all of which were religious in nature. Cafes, coffee shops, shopping malls, repurposed small town movie theaters, Chattanooga's National Guard Armory, and the UTC Fine Arts Center provided a variety of music styles.

In recent years, venues like Track 29, the Signal, and Songbirds South proved that Chattanooga music fans have a strong appetite for live shows.

Here are some highlights of Chattanooga area shows at various venues:

1937-1940 Archie Campbell, George Gobel and others performed at WDOD Radio Playhouse, 526 Market Street (later known as the Capital Theater)

10/31/44 Eddy Arnold at Peerless Auditorium in Rossville, Georgia

7/4/51 Jackie Brenston, Ike Turner at American Legion Hall, E. 9th St.

10/14/66 Ray Charles at Warner Park Fieldhouse

4/24/69 Guy Lombardo and his Royal Canadians at Cleveland State's Field House

12/3/77 Anita Bryant at Worldwide Assembly Tabernacle in Cleveland, TN

3/24/84 George Strait at Calhoun GA Municipal Auditorium

George Strait at the Calhoun, Georgia Municipal Auditorium in 1983. (Cindy Lowery)

5/5/84 Vern Gosdin at Playhouse 75 in Tunnel Hill, GA

8/31/84 Bend Sinister and Musical Moose at Knights of Columbus Hall on 8th Street, Chattanooga

8/24/85 Vern Gosdin at Country Junction USA in Dalton, GA

8/31/85 Dave and Sugar at Country Junction USA in Dalton, GA

9/28/85 John Schneider at Country Junction USA in Dalton, GA

10/11/85 Reba McEntire & Con Hunley at Country Junction USA in Dalton, GA

11/9/85 Ray Stevens at Country Junction USA in Dalton, GA

11/2/86 Sandi Patty at Collegedale Community Church

7/8/89 Alex Chilton at Michelangelo's at Miller Plaza

3/21/92 Hootie and the Blowfish at Michelangelo's at Miller Plaza

9/26/95 Pianist Floyd Cramer at Conn Center, Lee University in Cleveland

5/2/98 Michael English at Conn Center, Lee University in Cleveland

7/27/98 Lonestar at Hamilton Place Mall parking lot

12/16/98 Keith Harling at Big River Grille

1/25/99 Iris DeMent at Blue Angel Cafe on Frazier Avenue

8/3/02 Davy Jones at Hamilton Place Mall

10/3/02 Eric Heatherly at The Chattanoogan

11/1/02 Matraca Berg at Bessie Smith Hall

1/10/03 Ronnie McDowell, Drifters at Wink Theater in Dalton, GA

2/22/03 T. Graham Brown at Wink Theater in Dalton, GA

5/2/03 Keith Harling at Read House

7/12/03 Janie Fricke at Wink Theater in Dalton, GA

8/16/03 Justin Guarini at Hamilton Place Mall

8/16/03 Ronnie McDowell at Wink Theater in Dalton, GA

10/4/03 Mallory Hope at Wink Theater in Dalton, GA

11/15/03 Percy Sledge at Wink Theater in Dalton, GA

12/6/03 Toby Mac at Club Fathom in downtown Chattanooga

4/24/04 Raymond Fairchild & Maggie Valley Boys and Randall Franks at Wink Theater in Dalton, GA

5/15/04 David Frizzell at Wink Theater in Dalton, GA

8/15/04 Anthony Burger at Brainerd United Methodist Church

12/25/04 Ruben Studdard at The Chattanoogan

2/12/05 Ronnie McDowell, DJ Fontana, Mallory Hope at Wink Theater in Dalton, GA

10/22/05 Natasha Bedingfield at Sir Goony's Family Fun Center on Brainerd Road

3/24/06 Bo Bice at Club Fathom in downtown Chattanooga

4/14/07 Dottie Rambo, Randall Franks, Jeff Hullender at Ringgold United Methodist Church

5/11/07 Marksmen Quartet, Randall Franks, at Ringgold Depot

7/26/07 John Anderson, Heirline, Roger Alan Wade at Northwest Ga. Bank Amphitheater

8/23/08 Ruben Studdard at Bessie Smith Hall for Heritage Music Festival

11/13/09 Stella Parton, Randall Franks at Ringgold Depot

1/28/10 Joe and Vickie Price at Mud Pie on Frazier Avenue

8/21/10 Bobby Blue Bland at Bessie Smith Hall

2011 Sonny Schroyer and Ben Jones of "Dukes of Hazzard,"and Randall Franks of "In the Heat of the Night" appear at tornado relief fundraiser at Northwest Georgia Amphitheater

8/27/13 Cody Simpson at Hamilton Place Mall

9/19/14 Village People at Museum Center at Five Points, Cleveland, TN

7/22/15 Henry Cho (comedian) at Silverdale Baptist Church

12/14/15 Forester Sisters reunion at Church on Main in Chattanooga

8/5/17 Tiffany at Hamilton Place Mall

8/24/17 Kool Moe Dee at Bessie Smith Cultural Center

10/5/17 Gladys Knight at LDS Church in Ooltewah

2/10/18 Mimi Kennedy (with Bob Bernhardt) in "Love Letters" at Theatre Centre

5/12/18 Martha Reeves at Chattanooga Theatre Centre

5/18/18 Confederate Railroad at Crescent City Tavern in Dalton, GA

9/13/18 Kevin Whalum at Bessie Smith Cultural Center

9/28/18 John Crist at City Church in Chattanooga

2/28/19 Guy Penrod at Redemption to the Nations Church on Bailey Avenue in Chattanooga

6/21/19 Bill Anderson at Princess Theater in South Pittsburg, TN

8/2/19 Alessia Cara at Hamilton Place Mall

9/6/19 Mitch Ryder performed at Cadek Hall at UTC. Ryder moved to the Chattanooga area with his wife Megan, a north Georgia native, in 2017.

9/14/19 John Schneider, Smith and Wesley, Cody McCarver, Randall Franks at Northwest Georgia Amphitheater

12/21/19 John Schneider at Princess Theater in South Pittsburg, TN

2/8/20 Linda Davis at Princess Theater in South Pittsburg, TN

Abba's House on Hixson Pike

4/2/06 David Phelps

2/29/08 Mark Lowry

The Forester Sisters of Lookout Mountain, Georgia during their 2015 Holiday Reunion show at the Church on Main in Chattanooga

3/21/08 McKameys, Inspirations

4/15/10 Big Daddy Weave

6/4/10 Phil Stacey, Melinda Doolittle

9/23/10 Steven Curtis Chapman

3/5/11 Chris Tomlin

9/23/12 Tim Hawkins

2/15/13 Erik Estrada at showing of movie "Finding Faith"

4/21/13 Third Day

4/22/16 Sandi Patty

4/9/17 Chonda Pierce

6/25/17 Sandi Patty

1/21/18 Tim Hawkins

7/8/18 Josh Turner

11/16/18 Chonda Pierce

Barking Legs Theater (Dodds Avenue)

1/9/04 Norman Blake

10/20/07 Michael Cleveland

10/9/15 Col. Bruce Hampton

3/9/19 John Cowan Band

5/10/19 David Grier

10/8/19 Ben Curtis, McCallie School class of 1999 and former "Dell Dude" in TV commercials, played with his band Dirty Mae

Charles & Myrtle's Coffee House (McBrien Rd. in East Ridge)

2/3/07 Marshall Chapman

9/22/07 Marshall Chapman

3/22/08 Susan Taylor, Jerre Haskew and Dalton Roberts

4/14/18 Melanie (Safka)

Chattanooga Billiard Club East, Jordan Drive (US-101 High Noon Saloon)

6/27/00 Eric Heatherly

9/14/05 Aaron Tippin

Sept. 2009 Phil Vassar at US-101 High Noon Saloon

1/20/11 Craig Campbell

11/16/11 Casey James

5/24/12 Easton Corbin

1/16/13 Kacey Musgraves

1/22/14 Parmalee

5/28/14 Scotty McCreery

10/22/14 Kristian Bush

(E.G. Kight also played the CBC frequently between 1998 and 2005)

Colonnade in Ringgold, GA

11/29/01 Hovie Lister & Statesmen Quartet

4/13/02 Ronnie McDowell

Ronnie McDowell has appeared on Chattanooga area stages frequently since scoring his first hit in 1977. He is pictured here at the Colonnade in Ringgold in 2017. (Jack Mullins)

7/23/05 Danny Davis & Nashville Brass

4/20/07 Ronnie McDowell

5/28/10 James Gregory

3/16/17 Gene Watson

4/13/17 Ronnie McDowell

Each December from 2001 to 2019, James Rogers performed a Christmas concert

Greater Chattanooga Music Hall near Market St. Bridge (formerly the Rivers Edge)

9/8/78 Delbert McClinton

9/23/78 John Hartford

10/7/78 John Prine

11/5/78 Bellamy Brothers

11/11/78 Norman Blake

12/2/78 Eddie Money

12/16/78 Earl Scruggs Revue

12/30/78 Wet Willie

Lindsay Street Music Hall

9/27/09 Billy Joe Shaver

12/17/10 Charlie Louvin

National Guard Armory, Holtzclaw Avenue

5/20/61 Jim Nabors

2/23/62 Dion backed by local group Vivatones. He also was in a parade passing by several high schools that afternoon: Brainerd, Tyner, East Ridge and Central.

5/5/62 Hank Ballard and the Midnighters

11/7/70 Pacific Gas & Electric

Early 1971 ZZ Top

12/13/71 Ernest Tubb, Leona Williams, Claude King, Cal Smith

10/7/72 Mother's Finest

2/27/73 Lester Flatt, Leona Williams

12/16/73 Ernest Tubb, Texas Troubadours, Kenny Price, Leona Williams

2/17/84 Run DMC

12/14/84 White Animals

3/28/87 White Animals

4/8/94 Widespread Panic

11/30/94 Widespread Panic

12/14/94 White Animals

6/9/95 Kansas

1/3/95 Hootie and the Blowfish (attendance, 1500)

3/3/95 George Clinton P-Funk All Stars

11/22/95 Collective Soul

Revelry Room (at the Choo Choo, later became Songbirds South)

10/9/15 Jim Lauderdale

10/16/15 Revivalists

12/12/15 David Allan Coe

12/31/15 Velcro Pygmies

1/8/16 Mitch Rossell

5/16/16 Cracker

1/14/17 Steep Canyon Band

4/6/17 Smithfield

8/18/17 Mitch Rossell

The Signal (Chestnut Street)

2/16/18 St. Vincent

2/27/18 Gramatik

3/2/18 Riley Green, Channing Wilson

3/13/18 Matisyahu

3/17/18 Here Come The Mummies

3/23/18 Corey Smith

4/6/18 Cody Jinks

4/27/18 The Clutch

5/2/18 Buckethead

5/3/18 Breaking Benjamin

5/10/18 Aaron Watson

5/17/18 Chase Rice

5/22/18 Stone Temple Pilots

6/2/18 Fitz and the Tantrums

7/14/18 Kurt Vile

8/19/18 JJ Grey & Metro

8/31/18 Jimmy Eat World

9/20/18 Cherub

9/28/18 Chris Lane

10/20/18 Kip Moore

11/2/18 Gary Clark Jr.

11/8/18 LANCO

11/11/18 Dawes

11/24/18 Morgan Wallen

12/29/18 George Clinton's Parliament Funkadelic

1/22/19 Triumph Bonneville Icons

1/23/19 Corey Smith

2/12/19 Young the Giant

2/14/19 Travis Greene

2/16/19 Walk the Moon

3/22/19 Jacob Bryant

3/23/19 Cody Johnson

6/10/19 Insane Clown Posse

7/19/19 Warrant

8/6/19 Switchfoot

8/7/19 Gin Blossoms

8/22/19 Umphrey's McGee

10/5/19 Yacht Rock Revue

11/23/19 Abbey Road Live

2/7/20 Lauren Alaina

10/8/20 Whitey Morgan

10/30/20 Strung Like a Horse

11/13/20 Larry Fleet

11/14 10,000 Days

Lakeview Fort Oglethorpe High School graduate, and American Idol runner-up Lauren Alaina performed at the Signal in 2020. (Don Luzynski Photography)

11/18/20 Paul Cauthen

11/20/20 Corey Smith

11/27/20 Neon Moon

11/28/20 The Steel Woods with Dave Kennedy

12/4/20 Frank Foster

12/10/20 Three Star Revival

12/11/20 The Afternooners

12/15/20 Black Stone Cherry

12/19/20 Starlito

1/22/21 Lenox Hills

Suzy Bogguss is pictured at Songbirds Guitar Museum with Chris Clement in 2017. (Chris Clement)

Songbirds Guitar Museum, 35 Station Street

4/21/17 Dick Dale

6/30/17 Amber Carrington

7/28/17 Suzy Bogguss

8/17/17 Edwin McCain

10/17/17 BoDeans

12/1/17 Secret Sisters

1/6/18 Randall Bramlett

1/13/18 Tinsley Ellis

2/16/18 Kathy Mattea

2/21/18 Angie Aparo

3/1/18 Hal Ketchum, Brent Cobb

4/20/18 Steve Wariner

5/5/18 Dallas Walker

6/22/18 Ray Wylie Hubbard

8/16/18 Angie Aparo

9/20/18 Kim Richey

12/20/18 John Schneider

2/15/19 Suzy Bogguss

3/21/19 Little Texas

3/27/19 Kinky Friedman

6/20/19 Gretchen Peters

6/21/19 Josh Gilbert

6/26/19 Noam Pikelny, Stuart Duncan

10/11/19 Ray Wylie Hubbard

2/14/20 Kentucky Headhunters

Hal Ketchum at Songbirds in 2018. (Lori Elliott)

Songbirds South, 41 Station Street

12/14/17 Shooter Jennings

3/9/18 Velcro Pygmies

5/10/18 John Popper

7/17/18 Bacon Brothers (featuring Kevin Bacon)

8/1/18 Sister Hazel

8/9/18 Larry Fleet

9/12/18 Leo Kottke

10/19/18 Tinsley Ellis

11/30/18 Lee Roy Parnell

3/27/19 Brent Cobb

5/18/19 Nick Lowe

5/21/19 The Wailers

9/18/19 Ruston Kelly

9/21/19 Drivin' n' Cryin'

11/10/19 Shooter Jennings

12/21/19 Jimmy Hall

2/1/20 Mitch Rossell

Track 29 (at Chattanooga Choo Choo)

9/1/11 Jamey Johnson

9/9/11 Corey Smith

9/10/11 Drive By Truckers

10/4/11 Ghostland Observatory

10/7/11 Marc Broussard

10/13/11 Frankie Ballard

10/22/11 Lucinda Williams

11/6/11 NEEDTOBREATHE

11/7/11 John Hiatt

12/7/11 Lauren Alaina

12/22/11 Jamey Johnson

12/30/11 Avett Brothers

12/31/11 Dirty Guv'nahs

2/12/12 They Might Be Giants

2/23/12 Sam Bush

2/25/12 Wanda Jackson

3/1/12 Tommy Emmanuel

3/3/12 North Mississippi All-Stars

3/10/12 Jack White

3/13/12 Wood Brothers

3/14/12 Gavin DeGraw, David Nail, Gabe Dixon

3/15/12 Jamey Johnson

3/16/12 Terri Clark

3/17/12 Jason Isbell

3/24/12 Jake Owen

3/29/12 Pretty Lights

4/17/12 Galactic

4/22/12 Punch Brothers

5/1/12 Five Finger Death Punch

5/5/12 Clutch

5/11/12 Switchfoot

5/27/12 Seether

6/1/12 Todd Snider, Justin Townes Earle

6/28/12 Saving Abel

8/21/12 Ted Nugent

9/14/12 Corey Smith

9/26/12 Girl Talk

10/4/12 Jamey Johnson

10/12/12 Band of Horses

11/7/12 Lindsey Buckingham

11/10/12 Eli Young Band

11/13/12 Social Distortion

11/27/12 Surfjan Stevens

11/29/12 Blackberry Smoke

12/1/12 Dirty Guv'nahs

12/5/12 Lauren Alaina, Confederate Railroad

12/6/12 Dethlok

1/11/13 Jerrod Niemann

1/17/13 Robert Earl Keen

1/30/13 Dweezil Zappa

2/1/13 Down

2/20/13 Mimosa

3/8/13 Citizen Cope

4/22/13 Luke Bryan, Jon Pardi

4/24/13 Shooter Jennings

4/26/13 Asking Alexandria

4/30/13 Three Days Grace

5/4/13 Flaming Lips

5/9/13 Wallflowers

5/12/13 Bassnectar

5/17/13 Lamb of God

5/21/13 Black Crowes

5/30/13 Aaron Lewis

5/31/13 Big Boi, Killer Mike

6/3/13 Dropkick Murphys, Mahones, Old Man Markley

6/18/13 Edward Sharpe & Magnetic Zeros

6/27/13 Drive By Truckers

7/6/13 Jason Isbell

7/12/13 Toad the Wet Sprocket

7/13/13 Old Crow Medicine Show

7/25/13 Halestorm

8/25/13 Sara Bareilles

8/28/13 Puddle of Mudd

9/3/13 Here Come the Mummies

9/6/13 Arrested Development

9/24/13 Big Boi

10/3/13 Dwight Yoakam

10/7/13 Arctic Monkeys

10/9/13 Neutral Milk Hotel

10/16/13 Beats Antique

10/18/13 Neutral Milk Hotel

10/23/13 Datsuk

10/24/13 Steve Earle

10/29/13 Clutch

11/12/13 Steve Vai

11/20/13 Florida Georgia Line

12/4/13 Victor Wooten

12/7/13 Trombone Shorty

12/10/13 Goo Goo Dolls

12/12/13 Infamous Stringdusters

12/13/13 Kacey Musgraves

1/17/14 Blackberry Smoke

1/21/14 Tedeschi Trucks Band

1/29/14 Umphrey's McGee

2/7/14 Eli Young Band

2/16/14 The Floozies

2/25/14 Steep Canyon Rangers

3/3/14 Switchfoot

3/15/14 Jason Isbell

3/17/14 Indigo Girls

3/22/14 Juicy J

3/28/14 Dirty Guv'nahs

4/1/14 Umphrey's McGee

4/17/14 Dustin Lynch

4/21/14 Nickel Creek, Secret Sisters

4/27/14 Volbeat

5/8/14 311

5/10/14 Ghost

5/15/14 David Nail

5/17/14 Conor Oberst

5/23/14 Tegan and Sara

6/30/14 Lindsey Stirling

8/19/14 Chevelle

9/5/14 Justin Townes Earle

9/18/14 St. Paul and the Broken Bones

10/12/14 Blues Traveler

10/17/14 Ben Rector

10/18/14 Big Gigantic

10/20/14 Julian Casablancas

10/21/14 Arnon Amarth

10/23/14 Jimmy Eat World

10/29/14 STS9

10/30/14 Moon Taxi

11/5/14 Neon Trees

11/6/14 OAR featuring Andy Grammer

11/8/14 Robin Trower

11/11/14 Halestorm

11/18/14 RaeLynn

11/28/14 The 1975

12/4/14 Bone Thugs-N-Harmony

12/26/14 The 1975

12/27/14 Trampled by Turtles

1/9/15 Kansas

1/14/15 Rebelation

1/15/15 Paper Diamond

1/23/15 Corey Smith

1/27/15 Josh Turner

2/4/15 Umphrey's McGee

2/17/15 Kennedy Jones

3/9/15 Ryan Bingham

3/10/15 Modest Mouse

3/21/15 Die Antwoord

3/26/15 J. Roddy Walston

3/27/15 Keller Williams

4/1/15 War on Drugs

4/16/15 Jason Isbell, Strand of Oaks

4/17/15 So Mo

4/20/15 Bill Burr (comedian)

4/28/15 Five Finger Death Punch

4/29/15 In This Moment

4/30/15 Dirty Heads

5/1/15 Keb Mo'

5/2/15 Breaking Benjamin, Young Guns

5/5/15 Umphrey's McGee

5/9/15 Marilyn Manson

6/24/15 Indigo Girls

8/1/15 Raekwon

8/2/15 Coal Chamber

8/15/15 Eli Young Band

8/25/15 Blues Traveler

9/25/15 Cherub

9/26/15 Beats Antique

10/4/15 Seether

10/5/15 Godsmack

10/9/15 Mat Kearney

10/10/15 Chase Rice, Cadillac Three

10/17/15 Maddie & Tae

10/29/15 David Nail

10/31/15 Moon Taxi

11/12/15 Drew Holcomb

11/19/15 Drive By Truckers

11/27/15 Collective Soul

12/31/15 Here Come the Mummies

1/3/16 Chris Stapleton

1/22/16 Jamey Johnson

2/7/16 Papadosio

2/13/16 Mutemath

3/3/16 Kevin Gates

4/1/16 Ben Rector

4/8/16 Tech N9ne

4/14/16 Datsik

4/25/16 Alabama Shakes

4/27/16 Breaking Benjamin

4/29/16 Cypress Hill

5/2/16 Tesla

5/6/16 Bullet for my Valentine

5/12/16 Ghost

5/18/16 Shinedown

6/20/16 Silversun Pickups

6/30/16 Eli Young Band

7/3/16 Ani DeFranco

9/24/16 Judah and the Lion

9/25/16 Schoolboy Q

10/5/16 Umphrey's McGee

10/8/16 Switchfoot

10/21/16 Kane Brown "birthday bash"

10/22/16 Band of Horses

10/31/16 Moon Taxi

11/10/16 Old Dominion

10/22/16 Band of Horses

11/5/16 So Mo

12/14/16 St. Paul and the Broken Bones

1/7/17 Jamey Johnson

1/28/17 Tedeschi Trucks Band

3/7/17 Jimmy Eat World

3/20/17 Connor Oberst

4/20/17 Jason Isbell

4/25/27 STS9

4/28/17 Paula Poundstone

5/3/17 Chevelles

5/4/17 Drive-By Truckers

Kane Brown attended several schools in Chattanooga and North Georgia, including Dalton State College, before hitting it big in country music. He attracted a big crowd to Track 29 on his 23rd birthday in 2016. (RCA Records)

Frequent Chattanooga visitors the Drive-By Truckers, based in Athens, Georgia, played the final show at Track 29 in 2017. (Big Hassle Media)

UTC Fine Arts Center

10/23/80 Marcel Marceau

1/14/82 Paul Winter Consort

2/16/84 Billy Taylor Trio

9/12/85 Gary Burton Quartet

9/10/87 Dave Brubeck

9/22/89 Freddie Hubbard

11/18/91 Al Hirt

1/25/95 Wynton Marsalis Quartet

2/25/95 Leo Kottke

3/2/96 Bill Crofut and Chris Brubeck

4/6/97 Cleo Laine

10/30/97 Budapest Strings

3/26/99 Butch Thompson Trio

11/8/99 Peter Shickele

9/30/01 T.S. Monk

9/20/04 Capitol Steps

11/1/04 Anthony Zerbe

1/18/05 Mark O'Connor

2/5/06 Statesmen of Jazz

2/13/07 Juilliard String Quartet

2/20/08 Henry Rollins

3/3/08 Second City

3/20/08 Clark Terry & Statesmen of Jazz

9/11/08 Mark Russell

10/27/08 Vienna Boys Choir

9/24/10 Kathy Mattea

11/6/10 Anthony Zerbe

3/29/11 SF Jazz Collective

2/16/12 Ladysmith Black Mambazo

9/11/12 Secret Sisters

10/16/12 Julian Sands

9/23/13 Blind Boys of Alabama

9/9/14 Ramsey Lewis

11/5/14 Dave Mason

2/24/15 Rory Block

2/14/16 BeauSoleil avec Michael Doucet

9/16/16 Rosanne Cash

1/24/17 Julian Sands

3/8/18 Malpass Brothers

CHAPTER 14

Movies and Music Videos filmed in the Chattanooga area

Although Chattanooga, and the surrounding area, has never been a hotbed of motion picture activity, we've had our moments. Legendary filmmakers like Walt Disney, Francis Ford Coppola, George Lucas, and John Carpenter have been on site for various movie projects.

Stars as bright as Harrison Ford, James Caan, Mark Hamill, Jeff Bridges, Keith Carradine, Robert Pattinson, Reese Witherspoon, and Chadwick Boseman have starred in movies filmed in the Chattanooga area.

Chattanooga's scenery, railroad history, bridges, and climate have helped attract some productions. Historic Engel Stadium has been the backdrop for two major motion pictures and one music video.

Movies:

"Keep Your Powder Dry" portions shot summer 1944 at Women's Army Auxiliary Corps Fort Oglethorpe)

"Davy Crockett, King of the Wild Frontier" (1954) at Baylor School and Williams Island, with Fess Parker and Buddy Ebsen

"Light in the Forest" (July 1957) at Hales Bar area of the Tennessee River in Marion County, and at Watts Bar Lake, with Fess Parker, James MacArthur, Carol Lynley, Iron Eyes Cody, and Rafael Campos. Walt Disney was present at the beginning of filming, and was disappointed to learn that reporters had been made aware of his arrival. Cast and crew stayed at the Read House.

"The Rain People: (May 1968) shot several scenes at Ruby Falls and in downtown Chattanooga during the Armed Forces Day parade on May

17, 1968. James Caan and Shirley Knight were in the scenes. Francis Ford Coppola ("The Godfather") directed the film, and George Lucas ("Star Wars") assisted him. Both were in Chattanooga for the filming.

"The Night the Lights Went Out in Georgia," (also in Dade and Catoosa County, GA) Kristy McNichol, Mark Hamill, Dennis Quaid, Don Stroud (1980)

"Starman," Jeff Bridges, Karen Allen (1984) directed by John Carpenter ("Halloween")

"The Pete Gray Story" ("A Winner Never Quits") in Chattanooga and South Pittsburg, Keith Carradine, Dennis Weaver, Mare Winningham, Ed O'Neill (1985)

Spectators like Debbie Born were able to capture long-range shots of Robert Pattinson during the Catoosa County shoot of "Water for Elephants" in 2010. (Debbie Born)

"The Curse" (formerly known as "The Farm") included scenes shot at Apple Valley Orchard in Cleveland, TN. It was directed by David Keith, and actors included Wil Wheaton, Claude Akins, and John Schneider. Most of the shooting took place in Tellico Plains in Monroe County, TN. (1986).

"Dutch" Ed O'Neill (1990) Portions were shot in Chattanooga

"Love Potion # 9" (1991) Many interior scenes were shot in the Radisson Read House

"Fled" (1996) includes a scene filmed at Tennessee Valley Railroad Museum

"The Adventures of Ociee Nash" (2002) includes scenes filmed at Tennessee Valley Railroad Museum

"Heaven's Fall" (2004) included scenes filmed in Chattanooga

The Long family of Chatsworth, Georgia visited the Ellen DeGeneres Show in 2012 to talk about the "Bully" movie. (L–R: Troy, Teryn, David and Tina Long, with Ellen DeGeneres and a portrait of Tyler Long).

Chadwick Boseman, who played baseball star Jackie Robinson in "42" is pictured with Chattanooga resident Gary Miller, who played an umpire. Miller has appeared in dozens of motion pictures, usually as an extra or a small speaking part. (Gary Miller)

"Leatherheads" (March 2007) featured George Clooney in a scene filmed at Tennessee Valley Railroad Museum. Clooney was in Chattanooga one day, March 12, 2007.

"Water for Elephants" Robert Pattinson, Reese Witherspoon (2010), filmed partially in Catoosa County, GA

"Bully" a documentary filmed partially in Chatsworth, Georgia features the Long family (David, Tina, Troy, and Teryn) discussing the aftermath of their son Tyler's suicide in 2009, due to bullying. (2012)

"42" Chadwick Boseman and Harrison Ford filmed much of the movie at Engel Stadium (2012)

****"The Girl Who Spelled Freedom" (not shot in Chattanooga, but based on the life of local resident Linn Yann) (1986)

Tim McGraw filmed his 2012 music video "Truck Yeah" in Chattanooga. (WRCB)

Music Videos:

Alabama "Cheap Seats" at Engel Stadium (1994)

Tim McGraw "Truck Yeah" (Aug. 21, 2012)

Brett Young "In Case You Didn't Know" (2017)

For King and Country "God Only Knows" (2018)

About David Carroll

Dav64 Carroll is an award-winning journalist who has worked in Chattanooga television and radio for more than forty years. In addition to his broadcast work, he writes a weekly newspaper column, has a website (ChattanoogaRadioTV.com), and has authored two other books, *Chattanooga Radio and Television* (Arcadia Publishing, 2011) and *Volunteer Bama Dawg* (Fresh Ink Group, 2016). He and his wife Cindy have two sons, Chris and Vince, and make their home in Chattanooga.

Index

Duke Jupiter 288
Duke of Paducah 31, 44, 46, 48, 54, 58, 85, 88, 243, 244
Dukes of Dixieland 322
Dukes of Hazzard 264, 474, 499, 518, 541, 580
Duncan, Arne 455
Duncan, Arthur 79, 85, 120
Duncan, Bryan 131
Duncan, Deanna 468, 469
Duncan, Johnny 88
Duncan, Stuart 591
Duncan, Whitney 147
Dungy, Tony 418
Dunham, Jeff 153, 167, 571, 572
DUNHAM, JEFF 299
Dunn, Adam 417, 439
Dunn, Clare 156
Dunn, Gov. Winfield 446, 451, 488
Dunn, Holly 363, 364, 365
Dunninger 28
Dunn, Joe Lee 397
Dunn, John Randall 5
Dunn, Ronnie 218
Dunn, Winfield 181
Durham, Eddie 27
Durocher, Leo 384
Dye, Pat 402
Dye, Pete 440
Dykeman, Wilma 487, 488, 494, 496, 508
Dylan, Bob 123, 130, 133, 225, 230, 315, 316, 350, 376

E

Eagle, Johnny 73
Eagles 218, 223
Ealey, Theodis 330
Earhart, Amelia 474, 477
Earl Carroll Vanities 31
Earle, Justin Townes 221, 557, 563, 564, 594, 598
Earles, Jason 542
Earle, Steve 161, 203, 293, 356, 365, 596
Earle, Sylvia 538
Earl Scruggs Family & Friends 208
Earl Scruggs Revue 87, 95, 314, 585
Earnhardt Jr., Dale 429
Earth 94, 97
Earthquake 147
Earth Wind and Fire 95, 159, 325, 327
East, Dan 257
Eastgate Mall 395
Echaniz, Jose 8

Eckstine, Billy 42, 45
Eddie, Country Boy 62
Eddie & Gerald Levert 144
Eddington, Jelani 156
Eddy, Duane 57
Eddy, Nelson 19, 20, 23, 34, 179
Eden, Barbara 129
Edgar Winter Group 96, 556
Edgerton, Clyde 497
Edmonds, Babyface 370
Edwards, Dennis 290
Edward Sharpe & Magnetic Zeros 596
Edwards, Jonathan 192
Edwards, Ryan 512
Eight Days After 359
Eilperin, Juliet 538
Eisenhower, Dwight D. 463
Eisenhower for President 42
ela Fleck and Flecktones 209
Elbert, Donnie 53
Elder, Donnie 402
Eldredge, Brett 328
Elevation Worship 231
Eley, Bryan 269, 276
Elf the Musical 155
Elijah 13
Eli Young Band 165, 279, 595, 597
Ellen DeGeneres Show 608
Elliman, Yvonne 87
Ellington, Duke 15, 16, 20, 22, 33
Elliott, Lori 592
Ellis Brothers 273
Ellis, Dale 403
Ellis, Tinsley 202, 326, 330, 341, 561, 566, 591, 593
Ellis, Victor 421
Elman, Mischa 306
Elm Hill Meats 176
ELO 346
Elvin Bishop 97
Elvis 349
Elway, John 440
Ely, Joe 210, 355, 558
Emancipation Day 58
Emery, Ralph 76, 95, 99, 364, 365, 495
Emmanuel, Tommy 594
Emmons, Blake 192, 252, 255
Emmons, Kent 526
Emotions 100
Emotions, The 368
Encarnacion, Edwin 439
Enchantment 101

Fricke, Janie 104, 112, 148, 288, 290, 365, 502, 579
Friday's Promise 358
Friedan, Betty 495
Friedman, Kinky 93, 591
Friedman, Thomas 218
Friends 166
Frijid Pink 84
Frisch, Frankie 384, 438
Frist, Bill 453
Frist, Sen. Bill 451, 452, 453
Frizzell, David 109, 113, 549, 550, 580
Frizzell, Lefty 62, 69
Frye Band 238
Fuller, Clyde 510
Fuller, Craig 338
Fuller, Joe "Dixie" 318
Fuller, Millard 494
Fulmer, Phil 147, 421, 430, 536
Fulmer, Philip 410, 420, 432
Fulmer, Phillip 411, 415, 416, 422, 427, 431, 432
Fulson, Lowell 46
Funkadelic 99, 113
Funny Girl 80
Funny Page 549
Furillo, Carl 389
Furkusny, Rudolf 47
Fusebox 359

G

Gable, Dan 397
Gaffigan, Jim 219
Gaffney, Paul "Showtime" 439
GA Golf and Country Club 471
Gail, Linda 80
Gaines, Dean 199
Gaines, Ernest 502
Gaither, Bill 130, 155
GAITHER, BILL 297
Gaither Family 283
GAITHER FAMILY 297, 299
Gaither Vocal Band 155, 157, 363
Galactic 354, 594
Galifinakis, Zach 525
Gallagher 119, 123, 128, 131, 132, 189, 192, 193, 312, 572
Galli-Curci, Amelita 7
Galloway, Don 88, 97
Galloways 140, 207
Gambler, The 283
Gamma 105
Gant, Ron 409

Gap Band 109, 116, 210, 308, 314, 326
GAP BAND 290
Garber, Gene 401
Garber, Jan 17, 18, 20, 23
Gardell, Billy 570
Garden, Mary 6, 7
Gardner, "Brother Dave" 173, 174, 178, 179
Gardner, Brother Dave" 179
Gardner, Dave 58
Garfield, Andrew 514
Garfield, James 459
Garfunkel, Art 166, 222, 326
Garner, Jay 483
Garrett, Betty 182
Garrett, George 502
Garrett, Leif 546
Garroway, Dave 481
Garson, Greer 24, 479
Gary, John 119, 121, 129, 179
Gary Lewis and the Playboys 66, 266
Gary Lewis & Playboys 69, 76, 553
Gary Lewis & the Playboys 207
Gary Puckett & Union Gap 78
Gates, Bill 528
Gates, David 325
Gates, Lucy 306
Gatlin Brothers 324, 325, 365
GATLIN BROTHERS 290
Gatlin, Larry 99, 207, 282
Gattis, Evan 427, 439
Gawvi 360
Gayden, Mac 355
Gaye, Marvin 63, 66, 311, 312, 349
Gayle, Crystal 87, 92, 97, 196, 241, 252, 290, 322, 368
Gaynor, Mitzi 115
Gearrin, Cory 418, 426, 427
Geezinslaw Brothers 63
Gehrig, Lou 379, 382, 383, 384, 438
Gehringer, Charlie 383
Gems 108
Gene Cotton and Overland 568
Gene & Debbe 79
Gene Kelly's Salute to Broadway 185
Gene Pitney's Bonanza of Stars 68
General Electric 468
Gentle Giant 92
Gentry, Teddy 110, 314, 332, 493
Geoff Moore & the Distance 133
George Clinton & P-Funk 546
George Clinton P-Funk All Stars 586
George Clinton's Parliament Funkadelic 588

Golden, Arthur 209, 510, 511
Golden Gateway 177
Golden Gloves 19, 53, 82
Golden Gloves boxing 11
Golden Gloves Boxing 24, 33
Golden West Cowboys 29, 32
Golden, William Lee 271, 363, 365
Goldovsky Grand Opera 65
Goldovsky Opera 63
Goldsboro, Bobby 66, 68, 324
Goldthwait, Bobcat 570, 571
Goldwater, Barry 65, 445, 464
Goldwater, Sen. Barry 57, 445
Gomer Pyle 51, 69, 123, 475, 481
Gomer Pyle USMC 51
Gone with the Wind 173
Gone With The Wind 476
Gonzales, Pancho 387
Gonzalez, Fredi 429
Goodall, Dame Jane 537
Goodell, Dr. Jane 204
Gooden, Sam 518, 520, 526, 532, 549
Goodeve, Grant 542
Good Friday Sing 139, 140
Gooding Sr., Cuba 139
Goodman 292, 314
Goodman, Benny 28, 42, 186, 319, 323
Goodman, Dody 196
Goodman, John 181, 186
Goodman, Vestal 297
Good Morning Miss Bliss 499
Goodrich, Gail 401
Goodwin, Doris Kearns 512
Goo Goo Dolls 146, 225, 234, 328, 597
Goosebumps 135
Goose Creek Symphony 81, 89, 92, 93, 94, 95, 96,
    127, 326, 327, 338, 344, 353, 375, 559
GOP 102
Gordon, Dee 439
Gordon, Phil 419
Gore, Al 452, 467
Gore Jr., Albert 441
Gore, Lesley 68
Gore, Rep. Albert 443
Gore, Sen. Al 449
Gore Sr., Albert 447
Gore Sr, Sen. Albert 446
Gore Sr., Sen. Albert 85, 443, 446
Gore, Tipper 452, 494, 538
Gore, Vice President Al 202, 538
Gorgeous George 480
Gorgeous George Band 65

Gorka, John 325
Gosdin, Vern 334, 362, 363, 364, 549, 551, 579
Goslin, Goose 383
Gospel Concert 44
Gospel Melody Quartet 45
Gottfried, Brian 391, 427
Got to Give It Up 311
Goulet, Robert 197, 199, 202
Governor's Lounge 544, 549, 554, 555
Gov. George & Cornelia Wallace 88
Gov. George Wallace Stand Up for America 76
Gov't Mule 296, 298, 328, 567
Govt. Mule 556
Go West 292
Grace Baptist Academy 433
Grace, Jamie 360
Gracin, Josh 279, 337, 338
Graham, Billy 474, 477, 501
Graham Central Station 96
Graham, Franklin 526
Graham, Larry 135
Graham, Rev Billy 29
Graham, Rev. Billy 20, 30, 44, 312, 314, 479, 480,
    500, 503
Graham, Rev. Franklin 504
Graham, Sen. Lindsey 452
Graham, Virginia 185
Graham, Will 359
Gramatik 587
Grambling University 406
GRAMMER, ANDY 301
Grammer, Billy 66, 243, 244, 247, 250
Gramm, Sen. Phil 450
Grand Funk 93
Grand Ole Opry 31, 32, 35, 38, 40, 43, 44, 45, 46,
    47, 48, 54, 62, 65, 66, 74, 174, 239, 474
Grandpa Jones 58, 79, 257, 333, 364
Grandpappy 238, 241
Grand Terrace Orchestra 14
Grant, Amy 116, 121, 123, 135, 143, 153, 210,
    233, 283, 494
GRANT, AMY 295, 296
Grant, Jim "Mudcat" 416
Grant, Mudcat 416
Grant, Natalie 278, 280, 358, 359
Gran Torino 545, 546, 567
Grant, Ulysses S. 459
Grascals 339, 351
Grassroots 81, 84, 85, 88, 275, 292, 325, 326,
    328, 560
Grateful Dead 332
Graveure, Louis 5, 6

Tri-County Hospital 446
Trina 299
Trinity Baptist Church 496
Tri-Octaves 217
Triple H 506
Trippi, Charley 389
Tritt, Travis 122, 125, 128, 138, 143, 163, 208,
        215, 220, 221, 229, 232, 324, 326, 364,
        365, 366, 551
TRITT, TRAVIS 295, 296
Triumph 104, 561
Triumphant 159
Triumphant Quartet 155, 164, 169, 218
Triumph Bonneville Icons 588
Trombone Shorty 353, 597
Trombone Shorty Andrews 330
Troop 294
Troupe, Ben 418
Trout, Dizzy 385
Trower, Robin 97, 558, 598
Troy, Doris 62
Troyer, Verne 542
Trucks, Derek 337, 566
Trucks, Virgil 401, 406
Truman Brothers 156
Truman, Harry S 463
Truman, Margaret 41
Truman, President Harry 443
Truman, President Harry S 516
Trump, Donald 471
Trump Jr., Donald 457
Trump, Marla Maples 504
Trump, President 456, 457
Trump, Tiffany 504
Tubb, Ernest 26, 40, 44, 58, 77, 242, 250, 251,
        259, 261, 586
Tubb, Justin 75, 242, 247, 259
Tuck and Patti 355
Tucker, Chris 201, 210, 573
Tucker, Forrest 187
Tucker, Richard 66, 183
Tucker, Tanya 128, 259, 266, 324, 335, 364
Tucker, Tommy 32
Tuck & Patti 559
Tufano, Dennis 339
Tugman, Kathy 329
Tuller, Jorge 191
Tulloch, Stephen 420
Tune, Tommy 206, 210
Tuohy, Leigh Ann 521, 525
Turini, Ronald 62
Turley, Bob 401, 406

Turner, Big Joe 48
Turner, Ike 577
Turner, Jim 120, 408
Turner, Joe 46, 47, 48
Turner, Josh 210, 222, 279, 327, 339, 370, 583,
        599
Turner, Justin 439
Turner Nichols Band 273
Turner, Ted 189, 503, 511, 521, 534
Turner, Tina 283
TURNER, TINA 291, 292
Turning, The 359
Turnpike Troubadors 159
Turtle Derby 53
Turtles 68, 69, 192, 328
Turtles, The 326
TVA 45
Twain, Mark 200, 207, 501
TWAIN, SHANIA 297
Tweedy, Jeff 166
Twisted Sister 283, 291
Twister Alley 273
Twitty, Conway 76, 78, 80, 81, 85, 87, 89, 93, 95,
        97, 99, 101, 104, 106, 108, 109, 110, 112,
        113, 115, 117, 120, 283, 362, 363, 364
TWITTY, CONWAY 294
Twitty, Michael 270, 271
Two by Two 183
Two Fresh 563
Two Gentlemen of Verona 183
Tyler, Micah 360
Tyler, Ty 139
Tyminski, Dan 351
Tympany Five 28
Tyndall, Donnie 429
Tyner Academy 520, 526
Tyner High School 308
Tyrone Smith Revue 560
Tyson, Neil deGrasse 522

U

Udall, Stewart 450
Uecker, Bob 394
Uhry, Alfred 502
uilty Until Proven Innocent 144
Umphrey's McGee 588, 597, 599
UNC-Charlotte 437
Uncle Fester 12, 18
Uncle Lightnin' 326, 327, 353, 356
Undertaker 505, 506, 508, 509
Underwood, Carrie 284

Varnell, Chris 320
Vasconcellos, Martha 487
Vassar, Phil 139, 209, 583
Vaudeville Cafe 568
Vaughan, Sarah 47, 318, 322, 323
Vaughn, Linda 534
Veale, Bob 392
Vee, Bobby 68, 265
Veggie Tales Live 141, 146
Velasquez, Jaci 139, 276
Velcro Pygmies 564, 586, 592
Velvettes 65
Vereen, Ben 156, 368
Vernon, Mickey 387
Vertical Horizon 567
Verve Pipe 564
veteran reunions 11
Veterans Administration 448
Vice President George H.W. Bush 449
Victor Orchestra 12
Victory Parade 30
Vic Willis Trio 269
Vidale, Thea 146
Video Masters 407
Vienna Boys Choir 191, 221
Vienna on Parade 56
Vilas, Guillermo 403
VILAS, GUILLERMO 287
Vile, Kurt 557, 587
Village People 581
Villegas, Pablo 222
Vincent, Gene 52
Vincent, Rhonda 325, 327, 337, 351, 352
Vince Vance and the Valiants 265, 266
Vines, Ellsworth 17, 19
Vine Street 318
Vine Street Auditorium 568
Vine Street Market 533
Vinton, Bobby 323
Violent Femmes 346
Virdon, Bill 392
Vitaphone 8
Vivatones 245, 585
Vivian, Rev. C. T. 483
Vivia, Rev. C.T. 511
Vogues 68
Vogues, The 263
Voices of Lee 328
Volbeat 597
Volz, Greg 121, 335
Volz, Greg X. 120
Von Braun, Dr. Wernher 484

Vondells 248
Votto, Joey 439
Vronski and Babin 75
Vronsky and Babin 23
Vronsky & Babin 43
V-Roys 353

W

Wade, Bill 391
Wade, Roger Alan 220, 308, 326, 327, 328, 342, 357, 376, 534, 557, 580
WAGC 44
WAGC Teen Timers 34
Wagner, Glen 466
Wagner, Helen 491
Wagner Opera Company 35
Wagner, Robert 197, 204
Wagner, Roger 58
Wagoner, Porter 75, 79, 80, 84, 87, 88, 94, 240, 242, 243, 244, 245, 484
Wailers, The 593
Wain, Bea 19
Wainwright III, Loudon 354
Waite, Big Jim 48
Waite, John 203
Waits, Jim 41
Wake Forest University 387
Walcott, "Jersey Joe" 391
Waldenbooks 414
Wald, Jerry 32
Walker, Billy 77, 243, 244
Walker, Cas 25, 26
Walker, Clay 132, 280, 365, 536
Walker, Clint 489
Walker County Civic Center 414
Walker, Dallas 591
Walker, Debbie 401
Walker, Dixie 393
Walker, Harry "The Hat" 408
Walker, Herschel 431
Walker, Jerry Jeff 99, 325, 349
Walker, Jimmie "JJ" 569
Walker, Larry 438
Walker, Mayor Robert Kirk 122
Walker, Rube 388
Walker Sisters 102
Walker Theater 151, 159
Walking Tall 488
Walk Off The Earth 169
Walk the Moon 588
Wallace, George 115, 200, 368, 445, 446

Fresh Ink Group
Independent Multi-media Publisher
Fresh Ink Group / Push Pull Press / Voice of Indie

Hardcovers
Softcovers
All Ebook Platforms
Audiobooks
Worldwide Distribution

Indie Author Services
Book Development, Editing, Proofing
Graphic/Cover Design
Video/Trailer Production
Website Creation
Social Media Management
Writing Contests
Writers' Blogs
Podcasts

Authors
Editors
Artists
Experts
Professionals

FreshInkGroup.com

info@FreshInkGroup.com
Twitter: @FreshInkGroup
Facebook.com/FreshInkGroup
LinkedIn: Fresh Ink Group

Fresh Ink Group

IMAGES
of America
CHATTANOOGA RADIO
AND TELEVISION

David Carroll

Chattanooga Radio and Television provides an informative entertaining look at Chattanooga's broadcast history through the images and stories of its participants.

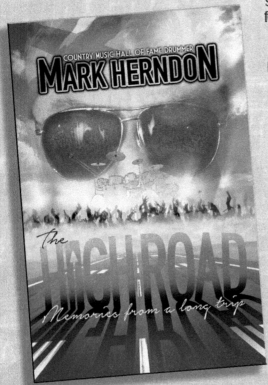

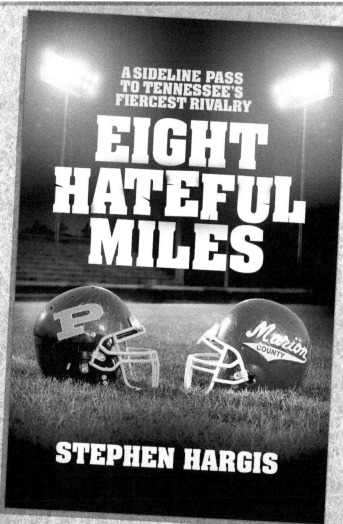

A SIDELINE PASS
TO TENNESSEE'S
FIERCEST RIVALRY

EIGHT HATEFUL MILES

STEPHEN HARGIS

Marion County and South
Pittsburg, Tennessee's fiercest high-school rivalry, 4 decades
of history by Chattanooga sports-writer Stephen Hargis in 400+
pages of stories with nearly a hundred color photos.

Printed in the USA
CPSIA information can be obtained
at www.ICGtesting.com
JSHW080738051223
52912JS00002B/2